Opritsa D. Popa

Bibliophiles and Bibliothieves

Cultural Property Studies
Schriften zum Kulturgüterschutz

Cultural Property Studies
Schriften zum Kulturgüterschutz

Edited by
Herausgegeben von

Opritsa D. Popa

Bibliophiles and Bibliothieves

The Search for the Hildebrandslied and the Willehalm Codex

With a preface by Winder McConnell

Walter de Gruyter · Berlin · New York
2003

Opritsa D. Popa is Distinguished Librarian at Shields Library, University of California, Davis

Cover illustration: Detail from the first leaf of the *Hildebrandslied*

∞ Printed on acid-free paper which falls within the guidelines of the ANSI to ensure permanence and durability.

Library of Congress Cataloging-in-Publication Data

Popa, Opritsa D.
Bibliophiles and bibliothieves : the search for the Hildebrandslied and the Willehalm Codex / by Opritsa D. Popa ; with a preface by Winder McConnell.
p. cm. – (Cultural property studies = Schriften zum Kulturgüterschutz)
Includes bibliographical references and index.
ISBN 3-11-017730-7 (Cloth : alk. paper)
1. World War, 1939-1945–Germany–Art and the war. 2. World War, 1939-1945–Germany–Destruction and pillage. 3. Art treasures in war–Germany. 4. Cultural property–Germany. I. Title. II. Series: Cultural property studies.
D810.A8P67 2003
940.53'18–dc22
2003019022

ISBN 3-11-017730-7

Bibliographic Information published by Die Deutsche Bibliothek

Die Deutsche Bibliothek lists this publication in the Deutsche Nationalbibliografie; detailed bibliographic data is available in the Internet at <http.//dnb.ddb.de>.

Printed in Germany
Cover: +malsy kommunikation und gestaltung, Bremen
Data Conversion: Werksatz Schmidt & Schulz, Gräfenhainichen
Printing and Binding: Hubert & Co, Göttingen

To the memory of Ardelia R. Hall and Edgar Breitenbach –
Champions in the recovery of war-looted art.

To the Directors of the Kassel State Library, 1945–1975,
And to their unwavering efforts to bring the manuscripts home.

Preface

Apart from the cost in human lives, war inevitably exacts a heavy toll on the cultural and spiritual life of those countries unfortunate enough to become the prime venues of hostilities. This is particularly true of conquered nations. The layman may be familiar with the story of the destruction of Carthage in 146 B.C. during the Punic Wars and, with it, the demise of many of the city's great libraries. A similar fate appears to have befallen the Royal Library in Alexandria, Egypt, when Caesar set fire to the Ptolemaic fleet in 48 B.C. The Daughter Library, or Sarapeum, supposedly suffered complete annihilation in 391 A.D., a victim of the Emperor Theodosius's order to destroy all the pagan temples in the city. During the Twentieth Century, hundreds of thousands of volumes and manuscripts were destroyed through bombing raids and artillery fire, most recently the University Library of Bucharest, Romania, during the overthrow of the Ceauşescu regime in 1989 (a library whose holdings Opritsa Popa has, in the interim, played a conspicuous role in restoring).

Less final than destruction, but often just as devastating to a nation's cultural heritage, is the looting of its artistic treasures. One particularly well documented chapter dealing with such "acquisitions" concerns the fate of thousands of principally Jewish-owned artworks seized during World War II by the Nazis throughout occupied Europe for private or public display within the German Reich. The recent book by Hector Feliciano, *The Lost Museum. The Nazi Conspiracy to Steal the World's Greatest Works of Art* (1995; English version 1997) traces the wartime and post-war fate of the private collections of five French-Jewish families: the Rothschilds, Rosenbergs, Bernheim-Jeunes, David-Weills, and Schlosses. Almost forty years ago, John Frankenheimer's film, "The Train," dramatized the efforts of a French Resistance leader (played by Burt Lancaster) to prevent a German unit (the commander played by Paul Scofield) from absconding in 1944 with the best of France's artistic works.

However, the story, or stories, of looting are nothing if not complex, nor are they confined to dictators and dictatorships. The Monuments, Fine Arts and Archives Specialist Officers of the Armed Forces of the United States, stationed in 1945 in Wiesbaden, Germany, and entrusted with the preserving and restoring to their rightful owners artworks looted or displaced in the course of the war, were appalled to receive from the Commanding General of the 7th Army on November 6, 1945 orders to prepare for shipment to the U.S.A. "a selection of at least two zero zero German works of art of greatest importance ...." Their written protest, sent one day following receipt of the aforementioned order and known as the Wiesbaden Manifesto, while not effective in putting an immediate halt to the looting, created enough of a stir in America that the Truman administration was forced to re-think its position on the matter. No further shipments followed and the two hundred and two artworks actually sent to the U.S.A. were returned to Germany four years later.

If government-sponsored looting by the U.S. Armed Forces had been checked, this was by no means the case on the individual level. Tens of thousands of items found their way out of Germany and back to the United States through the Army parcel post or in the trunks of demobilized GIs. In *Bibliophiles and Bibliothieves,* Opritsa Popa has documented what might justifiably be described as the most celebrated case of looting of two German cultural treasures by a member of the U.S. Army at the end of World War II and their subsequent odyssey across both an ocean and a continent: the pilfering from a cellar in Bad Wildungen of the ninth-century *Liber Sapientiae*, containing the two leaves of the oldest extant German heroic poem, the Old High German *Hildebrandslied*, along with the fourteenth-century illuminated *Willehalm* codex, both of which had been removed from the State Library in Kassel for protection from bombing raids.

There are few scholarly works that also read like detective novels. This is one of those few, and while it should appeal to aficionados of the latter genre, it will most certainly be of immense interest to professors and students of German Studies throughout the world. The author's research has been painstakingly meticulous. The reader moves from her overview of wartime Europe through the efforts of German librarians, administrators, and art connoisseurs to protect the cultural heritage of their homeland (as well as of numerous other countries) from the ravages of combat, to the untiring work of the civil engineers, librarians, and art historians of the American Monuments, Fine Arts and Archives (MFA&A) Corps, particularly the Director of the Wiesbaden Collecting Point, Walter Ings Farmer, to the domiciles of the "rich and famous" on both the Atlantic and Pacific Coast of the United States where the aforementioned treasures came to reside, at least temporarily. This is, simultaneously, a story of the book-collecting world of the United States in the first half of the twentieth century and of some of its most prominent representatives, foremost among them A. S. W. Rosenbach of New York, who bought both the *Liber Sapientiae* and the *Willehalm* codex from Bud Berman, a former lieutenant in the U.S. Army. It is to Opritsa Popa's credit that we now know the identity of the individual who brought these priceless manuscripts to the United States from occupied Germany. She has fully documented the efforts of, in particular, Ardelia Ripley Hall of the State Department, and Edgar Breitenbach, former Chief of the Prints and Photograph Division of the Library of Congress, to insure that works stolen from Germany were restored to their appropriate owners, and of library directors Wilhelm Hopf and Dieter Hennig in Kassel to reclaim their lost treasures.

It is a "detective story" with a happy ending. The second leaf of the *Hildebrandslied* was located in California and returned, along with the *Liber Sapientiae*, on March 25, 1955 to the library in Kassel. It would be sixteen and a half more years before, on September 22, 1972, the first leaf of the *Hildebrandslied*, along with the fourteenth-century *Willehalm Codex,* both located in the Rosenbach Museum and Library, would be turned over to Library Director Dieter Hennig in Philadelphia, who would bring them back to Kassel.

As a young graduate student at the University of Kansas in Fall, 1967, I read for the first time Professor Carl Selmer's 1955 account of his re-discovery of the *Hildebrandslied* in America in November, 1945 in New York. Needless to say, all of the details of this manuscript's prior and subsequent odyssey were, at the time, completely unknown to me. Now, nearing the conclusion of my career in German Studies, I am particularly indebted to Opritsa Popa for having filled in all of the gaps regarding what has undoubtedly been one of the most fascinating mysteries in the realm of *Germanistik*, and for contributing to the scholarship of older German literature one of the most significant books to appear in some time.

Davis, California
February 2003

Winder McConnell

Contents

List of Illustrations and Captions

Introduction and Acknowledgments

War is one of the greatest enemies of books. Ignorance is another. During the Second World War, German troops torched hundreds of libraries and destroyed nearly 200 million volumes. When the tide turned most German library buildings were lost in Allied bombing raids and millions of books fell victim to fire and plunder. In this as in all other wars, the maxim *To the victor go the spoils*, was generally accepted. No sooner had Soviet armed forces marched into East Prussia, then Marshal Stalin ordered his Red Army Trophy Brigades to use library looting as punishment for the immense losses suffered at the hands of the Nazis. Breaking with historical tradition, General Eisenhower ordered his advancing troops to preserve and respect the symbols of culture encountered on enemy territory. Officers of his US Monuments, Fine Arts, & Archives Corps were dispatched to protect art caught in the crossfire. When the guns fell silent, they collected, restored, and repatriated thousands of cultural treasures found hidden in mineshafts, churches, or air raid shelters.

But not all servicemen complied with the Supreme Commander's order. Some used the cover of war as an opportunity for personal enrichment. The relatively sturdy and transportable manuscripts and incunabula were among the most desirable war-trophies. Those who indulged in the sport of book liberating returned home with splendid souvenirs: masterfully bound volumes, venerable old codices, illuminated Bibles, or Horae with delicate miniatures.

The defacement, destruction, or scattering of medieval manuscripts is not a modern-day phenomenon. Their history is replete with violence and fraught with forced wanderings. Only a fraction of the once bountiful output of medieval scriptoria has endured to reach our century. These precious survivors were passed from hand to hand, sometimes lovingly as scholarly gifts, more often violently as loot or war-trophies. Perhaps the greatest single loss to literature resulting from the Second World War was the theft and defacement of the ninth-century *Hildebrandslied*, the oldest extant heroic poem ever found on German soil. One other codex vanished from the same box and bunker: the lavishly illustrated fourteenth-century *Willehalm Codex*. *Bibliophiles and Bibliothieves* attempts to trace the war and hostage years of these two priceless manuscripts.

The book draws on a wealth of newly uncovered material. In 1998, the *Universitätsbibliothek Kassel, Murhardsche Bibliothek und Landesbibliothek der Stadt Kassel* released to the University of California, Davis Library hundreds of letters, clippings, and testimonials relating to the post-war hunt for *Hildebrandslied* and *Willehalm Codex*. Until 1998 this information had been considered sensitive and kept confidential. The Kassel documents span the years 1943 to 1975 and reflect the unrelenting search efforts of five dedicated library directors. The papers, collated in six sizable dossiers, are identified in the footnotes and in the bibliography as *Hildebrandlied* 1 through 6. From this never before seen material, supplemented through declassified US government documents, published sources, interviews with survivors and descendents, and through papers found in private hands, a fascinating story emerges, a tale that begins in misery, spoliation and greed, and ends in cooperation and respect for the cultural heritage of a nation.

Work on the saga of the *Hildebrandslied* and *Willehalm Codex* would have never been possible without the approval and support of Dr. Konrad Wiedemann, Director of the *Landes- und Murhardsche Bibliothek der Stadt Kassel*. Dr. Wiedemann provided open access to the Kassel *Hildebrandslied* file, unique photographs from his Library's archives, and important clarifications to historical events. This book owes him its very existence. Heartfelt thanks go to Dr. Dieter Hennig, former Director of the same library. His meticulous documentation and organization of the Kassel *Hildebrandslied* file made the author's research a breeze. I am most thankful to Dr. Hennig for his many invaluable insights, editorial comments, and for his gracious support.

I would like to express my gratitude to Dr. Derick Dreher, Director of the Rosenbach Museum & Library, for the release of documents relating to the 1945 New York sale of the manuscripts. Without this information, the story of the *Hildebrandslied* would have remained unfinished. Recognition is due to Monsignor Francis J. Weber for an important selection of documents from the Archives of the Los Angeles Archdiocese; to Irene Selmer Griffith, daughter of Dr. Carl Selmer, for her touching recollections about her father; and to Peter de la Garza and Ben R. Tucker for their unique and insightful explanations. I was privileged to speak to Jennifer Shank, daughter of Dr. Edgar Breitenbach, and interview Dr. Werner Gundersheimer, who contributed significant knowledge on the 1972 discovery and return of the manuscripts. My thanks go out to Justin and William H. Twaddell for the use of unpublished materials from their father's archive, and to Dr. Arnold Price for essential clarifications. Special tribute is due to Mayor Margaret Planton-Farmer for her friendly support, and to librarians Josephus Nelson and Grant Harris of the Library of Congress, for helping me connect with key people.

I could not have completed the book without the assistance of my dear colleagues, Miriam Hull, Noel Peattie, and Beatrice Crockett. Their probing questions, editorial comments, and their many corrections have substantially improved the quality of the manuscript. I have been the happy recipient of much friendship and advice from Dr. Winder McConnell, Chairman of the Department of German and Russian at University of California, Davis, who generously contributed his vast erudition, expertise, and precious time. For his critique and for his words of encouragement, I will remain forever grateful. Heartfelt thanks go to Associate University Librarians Clinton Howard and George

Bynon for their continued interest and support. I am pleased to acknowledge the financial assistance of the Librarian Association of the University of California (LAUC), and its Davis Division (LAUC-D), and of the Academic Federation of the University of California, Davis.

To my dear friend Andrew Farkas, Director of Libraries, University of Northern Florida, Godfather and co-instigator of this book, I pledge my gratitude. He was my close advisor throughout the many stages of the project. His buoyancy and wit helped me gloss over those unavoidable dark moments of doubt. And last but never least, my greatest thanks go to my husband, the soul of this book, who mercilessly nagged, preached, and pushed me, first to undertake the project, and then to stay the course.

It is my hope that the reader will find the dramatic account of the search for the *Hildebrandslied* and the *Willehalm Codex*, not only justified, but also instructive and engaging.

Davis, California | Opritsa D. Popa
March 2003

Liber Sapientiae and *Willehalm Codex*, 1939-2002 - A Chronology

September 2, 1939

Kassel State Library Director Dr. Hans Peter des Coudres relocates twenty valuable manuscripts from the *Landesbibliothek Kassel* to the vault of the local Credit Bank. The *Liber Sapientiae* (with the *Hildebrandslied* written on its fly-leaves) and the *Willehalm Codex* are among the twenty.

September 8/9, 1941

British air strikes on Kassel. The Library is hit. Three hundred fifty thousand library volumes are lost.

April 1, 1942

Dr. Hermann Baldewein is appointed Acting Library Director.

August 30, 1943

Former library director Dr. Wilhelm Hopf relocates the *Liber Sapientiae* and the *Willehalm Codex* to a bomb shelter in the nearby resort-town of Bad Wildungen.

October 22, 1943

Kassel is destroyed in a devastating British bombardment.

March 31, 1945

US troops enter Bad Wildungen.

April, 1945

The Bad Wildungen bomb shelter is looted. The wooden chest with the two manuscripts together with several large Kassel Museum canvases vanishes.

1945

Dr. Wilhelm Hopf is reinstated as library director.

August 14, 1945

The US Military Government conducts a brief investigation into the looting. The case is closed due to lack of evidence.

November 10, 1945

The Rosenbach Company acquires the two Kassel manuscripts from a returning US officer. The first leaf of the *Hildebrandslied* with the library's ownership stamp is removed. Days later, the codex is offered for sale to the Pierpont Morgan Library. Professor Carl Selmer identifies the ballad and the Morgan Library returns the stolen manuscript to Rosenbach with a warning.

November 1, 1949

Dr. Wolf von Both is appointed Director of the Kassel State Library, succeeding Dr. Wilhelm Hopf.

March and May, 1950

The *Liber Sapientiae* is sold to Estelle Doheny of Los Angeles, California. A journal article on the Doheny collection mentions the lost *Liber Sapientiae.*

November, 1951

Kassel Murhard librarian Dr. Gerhard Liebers alerts the US Department of State that the stolen *Hildebrandslied* codex has resurfaced in New York City. Department of State art historian Ardelia R. Hall opens an investigation.

June 13, 1952

The US Bureau of Customs investigates the Rosenbach Company. The interview fails to produce any new leads.

July 1, 1952

Dr. A. S. W. Rosenbach dies.

March 5, 1953

Philip Rosenbach dies. The Rosenbach home and library becomes a public museum and research institution.

August 14, 1953

Ardelia Hall recovers the *Liber Sapientiae* from the Doheny Memorial Library in Camarillo, California.

September 10, 1954

Ardelia Hall returns the *Liber Sapientiae* to the German Cultural Attaché in Washington, DC. The codex is lacking its first leaf with the beginning verses of the *Hildebrandslied.*

March 22, 1955

The mutilated codex is shipped back to Germany and returned to Kassel.

April 30, 1959

Dr. Ludwig Denecke is appointed Director of the *Landesbibliothek Kassel*, succeeding Dr. Wolf von Both.

January 30 and July 12, 13, 1961

Ardelia Hall interviews Gretel Mayer, a former Rosenbach employee, who claims to have witnessed the sale and purchase of the Kassel manuscripts in New York, in November of 1945. She identifies the seller as a returning US officer.

May 1, 1968

Dr. Dieter Hennig is appointed Director of the recently merged Murhard and Kassel State Library, succeeding Dr. Ludwig Denecke.

December 30, 1971

The Department of State officially closes its investigation into the looting of the Kassel manuscripts.

February 3, 1972

Lessing J. Rosenwald, President of the Rosenbach Foundation, acknowledges the presence of Leaf One of the *Hildebrandslied* in the collection of the Rosenbach Museum & Library.

March 3, 1972

The Rosenbach curator discovers the *Willehalm Codex* among the Museum's uncataloged holdings.

September 22, 1972

Both manuscripts are returned to Dr. Hennig in a festive ceremony in Philadelphia.

January 3, 2002

The Rosenbach Museum & Library releases a cache of documents pertaining to the 1945 sale of the *Liber Sapientiae* and the *Willehalm Codex*, revealing for the fist time the name of the seller, the date, and the sales price of the manuscripts.

Chapter 1: "They've Sown the Wind And Now They Reap the Whirlwind."

Hosea 8:7

First light was tardy. Only around seven-thirty did it reluctantly seep through the fleecy fog still tangled in naked branches.[1] At Bomber Command Headquarters, west of London, Air Chief Marshal Sir Arthur T. Harris left his office at daybreak and walked hurriedly down the narrow beech-lined alley that led to the underground operation room.[2] His meteorological officer was waiting, weather charts unfurled. The day's reports called for continued electrical storms across the English Channel but for much-improved visibility over the Continent.[3] Hunched over the large map, Sir Arthur let his index finger glide slowly across Europe, and brought it to rest on a dot in the heart of Germany: Kassel. The raid was on.[4] Bomb release time, 2055 hours.

During morning briefings, aircrews in East and Central England were apprised of the mission. Information sheets and target maps were distributed. Kassel, the capital of Hesse-Nassau, population 216,000, was nestled in the Fulda valley. A busy railway junction, it connected northern seaports to industrial centers in the Ruhr and to all major cities of the Reich. The target map, dotted with small bombing objectives, displayed a clearly marked bull's eye: Henschel & Sohn, the most important train and motor vehicle factory in Europe. Of late, Henschel manufactured far more than locomotives and trucks. It churned out a steady stream of fighting vehicles: Tiger tanks, Stuka dive-bombers,[5] and land-to-air

---

1 *Times (London)*, October 22, 1943, p. 5. On October 22, 1943 the sun rose at 7:34 a. m.

2 Ralph Barker, *The RAF at War* (Alexandria, VA: Time-Life Books, 1981), 96, 100.

3 "More air blows at enemy. Another 1,500 tons on Kassel," *Times* (London), October 25, 1943, p. 4: "The weather was once more unfavorable, thick clouds, icy conditions, and electric storms being encountered most of the way. Over Kassel visibility was much better."

4 Barker, 101 describing how Cologne was chosen as a bombing target seventeen months earlier (on May 30, 1942) by Air Chief Marshal Sir Arthur T. Harris.
Note: The sequence of events relating to the bombardment of Kassel on October 22, 1943 is based on the chronology of Werner Dettmar, in *Die Zerstörung Kassels im Oktober 1943: Eine Dokumentation* (The Destruction of Kassel in October of 1943: A documentation) (Fuldabrück: Hesse, 1983), and on the eyewitness account of Georg Fiedler, the warden responsible for the civil defense of the Murhard Library. See: "Hildebrandlied 2," documents from the archives of the Gesamthochschul-Bibliothek Kassel – Landesbibliothek und Murhardsche Bibliothek der Stadt Kassel, deposited with the University of California, Davis, Shields Library, Department of Special Collections. Terrorangriff auf Kassel am 22.10.43 von 20–21:30 Uhr (Terror attack on Kassel on 10/22/43, from 8:00 to 9:30 p.m.). September 16, 1974. Copy of the 1943 eyewitness report of Georg Fiedler.

5 Stuka is short for *Sturzkampfflugzeug*, or dive-bomber.

rockets.[6] Its plants were under the direct control of the Wehrmacht,[7] and its name had become synonymous with armament production. At the very top of the target map a warning in bold print reminded pilots that this information was secret, to be memorized and destroyed.[8] On thirty-eight British airfields, an armada of 600 Lancaster, Stirling, and Halifax bombers began final preparations for attack.[9] Watches were synchronized. Later on that night, Kassel, Hitler's busy blacksmith shop would cease to exist.

It was Friday, October 22, 1943 and all through the morning hours, German radio surveillance detected increased communication between British airfields, a clear indication that a major raid was in the making. The bombing terror inflicted on Coventry, Birmingham, and London was coming home to roost. Since early spring, the British Royal Air Force had launched one devastating raid after another. Industrial installations in the Ruhr, oil refineries in the northwest, shipyards and submarine pens on the shores of the Baltic and North Sea had been pounded again and again. Flying deep into the German heartland, British bombing missions were now targeting densely populated centers, Essen, Mannheim, Lübeck, Rostock, Cologne, Münster, and Berlin. In July and August, Operation Gomorrah, a series of raids known to the people of Hamburg as *die Katastrophe*, had killed 50,000 civilians and had left the Hanseatic city in ruins. Survivors told harrowing stories of sweeping firestorms, and ghastly destruction.[10] While the *Luftwaffe* could no longer stem these raids, it did make each one very costly. With every attack, British bombers had to pierce through the Kamm-

---

[6] Reinhard Henschel, *Gleise und Nebengleise: Von meines Vaters Lokomotiven zu geheimen Missionen. Ein Mann besichtigt eine vergangene Zeit* (Tracks and sidetracks: From my father's locomotives to secret missions. A man contemplates a time gone by) (Bern: Scherz, 1983), 220.
Note: While very important, Henschel & Sohn was not the only armament purveyor of Kassel. There was also Gerhard Fieseler, a firm manufacturing Storch, Messerschmitt and Focke-Wulf fighter planes, flame-throwers, special military vehicles, and V1 bombers. Additionally, there was Wegemann, a producer of heavy tanks. Other Kassel companies supplied the war machine with boots, tent squares, and optical and medical instruments. A description of Kassel's contributions to the war effort can be found in *Volksgemeinschaft und Volksfeinde: Kassel 1933–1945. Eine Dokumentation* (Folk community and Folk enemies: Kassel 1933–1945. A documentation), Jörg Kammler, Dietfried Krause-Vilmar, Siegfried Kujawski, Wolfgang Prinz, and Robert Wilmsmeier, eds. (Fuldabrück: Hesse, 1984), 384, 428.

[7] Carl-Friedrich Baumann, *175 Jahre Henschel: Der ständige Weg in die Zukunft; 1810–1985* (175 years of Henschel: The persistent path toward the future: 1810–1985) (Moers: Steiger, 1985), 74.

[8] Dettmar, 80–81.

[9] Ibid., 96.

[10] Barker, 96–97: "Harris was free of scruples about bombing civilians who happened to be in the area. No nation fighting for its life, he argued, could be squeamish about its methods. Besides, Harris believed that bombing could obviate land confrontation and save the lives of many thousand of allied soldiers."

huber Line, a formidable wall of spotlights, anti-aircraft guns, and night fighters.[11] Many did not return.

By five-thirty in the afternoon, on airfields in Yorkshire, Lincolnshire and East Anglia, the grand armada was ready for take off.[12] On the other side of the channel the German air defense system was lying in wait. The probing eyes of the Freya and Würzburg radars,[13] which speckled the coast of occupied Europe, scanned the horizon intently. No sooner had the first bomber stream reached the dunes of the Dutch coastline than German night-fighters were airborne, ground defenses activated, and radar was plotting altitude, speed and direction, determined to identify the target city: it could be Aachen, Koblenz, or Frankfurt. Abruptly over Aachen, the dark bomber galaxy turned south, direction Koblenz. Fifteen minutes later, the formation changed course once more, and appeared headed for Frankfurt. German night-fighters rushed to the defense of the city.

In Kassel, it was the end of a golden day, bathed in that soft, consoling light that sometimes marks the end of the clement season. Reports from the Eastern Front were increasingly worrisome. Since the beginning of the year, the German offensive had suffered one setback after another. In January, the Russians had broken through the stranglehold on Leningrad, and only days later, on the frozen steppes between Volga and Don, Field Marshal Friedrich von Paulus and his Sixth Army had been forced to surrender.[14] The bloody battle of Stalingrad had marked the first stunning defeat of the Nazi war machine: seventy thousand Germans killed, 91,000 captured. The three days of national mourning were followed by an order for total mobilization: all men aged sixteen to sixty-five and all women seventeen to forty-five were summoned to defend the swastika. Vibrant Kassel had shriveled to a city of old folks and children. The brutality unleashed upon the world by Hitler and his all-too-willing followers was beginning to recoil upon Germany. And while Nazi propaganda continued its tirades of triumph and revenge, on this autumn afternoon in 1943, only a die-hard few still clung to the myth of the final victory.

---

11 Major General Josef Kammhuber had set up the German night air defense system in July of 1940. It was a firewall that stretched from Denmark to southern France.

12 Dettmar, 102.

13 The German radar consisted of a long wave aircraft reporting system called Freya, and a guidance system called Würzburg. The radar Freya was named after Freyja, the Norse goddess of dawn. Similarly to radar, the guardian of her necklace could see to the horizon in day or night.

14 Friedrich von Paulus, commander of the German Sixth Army in the Battle of Stalingrad, surrendered to the Russians against Hitler's orders. Almost all his surviving 91,000 soldiers were captured and sent to labor camps in Siberia. Prisoner von Paulus joined a league of German communists and ended up broadcasting anti-Nazi propaganda for Stalin. He was freed in 1951.

In the four years since the onset of the war, Kassel had grown accustomed to the plaintive wail of sirens.[15] Yet with one disastrous exception the thousand-year-old city had escaped major destruction. Two years earlier, during the night of September 8, 1941, a devastating British bombardment[16] had hit several armament factories, and had destroyed the railway station, the jewel-like Red Palace, and the stately Museum Fridericianum, home of the *Landesbibliothek*, the Kassel State Library.[17] Three hundred fifty thousand books had gone up in flames that night, seven-eighth of the library's entire book collection, irreplaceable incunabula, unique records, and rare works of art, law, and geography. Scorching temperatures had turned the fireproof steel cabinets of the manuscript collection into furnaces. In drawer after steel drawer, the ancient vellum leaves had blistered, shrunk, and shriveled.[18] Fortunately, some of the library's most valuable possessions were not in the building. On the second day of the war, September 2, 1939, library director Hans Peter des Coudres had prudently evacuated twenty of his most precious manuscripts to the underground vault of the Kassel *Landeskreditkasse*, the Hesse Credit Bank. Among the twenty evacuees was the library's crown jewel, the ninth-century *Hildebrandslied,*[19] the earliest extant epic poem in the German language.

Hans Peter des Coudres, the crafty director of the Kassel *Landesbibliothek*, was a member of the Nazi Party. He had joined in 1930 three years before Hitler's ascent to power, and this early political affiliation had earned him important pro-

---

15 Dettmar, 71. By the end of October of 1943, air raid sirens had sounded in Kassel over two hundred times.

16 "Kassel bombed by 100 aircraft." *Times* (London), September 10, 1941, p. 4, col. C: "Great destruction and fires beyond counting were left by the R.A.F. in Monday night's heavy attack on Kassel, in which nearly 100 aircraft took part. ... The attack was sharp, sudden, and heavy, and even before the main force of bombers had arrived there were many fires to signal our immediate success."

17 The Fridericianum, the first public museum of continental Europe, was named after Landgrave (Count) Friedrich I. Using the British Museum as a model, architect Simon Louis du Ry built the Fridericianum in 1779. Six statues representing philosophy, painting, architecture, sculpture, historiography, and astronomy adorned its facade. The museum brought together under one roof amazing displays from all fields of knowledge. The Landgrave's library was its centerpiece.
Note: For reasons of brevity and simplicity, throughout the text the designation "Kassel State Library" will be used in lieu of than the more accurate designation of "Hesse State Library in Kassel" or "Provincial Library of Kassel" (Landesbibliothek Kassel).

18 Hartmut Broszinski, *Kasseler Handschriftenschätze* (Kassel manuscript treasures) (Kassel: Johannes Stauda, 1985), 17.

19 *Handbuch der historischen Buchbestände in Deutschland* (Handbook of historical book collections in Germany), editor Bernhard Fabian, vol. 5 (Hildesheim: Olms-Weidmann, 1992), 319.

fessional rewards.[20] The day after the invasion of Poland, however, the library director had found himself caught on the horns of a political and professional dilemma. As head of the library, he had to protect his unique manuscripts from the dangers of war. Yet as a loyal Party member, he had to represent Germany's brazen image of invincibility. His evacuation order issued on the very day when German tanks were blasting their way through Polish lines seemed oddly defensive.

Banking perhaps on his good standing with the local Party leadership, des Coudres had set aside all thought of political risk and had proceeded with his evacuation plan. Mundane details, such as finding suitable packing material, had turned out to be more difficult than anticipated. At least two of the codices, the ninth-century *Hildebrandslied*, and the fourteenth-century illuminated *Willehalm Codex*, required special handling and care. Unable to find an adequate library crate, des Coudres had ended up using a sturdy wooden chest, inherited from his father. He had the two manuscripts wrapped in parchment paper and placed in the chest, which he then secured with two strong locks.[21] On September 2, 1939, a scant sixteen days before he was called up for his military duty,[22] des Coudres had carried the box to the Hesse Credit Bank on the *Ständeplatz*, not far from the Library. He had stored it in the underground vault, and had notified the *Landeshauptmann*, the Head of the Communal Administration of the District of

---

20 Hans-Gerd Happel in his *Das wissenschaftliche Bibliothekswesen im Nationalsozialismus: unter besonderer Berücksichtigung der Universitätsbibliotheken* (Scholarly librarianship during National Socialism: with special emphasis on university libraries) (Munich: Saur, 1989), 28, notes that des Coudres had been a member of the National Socialist Party since 1930. Hans-Oskar Weber comments on Director des Coudres's professional and political ascent in his chapter "Landesbibliothek Kassel 1938" (State Library Kassel 1938) In: *Bibliotheken während des Nationalsozialismus*, part 1, Peter Vodosek and Manfred Komorowski, eds. (Wiesbaden: Harrassowitz, 1989), 369–70: "Sogleich nach dem Fachexamen übernahm er die 'Bibliothek der Gesellschaft zur Förderung und Pflege deutscher Kulturdenkmäler' auf der Wewelsburg im Kreis Büren in der Gegend von Paderborn. Laut *Ex Bibliotheca Cassellana* war er dort 'Leiter der Bibliothek der Schutzstaffel der NSDAP'. Die Wewelsburg war damals wohl eine SS-Führerschule. ... Über seine politische Belastung kann ich nichts sagen; immerhin wurde er 1950 Leiter der Bibliothek des Bundesgerichtshofs." (Immediately after taking his qualifying examinations, he assumed responsibility for the 'Library of the Society for the Advancement and Cultivation of German Cultural Property' in Wewelsburg, in the district Büren, close to the city of Paderborn. According to *Ex Bibliotheca Cassellana* he was the 'head of the SS Party Library.' Wewelsburg was then an SS elite academy. ... I cannot judge his political culpability; after all, in 1950 he was appointed director of the library of the Federal Court of Justice.)
Note: Unless otherwise noted, the author has provided all translations.

21 "Hildebrandlied 1," documents from the archives ... sworn testimony of H. P. des Coudres, December 22, 1970.

22 *Ex Bibliotheca Cassellana: 400 Jahre Landesbibliothek, 20. 11. 1580–20. 11. 1980* (From the Kassel Library: 400 years of State Library, 11/20/1580–11/20/1980), editor Hans-Jürgen Kahlfuß (Kassel: Gesamthochschul-Bibliothek-Kassel, Landesbibliothek und Murhardsche Bibliothek der Stadt Kassel, 1980), 95.

Kassel, about the evacuation. A note in his diary recorded the date, contents, packaging method, and sundry details related to the transfer.[23] He must have felt at peace knowing that at least twenty of his treasures were better protected.

As feared, the immediate reaction of the Party elite had been one of accusation and condemnation. In the eyes of *Gauleiter* Karl Weinrich,[24] the senior area administrative commander, the librarian's action revealed distrust in German air superiority and implicitly in the effectiveness of the city's civil defense, which was under the *Gauleiter's* command. Des Coudres had been branded a man harboring defeatist attitudes,[25] a hostile accusation that could have cost him far more than his post.[26] Two years later, during the night of September 8, 1941, when

---

23 "Hildebrandlied 1," documents from the archives. ... Sworn testimony of H. P. des Coudres, January 12, 1971.

24 Karl Höffkes, *Hitlers politische Generale: Die Gauleiter des Dritten Reiches. Ein biographisches Nachschlagewerk* (Hitler's political generals. The Gauleiters of the Third Reich. A biographical reference book) (Tübingen: Grabert, 1986), 383–85, and Peter Hüttenberger, *Die Gauleiter: Studie zum Wandel des Machtgefüges in der NSDAP* (The Gauleiters: An analysis of the transformation of the Nazi power structure) Schriftreihe der Vierteljahreshefte für Zeitgeschichte, 19 (Stuttgart: Deutsche Verlagsanstalt, 1969), 209. Both authors describe how later Weinrich himself ran into trouble with the Nazis. The Gauleiter was severely criticized after the October 22, 1943 bombardment. He had been out of town, attending a Party meeting, and had not returned to the devastated city until the next day. Goebbels took a very dim view of Weinrich's leadership qualities. "During a conference with the responsible authorities, in the course of which reports were made on each question involved, I learned how little had been done. Weinrich played a very sorry role. He hadn't the faintest idea of the actual facts, didn't even know who was to talk at the conference, and forever had to question others so as to be able to reply to me. I shall certainly report to the Fuehrer the pitiful role he played as Gauleiter and urge that he be quickly replaced." See: Joseph Goebbels, *The Goebbels Diaries, 1942–1943.* Louis P. Lochner, editor and translator (Garden City, New York: Doubleday, 1948), 497. Indeed, Karl Gerland soon replaced Weinrich. For a biographical sketch of Weinrich and Gerland see the Appendix.

25 "Hildebrandlied 4," documents from the archives. ... Letter of D. Hennig to H.-O. Weber, October 9, 1972.

26 Defeatism was a crime that carried severe penalties. Karl-Heinz Brackmann, *NS-Deutsch: "Selbstverständliche" Begriffe und Schlagwörter aus der Zeit des Nationalsozialismus* (Nazi-German: Common concepts and expressions of the National Socialist era) (Straelen/Niederrhein: Straelener Manuskripte, 1988), 46, states that expressions of doubt in the final victory or in the strength of the *Wehrmacht* were severely punished. So was public display of fear of bombardments. A case in point was the punishment of artist Constantin Gerhardinger (1888–1970). Hitler, who admired the work of the painter, had given him an Honorary Professorship. But when Gerhardinger, fearing bombardments, refused to participate in the 1943 Art Exhibit in Munich, Hitler took away his professorship and dismissing him from the Academy. In the period after January 1943, death sentences were imposed on civilians who expressed demoralizing opinions. Marlis G. Steinert, *Hitlers Krieg und die Deutschen. Stimmung und Haltung der deutschen Bevölkerung im Zweiten Weltkrieg* (Hitler's war and the Germans. Public mood and attitude of the German people during the Second World War) (Düsseldorf: Econ, 1970), 423, for instance, mentions the execution of councilman Dr. Theodor Korselt of Rostock, who had ventured to say in a streetcar that Hitler ought to

the other codices shriveled, blistered and burned in their incandescent steel coffins, the library director's prudent and timely decision had been amply affirmed.[27]

During des Coudres's military service, the administration of the library was turned over to another trustworthy political appointee.[28] Dr. Hermann Baldewein, the new deputy director, was rumored to be a member of the *Sicherheitsdienst*, the SS intelligence.[29] Barely thirty months out of library training, Baldewein had limited administrative experience.[30] At the time of his appointment, the library was in crisis. The British bombardment had left the Fridericianum in ruins. Thousands of fire and water damaged volumes demanded immediate attention. Journal subscriptions had to be reactivated, and gaps filled. Replacement copies had to be identified, purchased, catalogued, and housed.[31] The library's acquisition and cataloging departments had to be relocated to offices of the Murhard Library, the second largest research library in Kassel. The beleaguered Baldewein needed assistance. For the mammoth acquisition work alone, he needed an experienced professional for whom knowledge of donors, of regional collections, and of the antiquarian book-trade was second nature, a person whose devotion to the *Landesbibliothek* was absolute. The expert Baldewein needed was already

---

resign. Another example was set with the execution of the youngest sister of writer Erich Maria Remarque. Elfriede Scholtz was arrested for defeatist statements and decapitated on December 16, 1943.

27 The *Landesbibliothek Kassel* was the first German library to be bombarded and destroyed during the Second World War.

28 Between 1939 and 1942, senior librarian Dr. Friedrich Israël was deputy director of the library. (*Ex Bibliotheca Cassellana*, 31) Hans-Oskar Weber, 370, explains that the diacritical mark on the *e* in the name Israël denoted Aryan descent. This is perhaps why Dr. Israël, in spite of his Jewish sounding name, was allowed to continue working in a professional capacity. In April of 1942, Dr. Israël was asked to accompany the Kassel manuscript collection to its evacuation site in Marburg, where he remained until 1948. (*Ex Bibliotheca Cassellana*, 39).

29 Hans-Oskar Weber, 372. Weber remarks that although Baldewein was rumored to be a member of the SD and an agent, he never took action against library colleagues denounced by informers. In 1945, as punishment for his Nazi past, Baldewein was dismissed without compensation.

30 *Ex Bibliotheca Cassellana*, 95.
Note: Happel, 29–30, lists the educational, political, and racial requirements necessary to become a research librarian under National Socialism: To enroll in library training, a candidate had to have a doctoral degree, be a member of the Nazi Party, and, if married, the spouse had to be of Aryan bloodline. The candidate had to declare that he was not a member of a Lodge or of any similar organization. Once the candidate's dossier was completed it was sent for verification and approval to the Reich's Ministry for Education in Berlin. If approved, the candidate, now called a *Bibliotheksreferendar* (library postulant), had to enroll in a two-year program of library instruction and political studies. This training was concluded with a comprehensive examination. The successful postulant received the title *Bibliotheksassessor* (assistant librarian).

31 *Ex Bibliotheca Cassellana*, 39–40.

in the building, working quietly as a part-time bibliographer. He was Dr. Wilhelm Hopf, the sixty-five-year-old former director of the Kassel State Library, whom the Nazis had demoted.

No one knew the Kassel *Landesbibliothek* better than Dr. Hopf. Mild-mannered and self-effacing he was recognized throughout the library world as a scholar of history, and admired for his bibliographic knowledge and organizational skills. Wilhelm Hopf had spent his entire professional life in the Kassel library. He had risen through the ranks from assistant librarian in 1912, to specialist in 1920, and had become director in 1921. Keenly interested in Hesse's past, he presided over the Society for Hesse History and Culture and was an active contributor to scholarly journals.[32]

Unlike des Coudres and Baldewein, Hopf was not favorably regarded in Nazi circles. In 1933, when the library was given the mandate to collect the documents of the National Socialist movement, Director Hopf refused, arguing that the Library's collecting emphasis excluded the field of political science.[33] The Party elite also remembered one other affront: in 1937 Hopf thwarted an attempt to offer the library's most precious manuscript, the *Hildebrandslied*, as a gift to the Führer.[34] That very same year, Hopf issued a faithful facsimile edition of the heroic warrior ballad.[35] Printed in a short run of only 200 copies, it was defensively dedicated to *Adolf Hitler, the Führer*.

Actions such as these did not help Hopf's political standing. Even more disturbing than his deeds were his philosophical views. Wilhelm Hopf was a freemason, a leader in the Kassel Masonic Friendship Lodge.[36] The ideas advanced by freemasons were antithetical to National Socialist thinking. In the eyes of the Nazis,

---

32 Eduard Brauns, "Wilhelm Hopf: Verzeichnis seiner Schriften" (Wilhelm Hopf, a bibliography), *Zeitschrift des Vereins für Hessische Geschichte und Landeskunde* 63 (1952): 128–134.

33 *Ex Bibliotheca Cassellana*, 26.

34 "Zurück ohne finanzielle Forderungen. *Hildebrandslied und Willehalm* daheim" (Back without financial compensation: The *Hildebrandslied* and the *Willehalm* are home) *Hessische Allgemeine*, 30 September 1972: "Dank wurde ... auch Dr. Wilhelm Hopf gesagt. Er hat seinerzeit verhindert, daß das Hildebrandslied Adolf Hitler geschenkt wurde." (Gratitude was also expressed ... to Dr. Wilhelm Hopf. At the time, he thwarted an attempt to offer the Hildebrandslied as a gift to Adolf Hitler.)

35 This facsimile edition was created mainly to protect the original from use, abuse and deterioration. In his foreword to *Das Hildebrandslied* (Kassel: Der Landeshauptmann in Hessen, 1937) Wilhelm Traupel, the Landeshauptmann of Hesse-Nassau, reminded his readers that in the past scholars had applied chemicals directly onto the vellum leaf to make faded text briefly legible. As exposure to heat, humidity, and light contributed to the progressive deterioration of the manuscript, the library administration decided to replace the original, which until then was on display, with the 1937 facsimile.

36 Adolf Kallweit, *Die Freimauerei in Hessen-Kassel: Königliche Kunst durch zwei Jahrhunderte, von 1743–1965* (The Freemasons in Hesse-Kassel: Royal art spanning two centuries, from 1743–1965) (Baden-Baden: Agis, 1966), 40, 78, and 85, and *Ex Bibliotheca Cassellana*, 26.

a person harboring such beliefs had no place at the helm of an important educational institution of the Third Reich. Notwithstanding life-long contributions to city and library, Hopf was declared unfit as director, and in 1938 forced to resign not only his position but also the presidency of the historical society.[37] Three years later, in the aftermath of the 1941 British bombardment, deputy director Baldewein had no choice but to ask Dr. Hopf to reassume some of his former administrative and professional responsibilities.

Hopf did not hesitate to take on the Herculean task. His intimate knowledge of antiquarian stock and trade allowed him to find rare replacement copies. He solicited and received valuable donations from private collectors, and duplicates from regional libraries.[38] Under his care, the empty shelves slowly began filling up again. Heat, fire, and water had ravaged the library's manuscript collection, and efforts were underway to evacuate the remnants to the neighboring city of Marburg. Fortunately, twenty of its most precious holdings, hidden in the underground bank vault, had survived the 1941 attack. But as bombardments increased in frequency and intensity, that storage area was no longer deemed secure. A safer evacuation site had to be found without delay. British bombers often targeted city centers, with their highly flammable wooden structures.[39] Conflagrations disrupted work schedules and hampered armament production.

An unexpected opportunity presented itself toward the end of summer 1943, when Rudolf Helm, curator of the *Landesmuseum*, the Provincial Museum of Kassel, offered to let the library share space in a remote air raid shelter. On August 30, Wilhelm Hopf retrieved the wooden chest from the bank-vault and moved it out of harm's way, some thirty miles southwest of Kassel to the resort town of Bad Wildungen.[40]

* * *

The setting autumnal sun coated the houses of the historic town center, *die Altstadt*, in hues of fluid gold. Since early October it had been abnormally quiet: no

---

[37] *Ex Bibliotheca Cassellana*, 92. On March 31, 1938 Hopf was compelled to take early retirement and was forced to resign from the presidency of the Society for Hesse History and Culture. In Alexandra Habermann, Rainer Klemmt, and Frauke Siefkes, "Lexikon deutscher wissenschaftlicher Bibliothekare, 1925–1980" (Bio-bibliographic dictionary of German academic librarians, 1925–1980), *Zeitschrift für Bibliothekswesen und Bibliographie*, Sonderheft 42 (Frankfurt am Main: Klostermann, 1985), 136, it is stated: "1938 wurde Hopf wegen seiner Mitgliedschaft in einer Loge vorzeitig in den Ruhestand versetzt." (In 1938 Hopf was forced to take early retirement due to his membership in the Lodge.)

[38] *Ex Bibliotheca Cassellana*, 40.

[39] Barker, 98.

[40] "Hildebrandlied 1," documents from the archives. ... Letter of W. Hopf to the Landeshauptmann, March 6, 1946. Before transferring the chest, Hopf obtained permission from the deputy Landeshauptmann, Dr. Otto Schellmann.

sirens and no sound of enemy planes in the skies above. Kassel was aching for a period of respite. A good harvest held a promise of higher food rations.[41] Enticing performances posted at the State Theater reinforced the illusion of normalcy: *Walküre, The Barber of Seville, Zar und Zimmermann.*[42] Over at the Königsplatz, the fantasy color film *Münchhausen*[43] had opened to rave reviews, while at the Palace Theater, near the railway station, the comedy *Zwei glückliche Menschen*, Two happy people, with film stars Magda Schneider and Wolf Albach-Retty, was drawing a crowd.[44] Just as in autumns past, after the movie, one could perhaps stop for plum cake and tea at the *Residenzcafé* close to the library. A lively, all-girl band was playing, and the light-hearted music offered a welcome escape from wartime worries.[45]

Around seven o'clock, house warden Georg Fiedler set out on his nightly inspection rounds. He and his wife were responsible for the civil defense of the Murhard Library.

Fiedler checked on all floors for the mandatory supplies of sand and water. Air raid precautions had been well rehearsed and had proven highly effective. The *Selbstschutz*, the self-protection system, organized army style, had ranks ranging from house staff, like Fiedler, to *Luftschutzleiter*, head air raid warden, who reported directly to the Chief of Police.[46] Everything seemed in perfect order. Exceptionally that evening, there was additional help on hand: Fräulein Schaller, Fräulein Heinlein, and the recently drafted schoolboy Möller were sharing fire-watch duties. Soon after eight o'clock, seven other people joined their small contingent: Herr Kind from the Department of Construction, Herr Meyer from Measurements, and five reservists. It was a balmy evening. Shreds of music drifted up from the coffeehouse in the square.

---

[41] Dettmar, 256.

[42] Ibid., 26.

[43] *Münchhausen*, a film with superb special effects, was released on March 3, 1943. The screenplay was by Berthold Bürger, a pseudonym for Erich Kästner. The Nazis had banned Kästner's books. On May 10, 1933, his works had been publicly burned together with other "un-German" writings by Brecht, Döblin, Heinrich and Thomas Mann, Hemingway, and Joyce. Kästner was twice arrested, and twice set free after interrogation. While he was forbidden to write in Germany, he was permitted to publish abroad so as to bring in hard currency. UFA, the German film studios, must have used this loophole to hire him for the *Münchhausen* screenplay. The incident however was reported to Hitler, who thereupon slapped Kästner with a total writing ban, extending to all countries.

[44] Dettmar, 26.

[45] Ibid., 119.

[46] Gordon Musgrove, *Operation Gomorrah: the Hamburg Firestorm Raids* (London: Jane's, 1981), 68.

Fig. 1. The Library in the Museum Fridericianum, 1779–1941
(Archives of the Universitätsbibliothek Kassel – Landesbibliothek und Murhardsche Bibliothek der Stadt Kassel – Reproduced by permission)

At eight seventeen a sudden shriek of sirens shattered the peace of the night. The *Kleinalarm*, the early signal, gave warning that enemy planes were less than thirty minutes away. The wave of British bombers had once again changed course and was now rapidly bearing down on Kassel. Abruptly as it had started, the *Kleinalarm* broke off, and the sudden silence griped the city by the throat. Only an occasional patter of rushing footsteps dotted the void: people caught in the streets scurrying to the nearest bomb-shelter. The unnatural stillness soon gave way to the ominous crescendo of the second siren, the *Fliegeralarm,* wailing of imminent danger.

Fiedler and his group hurriedly made their way to the library's cellar and hunkered down in the darkness.[47] From the west, a threatening drone was rapidly increasing to a roar. Moments later, anti-aircraft guns greeted the enemy planes with a thundering barrage of fire. Between bursts of flack, Georg Fiedler heard in horror the eerie whistle of falling bombs. The earth shook under the powerful

---

[47] The dramatic account of the British air raid is gleaned from house-warden G. Fiedler's report. See "Hildebrandlied 2," documents from the archives. ... Terrorangriff auf Kassel am 22.10.43 von 20–21:30 Uhr (Terror attack on Kassel on 10/22/43, from 8:00 to 9:30 p.m.). September 16, 1974, copy of the 1943 testimonial filed by Georg Fiedler.

force of the direct hit. The explosion ripped through the basement, hurling him and the others across the room. Windows and doors were blown off. It seemed as if above them the building had collapsed, and had buried them alive. Terrified, they tried crawling out of the basement, feeling their way along the pitch-black corridor, groping for the staircase. A second blast threw them backwards. Acrid clouds of soot belched up. A small projectile, a library stamp, hit Fiedler's wife in the face. The first wave of bombings lasted an eternity. Finally, during a pause, Fiedler and his helpers managed to clamber out. The library was still standing but its sheared-off roof and gables littered the pavement. The reprieve was short-lived and they had to dash back to the relative security of their smoke-filled cellar.

When they reemerged close to one hour later, the library was on fire. Oxygen-hungry flames swashed through its halls, devouring books and furniture. Kind, Meyer and the reservists were in a state of panic. The entire city was burning; their homes and families were threatened. They had to leave. Fiedler pleaded with them: the catalog, help save the catalog, it is the library's memory. Reluctantly the reservists followed him to the catalog hall, which had remained miraculously intact. Later, alone with only the women and the schoolboy, Fiedler struggled to put out hot spots, and prevent flames from uniting. With their meager supplies of sand and water, they kept fires at bay, off the ground floor, off the staircase, and out of an entry room, all filled with books.

Beyond the library, firestorms swept through the narrow streets of the *Altstadt*, setting cobblestones and buildings aglow. Walls of flames roared by, consuming everything in their path. In the Town Hall, the city archives had caught fire and were burning out of control.[48] The Credit Bank, where only days earlier the manuscripts lay hidden, was an incandescent skeleton, its orange tentacles reaching out angrily into the bloody sky. Structures collapsed blocking escape routes. Trapped in the bomb-shelters, thousands asphyxiated. Those who climbed out were cremated in the alleys. When dawn finally broke, light could not pierce through the heavy blanket of smoke hovering over the smoldering ruins of the *Altstadt*. *The Sunday Express* recorded the victory:

> Seldom, if ever, has a force composed solely of four engine bombers been used against a single target in such strength as that which last night showered its heaviest bombs on Kassel. ... In thirty-five minutes they dropped a load of more than 1,500 tons. ... From preliminary reports there is good reason to believe that the target was very successfully dealt with... Flames rose up 4,000 ft.[49]

---

[48] Leslie I. Poste, "The Development of U.S. Protection of Libraries and Archives in Europe During World War II" (Dissertation, University of Chicago, 1958), 233.

[49] "Kassel (1,500 Tons) Is Latest R.A.F. Target." *Sunday Express* (London), October 24, 1943. Sir Arthur Harris in his *Bomber Offensive* (London, Collins, 1947) 185, remembers that: "In a devastating attack on Kassel on the night of October 22nd–23rd, more than 90 per cent of the whole bomb load fell on the target."

Fig. 2. 1944 Map of Germany with Allied Occupation Zones.
(Adapted from: US Military Academy. Department of History. Campaign atlas to the Second World War: Europe and the Mediterranean. New York: The Academy, 1980. Adaptation created by the author).

Seven days after the attack, British reconnaissance planes reported fires still burning in Kassel.[50] What had taken 1,000 years to build had vanished in the span of fifty-five minutes.[51] Ten thousand people had perished. In the wake of the immense tragedy, the fate of books and manuscripts seemed utterly irrelevant. And yet, Director Hopf must have found some solace knowing that his most precious wards were safe, sealed in their gray wooden box, cloistered in a deep, cool cellar, afar from this fiery hellhole.

---

50 Dettmar, 153, citing paragraph 18 of the official Bomber Command report.

51 Ibid, 141 and Goebbels, 497: "The impression is devastating. The entire center of the city and most of the outlying sections have been destroyed. A gruesome picture strikes the eye. The destruction here can be compared only with that of Hamburg. A catastrophic fire of vast extent has run its unhindered course."

Chapter 2: "Habent Sua Fata Libelli" – Books Have Their Own Destiny

Terentianus Maurus

In a valley, hugged by the slopes of the Vogelsberg and Rhön, in the province of Hesse, lies the city of Fulda. For centuries, the beauty of its baroque architecture has enchanted artists and travelers alike. A majestic cathedral, its slender sand-colored towers reaching out towards eternity, dominates the city center. In spite of its eighteenth-century baroque appearance, Fulda's roots extend far deeper into history. Religious services have been continuously offered on the site of its cathedral for more then twelve hundred years.[1]

In the eighth century, Boniface, an English monk of great conviction and learning, came to this part of the world intent on converting the heathen Germanic tribes. Sustained in his efforts by a succession of popes and Frankish kings, Boniface established Christian communities throughout today's Bavaria, Hesse, and Thuringia. In 744 he sent out his pupil Sturmius and seven of his brethren in search of a suitable place for a new monastery. In a narrow vale, in the middle of a dense oak forest, the monk Sturmius planted his cross, marking the chosen spot. He named the future monastery after the adjacent river: Fulda.

Boniface used his great influence in Rome and Aachen to secure for his new monastery exemptions from episcopate authority and feudal obligations. Fulda became the third abbey, after Bobbio in Italy and Saint-Denis in France,[2] to be subordinated solely to pope and king. Boniface endowed the cloister library with precious personal books acquired during years of pilgrimage, study and preaching.

Eleven years later, in 755, on the plains of Dokkum in Holland, the seventy-five-year-old Boniface and his small group of believers were put to the sword by the Friesians they had set out to convert. Boniface's martyrdom earned him a place among the communion of saints. He was canonized and is venerated to this day as the Apostle of the Germans. Equally important, his erudition and passion for books earned him a place in the history of culture and libraries. To Boniface we owe the founding of one of the most important learning centers in Europe and the creation of one of the most glorious monastic libraries of the Carolingian Renaissance.

---

1 *Der Dom zu Fulda* (The Fulda Cathedral) (Fulda: Parzeller, 1973), 3.

2 *Hesse und Thüringen – Von den Anfängen bis zur Reformation: Eine Ausstellung des Landes Hessen* (Hesse and Thuringia – From the beginning to the Reformation: An exhibit of the province of Hesse) (Marburg: Historische Kommission für Hessen, 1992), 111. Bobio was exempted from episcopal jurisdiction in 628, and Saint-Denis in 757.

According to his wishes, Saint Boniface was laid to rest in his beloved Fulda. His tomb became a place of worship and pilgrimage. Precious gifts of manuscripts, gold and silver, and numerous bequests of land and properties poured in, making Fulda one of the wealthiest abbeys in Germany. A monumental Romanesque church modeled after Saint Peter's basilica in Rome, rose above his crypt. By the dawn of the ninth century, 5,000 people toiled in the service of the abbey and 134 monks called it home.[3] This is the place on which today's baroque cathedral stands.

In 789, a remarkable letter, written by Charlemagne to Baugulf, second abbot of Fulda, marked a turning point in the educational system of the kingdom. In his letter, Charlemagne urged the abbot to institute a teaching program that stressed literacy and biblical studies, and promoted literature and the sciences. Known as the *Epistola de Litteris Colendis,* Letter on the Promotion of Literary Culture, it is regarded as the central document of the Carolingian educational reform policy, and at the same time, as the founding document of Fulda's cloister school.[4] From the four corners of Europe students began beating a path to the gates of the abbey. Here they learned to read and write, studied Latin, and explored not only the works of church fathers[5] but also the masterpieces of secular authors.[6] In the first decades of the ninth century, Fulda emerged as the most important seat of learning in Europe.[7]

No scholarship can flourish without the support of a library, and Fulda was no exception. Its magnificent book collections acquired through donations and enriched through reproductions were the wonder of the medieval world. Charlemagne himself is said to have endowed Fulda with books.[8] The cloister library, patterned after the Benedictine library of Saint Martin in Tours, thrived under Rabanus Maurus, theologian, scholar, teacher, writer, and abbot between the years 822 and 842. Under his direction and care the library collections are said to

---

3 *Dictionary of the Middle Ages*, editor Joseph R. Strayer (New York: Scribner, 1982–1989), v. 5, 311.

4 Thomas Martin, "Bemerkungen zur 'Epistola de Litteris Colendis'" (Commentaries to the 'Epistola de Litteris Colendis'), *Archiv für Diplomatik: Schriftgeschichte, Siegel- und Waffenkunde* 31 (1985): 270–72.

5 Gangolf Schrimpf, *Mittelalterliche Bücherverzeichnisse des Klosters Fulda und andere Beiträge zur Geschichte der Bibliothek des Klosters Fulda im Mittelalter* (Medieval book catalogs of the monastery Fulda and other contributions on the history of the Fulda monastic library in the Middle Ages) (Frankfurt am Main: Knecht, 1992), I.

6 *Dictionary of the Middle Ages*, vol. 5, 312.

7 Karl Christ, *The Handbook of Medieval Library History,* translated and edited by Theophil M. Otto (Metuchen: Scarecrow, 1984), 143.

8 James Westfall Thompson, *The Medieval Library* (Chicago: University of Chicago Press, 1939), 58.

have numbered more books than could ever be counted.[9] In one of his letters, Rabanus praised the library as one that offered all the writings God had given to men and all the wisdom the world had produced from the beginnings of time.[10] It is during his tenure as abbot that the *Hildebrandslied* was copied in his scriptorium and shelved in his library.

From surviving fragmentary catalogs and inventories and from contemporary correspondence of clergy and scholars we can partially reconstruct the library's holdings. It certainly must have included many theological writings, biblical texts and commentaries, hagiographies, and works of ascetic literature, used in worship and instruction. However, what made Fulda so important and so astoundingly rich was the inclusion of the literature of Latin antiquity[11] and of secular books ranging from agriculture and architecture to military subjects.[12] While only eleven hundred of its manuscripts can be authenticated through records, it is believed that at its peak the library boasted some 2,000 volumes. Fulda excelled in one other area: it preserved through reproduction texts in the Old High German language, of which a handful survived to this day.[13] Among them was the best-known gift of Fulda to posterity, *Das Hildebrandslied.*

The monastic library was housed within or nearby the abbey's church building.[14] Locked bookcases, filled with vertically shelved manuscripts, lined its walls.[15] Individual desks, nestled in the bays of windows, must have offered readers full advantage of natural light and seclusion. The library's collections were augmented by copies produced in the abbey's scriptorium, which functioned much like a medieval publishing house,[16] copying for its own needs and accepting commis-

---

9 *Monumenta Germaniae Historica Inde Ab Anno Christi Quingentesimo Usque Ad Annum Millesimum Et Quingentesimum. Scriptorum,* vol. 13 (Hanover: Hahn, 1926–1934), 273.

10 *Monumenta Germaniae Historica Inde Ab Anno Christi Quingentesimo Usque Ad Annum Millesimum Et Quingentesimum. Poetarum Latinorum Medii Aevii* (Leipzig: Hiersemann, 1880–), 2 and 187.

11 Christ, 145: "In the saga of the survival of ancient literature, Fulda occupies a prominent place. Authors such as Cicero, Servius' edition of Virgil, Columnella, Vitruvius, the grammarians, especially the historians Suetonius, Ammianus Marcellinus, Justin, Hegesippus, and probably Tacitus, to name only the most important, were associated with Fulda."

12 Schrimpf, 95.

13 The seven texts known to have been recorded in Fulda are: the *Hildebrandslied*, the Old High German translation of Tatian's *Evangelienharmonie*, *Fränkisches Taufgelöbnis*, *Fuldaer Beichte*, *Hammelburger Markbeschreibung*, *Basler Rezepte* and the fragments of *Lex Salica.*

14 Schrimpf, 179.

15 Florence Edler de Rover, "The Scriptorium." In: *The Medieval Library.* James Westfall Thompson (Chicago: University of Chicago Press, 1939), 595.

16 *Fuldische Handschriften aus Hessen mit weiteren Leihgaben aus Basel, Oslo, dem Vatikan und Wolfenbüttel. Katalog zur Ausstellung anläßlich des Jubiläums '1250 Jahre Fulda.' Hessische Landesbibliothek Fulda, 19. April bis 31. May 1994* (Fulda manuscripts from Hesse with addi-

sions from monasteries, libraries, and wealthy patrons. At the time of Abbot Sturmius the scriptorium seated as many as forty scribes.[17] Here, devotion, prayers, diligence, and talent converged to produce works of extraordinary beauty. From dawn to dusk, copyists, artists, and artisans transcribed existing text onto smooth, wheat-colored parchment leaves, and adorned the leaves with elegant rubrics and illuminations.

Work was done during daylight, since candles presented too great a fire hazard. A librarian assigned specific daily tasks to the scribes. First, the vellum leaf was scraped clean and smoothed with pumice. Then lines were drawn with a sharp metal stylus: vertically, to mark the margins, and horizontally to keep the writing straight. The monks worked in complete silence at desks tilted in an almost vertical plane. Hunched over the smooth parchment sheets, they painstakingly transcribed their assigned texts, with a sharpened goose quill moistened in ink made of gall, sulfuric acid, gum, and sometimes wine.[18] Since vellum leaves were expensive, every inch of the surface was used to its fullest. A series of completed leaves was folded and sewn together to form a book. If there were to be a binding, it was usually made of vellum or of wooden boards covered with leather. This hand-made book, known as the codex, is one of the most precious offerings of the Middle Ages. Each codex, whether large or small, whether simple or adorned, is a unique and intensely personal creation, a gift to those who study, travel, minister, or pray.[19]

At the turn of the eighth century, the writing used in the Fulda scriptorium changed gradually from the angular and elegant style known as the Anglo-Saxon minuscule, to a lettering simple and rounded in appearance called the Carolingian minuscule.[20] By comparing script elements and studying the transition to this new writing style, researchers were able to establish a fairly accurate dating system for the works duplicated or created at the abbey.

---

tional loans from Basel, Oslo, the Vatican, and Wolfenbüttel. Catalog of the exhibit of the jubilee '1250 Years of Fulda.' Hesse State Library, April 19 to May 31, 1994), Hartmut Broszinski and Sirka Heyne, eds. (Fulda: Hessische Landesbibliothek, 1994), 7.

17 Thompson, 51.

18 Some "recipes" for medieval ink can be found in Wilhelm Wattenbach, *Das Schriftwesen im Mittelalter* (Writing in the Middle Ages) (Leipzig: Hirzel, 1875), 198–99; Falcone Madan, *Books in Manuscript: A Short Introduction to Their Study and Use; With a Chapter on Records* (London: Kegan Paul, Trench, Trubner and Co., 1893), 16–17; and Javier Garcia-Guinea, et al., "Framboidal Pyrites in Antique Books," *Nature* 388, no. 6643 (1997): 631. Thompson, 601, footnote 31, writes that it was "made by a mixture of soot or bone black with gum and water, from iron fillings and oak bark, or gall nuts boiled in vinegar."

19 For a description of medieval scriptoria, see Edler de Rover, 594–612.

20 Harmut Broszinski, *Kasseler Handschriftenschätze* (Kassel manuscript treasures), Pretiosa Cassellana (Kassel: Johannes Stauda, 1985), 140.

More than eleven hundred years ago two Fulda monks laboriously copied the text of an old Germanic warrior ballad onto the blank pages of an existing religious codex.[21] This codex, known as the *Liber Sapientiae*, The Book of Wisdom, dated from the end of the eighth century, and already contained biblical texts ascribed to the Wisdom of Solomon and of Jesus Son of Sirach. Some of its pages had been left vacant, and the monks conscientiously filled the empty spaces with prayers and other small writings, until only two pages were left:[22] the frontal surface of the first leaf and the very last surface of the end leaf, in other words the top and the bottom of the book. Starting on the front of the first leaf and skipping to the back, the two monks copied onto these last empty pages of the codex the text of the tragic story of Hildebrand. The space was limited, and thus the ending of the ballad, if indeed there ever were one, was either written on a loose leaf now lost or remained unrecorded.

Even a superficial glance through textbooks of German literary history reveals the prominent place of this brief text in the consciousness of a nation. Most textbooks open with the *Hildebrandslied.* It is the oldest extant heroic poem of German literature and the only surviving one on German soil. No other echo of Germanic oral poetry has ever reached our time. And while other ancient texts exist in multiple versions and copies, in this case history has conspired to save only one: this presumed fragmentary text copied in Fulda and later preserved in Kassel. The popular ballad must have been created in Northern Italy, around the year 600 and wandered in a northerly direction by word-of-mouth, from city to city, from court to court. Eventually it crossed the Alps, traversed the expanses of today's Germany, skipped over the North Sea, and came to rest on the plains of Scandinavia.[23] Midway on its long journey, around the early decades of the ninth century, its alliterative verses were anchored into script at the abbey of Fulda. No other written record of this or any other old Germanic heroic poem has ever been found.[24]

---

21 Hanns Fischer in *Schrifttafeln zum althochdeutschen Lesebuch* (Tables to the Old High German textbook) (Tübingen: Max Niemeyer, 1966), 14, quotes Bernhard Bischoff, who dated the *Hildebrandslied* to the third decade of the ninth century.

22 *Manuscripta Theologica: Die Handschriften in Folio* (Manuscripta Theologica: The folio manuscripts) editor Konrad Wiedemann, Handschriften der Gesamthochschul-Bibliothek Kassel – Landesbibliothek und Murhardsche Bibliothek der Stadt Kassel, 1,1 (Wiesbaden: Harrassowitz, 1994), 72, citing a letter of Bernhard Bischoff.

23 Dieter Hennig, "Zur Rückführung zweier Handschriften der Murhardschen Bibliothek der Stadt Kassel und Landesbibliothek" (On the return of two manuscripts belonging to the Murhard Library of the City of Kassel and State Library), *Zeitschrift für Bibliothekswesen und Bibliographie* 20, no. 1 (1973): 25.

24 Frederick Norman, *Three Essays on the Hildebrandslied* (London: University of London, 1973), 9.

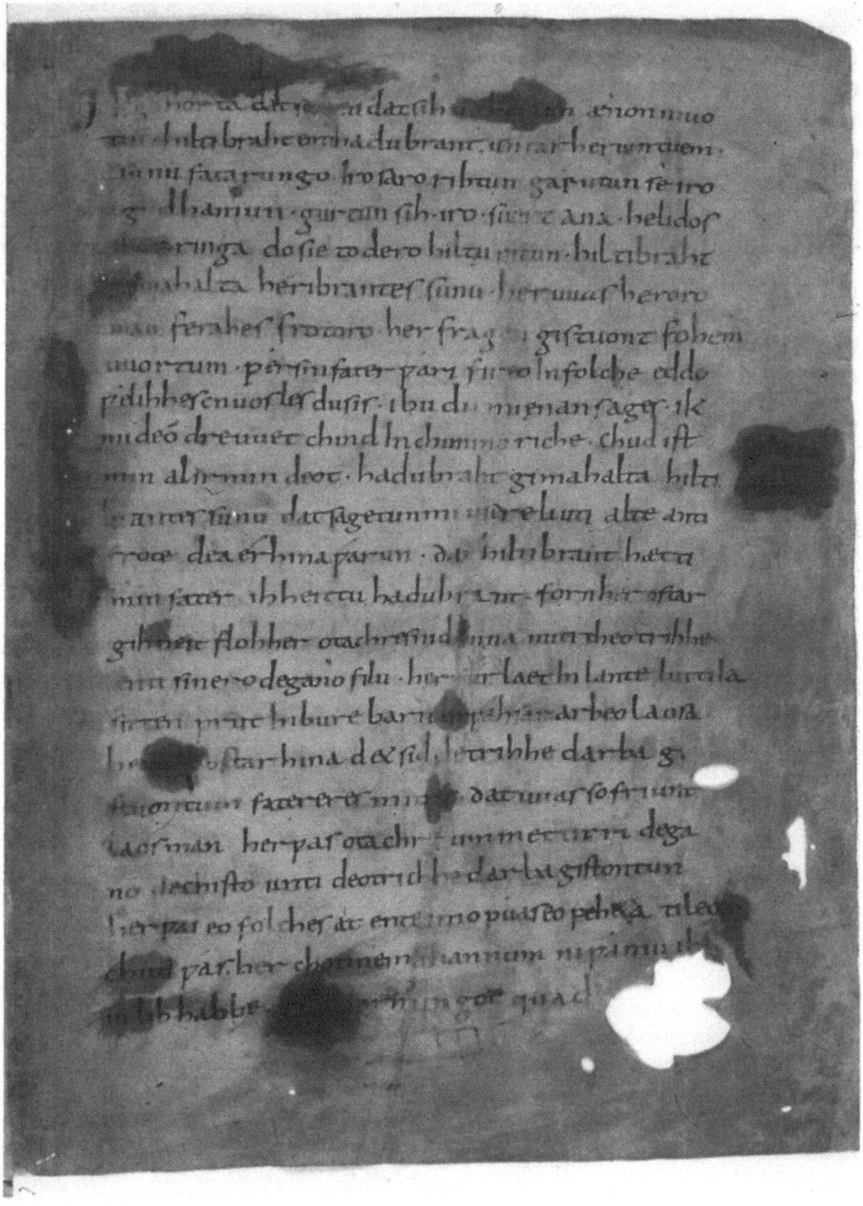

Fig. 3. Hildebrandslied, Leaf One – 2° Ms. theol. 54/1ʳ.
(Archives of the Universitätsbibliothek Kassel Landesbibliothek und Murhardsche Bibliothek der Stadt Kassel – Reproduced by permission)

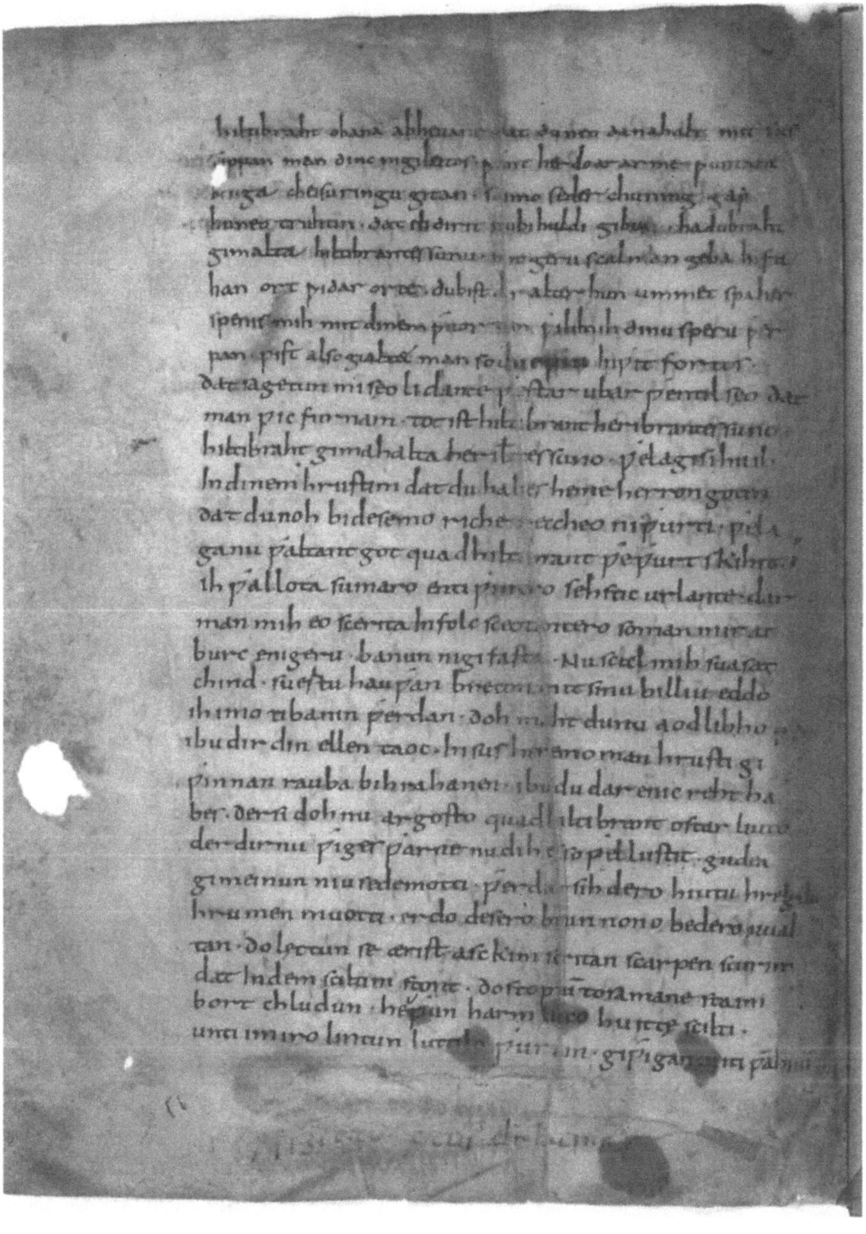

Fig. 4. Hildebrandslied, Leaf One 2° Ms. theol. 54/76ᵛ.
(Archives of the Universitätsbibliothek Kassel Landesbibliothek und Murhardsche Bibliothek der Stadt Kassel Reproduced by permission)

The oral tradition of the poem resonates from the opening verse, from that ritualized phrase, which German school children once used to learn by heart. It sounds like a beguiling invitation, a call that captures the attention and lures the listener into its realm of wonder: "*Ik gihorta dat seggen. ...*" I once heard it said ... Once upon a time. ...

Once upon a time, Hildebrand, the warrior hero, returned to his homeland after an absence of thirty years, sixty summers and winters. As a young man he had joined the armies of the Ostrogoth King, Theodoric the Great. He had bravely fought in every battle. Now, in the twilight of his years, Hildebrand heads home with a small troop of men. Unexpectedly, at the border, an armed patrol led by a young and brazen warrior blocks his way. The two leaders ride forward, sizing each other up, armor on, swords buckled over their chain mail. Behind them, in tense anticipation, their loyal warriors await their orders. The elder and more seasoned Hildebrand breaks the silence. He demands to know the young man's bloodline, for he remembers everyone in this kingdom, every name, and every ancestry. The young warrior defiantly tells him: he is Hadubrand, Hildebrand's son. Long ago, his father, who must have loved battle more than home and hearth, deserted him and his mother and followed his master. Wife and infant were thus deprived of rank and rightful inheritance. Hildebrand must be dead by now, fallen in battle. Sailors, traveling across the Mediterranean Sea, had brought him the news. How else could his absence be explained?

The two armies silently listen to the bitter charges. Unknowingly, Hadubrand confronts his own father and indicts his actions. Calling upon God in Heaven as a witness, Hildebrand attempts to tell his son that he is his father. In a desperate gesture of reconciliation, he offers Hadubrand a gift of gold: his precious armbands received for bravery from Attila, King of the Huns. But the suspicious young man rejects both explanation and gift. In front of his cohort he, the abandoned, the fatherless son, cannot show weakness, cannot lay down his weapons to reach for the bribe. This old and cowardly Hun must want to deceive him. Treachery must be the weapon that has kept him alive for so long. He will take the gifts, but only with the point of his spear.

Hildebrand's honor is gravely wounded. His warriors have heard the humiliating insults. He is trapped between kinship and honor. Once again he calls upon God Almighty, whose cruel fate he can no longer escape. The fight must take place. And so father and son clash in a life and death struggle.

The poem falls silent, its tragic ending untold. However, the listener senses that there is only one possible outcome. The old warrior Hildebrand is destined to kill his only son, to destroy his own lineage. In an ironic twist, his name will be carried on by the lonely voice of the wandering ballad, which will narrate his tragic destiny, and will endow him with a bloodstained immortality.

In its masterfully tight construction of only sixty-eight alliterative verses, the *Hildebrandslied* encapsulates a dramatic scene of ancient Germanic life. The abundance of emotions, ranging from hope, suspicion, and anger, to agony, and resignation, is as poignant today as it must have been some twelve hundred years ago. The listener is a silent witness, standing among the soldiers, watching the encounter between father and son, observing their demeanor and eavesdropping on their ill-fated argument. The tense dialogue offers a unique insight into the Germanic code of honor, social organization, family relations, and their concept of destiny, of guilt and punishment. The tragedy of Hildebrand, the father destined to murder his son, is timeless and universal.

Two scribes took turns copying from an original text recorded either on parchment or on wax tablets.[25] They reproduced it in the prevailing rounded Carolingian minuscule and interspersed it with letters of the older, more angular Anglo-Saxon script. It is this mixture of writing elements that has allowed modern scholars to ascribe to the ballad a fairly precise date: the third to fourth decade of the ninth century.[26] The first monk seems hesitant, erasing, re-writing, and mistakenly repeating words already copied. His letters are big and broad. At the beginning of the second leaf, a second hand takes over. This second monk writes in small letters, neat and clean, with no erasures.[27] After only seven-and-one-half lines, the first monk reclaims the quill and continues, his writing becoming narrower and narrower, as if he were intent to fit the full text of the poem onto the remaining space. At the end, he appears to give up. We may never know if a third, loose page was used to record the remaining verses. The tragic conclusion of the *Hildebrandslied* has never been found.

The identity of the scribes remains to this day a mystery. Their handwriting could never again be traced through the codices copied at the cloister.[28] No one

---

25 Ludwig Denecke, "Die erste Niederschrift des Hildebrandliedes – Aus mündlicher Überlieferung auf Wachstafeln?" (The first recording of the Hildebrandslied – from oral transmission on wax tables?), *Neophilologus: An International Journal of Modern and Mediaeval Language and Literature* 62, no. 1 (1978): 106–107.
Note: These tablets were made of short planks of wood in a raised frame, covered with black wax. The scribe wrote on the wax surface with a sharp stylus. Each letter groove made the underlying wood visible. Wax tablets were very practical. The wood blocks could be easily reused or stacked to form a codex.

26 *Handschriftarchiv Bernhard Bischoff (1906–1991):(Bibliothek der Monumenta Germaniae Historica, Hs. C 1, C 2).* (Manuscript Archive of Bernhard Bischoff). Editor Arno Mentzel-Reuters. (Munich: Bibliothek der Monumenta Germaniae Historica, 1997). Microfiche-Edition. Hs C1 XLI. Fiche 17, Kassel; Landes- und Murhardsche Bibliothek. 1. Korrespondenz; Notizen zu einzelnen Hss. Segment 1.4–6: Durchschlag des Anwortsschreibens v. B. Bischoff and Dr. Hennig v. 21. X. 1973 mit detaillierter Begründung seines Datierungsansatzes. (Carbon copy of B. Bischoff's response to Dr. Hennig, October 21, 1973, with detailed reasoning of his date assessment.)

27 Helmich van der Kolk, *Das Hildebrandlied: Eine forschungsgeschichtliche Darstellung* (The Song of Hildebrand: A research history) (Amsterdam: Scheltema & Holkema, 1967), 10.

28 *Das Hildebrandlied: der Kasseler Handschrift mit einer Einführung von Hartmut Broszinski* (The Song of Hildebrand. Facsimile of the manuscript from Kassel with an introduction by

knows why the monks chose to record this particular song. Perhaps the *Hildebrandslied* was part of a larger collection of heathen ballads gathered on orders of Charlemagne.[29] Perhaps it was a simple writing exercise. Many other questions remain to this day the focus of intense scholarly research and speculation. Why, for instance, was this heroic poem written on the blank pages of a codex dedicated to liturgical writings? Why did two hands take turns copying a relatively brief text? And why did they brake off before recording the ending? Or did they?[30] Could it be that the original text, from which they were copying, was fragmentary as well?

What is known is that for nine centuries the *Liber Sapientiae* with the *Hildebrandslied* written on its flyleaves remained shelved in the cloister library. It was there when the Franks and the Saxons chose Henry the First as King of Germany in 918. It was there in the year 1000 when Leif Ericson landed on the coast of Newfoundland, and when the Persian poet Firdausi wrote *Shah-nameh.* It was there when Thomas Becket was born and when he was murdered in 1170, when Dante loved Beatrice and Leonardo painted the Mona Lisa. The *Liber Sapientiae* was frequently used: creases in its flyleaves indicate that it was shelved and re-shelved carelessly, jammed between other books.[31] Only much later was the codex fitted with its own leather-covered boards.[32]

The beginning of the fifteenth century marked the decline of the illustrious Fulda library. Theft, abuse of scholarly privileges, and inter-monastic book lending contributed to the erosion of its collection. The decline was hastened by the discovery of movable type. Gutenberg's printing press eliminated the arduous labor of the scribe replacing the codex with the much cheaper printed book, the

---

Hartmut Broszinski), second edition, Pretiosa Cassellana (Kassel: Johannes Stauda, 1985), [23].

29 Broszinski, 144.

30 Alain Renoir, "The Kassel manuscript and the conclusion of the Hildebrandslied," *Manuscripta,* 23 (1979): 104–108. Renoir argues that the Kassel Hildebrandslied is a complete text and not a fragment.

31 Broszinski, 139: "Beide Blätter des Hildebrandliedes weisen vertikale Quetschfalten auf, ein deutlicher Hinweis darauf, daß der Band lange ohne Einband zwischen anderen Büchern stand; beim Herausnehmen und Einstellen knickten diese äußeren Blätter ein." (Both pages of the Hildebrandslied show vertical creases, clear proof that for a long period of time the volume was shelved without covers between other books. When it was retrieved and re-shelved, these outside leaves became wrinkled.)

32 "Hildebrandlied 4," documents from the archives of the Gesamthochschul-Bibliothek Kassel – Landesbibliothek und Murhardsche Bibliothek der Stadt Kassel, deposited with the University of California, Davis, Shields Library, Department of Special Collections. Letter of D. Hennig to U. Winter, November 28, 1972. Hennig states that at the end of the Middle Ages the codex was bound in wood boards covered in leather. Broszinski, 139, cites Ernst Kyriss and Ilse Schunke, 1973, who date the binding to the fifteenth century. Wiedemann, however, in *Manuscripta Theologica,* 72, dates it to the ninth/tenth century.

incunabulum. In 1632, during the Thirty-Years'-War, the cloister library suffered its fatal blow: Hessian soldiers destroyed the monastery and plundered the library. Some of the stolen manuscripts were eventually found and returned to the Hessian Landgraves in Kassel. One of the few Fulda codices, which ended up in the Kassel Court Library, was a plain looking volume called the *Liber Sapientiae*, a miracle since of the 2,000 manuscripts that once graced the monastic library of Fulda, only ninety-five codices and 150 scraps of parchment survived.[33]

In the second decade of the eighteenth-century, close to a hundred years since the demise of the Fulda library, a Kassel librarian came across the *Liber Sapientiae* and noticed the ballad inscribed on its flyleaves. Johann Hermann Schmincke showed his curious find to Johann Georg Eckhardt, a highly regarded scholar. On Schmincke's advice, Eckhardt issued in 1729 a Latin translation and a reproduction of the first fourteen lines. His discovery, however, remained largely unnoticed for another eighty years, when the Grimm Brothers, the most illustrious librarians in Kassel's history, made the ballad known to the world. In 1812, nearly a thousand years after it was copied in Fulda, the Grimm Brothers, who had just published their famous anthology of fairy tales, issued the first in-depth study of the poem. They named the untitled heroic ballad *Das Hildebrands-Lied*, The Song of Hildebrand. It is to their extensive research that we owe the revival of this epic monument of the Germanic past.[34]

The discovery of the *Hildebrandslied* captured the imagination of scholars worldwide and soon the poem became the focus of literary, historical, and linguistic studies and debates.[35] With fame came abuse. Researchers obtained permission to conduct experiments on the faded text hoping to decipher illegible sections. They resorted to chemicals, which, when applied to the vellum, made faint letters visible for brief periods of time. These experiments left dark shadows on the parchment, obscuring possibly forever portions of the writing.[36]

---

33 *Fuldische Handschriften aus Hessen ..., 11.*

34 Ernst S. Dick, "The Grimms' Hildebrandslied," In: *The Grimm Brothers and the Germanic Past*, editor Elmer H. Antonsen (Amsterdam: John Benjamins, 1990), 72.

35 Fame is often followed by forgery. Philipp Wehner, a Fulda librarian, secretly revealed to a group of amateur friends that he owned a parchment scroll with the complete text of the *Hildebrandslied*, including those never before seen verses depicting the tragic killing of Hadubrand. He showed them what seemed to be an ancient vellum scroll, penned in Carolingian minuscule. But after his death, extensive searches financed by the Grimm Brothers did not find any trace of that mysterious scroll. Today the scholarly consensus is that Wehner's so-called complete *Hildebrandslied* was a hoax. See: Wilhelm Schoof, "Die verlorene Handschrift" (The lost manuscript), *Wörter und Sachen: Zeitschrift für indogermanische Sprachwissenschaft, Volksbildung und Kulturgeschichte. Neue Folge.* 3 (21) (1940): 53- 60; and also Denecke, "Die zweite Handschrift des Hildebrandliedes" (The second manuscript of the Hildebrandlied) *Anzeiger für Deutsches Altertum und Deutsche Literatur.* 83 (1972): 227–29.

36 Broszinski, 145.

Fig. 5. Willehalm Codex – 2° Ms. poet. 1/7ᵛ.
(Archives of the Universitätsbibliothek Kassel – Landesbibliothek und Murhardsche Bibliothek der Stadt Kassel – Reproduced by permission)

Fig. 6. Willehalm Codex – 2° Ms. poet. 1/25r.
(Archives of the Universitätsbibliothek Kassel – Landesbibliothek und Murhardsche Bibliothek der Stadt Kassel – Reproduced by permission)

Through secularization and bequests, the Kassel Court Library blossomed into one of the most prestigious collections of medieval texts in Germany, equaled only by those in Gotha, Wolfenbüttel, or Heidelberg. The Grimm Brothers modernized the old court library and transformed it into a first-class research facility. Under their wise acquisition policy valuable books, manuscripts, and scholarly reference sources were steadily added. The 1831 Hesse Constitution granted the old Kassel Court Library the status of *Landesbibliothek*, State Library.[37]

With the Kassel collections of the Landgraves, the *Landesbibliothek* also inherited another volume: one of the most lavishly illuminated secular manuscripts of the Middle Ages, the *Willehalm Codex*. Landgrave Heinrich II of Hesse had commissioned this sumptuous, oversize codex in 1334, in honor of Saint Wilhelm Marchionis, believed to be his ancestor. It must have been one of the showpieces of his court, a source of pride, a proof of wealth, a testimony to his illustrious ancestry and fame. An inscription at the end of the manuscript identified Landgrave Heinrich II as the owner and ordained that this codex never leave his library and that it remain in perpetuity in the custody of the his heirs. The nineteenth-century successor of the Kassel Court Library, the *Landesbibliothek*, thus became heir to, and rightful owner of, the *Willehalm Codex*.

The *Willehalm* manuscript is believed to be a product of the Fritzlar scriptorium, a monastery founded by Boniface.[38] It consists of 396 vellum leaves of the highest quality, with text written in two columns. The handwriting is even, firm, and elegant, and adorned with beautifully decorated initials. Of the 479 miniatures planned,[39] only thirty-three were completed, another twenty-nine sketched and colored, and the balance framed or left vacant. This unfinished manuscript is very important, since it offers a unique window into the process of book production and illumination in medieval scriptoria.[40]

---

[37] For the history of the Library and its collections see Wilhelm Hopf, editor, *Die Landesbibliothek Kassel, 1580–1930* (The Kassel State Library: 1580–1930) (Marburg: N. G. Elwert, 1930). Also *Ex Bibliotheca Cassellana: 400 Jahre Landesbibliothek, 20.11.1580–20.11.1980* (From the Kassel Library: 400 years of State Library, 11/20/1580–11/20/1980), editor Hans-Jürgen Kahlfuß ([Kassel]: Gesamthochschul-Bibliothek-Kassel, Landesbibliothek und Murhardsche Bibliothek der Stadt Kassel, 1980), and *Handbuch der historischen Buchbestände in Deutschland* (Handbook of historical book collections in Germany), editor Bernhard Fabian, vol. 5, s. v. "Kassel" (Hildesheim: Olms-Weidmann, 1992).

[38] Ursula Winter, "Hildebrandlied und Willehalm-Codex: Zwei Handschriften der Landesbibliothek Kassel und ihre Schicksale" (The Lay of Hildebrand and the Willehalm Codex: Two manuscripts of the Kassel State Library and their fate), *Marginalien: Zeitschrift für Buchkunst und Bibliophilie* 56 (1974): 61; and Broszinski, 155.

[39] "Hildebrandlied 2," documents from the archives. ... Zum Kasseler *Willehalm-Codex*. Description by Dr. Kunz, March 17, 1972.

[40] Broszinski, 151.

Five hundred years younger than the *Hildebrandslied*, the Kassel *Willehalm* consists of three interconnected courtly adventures set against a background of conflict between Christianity and Islam. The prologue, *Arabel*, the story of a pagan queen, is the work of Ulrich von dem Türlin. It is followed by the adventures of *Willehalm*, the paladin of Charlemagne. The author is Wolfram von Eschenbach, famous for *Parzival*, the most popular story of the Middle Ages. The trilogy ends with the tale of *Rennewart*, written by Ulrich von Türheim, which narrates the exploits of a valiant giant. Unlike to the *Hildebrandslied*, the story of *Willehalm* exists in multiple copies.[41] The Kassel rendition stands out through its inclusion of all three stories and its lavish pictorial treatment.[42]

History had been merciful to the two Kassel manuscripts. Unlike many others, they had survived conflict, looting, ignorance, and neglect. For a while, they had even enjoyed fame and the care of knowledgeable librarians. Now, trapped in their gray wooden chest, hidden in the darkness of a small-town air raid shelter, the two codices were once again facing the menace of war.

---

[41] Ibid.,150. There are twelve complete manuscripts and fifty-nine fragments.

[42] Joan A. Holladay, *Illuminating the Epic: The Kassel 'Willehalm Codex' and the Landgraves of Hesse in the Early Fourteenth Century* (Seattle: College Art Association and University of Washington Press, 1996), 84: "The large scale of the illumination cycle and the mannered elegance of the painting style put Heinrich's manuscript in the category of luxury books to which art historians devote their attention. These features give the Kassel codex an important place in the histories of German and secular illumination."

Chapter 3: Countdown to Surrender

New Year's Day 1945 greeted Kassel with a hailstorm of phosphorous and incendiary bombs. In wave after wave, 800 planes mercilessly pounded a city already in ruins.[1] Terrified people fought their way into the relative security of the few remaining shelters. For seemingly endless hours, delayed explosions kept them cowering underground, anguished and powerless, gasping for air, body pressed against body.[2] No one knew what daybreak would bring or how many would reemerge to resume a miserable existence. After every attack, obituaries were published in batches, scattered over several newspaper issues, so as not to sap the morale of those sorrowful souls condemned to live through the next harrowing night.[3] This New Year's raid was the thirty-seventh major attack on Kassel and there would be ten more before the end of winter.

Five years had passed since German tanks had blasted their way eastwards, gun-barrels pointed toward Moscow. For a while, a string of stunning victories seemed to confirm the Nazi claim to military, racial, and technological superiority. But then, on the banks of the Volga, the tide had turned. The unstoppable counteroffensive had tightened its noose around Germany's neck, bringing the specter of death and destruction back to the source. Fifty million lives, that was the price of Hitler's aggression. Of these, six million were Germans, and close to thirty thousand residents of Kassel.[4]

January 1945 made its début with bitter winds and glacial temperatures. Kassel's streets were coated with sheets of ice. The newly fallen snow partially softened the outlines of the cavernous wounds inflicted by relentless aerial attacks. The city's lights had long gone out. Darkness reigned from dusk to dawn. Here and there smoldering fires glowed among the ruins, pools of blood on the untarnished white. The iron grip of fear, frost, and famine paralyzed the city. The official food ration per person was 1,600 calories a day,[5] but reality was quite different. Potatoes, vegetables, and sugar were scarce, meat and bread a luxury. Since

---

1 *"Bis 5 Minuten nach Zwölf." "Letzte Kriegstage 1945 in Kassel in Tagebüchern und anderen zeitgenössischen Quellen"* (Five minutes past midnight: The last days of the war in 1945 in Kassel reflected in diaries and other contemporary sources), editor Frank-Roland Klaube, Kasseler Quellen und Studien, Kleine Reihe, vol. 5 (Marburg: Jonas, 1995), 12.

2 Ibid., 46.

3 Ibid., 27.

4 *Volksgemeinschaft und Volksfeinde: Kassel 1933–1945. Eine Dokumentation* (Folk community and folk enemies: Kassel 1933–1945. A documentation), Jörg Kammler, Dietfried Krause-Vilmar, Siegfried Kujawski, Wolfgang Prinz, and Robert Wilmsmeier, eds. (Fuldabrück: Hesse, 1984), 407.

5 *Bis 5 Minuten nach Zwölf*, 82.

damaged mains could no longer be repaired, water was distributed by truck and carried by sled or improvised cart. The walk home on icy paths crossing mountains of debris was long and treacherous.

After each air raid, the starving searched the ruins for the hoarded reserves of the dead. The Nazi *Kurhessische Landeszeitung*, the only newspaper still published,[6] carried stern orders from *Gauleiter* Gerland[7] to surrender the stockpiles. But few could resist the temptation of a handful of potatoes, an apron full of coal. As raids reduced the number of hungry mouths, survivors were compensated with larger rations. Redistribution, however, did not extend to the foreign slave laborers. Obituaries of Russians, Czechs, Poles, French, Italians or Belgians listed emaciation as one of the causes of death.[8]

A constant state of fear, not entirely stemming from foreign enemy attacks, exacerbated the physical suffering. Since the beginning of the war, the shadow of the Gestapo was ever present.[9] Kassel's citizens were encouraged to denounce coworkers, friends, and neighbors. Reasons for reporting were not always ideological. Often petty disagreements were couched in political terms so as to give the Gestapo a reason to act.[10] Whispers of night raids, arrests, interrogations, and torture perpetuated a climate of terror.

If German civilians were suffering the nightmare of bombing-raids, hunger, cold, and fear, an even greater peril was threatening Kassel's Jewish community: the threat of extinction. Engrossed in their fight for survival, Kassel's Christian

---

6 Ibid., 18: "Nach dem 22. Oktober, 1943 erschien in Kassel nur noch eine Tageszeitung, die nationalsozialistische 'Kurhessische Landeszeitung.'" (After October 22, 1943 only one daily newspaper was published in Kassel, the Nazi "Kurhessische Landeszeitung.")

7 Karl Höffkes, *Hitlers politische Generale: Die Gauleiter des Dritten Reiches. Ein biographisches Nachschlagewerk* (Hitler's political generals. The Gauleiters of the Third Reich. A biographical reference book) (Tübingen: Grabert, 1986), 83–85.

8 *Bis 5 Minuten nach Zwölf*, 53, 89.

9 Hans-Oskar Weber, "Landesbibliothek Kassel 1938" (State Library Kassel 1938), in: *Bibliotheken während des Nationalsozialismus*, part 1, Peter Vodosek and Manfred Komorowski, eds. (Wiesbaden: Harrassowitz, 1989), 371–72, footnote 7, comments on the situation in Kassel: "Es war ein offenes Geheimnis, daß sich in jedem Betrieb (und in größeren Wohnhäusern) mindestens ein Vertrauensmann (dieser konnte auch weiblichen Geschlechts sein und hieß dennoch so) befand, Partei- oder besser noch SD-Mitglied oder -Beauftragter, der seine Ohren offenzuhalten, und Meldenswertes, besonders 'Zersetzendes', weiterzugeben hatte. Wer das in einem Betrieb war, konnte oft nur vermutet werden; unter vorgehaltener Hand sprach man vom Spitzel." (It was an open secret that each workplace (and each larger apartment house) had at least one trustworthy man (this designation could also be given to a woman, also referred to as a 'Vertrauensmann'), a Party member, Security Service member, or agent, who spied on others and reported newsworthy developments, especially rumors considered pernicious. The identity of this person in the workplace was only suspected. Secretly people whispered about the informer.)

10 *Volksgemeinschaft und Volksfeinde*, 288.

residents had turned a blind eye to the plight of their Jewish neighbors. For six hundred years, Kassel's Jews had been part and parcel of the city's social fabric. The illusion of belonging to one and the same community was shattered in 1937 when a "J" was stamped on their identity cards. In time, a succession of decrees, laws, and ordinances identified them as the nation's greatest enemy.

Kassel was known as the birthplace of *Kristallnacht,* the Night of Broken Glass. Leaders of the SS and SA were quick to remind one and all that the pogrom, which later swept over the country, had ignited two days earlier right there, in the streets of Kassel.[11] On the morning of November 7, 1938 a young Jew from Hanover, whose parents had been deported, killed a German diplomat in Paris. That night, some thirty thugs burst into the Kassel synagogue, dragged out its Torah scrolls and ceremonial objects, and set them on fire. Police stood idly by as the mob rampaged through the Jewish quarter destroying homes and businesses. The *Kurhessische Landeszeitung* commended the violence as a spontaneous protest against the murder in Paris. Two days later at a Nazi meeting in Munich, Joseph Goebbels, Hitler's Chief of Propaganda praised the initiative. This was the call for *Kristallnacht*, the night of November 9, 1938, when all across Germany Nazi hoodlums wreaked havoc: one hundred ninety-one synagogues were destroyed, Jewish businesses were ransacked, thirty-six people were killed, and many were arrested and sent to concentration camps. Of these, 258 were Kassel Jews.[12]

In neighboring Frankfurt am Main, with the largest Jewish population after Berlin, the pogrom raged with ferocity. The Nazis torched a synagogue, and then slashed and burned their way through Jewish cultural institutions and private homes. Herman Samuel Gundersheimer, curator of the Rothschild Museum, watched as his priceless collections were vandalized.[13] The museum displayed one thousand years of continuous Jewish life on Germany's soil. His son Werner was only a small child, yet the images of brutality relived over and over again through his parents' memories, remained forever seared in his heart.[14] The horrors of *Kristallnacht* shaped a boy's burgeoning belief system. Thirty-four years later, Kassel, birthplace of the pogrom and home of the *Hildebrandslied*, would benefit from these convictions painfully acquired by a child.

Kristallnacht was the turning point in Hitler's war against the Jews.[15] Thereafter Kassel Jews were stripped of their possessions and identity. They were deprived

---

11 Ibid., 11.

12 Ibid., 248.

13 Rita Thalmann and Emmanuel Feinermann, *Crystal Night: 9–10 November 1938,* translated by Gilles Cremonesi (London: Thames and Hudson, 1974), 76.

14 Werner Gundersheimer, "Kristallnacht Revisited: A Nightmare, a Legacy." *Washington Post*, November 9, 1988, A10.

15 Ibid.

of control over their own assets, and barred from participating in the professional, cultural, and social life of the city. Beginning in 1941, Jews were forced to wear a clearly visible yellow Star of David on their chests.[16] Emigration was no longer an option and fleeing the country was tantamount to suicide. Three mass deportations to Riga, Lublin-Majdanek and Theresienstadt *cleansed* Kassel of its Jewish citizenry. One thousand and seven perished.[17] Of the ninety-nine Kassel Jews deported to Majdanek in the summer of 1942, not a single one returned.[18]

* * *

Since May of 1942, Dr. Wilhelm Hopf and the surviving volumes of his Hesse history collection had found temporary refuge in a mid-town museum, known today as *Die Neue Galerie.*[19] The building was vacant, dark and unheated, its masterpieces crated and stored in distant repositories. In between bombardments, Hopf continued his work of acquisition, cataloging and public service. He remained determined to keep his section open and offer services to those wanting to read.[20] His patrons deserved an island of normalcy in a world gone mad. Since he was the only senior librarian still active, all professional responsibilities and management functions fell squarely onto his shoulders.[21]

Periodically, Hopf traveled the short distance to Bad Wildungen to check on the state of his manuscripts and on the Kassel art collections. He and Rudolf Helm, curator of the *Landesmuseum*, took turns inspecting the cellar. The city of Bad Wildungen was one of the richest war-repositories of the region. Fifteen art institutions, most notably the Frankfurt Staedel Museum, were using its cellars as air raid shelters.[22] Journeys to Bad Wildungen must have offered a pleasant

---

16 *Volksgemeinschaft und Volksfeinde*, 260.

17 *Namen und Schicksale der Juden Kassels, 1933–1945. Ein Gedenkbuch* (Names and fate of Kassel Jews, 1933–1945. A memorial), Beate Kleiner and Wolfgang Prinz, eds. (Kassel: Magistrat der Stadt Kassel – Stadtarchiv, 1986), 246.

18 *Volksgemeinschaft und Volksfeinde*, 229.

19 *Ex Bibliotheca Cassellana: 400 Jahre Landesbibliothek, 20.11.1580–20.11.1980* (From the Kassel Library: 400 years of State Library, 11/20/1580–11/20/1980). Hans-Jürgen Kahlfuß, editor ([Kassel]: Gesamthochschul-Bibliothek-Kassel, Landesbibliothek und Murhardsche Bibliothek der Stadt Kassel, 1980), 40.
Note: Heinrich von Dehn-Rotfelsen built this Gallery in 1871–1877 to house the Kassel collection of Old Masters. At the time, it was referred to as *Die Gemäldegalerie*. Today it is called *Die Neue Galerie* and exhibits paintings from 1750 to the present, with special emphasis on local artists.

20 *Ex Bibliotheca Cassellana*, 41.

21 Ibid., 43.

22 "Paintings from Bad Wildungen Repository, 1951–1961," US Department of State, records maintained by the Fine Arts and Monuments Adviser, 1945–61, Ardelia Hall Collection. Record Group 59, Lot 62D4, Box 9, National Archives and Records Administration. File note. April 20, 1955.

respite from hardships, tedious routines, and unrelenting worries. As the train slowly made its way southwest through the Waldeck region the landscape changed from rubble and ruin to softly rolling hills and dark green forests. Out there in the countryside, one could almost forget the tragedy of war.

Bad Wildungen, a fashionable health spa, had remained relatively untouched by the bombing. Its medieval origins were evident in the vestiges of its massive defending walls and monumental watchtowers. Rising above its *Altstadt* was the City Church, the *Stadtkirche*, admired for its altarpiece with a poignant crucifixion scene. The potency of the spa's healing waters used in cures ranging from kidney disorders to heart and circulation problems was well known since the Middle Ages. Around the turn of the twentieth century, the city had blossomed into an international health resort with a guest list of European celebrities. Heinrich Schliemann, of Trojan fame, the writer Gerhart Hauptmann, the royal family of the Netherlands, Paris banker Edmund von Rothschild, members of the Czar's family, Russian nobility and trendy European artists, all flocked to Bad Wildungen to relax, socialize, and take the waters.[23]

On July 7, 1944, it was Dr. Hopf's turn to inspect the evacuation site.[24] Just as in summers past, garlands of flowers cascaded from most every windowsill softening the austerity of the half-timbered houses. The days of ritualized cure and leisurely promenades were long gone. The war had left its ugly imprint even on this idyllic vacation spot. The once elegant clinics, hotels, and mineral baths had been converted to military hospitals. Instead of literati and royalty, 4,000 wounded soldiers inhabited the wards.[25]

One of the spa's mid-nineteenth-century inns was the stately Hotel Goecke. Its upper floors housed the resort town's administrative offices, and, since the beginning of the war, its deep basement was used as an air raid shelter. The Goecke cellar filled with masterpieces had been placed under the care of Hubert Vonhoff, a member of the *Heimschutz*, the Hesse Home Guard. Hubert however had been drafted and was now fighting on the Eastern Front. During his conscription his wife kept a vigilant eye on the hotel's cellar, brimming with artwork. It was a weighty responsibility, in which the efficient Frau Vonhoff took great pride. While most other city bunkers were under the administration of Bad Wildungen museum director Felix Pusch, Hotel Goecke was exclusively under her care.[26]

---

[23] Fritz Kesting, *Stadt und Bad Wildungen im Wandel der Zeit* (The history of the city and spa Wildungen) (Bad Wildungen: Wilhelm Bing, 1968), 215–16.

[24] "Hildebrandlied 1," documents from the archives. ... Declaration of W. Hopf, June 20, 1945.

[25] Kesting, 101.

[26] "Paintings from Bad Wildungen Repository 1951–1961," US Department of State, records ... File note. April 20, 1955. "The repository was, unfortunately, left unguarded by the re-

As always, Dr. Hopf began his visitation with a review of the cellar temperature data, recorded three times daily by the meticulous Frau Vonhoff, and then went down to the basement to visually inspect Helm's artwork and his own crate with manuscripts.[27] In spite of warm weather, the cellar had remained cool and dry. He found his wooden chest securely locked and undisturbed, right where he had left it, under a protective wall spur.[28] He had chosen that inconspicuous spot with the greatest of care. The recess provided camouflage and additional protection against air raids. Helm's museum pieces were all in perfect order. His tour of duty satisfactory concluded, Dr. Hopf prepared to return to Kassel.[29] This was to be the last time that he would see the gray wooden chest with the two priceless manuscripts.

On a hill overlooking Kassel, rises the proud eighteenth-century palace of Wilhelmshöhe, surrounded by its lush baroque gardens. During the summer months, the frothy waters of the gigantic Hercules Cascade tumble in tier after tier down the slopes of the Habichswald to reach the clear reflecting pool at the foot of the castle. Its secluded location on the western edge of town had so far saved it from aerial attacks. Its run of good luck ended on Monday night, January 29, 1945, when incendiary bombs hit palace. The fire spread quickly and soon engulfed the entire structure. A blustering northwest wind fanned the blaze, constantly renewing its strength.[30] The next day, a smoldering skeleton was left standing, a tragic symbol of the plight of an entire country.

Germany lay in ruins. The war was lost. Yet Hitler imposed one last sacrifice on his people. He ordered the exhausted civilian population to rise and defend every inch of the *Vaterland* to the last man and the last cartridge. This senseless edict took the form of the *Volkssturm*, the mobilization of the national militia. Outnumbered and outgunned, the very old and the very young were sent forth to contain, with little more than their bodies, an unstoppable Allied advance. Any sign of defeatism was punished by execution.

Dr. Hopf's colleague, Rudolf Helm, curator of the *Landesmuseum*, was one of these last-ditch defenders. Before leaving, he transferred the responsibility for the evacuated artwork to the *Oberpräsident*, the Governor of Hesse. In January of

---

sponsible German museum officials." And also: "Hildebrandlied 3," documents from the archives. ... Report of Koolman on the meeting with R. Pusch and H. Schleiermacher, April 15, 1972, in which Riza Pusch, widow of museum director Felix Pusch, declared that her husband was not responsible for the oversight of the Goecke cellar.

27 "Hildebrandlied 1," documents from the archives ... Statement of H. Hopf and W. von Both, February 8, 1952.

28 Ibid., Declaration of W. Hopf, June 20, 1945.

29 Ibid., Declaration of W. Hopf, August 2, 1952.

30 *Bis 5 Minuten nach Zwölf*, 67–69.

1945, in preparation for this suicidal resistance, Helm and the rest of the Kassel fighters were given each a handgun and three bullets. There were no military uniforms for the Kassel *Volkssturm*. Instead, they were offered a heap of rags, leftovers from an army surplus collection. After rummaging around, curator Helm found an officer's jacket from the First World War, and dyed SA[31] coat, but no pants, no cap, no gloves, and no footwear. Unlike other less fortunate comrades, he still owned a good pair of ski boots. He strapped them on and was one of the lucky soldiers who returned home from the Eastern Front with his ski boots still on.[32]

The relentless bombardments had forced Hopf and his librarians to move once again, this time to the offices of the Murhard Library, the second largest research library of Kassel.[33] The Murhard had been hit several times, but after hasty repairs some of the office space was still usable. Hopf's books and journals were long gone, some lost in bombing raids, others crated and scattered to the four corners of Hesse and beyond. For a while, he and two of his diehard librarians continued to show up for work. Without heat, electricity, or mail, and often without food or means of transportation, a regular schedule could hardly be sustained. Reluctantly, Hopf decided to suspend services. The *Landesbibliothek* would remain closed to the public until August of 1948.[34]

The unusually early spring of 1945 brought more misery than relief. Incessant rains turned the streets into rivers of mud. The ghastly stench of decomposing bodies, buried deep under the rubble, hung heavily over the devastated city. At night, the southern sky reflected an ominous glow, and the surrounding hills echoed with the menacing rumble of artillery fire.[35] The Ardennes counteroffensive had crumbled, and the path to Berlin was wide open. In March, American troops crossed the Rhine and Patton's Third Army began its advance through southern Hesse. In Kassel the mood of the people dithered between apathy and

---

31 Note: SA stands for *Sturmabteilung*, or Assault Division, a paramilitary organization of the Nazi Party, since 1939 charged with the training of the Home Guard units.

32 *Bis 5 Minuten nach Zwölf*, 59, citing Rudolf Helm's *Volkssturm-Saga* (Kassel: [Weber & Weidemeyer]), 1961. Published in manuscript, 1945/46.

33 *Handbuch der Historischen Buchbestände in Deutschland* (Handbook of historical book collections in Germany), editor Bernhard Fabian, vol. 5 (Hildesheim: Olms-Weidmann, 1992), 318–19.
Note: The brothers Friedrich (1778–1853) and Karl Murhard (1781–1863), descendants of an old Hessian merchant family, established and later endowed a library (named after them *Die Murhardsche Bibliothek der Stadt Kassel*), whose collections complemented those of the *Landesbibliothek*. Whereas the *Landesbibliothek* collected in the fields of history, regional history, classical and contemporary philology, archaeology, art, geography, theology, and law, the Murhard Library emphasized political sciences, economics, and pedagogy.

34 *Ex Bibliotheca Cassellana*, 46.

35 *Bis 5 Minuten nach Zwölf*, 151.

panic. Fear of a Nazi blood bath, terror of Russian brutality, and apprehension of American wrath alternated with exhausted resignation and weary helplessness.

Holy Week came early in 1945, and nature greeted the holiday with splashes of yellow forsythias and deep blue violets flowering among the ruins.[36] On Good Friday, Kassel came abuzz with rumors of a peaceful surrender. But instead, at nightfall, Hitler's Nero-Order was implemented.[37] Women and children were evacuated, plants, factories, and bridges were ordered blown up and the tattered *Volkssturm* was called to the trenches.[38]

German armed forces retreated from Bad Wildungen, abandoning the city to the mercy of the victor, be it Soviet or American. To defend a resort filled with thousands of wounded soldiers would have been suicidal. On March 31, Christian Albus perched atop the high tower of the *Stadtkirche,* spotted the approaching US troops. He signaled to the townsfolk huddled at the foot of the belfry. The people of Bad Wildungen poured out in the streets relieved that the final defeat was not at the hands of the Soviet Red Army. US troops swiftly took over City Hall[39] and declared the spa a restricted military zone.[40] Residents were ordered to vacate homes, inns, and hotels. US army units sealed off the quarter around the administration building, and occupied Hotel Goecke.[41] In the chaos of the early hours, private homes, inns, and hospitals were plundered. Furniture, silverware, carpets, medical instruments, all disappeared. The baroque library of Friedrichstein castle, up on the hill, was set on fire.[42]

Just before retreating, Hesse *Gauleiter* Gerland ordered the execution of anyone hoisting a white flag, and the murder of one hundred Gestapo prisoners. Days later, their machine-gunned bodies were discovered in a mass grave.[43] For Kassel the end came swiftly. On April 2, units of the US Third Army entered through devastated Wilhelmshöhe,[44] and on April 5, from all city windows white flags

---

36 Ibid., 187.

37 Part of Hitler's scorched-earth policy. As all hope was lost, it was Hitler's intention to take down with him Germany's entire infrastructure and leave nothing behind.

38 *Bis 5 Minuten nach Zwölf,* 199–200.

39 Kesting, 101.

40 Douglas Botting, *In the Ruins of the Reich* (London: Allen & Unwin, 1985), 70.
Note: General Omar Bradley, Twelfth US Army Group commander established his headquarters at the Fürstenhof Hotel in Bad Wildungen.

41 "Hildebrandlied 1," documents from the archives ... Summary decision, July 6, 1946.

42 Kesting, 100–102.

43 *Volksgemeinschaft und Volksfeinde,* 277, 462.

44 William Freeman Twaddell, "The Hildebrandslied Manuscript in the U.S.A., 1945–1972," *Journal of English and Germanic Philology* 73, no. 2 (1974): 157: "In the advance of US troops through eastern Hesse in the early spring of 1945, the regions around Kassel and Bad

were seen waving in the wind.[45] Surrender marked the Hour Zero, *die Stunde Null*, "... the moment of hiatus when the people of a nation ... ceased to exist, touched rock-bottom, when the hands of the stop-watch were reset to zero and began to tick towards an unthinkable future."[46] From deep underground, in a landscape of unspeakable destruction, Dr. Hopf and his surviving librarians, joined the crowds who emerged to greet the victors with silence and relief. The war was over.

Wildungen were secured by the following units of the Third Army: the 9th Armored Division of the V Corps, especially Combat Command B; the 6th Armored Division of the XX Corps, especially Combat Commands A and B. The garrison of Kassel surrendered to the 80th Division on 4 April. The following day, the 69th Division relieved the 80th Division, and Regimental Combat Team 271 remained to guard installations."

45 *Bis fünf Minuten nach Zwölf*, 218.

46 Botting, 94.

Chapter 4: "Protect and Respect These Symbols ..."

Dwight D. Eisenhower

While the war was raging in Europe, on the other side of the ocean, the United States museum community was growing increasingly concerned about the large-scale destruction of artistic and historic monuments. The bitter struggle against the Nazi aggressor had unleashed a hailstorm of bombardments. As a result, half the continent lay in ruins. The looming assault on Germany was causing the museum world even greater alarm. The Allied invasion was bound to cut through the very heart of historical Europe and in its path level irreplaceable landmarks. With no time to spare, curators from two of the most influential cultural organizations in the United States, the *American Defense-Harvard Group* and the *American Council of Learned Societies*, approached Secretary of War Henry L. Stimson[1] with a plea to safeguard the endangered symbols of European civilization.[2] Together with their petition they submitted a strategic plan. They sought to create a special organization to protect artworks in times of war. They recommended the formation of an elite corps of specialists to safeguard monuments caught in the crossfire, and the compilation of a roster of trustworthy European museum personnel to assist US troops in locating hidden art caches, and in conducting emergency restoration and restitution work. It was a bold vision that marked a complete departure from the time-honored war mentality of slash-and-burn and finders-keepers. It might have been too bold and too novel, for their appeal fell on deaf ears. The military establishment did not look kindly upon such well-intended, yet seemingly unrealistic recommendations. Safeguarding old buildings and artifacts in the heat of battle was considered not only impractical but downright inimical to military goals.

Notwithstanding modern day international agreements, destruction was largely tolerated as an unintended consequence of war, and spoliation as the privilege of

---

1 Henry L. Stimson (1867–1950) was twice Secretary of War: under President William Howard Taft (1911–1913) and under Presidents Franklin Roosevelt and Harry Truman (1940–1945).

2 *Civil Affairs and Military Government Activities in Connection With Monuments, Fine Arts, and Archives – The General Board, United States, Army, Forces in the European Theater* ([The General Board, USFET] [Bad Nauheim, Germany] [1945 or 1946]), 1–2: ... "On 8 December 1942, the Honorable Harlan F. Stone addressed a letter to the President concerning the creation of an organization to function under the auspices of the Government for the protection and conservation of works of art and of artistic or historic monuments and records in Europe. ... On 20 April 1943, the President was again approached ..." "On 15 March 1943, Professor Bell Dinsmoor of Columbia University, writing to the Secretary of War, enclosed a Memorandum relative to the military steps to be taken for the protection and salvage of artistic and historic monuments in Europe."

the conqueror. There was an abundance of historical precedents. Triumphant Roman legions had returned home laden with the fabled treasures of their vanquished enemies. Crusaders had sacked Constantinople, scattered its riches and carted off its relics. Napoleon had ruthlessly seized the cultural heritage of his vanquished enemies, and had encouraged his troops to partake in the spoils. "Voler, c'est malhonnête, le soldat trouve!"[3] was his permissive explanation for the forays perpetrated by his soldiers. Voltaire, in his cynical assessment of human behavior, had branded war a simple excuse for pillage[4] and the term *soldier* and *robber* as synonymous.[5]

But no matter how destructive the random raids of history had been, they did not begin to compare with the systematic and deliberate plunder carried out by Hitler and later emulated by Stalin. Hitler raided Europe and the Soviet Union with calculated method and clear purpose. The best pieces were earmarked for his German Reich Museum in Linz, a mammoth neoclassical ensemble. Architectural plans envisioned the largest cultural complex of all times, anchored by a mausoleum for German heroes, and surrounded by museums, theaters, libraries, archives, and academies. The creation of this Acropolis-on-the-Danube[6] was one of Hitler's most cherished projects. He tinkered with the model in his bunker until the very end, while the Red Army shelled Berlin. And once the Soviets invaded Germany, it was Stalin's turn to loot.

As bombings increased in destructive ferocity, the American curators decided to wait no more. The time had come to cut through the red tape and bring their appeal directly to the attention of the White House. In a letter to President Roosevelt signed by Chief Justice Harlan F. Stone of the US Supreme Court they outlined yet again the purposes and functions of their proposed organization. Astutely, this time they stressed not only their noble intent to salvage and preserve European art but also the political advantages that could be derived from

---

3 "Stealing would be dishonest, for a soldier merely finds!" Attributed to Napoleon during the campaign in Italy. Cited in: *Der Quedlinburger Schatz wieder vereint* (The Quedlinburg treasure together again), editor Dieter Kötzsche (Berlin: Kulturstiftung der Länder: Ars Nicolai, 1992), xv.

4 Voltaire, *Œuvres complètes de Voltaire* (Paris: Garnier Frères, 1877–1985), v. 28, *Mélanges VII, Dieu et les Hommes*, 431: "[M]ais il est clair que le grand but de la guerre était ... en un mot, de voler." (Yet it is obvious that the great goal of war was ... in a word, to pilfer.)

5 Voltaire, *Œuvres complètes de Voltaire* (Paris: Garnier Frères, 1877–1985), v. 19, *Dictionnaire philosophique III, Gouvernement,* 293: "... les noms de *soldat* et de *voleur* étaient souvent synonymes." (... the names of *soldier* and *robber* being often synonymous.)

6 S. Lane Faison Jr., "Transfer of Custody to the Germans," in: *The Spoils of War: World War II and Its Aftermath: The Loss, Reappearance, and Recovery of Cultural Property,* editor Elizabeth Simpson (New York: H. N. Abrams in association with the Bard Graduate Center for Studies in the Decorative Arts, 1997), 139.
Note: The city of Linz is on the Danube River.

the implementation of their program. A clearly adopted policy for the protection of art against destruction and spoliation, they explained, would go a long way to discredit Fascist accusations of American barbarity towards, and ignorance of European history and civilization. It would reinforce the belief that the United States was fighting to preserve the very symbols created by the genius of mankind.[7]

Roosevelt liked the plan. On June 23, 1943, he ordered the creation of the American Commission for the Protection and Salvage of Artistic and Historic Monuments in Europe.[8] It was a historic departure from the practices of the past: few leaders had ever championed the protection of art during armed conflict.[9] And no victor had ever considered returning war booty to victims and vanquished alike. Chaired by Owen J. Roberts, Justice of the US Supreme Court, it became known as the Roberts Commission or the RC, for short.[10]

---

7 *Report of the American Commission for the Protection and Salvage of Artistic and Historic Monuments in War Areas* (Washington: Government Printing Office, 1946), 1.

8 Ibid. 3. The offices of the newly created Commission were housed in the National Gallery of Art in Washington, DC. The Commission functioned for three years (1943–1946), held nine full meetings, and numerous subcommittee meetings. Additional consultations and communications were handled via telephone, telegraph, and letter.
Note: In May 1944, Great Britain established the British Commission on Preservation and Restitution of Works of Art, Archives and Other Material in Enemy Hands, known as the Macmillan Committee, which was mostly concerned with restitution of lost paintings. After liberation, French, Belgian, and Dutch commissions on recovery and return of works of art were also formed.

9 Leslie I. Poste, "The Development of U.S. Protection of Libraries and Archives in Europe During World War II" (Dissertation, University of Chicago, 1958), 165–169: "For the origin of this remarkable program [Poste refers here to the protection and preservation of cultural resources] ... we must give credit to both the Germans, despite their vandalism and looting activities, and to the British. *German Kunstschutz.* – At the time of the German campaign in western Europe in 1940, the *Oberkommando [des] Heeres* (German High Command, also known as the OKH) created the *Kunstschutz* in May 1940 ... The *Kunstschutz* had the mission of assisting the various fine arts administrations of the occupied territories in the preservation and protection of art, monuments, libraries, and archives from war damage. The *Kunstschutz* ... operated only in those countries under German Military Government, namely: France, Belgium, Jugoslavia, and Greece." On the British program, Poste describes the initiative of Major J. B. Ward Perkins and fellow archaeologist Brigadier Mortimer Wheeler, to safeguard Roman ruins during the capture of Tripoli in January of 1943, and the art-saving missions during the Allied campaign in Sicily and Italy.

10 For a history of the Commission see the *Report of the American Commission....* Also Harry L. Coles and Albert K. Weinberg, *Civil Affairs: Soldiers Become Governors.* United States Army in World War II, Special Studies, vol. 8 (Washington, D.C.: Office of the Chief of Military History, Department of the Army, 1964); and Ruth K. Mayer, "The Roberts Commission," in: Walter I Farmer. *The Safekeepers: A Memoir of the Arts at the End of World War II,* revised and prefaced by Klaus Goldmann, with an introduction by Margaret Farmer Planton (Berlin: de Gruyter, 2000), 123–43.

The newly created Commission consisted of seven specialized subcommittees.[11] Membership was prestigious and highly selective. To its Subcommittee on Books, Manuscripts and Other Printed and Written Material of Cultural Value, chaired by Librarian of Congress Archibald MacLeish and composed of only five distinguished advisers, Justice Roberts appointed a well respected and internationally recognized expert: the rare book collector and dealer Dr. A. S. W. Rosenbach.[12] In his hands and in those of his five other eminent colleagues, President Roosevelt placed his trust and the creation of a model policy designed to protect the written heritage of the human mind.

True to its agenda, the RC began by compiling a roster of officers and enlisted civil engineers, curators, librarians, and art historians. These were sent out into the war zone to safeguard threatened art and monuments.[13] They became known as the Monuments Men, members of an elite corps: the Monuments, Fine Arts and Archives (MFA&A). To strengthen their authority on the battlefield, Dwight D. Eisenhower, Allied Supreme Commander in Europe, issued on May 26, 1944, his now famous order governing rules of engagement:

> Shortly we will be fighting our way across the Continent of Europe in Battles designed to preserve our civilization. Inevitably, in the path of our advance will be found historical monuments and cultural centers, which symbolize to the world all that we are fighting to preserve.
>
> It is the responsibility of every commander to protect and respect these symbols whenever possible....
>
> ...There are many circumstances in which damage and destruction is not necessary and cannot be justified. In such cases, through the exercise of restraint and discipline, commanders will preserve centers and objects of historical and cultural significance. Civil Affairs Staffs at higher echelons will advise commanders of the locations of historical monuments of this type, both in advance of the front lines and in occupied areas. This information, together with the necessary instructions, will be passed down through command channels to all echelons.[14]

---

[11] *Report of the American Commission ...*, 7–8. The other six subcommittees were Definition of Works of Cultural Value and Property; Administration; Collection of Maps, Information and Description of Art Objects; Personnel; Art Instruction in Military Government Schools; and the Committee on Axis-Appropriated Property.

[12] Ibid., 8: "Its Advisers were Dr. Solon J. Buck, Dr. Waldo G. Leland, Dr. Henry M. Lydenberg, Dr. A. S. W. Rosenbach, and Mr. Lewis Hanke."
Note: Solon J. Buck (1884–1962) was a historian and archivist; Waldo Gifford Leland (1879– 1966) was a well known historian and archival theorist; Henry M. Lydenberg (1874–1960) was librarian and former director of the New York Public Library (1934–1941); Lewis Hanke (1905–1993) was the first director of a Hispanic foundation set up by Henry E. Huntington at the Library of Congress, and considered the father of the field of Latin American studies. The Chairman was Archibald MacLeish (1892–1982) a poet, lawyer, distinguished public servant, and Librarian of Congress from 1939 to 1944.

[13] *Civil Affairs and Military Government Activities ...*, 15.

[14] *The Papers of Dwight David Eisenhower: The War Years: III*, editor Alfred D. Chandler, Jr. (Baltimore: Johns Hopkins, 1970), 1890–91.

The small MFA&A contingent followed closely behind the Normandy invasion force. By the nature of their assignments its officers fell into two groups: Doers and Gatherers. The Doers, architects and engineers, were first out in the field identifying endangered monuments, exhorting artillery to spare cathedrals, castles, and villas, urging officers not to bivouac in historic places, soldiers not to deface buildings and statues, or destroy archives. After each battle, they rushed to shore up structures, perform quick repairs, protect exposed artwork from the elements, and prevent plunder. Their mission was difficult and dangerous. During the early days of the invasion, Captain Walter J. Huchthausen, a professor of art and architecture at the University of Michigan, and British Major Ronald E. Balfour of Kings College Cambridge were killed by sniper bullets.[15]

The Gatherers, museum curators, historians, archivists, and librarians, were the second wave of art protectors. Their work began only when the guns fell silent. Their post-combat role was to collect, identify, catalog, and return treasures hidden in war-repositories. To the art-loving Monuments Men the destructive tendencies of the fighting men were appalling and the lack of support from field commanders, grievous. To the troops and to the warlords, the pesky art-protectors, who seemed to get in the way of military operations, were a constant source of vexation.[16] Neither Doers nor Gatherers enjoyed much respect from GIs, who delighted in calling them "mousy Venus-fixers."[17]

When on March 7, 1945, US troops crossed at Remagen the last intact bridge spanning the Rhine, the Ludendorff, a bad situation became worse.[18] Angry

---

15 Poste, 194.

16 Gerald K. Haines, "Who Gives a Damn about Medieval Walls," *Prologue* 8, no. 2 (1976): 97–106, 100: "The situation these men found themselves in was novel: they had to explain, almost in the midst of battle, who they were, what they were trying to do, and why it was important. Their task was to give advice to field commanders, though they had no real authority, give first aid to badly injured art, though they had no repair materials, and inspect and report on the state of monuments ... though they had no transportation."

17 Ibid., 101.

18 Earl F. Ziemke, *The U.S. Army in the Occupation of Germany 1944–1946*, Army Historical Series, (Washington, DC: Center of Military History, United States Army, 1975), 199–200: "Lt. Col. Webb, SHAEF's (N.B. Supreme Headquarters, Allied Expeditionary Force) MFA&A adviser, toured the two British armies and US Ninth Army in March [N.B. 1945]. Pillage and wanton destruction, he concluded, were at least a combined effort, being as prevalent among British and Canadians as among Americans. At Juelich, he saw slashed pictures and cases of books from the Aachen library broken open and their contents strewn about by souvenir hunters. Aware that the prevailing mood was not one of kindliness toward Germans or their property, he pointed out that the German collections also contained looted art work which the Allies had pledged to restore to their rightful owners, and these pieces too were threatened. SHAEF G-5 forwarded Webb's report, adding, "It is appreciated that a certain amount of 'toughness' may be desirable in occupied territory and it is not suggested that we should instruct our troops to act in Germany as they have usually in liberated territory; nevertheless, it is important that Allied troops should not desecrate churches and

British, Canadian, and American soldiers seemed intent to punish not only the enemy but also its cultural symbols.

> Whatever inhibitions there had been regarding the use of property and the destruction of artistic works in Allied territory, they no longer applied. The military bore little or no respect for German works of art. Monuments were smashed, houses looted, buildings bulldozed, and paintings and statues destroyed.[19]

Just prior to inspection by MFA&A officers, in Jesberg, province of Hesse, where many files of the state archives of Marburg were stored, troops threw out thousands upon thousands of historical documents to make room for the military occupation force.[20] The combat soldiers must have considered the Supreme Commander's order to "protect and respect" inane, and could not have been overly anxious to enforce it.

While the Monuments Officers grappled with the damage of war and the destructive behavior of troops, across the ocean, in Washington, DC, the members of the Roberts Commission wrestled with their own set of problems. Waves of returning soldiers arrived at border points with knapsacks filled with war souvenirs.[21] Alarmed, the Roberts Commission applied pressure on the US Treasury Department to strengthen import controls, and as a result on June 8, 1944, Treasury Decision 51072 was implemented.[22] Customs agents were ordered to demand proof of origin for all art objects entering the country valued at $ 5 000 or more. But by then the number of illegal war souvenirs had reached staggering proportions. An increase of six to eight thousand inspectors was deemed necessary to cope with all incoming military luggage and parcel shipments. The additional manpower was never allocated. Beset by sheer volume, Customs Agents on duty could only performed occasional spot-checks. Treasury Decision 51072 might have been well intended and well timed, but in practice it remained unenforceable. Many a war souvenir slipped by undetected.[23]

---

should not destroy works of art looted from our allies." It was in fact not a good time to attempt to convert the troops into guardians of German culture. General Smith passed the Webb report on to the army groups with the slightly equivocal comment that looting had to be considered a less despicable offense on enemy territory but ought to be discouraged for the sake of the restitution policy."

19 Haines, 105–6.

20 *Civil Affairs and Military Government Activities* ..., 29.

21 *Report of the American Commission* ..., 9.

22 Lynn H. Nicholas, *The Rape of Europa: The Fate of Europe's Treasures in the Third Reich and the Second World War* (New York: Knopf, 1994), 276, quoting from the *Minutes of the RC meeting, February 3, 1944* (RG 239/5).
Note: Military Government Law 52, which was already on the books, prohibited sale, movement, transfer, concealment, or destruction of any work of art. Treasury Decision 51072 was supposed to stop the influx of stolen art into the US.

23 *Report of the American Commission* ..., 23: "At the meeting of the Commission in Septem-

Out in the field, the MFA&A corps was also suffering from inadequate manpower. In spite of repeated and insistent requests, the shortage of MFA&A personnel was never remedied.[24] All in all, the elite European contingent numbered 165 officers and enlisted men, and twenty-one civilians.[25] This handful of people was sent out to patrol the vast expanses of occupied Germany. At the end of April 1945, for instance, the area of the Twelfth Army Group,[26] extending over a surface of 47,000 square miles, had three Monuments Officers on active duty. Dispatched with the First Army, with some 15,000 square miles to patrol, in one of the richest cultural areas of the land, was one lonely officer with no transportation.[27] Logistical support was woefully inadequate: lists received from the RC describing cultural sites in need of protection were sometimes wrong and often outdated.[28] At times, even the most rudimentary supplies were lacking, such as signs designating Off Limit areas. To keep looters away, officers had to mark buildings with white tape indicating unexploded mines.[29] There was a dearth of drafting and technical equipment. The *Leicas* promised at the beginning of the operation were never procured. Officers, with a mandate to document destruction and provide evidence of repairs, went in the field with their own cameras or

---

ber 1944 Monsignor Griffiths, representing Archbishop Spellman, had called the attention of the American Commission to numerous reports of importation of objects of artistic and religious importance by members of the armed forces. ...Military Government Law 52, established during the period of the Supreme Commander's control in Europe and continued during the period of our Allied military government control in Germany and Italy, prohibited the exportation of works of art or other objects of cultural importance from the Theater. In June 1945 Mr. John A. Gilmore, then Assistant Secretary of the Commission, conferred in New York with representatives of the Bureau of Customs regarding the Treasury Department controls under T. D. 51072 with special relation to possible importations by the armed forces. The Customs authorities admitted that the extent of importation by members of the armed forces was considerable and that existing controls could only consist of spot-checking. ... A representative of the Customs Mail Division informed Mr. Gilmore that it would require 6,000 to 8,000 additional inspectors to screen completely parcel-post shipments from abroad. As these facts would indicate, the establishment of controls over these importations by armed forces was a tremendous problem."

24 *Civil Affairs and Military Government Activities* ..., 15.

25 Poste, 181.

26 Ibid., 191: "The Twelfth Army Group was under the command of Lieutenant General Omar Bradley. Armies and their commanders, at the time of the final offensive, comprising the Twelfth Army Group were the Third U.S. Army, Major General George S. Patton, Jr.: First U.S. Army, Lieutenant General Courtney H. Hodges; Fifteenth U.S. Army, Brigadier General Leonard T. Gerow; and Ninth U.S. Army, Lieutenant General William H. Simpson. Before the Twelfth Army Group became operational, it had been agreed that one Monuments, Fine Arts and Archives officer would be attached to the headquarters of each G-5 section at army level."

27 *Civil Affairs and Military Government Activities* ..., 25.

28 Ibid., 30–31.

29 Haines, 105.

with none at all.[30] The MFA&A mission looked great on paper and was worthy of the best traditions of the US Armed Forces, the Monuments Men seemed to enjoy support at the highest level of military echelons, but out there on the battlefield those guarantees did not match reality.

From resistance fighters, informants, and anti-Nazi museum personnel, the Monuments Men began gathering leads on hidden art caches. Ultimately fourteen hundred such repositories were discovered, with over fifteen million items, the largest art collection ever assembled in the history of warfare.[31] One third were objects looted on Hitler's orders and set aside for his super-museum in Linz. However, two thirds belonged to legitimate German museums, libraries, and churches, collections, which had been hastily evacuated for fear of fire, bombardments, and looting.[32]

The first post-operational task of the Monuments Men was to set up storehouses in which to gather the treasures. Two facilities, one in Munich and the other in Offenbach, were designated to receive art plundered from occupied territories or confiscated from Jews. A third one in Wiesbaden was assigned to house art belonging to German cultural institutions.[33] The Doers had concluded their mission. It was time for the Gatherers to begin collecting, identifying, cataloging, and returning millions of art objects displaced in the turmoil of war.

---

30 *Civil Affairs and Military Government Activities* ..., 30.

31 Michael J. Kurtz, "The End of the War and the Occupation of Germany, 1944–52. Laws and Conventions Enacted to Counter German Appropriations: The Allied Control Council." In: *The Spoils of War: World War II and Its Aftermath: The Loss, Reappearance, and Recovery of Cultural Property,* editor Elizabeth Simpson (New York: H.N. Abrams in association with the Bard Graduate Center for Studies in the Decorative Arts, 1977), 116.

32 Poste, 193.

33 Initially, numerous small collecting points were established. Over time these were reduced to four: Munich, Wiesbaden, Marburg, and Offenbach. In summer of 1946, the Marburg Collecting Point was closed. The remaining three were reorganized to house recovered art by type of provenance.

Chapter 5: Of US Safekeepers, Soviet Trophy Commissars and Marauding Allied Soldiers

In spring of 1945, Captain Walter I. Farmer, a thirty-five-year-old engineer from Cincinnati, Ohio, was stationed in Frankfurt am Main.[1] His army unit, which had just finished building bridges over the Rhine, had been reassigned to assemble cages for prisoners of war.[2] The task was singularly depressing. Evenings, Farmer found escape in the stories published by the *Stars and Stripes,* the daily newspaper of the US Armed Forces. What made the *Stars and Stripes* so captivating in spring of 1945 was its series on Hitler's hidden treasures. Since his regiment was on alert to return to the States for redeployment to the Pacific, Farmer, a student of architecture and interior design, decided to try his luck and offer his services to the men who guarded those riches, the Monuments Officers.

Desperately short of engineers, not to mention seasoned officers who knew their way around the military bureaucracy, the Monuments Men were only too eager to take Farmer up on his offer. After the briefest of interviews, he was ordered to report to Wiesbaden, and set up a repository for recovered German-owned art. The massive Wiesbaden *Landesmuseum,* the Provincial Museum, a gutted structure with blown out windows and doors, with no running water, heat or electricity, was designated as his storehouse, or in military parlance as his Central Collecting Point. There were only ninety days left to the start of the rainy season and waiting to be processed was a first shipment of 6,000 crates, filled with artifacts from Germany's leading museums: church articles from the medieval Guelph Treasure, masterpieces of Islamic art, coins of all periods, ethnologic rarities, early Christian and Byzantine collections, delicate East Asian sculptures, and boxes upon boxes with gems and jewelry. In one of the crates Farmer discovered the word-famous long-necked, one-eyed bust of the beautiful Nile-Queen Nefertiti. This batch was only a prelude. As bunker after bunker was emptied, more shipments arrived at Farmer's door, with contents ranging from the sublime to the bizarre. From an iron mine in Siegen Farmer received four hundred canvasses of old masters, together with the collections of the church treasuries of Metz, Aachen, Essen, Cologne, and Munich, and forty crates filled

[1] For the complete story of Farmer and his Frankfurt and Wiesbaden activities, see Walter I. Farmer, *The Safekeepers: A Memoir of the Arts at the End of World War II,* revised and prefaced by Klaus Goldmann, with an introduction by Margaret Farmer Planton. Cultural Property Studies (Berlin: de Gruyter, 2000)

[2] Walter I. Farmer, "Custody and Controversy at the Wiesbaden Collecting Point," in: *The Spoils of War: World War II and Its Aftermath: The Loss, Reappearance, and Recovery of Cultural Property,* editor Elizabeth Simpson (New York: H. N. Abrams in association with the Bard Graduate Center for Studies in the Decorative Arts, 1977), 131.

Fig. 9. Walter I. Farmer and Queen Nefertiti 1945
(Courtesy of Margaret Planton-Farmer)

with Beethoven manuscripts.[3] From the salt mine of Bernterode, northeast of Kassel, Farmer acquired the funeral caskets of Field Marshal von Hindenburg, that of the Soldier King Frederick William the First, and that of Frederick the Great.[4] Practically overnight, Walter Farmer, Cincinnati engineer and art student, had become the master of fabulous treasures, and his bombed-out building a real Ali Baba's cave.[5]

Farmer had no manpower, and no equipment. He needed laborers to patch up the *Landesmuseum*, armed security guards to watch over the spoils, specialists to inventory and care for the splendor in the crates. Necessity being the mother of invention, Farmer began by re-inventing himself. He discovered he had the courage and confidence of a seasoned organizer, the ingenuity of a creative administrator, the drive of an inspiring leader, and the heart of a principled protector of the cultural heritage of a vanquished nation.[6]

Finding employees with no prior Nazi affiliation in post-war Germany was no easy task. After a rigorous selection process, Farmer succeeded in assembling a trustworthy crew of engineers, day workers, and guards. He also hired a distinguished curator, Dr. Friedrich Bleibaum, a former art minister of pre-Nazi days, who had chosen early retirement rather than joining the Party.[7] Farmer had the *Landesmuseum* surrounded by a high fence, and used scavenged headlights from army jeeps as floodlights to illuminate the building by night.

> GI's guarded the perimeter of the building [he noted in his diary] German police guarded the galleries now used as storerooms. A secret policeman guarded the Germans and I guarded the guards.[8]

With security and personnel in place, Farmer's Wiesbaden Central Collecting Point opened for business on August 20, 1945, three short months after V-E Day.[9]

---

3 Leslie I. Poste, "The Development of U.S. Protection of Libraries and Archives in Europe During World War II" (Dissertation, University of Chicago, 1958), 218.

4 *Report of the American Commission for the Protection and Salvage of Artistic and Historic Monuments in War Areas* (Washington: Government Printing Office, 1946), 131.

5 Farmer, *Custody and Controversy*, 132.

6 Margaret Farmer Planton, Farmer's daughter, dubbed the Monuments Men *The Safekeepers*, a fitting designation for those indefatigable champions in the return of war-dispersed art.

7 Farmer, *The Safekeepers*, 40 and *Custody and Controversy*, 132.

8 Farmer, *Custody and Controversy*, 132.

9 *Monthly Report of Military Governor US Zone, Monuments, fine Arts and Archives*, no. 2, 20 September 1945, 2.
Note: V-E Days is short for *Victory in Europe Day*, celebrating May 8, 1945, the day of victory of the Allied Forces in World War II.

Across the Main River, in Offenbach, the Central Collecting Point for Judaica had also opened its doors. Mournfully, in row upon row, it displayed objects of every-day Jewish life, religion and culture pilfered from East European shtetl, impounded from Dutch and Belgian museums, confiscated from French or German Jews. In its cabinets bolted with iron bars there were letters, pictures, Torah scrolls, embroidered ark curtains, brass and silver menorahs, Passover plates, and precious books and manuscripts. For Captain Isaac Bencowitz, a Rockefeller Institute chemistry professor, and director of the Central Collecting Point, and for his staff, the daily work of sorting, cataloging, and finding the owners of these objects, was a poignant mission. Between March of 1946 and April of 1949 the Offenbach Archival Depot succeeded in returning to survivors, descendents, and museums over three million looted items.[10]

Further south, in Munich, at the third Central Collecting Point a lone Monuments Man, Captain Bernard Taper and a handful of weary helpers were sifting through art-filled containers evacuated from Berlin, recovered from southern Germany, or from the salt-mines of Austria.[11] The Munich Collecting Point was responsible for non-Jewish objects, confiscated from Nazi occupied territories, and for the so-called twice-looted art, items seized by the Nazis and then, at the end of the war, purloined by the local population.[12] The overworked Captain Taper was waging a loosing battle trying to follow up leads, interview suspects, and impound stolen goods.[13] Fortunately for him, help was on the way.

* * *

The US cargo plane skidded to a halt on the damp runway of a military airport near Marseilles.[14] Shivering and numb after the long, uncomfortable flight, Edgar

---

[10] Poste, 392. For a detailed description of the activities of the Offenbach Central Collecting Point, see Poste, 339–95.

[11] Elga Böhm, "Der Central Collecting Point – München: Erste Kunstsammelstelle nach Kriegsende" (The Central Collecting Point in Munich: First collecting point for art after the end of the war in 1945), *Kölner Museum Bulletin*, no. 4 (1987): 26. By February 1946, the Munich Central Collecting had inventoried twenty thousand crates containing some fifty thousand objects.

[12] Bernard Taper, "Investigating Art Looting for the MFA&A," in: *The Spoils of War: World War II and Its Aftermath: The Loss, Reappearance, and Recovery of Cultural Property,* editor Elizabeth Simpson (New York: H. N. Abrams in association with the Bard Center for Studies in the Decorative Arts, 1997), 136.

[13] Edgar Breitenbach, "Historical Survey of the Activities of the Intelligence Department, MFA&A Section, OMGB, 1946–1949," *College Art Journal* 9, no. 2 (1949–1950): 192: "Looking back, one must regret that in 1945 only one MFA&A officer from OMGUS was assigned to take care of art intelligence work, and that he had no counterpart in the Laender."

[14] The segment describing Edgar Breitenbach's post-war activities in Germany is closely based on his "Erinnerungen" (Recollections), in: *Bibliothek '76 International: Rückschau und Ausblick. Freundesgabe für Werner Mevissen zu seinem 65. Geburtstag am 16. April* (Bremen: Stadtbibliothek, 1976), 40–46.

Fig. 10. Edgar Breitenbach
(Courtesy of Jennifer Shank)

Breitenbach picked his way around the craggy airmail bags that had served him as cover and pillow, and staggered out into the drizzle of the gray morning. For days, his flight from Washington, DC had zigzagged across the ocean, stopping first in Bermuda, and then in the Azores, off the coast of Portugal. The plane was bound for Paris, but Paris was fogged in, and thus it was diverted to the dreary military airstrip, where Breitenbach was unceremoniously deplaned. He managed to hitch a flight to Frankfurt. On a late night in October 1945, eight years after fleeing his homeland, Edgar Breitenbach was about to set foot on German soil again. No longer a hunted Jew, he was returning with the US occupying forces to help sift through wreckage left in the wake of the hurricane.

Frankfurt am Main was a perfect illustration of the destructive force of that hurricane. Breitenbach's shifting emotions quickly froze into one solid clump of horror. What had happened to his city was abhorrent to mind and soul. The familiar web of narrow cobblestone streets with quaint houses and charming squares was gone. Here and there, the skeleton of a church, the twisted spike of a fountain, or an absurdly erect chimney shaft, brought back faint echoes of topical memories. Breitenbach followed a footpath that led through the wasteland to his old City Library. He found the shell of the building still standing, but behind that brave front, the body had crumbled, burying under the rubble the promise of his youth.[15]

Sixteen years earlier his future looked bright and secure. A summa cum laude doctoral degree in art history[16] and a rigorous training in librarianship led, in spite of a hiring freeze, to a coveted position of research librarian. All indicators pointed to a brilliant career ahead. But then Hitler came to power. The April 7, 1933 Law for the Restoration of the Professional Civil Service, which barred Jews from professional positions, wrenched Breitenbach from his scholarly world. He tried to find some other way to earn a living. In Basel, art historian and Holbein specialist Paul Ganz offered him a research position, but the Swiss denied him a work-permit. London was next where for a while he enjoyed asylum and employment. As Germany continued to spiral downward into hatred and war, Breitenbach took once more the uncertain path of exile. He crossed the ocean and accepted a temporary teaching position with Mills College, in Northern California. A year later, with no prospects of an extension, he joined a group of migrant workers picking fruit in the orchards of the Northwest. Hope and cash were almost gone when a job opened at the Federal Communications Commission and he was hired as monitor for German short-wave transmissions. A grateful Breitenbach formally adopted the country, which had given him work and sanctuary. At the end of war, the Monuments, Fine Arts and Archives corps recruited him and sent him back to Germany.

Breitenbach joined the beleaguered Captain Taper at the Munich Central Collecting Point, as the second intelligence officers responsible for finding displaced, misplaced, and looted artwork.[17] In Munich, as almost everywhere else

---

15 Poste, 282: "Of the 800,000 volumes and 450,000 dissertations formerly held by the Stadtbibliothek, only 250,000 volumes and 10,000 dissertations survived."

16 His dissertation was titled *Speculum Humanae Salvationis, Eine Typengeschichtliche Untersuchung*, (Speculum Humanae Salvationis: A typological historical study) (Strassburg: Heitz, 1930).

17 Taper, 135.

in post-war Germany, the black market was booming. Hunger drove people to desperate barter of family heirlooms. Art objects, looted in the rubble of the Reich, were offered for sale with little concern for legality, provenance, or destination. The trade had spawn gangs of middlemen and dubious dealers, who feverishly bought and sold paintings, sculptures, and tapestries, carpets, books, and jewelry, anything and everything portable. Breitenbach, who could easily pass for a local, followed the peddlers to the bohemian Munich district of Schwabing, where, day-in and day-out, he watched them haggle openly at street-corners over long lists of art-objects. Breitenbach's interest in the Schwabing merchandise was keen. His assignment was to recover the canvasses of the Adolphe Schloss Collection, a gathering of small paintings of seventeenth-century Dutch and Flemish masters acquired by Hitler and stored in the Munich *Führerbau,* the Führer Building. In the early hours of the US occupation, the starving population had stormed that building in search of food and liquor. After the mob had pilfered all provisions, it had gone on to better spoils. Furnishings, drapes, books, statuary and finally the canvases of a Jewish commodities merchant from alsace named Adolphe Schloss, all had disappeared.

Breitenbach slipped into his sleuthing role with thespian flair and fiendish creativity. Out in the field he was known as *der Bilderschreck*, the paintings-terror. He patrolled the back streets of Schwabing or roamed the villages around Berchtesgaden dressed in lederhosen[18] and speaking a thick Hamburg lingo, which was dulled by the presence of a stubby pipe forever dangling from the corner of his mouth.[19] He was masterful in wringing information from cliquish peasants, sleazy informers, and reluctant locals. One of his favorite techniques was to stop for a bite in some small watering hole and strike up a conversation with the owner. He would adroitly steer the chat to the dramatic events of the American invasion and gingerly ask if the owner had been in the *Führerbau*, in search of ... here a hand motion would convey the internationally recognized sign for booze. More often than not, the boisterous owner would launch into a vivid narrative of that action-filled night. Breitenbach would go on asking about those small paintings, which disappeared from the basement. The talkative bar-owner would eagerly finger some annoying patron, who in turn would angrily denounce the bar-owner. After three years of patient work, Breitenbach managed to recover half of the looted Schloss Collection. His only regret was that Army regulations did not permit him to offer food and cigarettes as incentives. He would have been far more successful.

* * *

When it came to the control and disposition of the cultural heritage of their vanquished enemy, the victors, Marshal Stalin and President Roosevelt were not of

---

[18] Lynn H. Nicholas, *The Rape of Europa: The Fate of Europe's Treasures in the Third Reich and the Second World War* (New York: Knopf, 1994), 429.

[19] Taper, 137.

one mind. Unlike its US ally, the Soviet Government was determined to use spoliation as a tool to punish Germany for the immense losses it had suffered during the war.[20] While US Monuments Men grappled with problems of recovery, preservation and restitution, Soviet curators compiled wish lists of German owned art. No sooner had Soviet tanks rolled across the Oder River, than Stalin loosed his Red Army Trophy Brigades, the enforcers of his policy of art plunder. The uniformed Soviet curators descended upon museums and libraries, brandishing their lists of valuable items. With lightning speed they crated, loaded and shipped back home trainload upon trainload of fabulous loot.[21] Just as Hitler before him, Stalin planned to build an immense museum dedicated to his spoils. It never materialized since the dictator soon discovered that his grandiose vision violated international agreements to which he was a signatory.[22] The beautiful booty remained hidden in Soviet cellars and secret hideouts. And although Khrushchev returned selected pieces to East Germany in 1955, millions of books and archival documents, and thousands of paintings are to this day shadowy prisoners of former Soviet states.

---

[20] See Poste, 266: "Entirely apart from the looting carried out by individual soldiers and units, there was an official commission, referred to as the 'Trophy Commission,' which functioned in violation of Article 56 of the Hague Convention (IV) of 1907 almost as soon as the Russians gained control of their sector of Berlin." Also: *U.S. seeks to replace cultural property displaced during World War II*, Department of State Bulletin, 25, no. 635 (1951), 345: "Restitution in kind or replacement of cultural property of unique character was given consideration by Allied Control Council in Berlin in 1946 and early in 1947. A quadripartite agreement for implementation of such a policy, however, was never concluded. American policy in the 1947 directive to the Commander-in-Chief of the United States Forces of Occupation (JCS 1779, July 11, 1947) prohibited replacement of cultural property from Germany's cultural heritage. ... A special resolution opposing the use of works of art as replacement or reparations material was unanimously approved by the *American Commission for the Protection and Salvage of Artistic and Historic Monuments in the War Areas* at its final meeting on June 20, 1946. It was recommended that 'cultural objects belonging to any country or individual should not be considered or involved in reparations settlements growing out of World War II.'"

[21] For a detailed description of the Soviet plunder see Konstantin Akinsha and Grigorii Kozlov, *Beautiful Loot: The Soviet Plunder of Europe's Art Treasures* (New York: Random House, 1995).

[22] See, for instance, the *Inter-Allied Declaration against Dispossession Committed in Territories under Enemy Occupation or Control*, signed at London on January 4, 1943. Issued as Department of State Publication 2530, and cited in: Elizabeth Simpson, editor, *The Spoils of War: World War II and Its Aftermath: The Loss, Reappearance, and Recovery of Cultural Property* (New York: H. N. Abrams in association with the Bard Graduate Center for Studies in Decorative Arts, 1977), 287. This declaration, signed by the Soviet Union, the USA, Great Britain, Poland and others, stipulated that "the Governments making this Declaration ... reserve all rights to declare invalid any transfer of, or dealings with, property ... which are or have been situated in the territories which have come under occupation and control. ... This warning applies whether such transfers or dealings have taken the form of open looting or plunder or of transactions apparently legal in form ..."

Library collections were high on the appropriation lists of Red Army Trophy commissars. Long before the end of the war, under directives from political leaders at the level of Molotov, Mikoyan and Beria,[23] Soviet librarians compiled detailed inventories of valuable books in German library collections. At the time of surrender, forty percent of German libraries fell into Soviet hands. While US Monuments Men struggled to identify and return German books to German libraries, Lieutenant Colonel Margarita Rudomino, founder of the State Library for Foreign Literature in Moscow, spearheaded the great Soviet book removal. A fierce communist, Rudomino considered spoliation a righteous act of compensation. On her wish list were collections that had to be confiscated, over and above the imposed reparation payments made by Germany.[24] A secret memorandum signed by Rudomino and recently discovered in the archives of the Moscow Union State Library for Foreign Literature acknowledges the success of her expedition: it yielded eleven million German books.[25] Of these, 50,000 handpicked

---

23 Ekaterina Genieva, "German Book Collections in Russian Libraries," in: *The Spoils of War: World War II and Its Aftermath: The Loss, Reappearance, and Recovery of Cultural Property*, editor Elizabeth Simpson (New York: H. N. Abrams in association with the Bard Graduate Center for Studies in the Decorative Arts, 1997), 222.
Note: Molotov, Mikoyan and Beria were three of the highest political leaders under Stalin. Vyacheslav Mikhailovich Molotov was the People's Commissar for Foreign Affairs; Lavrentii Beria was head of the People's Commissariat of Internal Affairs (NKVD), better known as the communist secret police; Anastas Mikoyan was deputy chairman of the Council of People's Commissars and, in his role as member of the State Defense Committee, also supervised the procurement and transport of supplies to the armed forces.

24 Ibid., 222: "However, it was not contrary to her will and her conscience that Margarita Rudomino was involved in sending to the Soviet Union the greatest legacy of the German people, the Deutsches Buch- und Schriftmuseum der Deutschen Bücherei (The German Museum of Books and Manuscripts). ... In the files of 1945, there is an interesting and rather lengthy document entitled 'List of certain German libraries whose holdings it is useful to make available to the USSR regardless of reparation payments in books by Germany to the Soviet Union.'"

25 Ibid.: "In the archives of my library there is a document signed by Rudomino stating that altogether about eleven million books were removed to the Soviet Union. Five million were sent to Moscow and Leningrad, two million to Minsk, three million to Kyiv (Kiev), and for one million a destination was not specified."
Note: A far more sinister intimation involving the son of Margarita Rudomino is also recorded by Genieva in the same article, 123: "The Gutenberg Bible [she writes] from the collection of the Deutsches Buch- und Schriftmuseum was hidden in the basement of the ancient family castle of Baron Raunstein. Right after the departure from the region of the American troops, the Raunsteins themselves reported the book's location to the Soviet military command. ... Believing in the strength of long-standing German-Russian cultural relations, they hoped that at some point in the future this great book would once again return to Germany. All that is known of the family's fate is that they disappeared at the end of the 1940s. Perhaps their secret is preserved in some yet unopened Russian archives. Thus the Raunsteins' Gutenberg Bible was brought to the USSR. Those who took this treasure to the USSR included the son of Margarita Rudomino, a twenty-year-old lieutenant also serving in Germany."

trophy-volumes were set aside for Rudomino's own Moscow library.[26] The balance ended up forgotten in the warehouses of distant provincial institutions.

Armed conflict and opportunistic plunder go hand in hand. In the lawlessness that grips a world at war, integrity is oftentimes suspended. Oblivious to general rules of engagement, ignorant of international agreements, and disrespectful of basic laws of morality, Allied soldiers, Soviet and American,[27] used the cover of war as an opportunity for personal enrichment. Unlike the systematic and deliberate looting campaigns of Hitler and Stalin, the forays of individual soldiers were accidental and random. The Russians starved for household items and consumer goods collected everything from radios, watches and kitchen utensils, to typewriters, bicycles, and mechanical gadgets. The more sophisticated Americans preferred collector items with good resale value:[28] coins, paintings, stamps,

---

[26] *Katalog der Drucke des XVI. Jahrhunderts aus den Beständen der VGBIL* (Catalog of 16th century imprints in the collection of the Union State Library for Foreign Literature VGBIL), E. A Korkmazova, and A. L. Ponomarev, compilors (Moscow: Rudomino, 1996), X.
Note: In 1996, The *Rudomino Library* published this annotated listing of sixteenth century imprints included in their collection. As the prefatory material attests, one third of the fifteen hundred books described were acquired as trophy literature. For many years Margarita Rudomino ruled unchallenged in the world of Soviet and East Block librarianship and as director of the *Union State Library for Foreign Literature*. She guarded to her death the secret of the volumes brought to the USSR, including that of the Gutenberg Bible. A quarter century after the war, her active participation in the pillage of German libraries was all but forgotten. History is very fickle in what it wants to reward, remember, denounce, forgive, or forget. In 1973, the international library world honored Rudomino by electing her vice-president for life to its highest forum, the *International Federation for Library Associations*. The existence of her hidden trophy books came to light only after the collapse of communism. At the time of her death, East German librarians eulogized her and praised her exemplary work in librarianship. (See: Jürgen Hering, "Restitution kriegsbedingt verlagerter Kulturgüter: Ein neues Kapitel zur Rückführung deutscher Bücher aus Rußland (Restitution of cultural property dispersed during the war: A new chapter in the return of German books from Russia)," in: *Bücher für die Wissenschaft: Bibliotheken zwischen Tradition und Fortschritt. Festschrift für Günter Gattermann zum 65. Geburtstag,* editor Gert Kaiser (München: K. G. Sauer, 1994), 293 and two obituaries: Joachim Wieder, "Margarita Ivanovna Rudomino (1900–1990), In Memoriam," *IFLA Journal* 16, no. 3 (1990): 304–6; and Friedhilde Krause and Tatjana Inokent'evna Skripkina, "Margarita Ivanovna Rudomino zum Gedenken (Margarita Ivanovna Rudomino in Memoriam)," *Zentralblatt für Bibliothekswesen* 104 (1990): 288–90. The Moscow *Foreign Literature Library* was renamed the *Margarita Rudomino All-Russian State Library of Foreign Literature*. The Russian Parliament has so far prohibited Russian librarians from returning their illegally seized war booty.

[27] Earl F. Ziemke, *The U.S. Army in the Occupation of Germany 1944–1946*, Army Historical Series, (Washington, DC: Center of Military History, United States Army, 1975), 199–200.

[28] Douglas Botting, *In the Ruins of the Reich* (London: Allen & Unwin, 1985), 176: "The Russians set off back in horse-carts piled high with anything down to harmoniums and lavatory-pans. The Americans, having less need for domestic appliances (which to the Russians were treasure on earth), went for collectors' items with investment potential – Napoleon's death-mask, lead solders from the War Museum, the Reichspost stamp collection, Goering's Mercedes, the Walther pistol with which Hitler shot himself. A few, however, took advantage of

jewelry, museum pieces, books and valuable manuscripts.[29] A few notorious robberies were exposed and brought to justice.[30] Most others were dismissed as regrettable but unavoidable mishaps of war.

One heist, which decades later generated sensational headlines, was that of the Quedlinburg treasure. At the close of the war, in a cave of the Altenburg mountain, outside the city of Quedlinburg, US Army Lieutenant Joe Tom Meador discovered the dazzling, thousand-year-old treasure of the city's cathedral. He stashed the delicate objects under his army coat and later sent them, wrapped in coarse brown paper, via Army parcel post, back home to Whitewright, Texas. The package slipped undetected through the hands of overworked US Customs Agents. In it were medieval reliquaries and artifacts belonging to illustrious German kings. But the most precious item of all was the *Samuhel Evangeliar*, a sumptuously illustrated ninth-century book of gospels. After the war, Meador returned to Texas to take over the family's hardware business. There, on the checkout counter at night, he stealthily displayed his liberated art to lure an occasional weekend lover. Close to half a century later, the German government succeeded in recovering part of the treasure after paying a hefty "finder's fee" to Meador's greedy heirs.[31]

---

the opportunity and the chaos of the time to make a killing in instant riches – jewels, money, gold. It was the dubious distinction of the American zones of Germany and Austria to play host to some of the greatest robberies in history, only one of which was ever brought to court."

29 Lucy S. Dawidowicz, *From That Place and Time: a Memoir, 1938–1947* (New York: Norton, 1989), 317: "In occupied Germany you couldn't prevent books from disappearing. Wherever there were books ... people pocketed them and carried them off."

30 A spectacular heist that culminated in a dramatic trial was that of the Hesse Crown Jewels. US Captain Kathleen Nash and her partner Colonel Jack Durant chanced one day upon the royal treasure, hidden behind a false wall in the cellar of a castle. It consisted of a twelve carat canary yellow diamond, emeralds, pearls, star sapphires and rubies, flatware encrusted with precious stones, watches, books, and medals. Nash cut the stones off their mounting, smuggled them into the United States, and hid them in a Chicago train-station locker. Upon discovering the loss, the Hesse family filed suit with American authorities in Frankfurt. The culprits were tracked down, arrested, tried, and sentenced to brief jail terms. Only one third of the multi-million dollar loot was ever recovered. (See: Nicholas, 254–55; Kenneth D. Alford *The Spoils of World War II: The American Military's Role in the Stealing of Europe's Treasures* (New York: Birch Lane, 1994) 111–214; and Botting, 176–77).

31 Several books were published on the subject. See: William H. Honan, *Treasure Hunt: A New York Times Reporter Tracks the Quedlinburg Hoard* (New York: Fromm, 1997); Siegfried Kogelfranz and Willi A. Korte, *Quedlinburg – Texas und Zurück: Schwarzhandel mit geraubter Kunst* (Quedlinburg –Texas and back: Black-marketeering with stolen art) (München: Knaur, 1994); Friedemann Goßlau, *Verloren, gefunden, heimgeholt: die Wiedervereinigung des Quedlinburger Domschatzes* (Lost, found, returned: the reunification of the Quedlinburg cloister treasure) (Quedlinburg: Quedlinburg Druck, 1996). There were also numerous newspaper and journal articles.

Most robberies were far less notorious than that of Joe Meador. A common souvenir hunter was William Braemer of North Sterling, Connecticut. From the salt mine of Heiligenroda in Thuringia, Breamer picked up seven sixteenth-century miniatures, four of which painted by the master of illumination, Simon Bening of Bruges.[32] The miniatures were part of a book of prayers, which belonged to the Kassel *Landesbibliothek*. After the war, Braemer sold his miniatures for a paltry one hundred dollars. His wife had found no pleasure in them since they did not match her living-room wallpaper. Years later, the miniatures were discovered hanging in the office of a Massachusetts carpet merchant and, in 1998, after a protracted legal battle, they were finally returned to Kassel.[33] Eleven years earlier that very same book-liberator William Braemer had been forced to acknowledge the theft of yet another item belonging to the Kassel *Landesbibliothek:* a valuable eleventh century Cicero manuscript, which he had picked up in a mineshaft in Springen, Hesse. Unlike the miniatures, the manuscript had found favor with Mrs. Braemen, who admired it greatly and dusted it regularly.[34]

In the agony of the final hours, the survival of the *Hildebrandslied* and the *Willehalm Codex*, hidden in the makeshift shelter of a small resort town, was in great jeopardy. The manuscripts were at the mercy of predatory raids, which were as erratic as bombings, as capricious as fire. Indeed, just three months after the fall of Kassel Dr. Wilhelm Hopf was notified that the Bad Wildungen repository had been ransacked and that his wooden chest was gone.[35]

---

[32] Simon Bening, an illustrious painter of Flanders, was born around 1483 and died in 1561. His hauntingly beautiful miniatures adorned books used in devotional readings.

[33] "Besitzgeschichte der Handschrift 4° Ms.math.50 Gebetbuch Herzogs Johann Albrecht von Mecklenburg" (History of Ownership of the Manuscript 4° Ms./math. 50 Book of Prayers of Prince Johann Albrecht of Mecklenburg), documents from the archives of the Gesamthochschul-Bibliothek Kassel – Landesbibliothek und Murhardsche Bibliothek der Stadt Kassel, deposited with the University of California, Davis, Shields Library, Department of Special Collections. A number of articles appeared in the US press on the Braemer case. See, for instance: "Kassel Gets Pictures Back, for a Price: Veteran's Reluctant Admission of Taking Plunder Clinches Case" *Art Newspaper* 9, no. 82 (1998): 7; "Why Did Leading US Museum Director Keep Mum Over Paintings Stolen From Kassel" *Art Newspaper* 8, no. 70 (1997): 14, and Walter V. Robinson, "Theft Admission Ends Tug-of-War over Artwork" *Boston Globe (*May 13, 1998): A1.

[34] "Cicero, Rückführung des Manuscripts" (Cicero, return of the manuscript), documents from the archives of the Gesamthochschul-Bibliothek Kassel – Landesbibliothek und Murhardsche Bibliothek der Stadt Kassel, deposited with the University of California, Davis, Shields Library, Department of Special Collections. Letter of E. von Kotzebue to Weizsäcker, November 1, 1979.

[35] "Hildebrandlied 1," documents from the archives of the Gesamthochschul-Bibliothek Kassel – Landesbibliothek und Murhardsche Bibliothek der Stadt Kassel, deposited with the University of California, Davis, Shields Library, Department of Special Collections. Summary decision, July 6, 1946.
Note: The date of the phone-call was June 20, 1945.

Chapter 6: "Enjoy the War, the Peace Is Going to be Terrible!"

1945 Graffito on a Berlin Wall

The telephone message was from Dr. Friedrich Bleibaum, Walter Farmer's new curator at the Central Collecting Point in Wiesbaden.[1] The news was appalling. If art repositories were plundered under the watch of US soldiers, Hopf did not even want to contemplate the fate of his other treasures, stored in safe-houses east of the Werra River, which had fallen into Soviet hands. Only days earlier Eduard Brauns, one of the two librarians still working for him, had suggested that he check on the state of the Bad Wildungen repository.[2] Although Brauns had not articulated the fear, Hopf must have sensed it was there, lurking behind the seemingly innocuous suggestion.

Unbeknownst to Brauns, Hopf had already tried to contact Frau Vonhoff, the hotel administrator, and Felix Pusch, the Bad Wildungen museum director. But under the draconian new rules of the US Military Occupation, he was forbidden to use the telephone. Writing was not an option either, since there was no mail service, and Germans were not permitted to travel more than six kilometers away from home.[3] It took one month before Hopf could even file a petition requesting authorization to check on his evacuation site. The response of the Military Government had been disconcerting. Bad Wildungen had been declared a restricted military zone, off limits to German civilians.[4] Worried, he had filed and re-filed his petition only to receive each time the same discouraging rebuff: access denied. The telephone call from Wiesbaden confirmed his worst appre-

---

1 "Hildebrandlied 1," documents from the archives of the Gesamthochschul-Bibliothek Kassel – Landesbibliothek und Murhardsche Bibliothek der Stadt Kassel, deposited with the University of California, Davis, Shields Library, Department of Special Collections. Summary decision, July 6, 1946.

2 "Hildebrandlied 2," documents from the archives. ... File note of E. Brauns, March 10, 1972.

3 Douglas Botting, *In the Ruins of the Reich* (London: Allen & Unwin, 1985), 94: "The Germans had no rights or authority of any kind. Their country was like a gigantic concentration camp in which they lived in enforced isolation from the world. Non-fraternization laws at first forbade them to converse with British or American soldiers except in the course of duty. They could not travel, send letters, or receive newspapers or books from abroad. They were subject to curfew. They could not use the telephone or travel more than six kilometers from their homes. Their bank accounts were frozen. They could be searched or seized and their property requisitioned at a moment's notice. Meetings of more than five people were prohibited. Males between 14 and 65 and females between 15 and 50 were liable to compulsory labour. They were defeated, disillusioned, demoralized. They were saddled with a history of which they were ashamed and treated as barbarians whether they had been Nazis or not."

4 "Nur die zweite Seite des Hildebrandsliedes kehrt zurück" (Only the second page of the Hildebrandslied returns), *Hessische Nachrichten* (September 13, 1954).

hensions: the Goecke cellar had been plundered and his wooden chest had vanished. Confined within his city limits, with no means of communication, and no assistance, Hopf was powerless, left only with suspicions and speculations. In the confusion of surrender any number of people could have gained access to the cellar, German and American soldiers, refugees, transients, locals. The odds of catching the thief months after the robbery were stacked against him. The loss of Kassel's most precious manuscripts was one more blow in the long chain of calamities that had befallen his country, his city, and his library. "Enjoy the war", sneered an inscription on a city wall, "the peace is going to be terrible."[5]

Indeed, if there were a defining symbol for Kassel in spring of 1945, it had to be the symbol of the ruin.[6] Three quarters of the city was rubble. Of the 216,000 pre-war inhabitants, a mere 70,000 emerged from the bomb shelters[7] to gaze upon a landscape not unlike Pompeii's. One could not grasp what was missing; one could only see devastation itself. When classifying German cities, post-war urban planners applied a dispassionate yardstick. They measured the amount of rubble that had to be cleared by each resident. On their scale Kassel ranked third, claiming its place right after Cologne and Dortmund, with thirty-five cubic yards of wreckage for every prewar inhabitant.[8]

Squatting in sordid cellars or in bombed-out ruins, the rubble-dwellers of Kassel clung to a life of unspeakable misery. The median family income was the lowest of all *Länder*[9] of the American Zone, and amounted to 120 Reich Mark a month. It did not even begin to cover basic survival needs.[10] Food rations had dropped to 804 calories a day,[11] a slow starvation diet.[12] Hunger was the domi-

---

5 Botting, [vi]. The wording of this graffito is the motto of his book *In the Ruins of the Reich*.

6 Hermann Glaser, Lutz von Pufendorf, and Michael Schöneich, eds., *So viel Anfang war nie: deutsche Städte 1945–1949* (There never were so many beginnings: German cities 1945–1949) (Berlin: Siedler, 1989), 9, citing Hans Werner Richter's *Literatur in the Interregnum*, In: *Der Ruf*, 15 (1947):10: "Das Kennzeichen unserer Zeit ist die Ruine. ... Die Ruine lebt in uns wie wir in ihr. Sie ist unsere neue Wirklichkeit, die gestaltet werden will." (The characteristic our time is the ruin ... The ruin lives within us as we life in it. It is our new reality, which strives to become form).

7 Herfried Homburg, *Kassel: Das geistige Profil einer tausendjährigen Stadt* (Kassel: spiritual profile of a thousand-year-old city) (Kassel: Schneider & Weber, 1969), 171.

8 Jeffry M. Diefendorf, *In the Wake of the War: The Reconstruction of German Cities After World War II* (New York: Oxford University Press, 1993), 15.

9 Land, plural Länder, is the name given to the constituent states (or provinces) of Germany. It was first introduced during the Weimar Republic (1919–1933).

10 *Public Opinion in Occupied Germany: The OMGUS Surveys, 1945–1949*, Anna J. Merritt and Richard L. Merritt, eds. (Urbana: University of Illinois Press, 1970), 132.

11 Botting, 102.

12 *The European Recovery Program: US/UK Occupied Areas of Germany, 1. April 1948–30 September 1948. Joint Report of the United States and United Kingdom Military Governors*

nant torment, stamped on emaciated faces and reflected in tragically enlarged *Hungeraugen,* famine eyes. The catatonic mindset of survivors was dubbed *urbane Endzeitstimmung*, urban doomsday outlook, a fitting aura of wretchedness that emanated from the Hour Zero, the hour of total collapse.[13]

The newly established US Military Government presided over staggering economic and social problems with no easy solutions. Thousands were homeless. Winter was approaching. Germans and waves upon waves of refugees had to be kept alive. Food riots and civil unrest could endanger not only the safety of the population but also that of the occupying forces. An economic recovery program had to be set in motion.[14] Aside from purely economic concerns, there were also pressing social programs demanding immediate implementation: demilitarization, denazification, and reeducation of Germans towards democracy. Yet the lofty ideals of democracy were utterly meaningless to a people tormented by hunger and cold.[15]

The exceedingly severe winter of 1945–1946, the continued food shortages, and the surrounding devastation sapped everyone's will to live. Despair must have been all too familiar to German librarians. Across the country their libraries lay in ruins. Terrorized by air raids, they had hastily evacuated their books to cellars, mines, cloisters, or farmhouses. Thousands of volumes had been lost in bombings or in transit. Others had suffered damage by fire, heat, humidity, molds, and rodents.[16] Vandalism, souvenir taking, and the expert removal work of the Red Army Trophy Brigades all had taken an enormous toll.

In Kassel, Dr. Hopf and his librarians fared no better. The Museum Fridericianum, the pre-war home of the *Landesbibliothek*, was a charred hull; *Die Neue Galerie*, their wartime refuge, hit by incendiary bombs and ravaged by fire, was in need of massive repair work. Most books had been destroyed in the bombardments of 1941 and 1943. The few surviving volumes were scattered throughout

---

(s. l.: Office of the Military Government for Germany (U.S.) and Control Commission for Germany (British Element), 1948), 26.

13 Glaser, 11.

14 *The European Recovery Program,* 25.

15 Ibid., 2.

16 A detailed census of libraries and collections in postwar Germany was conducted by Georg Leyh. See his *Die deutschen wissenschaftlichen Bibliotheken nach dem Krieg* (German scholarly libraries after the war) (Tübingen: Mohr, 1947). Hopf's report, 129–30, while factually grim, tries to maintain an upbeat tone. He notes that the surrounding walls of his bombed-out library are still standing, making reconstruction possible. As to his collections, he states that 350,000 of the 400,000 volumes had been lost during air raids, and that the surviving books were damaged by water. 70,000 new titles, however, had since been acquired. Most of the music and manuscript collections had survived, although several valuable codices had been lost. Hopf does not mention the losses by name. A partial reopening could be possible by fall of 1947.

Hesse and Thuringia. The Kalkhof estate, east of the Werra River, where the Grimm collection lay hidden, had fallen into Soviet hands. The *Hildebrandslied* and the *Willehalm* had vanished from their Bad Wildungen air raid shelter. Many of their former library colleagues, male and female, were either dead, missing, or were too weak to work.

There was one way out. Dr. Hopf could declare his library a total loss, abandon the utopia of rebuilding, and fade into retirement. But this was not his way. If there were to be a return to humanity, Hopf had to shoulder his share of the burden. As an institution of learning, his library had an obligation to nurture the fledgling beginnings of peace. Knowledge offered a beacon of hope, a sphere of clarity, and his history collections were a symbol of permanence and continuity. Somehow, the septuagenarian had to find the courage to rise above his own daily struggle for survival. Somehow he had to find a way to confront the challenges facing his library, and the will not just to live but also to start anew.

The first order of business was to conquer the rubble that choked his temporary offices in the Murhard Library.[17] The Murhard had suffered great damage, its roof was gone, snow and rainwater had ravaged its interior.[18] Next he had to find containers and trucks to retrieve his books from distant evacuation sites. Hopf needed shelving units, and library supplies. He needed workers to unpack the returning volumes, and librarians to sort and organize the salvaged collections. In a city where scarcely a building was left standing, he had to find shelter to protect his returning volumes from bad weather and further vandalism. And to attempt all this, he needed funding.

In record time, Hopf succeeded in re-leasing the first floor of the bombed-out *Neue Galerie*. It required extensive structural repairs and interior renovation, but for the time it offered a roof over his returning collections. He pounded on bureaucratic doors and recovered monies he knew had been set aside years earlier for library reconstruction. He petitioned the *Land* administration and secured nine librarian positions.[19] Once he had a modicum of space, funding, and manpower, he ferreted out a truck and with the help of Monuments Men, began bringing home his books on the history of Hesse, those precious volumes saved from the flames of 1941. Other collections followed. The waves of returning books were stacked in the Murhard Library and on the first floor of the *Neue*

---

17 The Murhard Library, established in 1845, collected in the fields of economics, pedagogy, and political sciences.

18 *Ex Bibliotheca Cassellana: 400 Jahre Landesbibliothek, 20.11.1580–20.11.1980* (From the Kassel Library: 400 years of State Library, 11/20/1580–11/20/1980), editor Hans-Jürgen Kahlfuß ([Kassel]: Gesamthochschul-Bibliothek-Kassel, Landesbibliothek und Murhardsche Bibliothek der Stadt Kassel, 1980), 42–43.

19 Ibid., 44.

Galerie.[20] Losses were small in number, but huge in importance. Aside from the *Hildebrandslied* and *Willehalm Codex*, word came that some of the manuscripts of the Brothers Grimm together with several irreplaceable codices had indeed vanished. The Kalkhof estate had been plundered by the Soviets and then pilfered by locals.[21] Daily difficulties and setbacks notwithstanding, Hopf remained stubbornly determined to reorganize, rebuild, and make his collections available to his readers. A functional library was a symbol of normalcy. This was to be his gift to his fellow survivors, his personal offering of hope.

Slowly the shattered city began showing timid signs of life. By fall of 1945 the newspaper *Hessische Nachrichten* was back on the stands; the State Theater premièred with Goethe's *Iphigenie* and at the Art Gallery, the Monuments Men prepared an exhibit of old masters.[22] Hopf was heartened by the decision of the American Military Occupation to reinstate him as director of the *Landesbibliothek*.[23] This was a fitting tribute to his unwavering civic and professional devotion and political integrity, but it hardly represented a change. With or without the official title, Hopf remained the very soul of his institution.

Stories began circulating about Bad Wildungen at the hour of surrender.[24] There were whispers that US soldiers had been on the prowl, searching for portable souvenirs, most notably books with illuminations.[25] In the confusion of the first hours hospitals, libraries, hotels, and air raid shelters had been ransacked. Troops had occupied the administration building and vandalized its cellar. Frau Vonhoff had reported the break-in to US authorities. Officer Rudolf Hörchner of the local police force had requested permission to inspect the air raid shelters, but his request was denied.[26]

---

20 Gerhard Liebers, "Die Bibliotheksverhältnisse in Kassel nach dem Kriege" (Library conditions in Kassel after the war), *Zentralblatt für Bibliothekswesen* 65, 9/10 (1951): 385.

21 *Manuscripta Theologica: Die Handschriften in Folio* (Manuscripta Theologica: The folio manuscripts), editor Konrad Wiedemann, Die Handschriften der Gesamthochschul-Bibliothek Kassel – Landesbibliothek und Murhardsche Bibliothek der Stadt Kassel, 1,1 (Wiesbaden: Harrassowitz, 1994), xxxiii; and "Hildebrandlied 1," documents from the archives of the Gesamthochschul-Bibliothek Kassel – Landesbibliothek und Murhardsche Bibliothek der Stadt Kassel, deposited with the University of California, Davis, Shields Library, Department of Special Collections. Declaration of W. Hopf, February 5, 1946.

22 Glaser, 116.

23 *Ex Bibliotheca Cassellana*, 43.

24 Note: Most documents surrounding the 1945 disappearance of the manuscripts were systematically collected by library director Dr. Dieter Hennig. To Dr. Hennig we owe the methodical search for clues and witnesses, and the organization of the papers in the six dossiers, which make up the Kassel *Hildebrandlied* file.

25 "Hildebrandlied 3," documents from the archives. ... Report of E. Koolman, April 15, 1972.

26 "Hildebrandlied 1," documents from the archives. ... Letter of R. Hörchner to D. Hennig, January 18, 1971.

Fig. 11. March 31, 1949 – Kassel State Library staff on the day Dr. Hopf retired. Dr. Wilhelm Hopf is sitting in the front row in the middle. Standing behind him is his successor, Dr. Wolf von Both
(Archives of the Universitätsbibliothek Kassel – Landesbibliothek und Murhardsche Bibliothek der Stadt Kassel – Reproduced by permission)

The perceived reluctance of the US Military Occupation to investigate reports of alleged looting by its troops fueled wild and angry speculations. A Bad Wildungen resident reported hearing a heated argument between three American Officers: Williams, Unschuld and Goldberg.[27] Williams, who had been in the Goecke cellar, had recognized the importance of the artwork. According to the Bad Wildungen eyewitness, Williams had tried to convince the other two to secure the premise and return its contents to the city of Kassel. But Unschuld and Goldberg had strongly disagreed. The way they saw it, these were spoils of war belonging to the victor. Did the officers confiscate the paintings and manuscripts? The Bad Wildungen witness, who preferred to remain anonymous, did not know.

[27] "Hildebrandlied 2," documents from the archives. … D. Hennig, File note, May 20, 1975. Note: A search through the roster of 1946 MFA&A officers, enlisted men, and civilians published in *Report of the American Commission for the Protection and Salvage of Artistic and Historic Monuments in War Areas* (Washington: Government Printing Office, 1946), 163–164, identified a Major Lewis S. Williams and a T/5 S. L. Goldberg. The name Unschuld does not appear on the list.

Another detail was gleaned from a letter written by Dr. Wolfgang Medding of Marburg. The scholar was trying to recover a personal carton with books and research notes left in Bad Wildungen. A prisoner of war, interned in the city, told Dr. Medding that little was left in the city's repositories. The POW knew this first hand. He had been ordered by US soldiers to load crate upon crate from the city's cellars onto trucks and drive them to the nearby airport in Fritzlar. There the POW had been forced to help put the crates on a plane.[28]

Suspicions also swirled around the nefarious deeds of a US Lieutenant with a ravenous appetite for beautiful objects. Officer Sinclair Robinson, who had been caught stealing a Rubens, a Lieberman, and a Canaletto, had forced the curator of the Frankfurt Staedel Museum at gunpoint to drive him to Bad Wildungen. Days later, thirteen large canvases belonging to the Kassel Art Gallery and Hopf's manuscripts were discovered missing.[29]

While Bad Wildungen remained cut off from the world, Frau Vonhoff, the administrator, struggled to safeguard the remaining artwork in her ransacked cellar. She had reported the break-in to US authorities, but no one had come to secure the premises or investigate the theft. US soldiers were still bivouacked on the upper floors of the building, and her unguarded basement was at their whim and mercy. Distressed by the indifference of the US Military Government, Frau Vonhoff appealed to local museum director Felix Pusch for assistance. Pusch, who was responsible for most other art repositories in the city, had his hands full. Three air raid shelters had been plundered,[30] and the Goecke repository was not his responsibility.[31] However, the museum director could not abandon Frau Vonhoff in her hour of need. He petitioned the Military Government for admittance to the Goecke basement and, after some delay, permission was granted.

To evacuate the cellar, Pusch needed more than good will and a permit. He needed a truck and husky helpers. He had neither, and military officials were not forthcoming with manpower and transportation. To his good fortune, his neighbor Heinrich Schleiermacher still had his horse-drawn wagon and, when asked, agreed to lend a hand. On April 25, 1945, Pusch and Schleiermacher pulled up in

---

[28] "Hildebrandlied 1," documents from the archives. ... Letter of W. Medding to W. Hopf, September 9, 1947.

[29] Kenneth D. Alford, *The Spoils of World War II: The American Military's Role in the Stealing of Europe's Treasures* (New York: Birch Lane, 1994), 17–30. During the military inquiry into his misdeeds, Robinson refused to answer any questions about his Bad Wildungen trip for reasons of self-incrimination. The recommendation for trial by court-martial for grand larceny was dismissed due to "the nature of the offenses, the age of Robinson, his military service, and the necessity of preserving the manpower of the Nation."

[30] "Hildebrandlied 1," documents from the archives. ... Letter from the offices of the Regierungspräsident Kassel, January 26, 1946.

[31] "Hildebrandlied 3," documents from the archives. ... Report of E. Koolman, April 15, 1972.

front of Hotel Goecke. Almost immediately, American soldiers surrounded the wagon, brandishing their weapons, barking unintelligible orders. Fearing a confrontation, Pusch, who did not speak a word of English, waved his evacuation permit and, followed by Schleiermacher, hurried down the stairs to the basement. The cellar was in disarray. The floor was littered with empty picture frames, smashed crates, and broken artwork.[32] Frightened by the surly demeanor of the guards, Pusch and Schleiermacher went swiftly about their work. They hauled all remnants of the art collection up the stairs, and loaded frames, boxes, and broken crates onto their buggy, with no receipt or inventory. With the wagon packed high, Schleiermacher cracked his whip and down the bumpy cobblestone road they raced, relieved to be alive, their fragile cargo rattling helter-skelter in the wagon-bed.

With the help of Schleiermacher, Pusch stored the salvaged objects as best he could at his workplace, a printing shop on Brunnenstraße 68. It might not have been a perfect refuge for the once proud museum collection, but it was far safer than the Goecke cellar. No one told him about the gray wooden box and thus he neither asked nor searched for it. As Bad Wildungen remained quarantined, he was unable to contact curator Helm in Kassel to tell him what had happened.

Close to two months later, on June 19, 1945, Rudolf Helm succeeded in placing a telephone call to Bad Wildungen.[33] Military occupation restrictions had been somewhat relaxed and the inter-city telephone system was once again functioning.[34] It was then that he learned from a distraught Pusch about the looting, the precipitous evacuation, and about the missing and damaged paintings. Worried, Helm asked about the chest with the manuscripts. Pusch was taken aback. He had no idea that the *Hildebrandslied* was in Bad Wildungen. He went searching through the salvaged objects hoping to find the box, but there was no trace of it. The loss had to be reported immediately to the Provincial Conservator for Hesse at the Central Collecting Point in Wiesbaden, he advised. The Monuments Officers in Wiesbaden were overseeing all regional repositories of German art. The very next day, Dr. Friedrich Bleibaum, Captain Farmer's curator in Wiesbaden, was duly notified, and he in turn telephoned Kassel with the terrible news.

In his official capacity as State Conservator for the Land of Hesse, curator Friedrich Bleibaum filed a request for a criminal investigation into the Bad Wildungen

---

32 Ibid., Report of E. Koolman, April 15, 1972.

33 "Hildebrandlied 1," documents from the archives ... Report of F. Pusch to the Military Government Bad Wildungen, June 27, 1945.

34 Earl F. Ziemke, The *U.S. Army in the Occupation of Germany 1944–1946*. Army Historical Series (Washington, D.C.: Center of Military History, United States Army, 1975), 272.

larceny.[35] In his petition to the US Military Government, Dr. Bleibaum described the enormous importance of the two manuscripts and appended reproductions of the *Hildebrandslied* pages and miniatures from the *Willehalm Codex*. It was a compelling effort to convince an otherwise overworked and indifferent military bureaucracy that these were no ordinary books, but masterpieces of art and literature of paramount importance to the German people and to world culture.

Before considering Bleibaum's request, the US Military Government needed confirmation that the manuscripts were truly missing from the war repository. Consequently, Bad Wildungen museum director Felix Pusch was ordered back to the cellar. On June 26, Pusch returned to the Goecke Hotel and this time the guards waved him casually in. The cellar was filled with piles of old administrative records. Undaunted, Pusch went to work. But after scrutinizing every scrap of paper and every sliver of wood, he was forced to acknowledge defeat. He filed a report with the Military Government confirming that, so far as he could determine, the crate with manuscripts was not in the cellar. He recommended however that the space be cleared and thoroughly inventoried.[36] Dr. Hopf, who could not trust a stranger with this last chance of finding a clue to the whereabouts of his treasures, petitioned to be the one assigned to the task. His request was ignored.

One month passed and then another. Finally, on August 14, 1945, close to five months after the looting, the Military Government declared itself ready to proceed with the official criminal investigation. The Provost Marshal of the Seventh Army forwarded a formal complaint of alleged theft to the Criminal Investigations Division. But the long awaited inquiry was disappointingly brief and superficial. The investigating officers were either disinclined, or unable to pursue allegations against purported looters. There was no probe into the misdeeds of Lieutenant Sinclair Robinson and his alleged Bad Wildungen excursion. There was no follow up on complaints regarding movement of crates out of the city, nor were there any interviews with officers rumored to have been in the Goecke cellar. The only person deposed was Museum Director Felix Pusch. Thereafter, the panel summarily concluded that the evidence was insufficient to warrant any further action. Although less then five months had passed since the occupation of Bad Wildungen, there were no records at hand to indicate which Divisions and Corps had been quartered in or around the administration building. Since

---

[35] "File Ms. of Hildebrandslied From Kassel," US Department of State. Records Maintained by the Fine Arts and Monuments Adviser, 1945–61, Ardelia Hall Collection, Record Group 59, Lot 62D4, Box 6, Item 2, National Archives and Records Administration. Letter of F. Bleibaum to the Military Government, Bad Wildungen, June 22, 1945.

[36] "Hildebrandlied 1," documents from the archives. ... Report of F. Pusch to the Military Government Bad Wildungen, June 27, 1945.

3

CONFIDENTIAL

CRIMINAL INVESTIGATIONS DIVISION

126

APO 758

This case originated at : Bad Wildungen, Germany	File No. 480-268 2 4 7th Army
Report made at : Alsfeld, Germany — Date when made : 15 Aug 1945	Period for which made : 14-15 Aug 1945
Title : Kreis Kassel Library, Kassel, Germany (Injured Party)	Character of case : Larceny of two Manuscripts 1. Hildobrandelied 2. Willehalm

Synopsis of facts :

On 14 Aug 1945 the Provost Marshal, 7th Army, forwarded a complaint alleging theft of two valuable manuscripts from the bunker of the Kurhotel, Bad Wildungen, Germany, where they had been placed for safe-keeping.

Neither officials of the Military Government nor the person responsible for the welfare of these manuscripts could state when, how, or by whom they had been taken and it could not be established that American troops were responsible for their removal.

Case closed.

DETAILS: see next page.

Report made by : WILLIAM H. KOOP, Agent, CID — ARTHUR H. PORCHE, JR., Agent, CID	Distribution of report :
Approved and forwarded : PHILIP J. [illegible]ENN, JR. Chief Agent	1- U.S. Claims Commission APO 758, US Army 1- Provost Marshal, 7th Army APO 758, US Army ~~1- TPM, CID, APO 887~~ 1- Files

CONFIDENTIAL

Fig. 12. Confidential report of the Criminal Investigations Division into the Larceny of the *Hildebrandslied* and the *Willehalm Codex*.
(Copy from the Archives of the Universitätsbibliothek Kassel – Landesbibliothek und Murhardsche Bibliothek der Stadt Kassel.)

there was no proof that American troops were responsible for the removal of the manuscripts, there were no leads to follow. On August 18, 1945, four days after the opening of the investigation, a confidential report was filed with the Military Government, Detachment Kassel, which ended in a two-word decision: *Case closed*.[37] As far as the US Military Government was concerned, this was the end of the road.

[37] Ibid., Criminal Investigation Division. Report of Agents Koop and Porche, Jr., August 15, 1945.

Chapter 7: Hope Deferred

"No historical grievance will rankle so long, as the removal of a part of the heritage of any nation."

Wiesbaden Manifesto

As 1945 was drawing to a close, US Army Captain Walter I. Farmer of the Wiesbaden Central Collecting Point found himself immersed in a sea of trouble. The search for the *Hildebrandslied* and Dr. Hopf's request to inventory the trash in the Goecke cellar were lost in the storm that threatened to engulf his work and destroy his military career. It had started quite innocently with an official visit from Washington. Colonel Harry McBride, Administrator of the National Gallery of Art, had come to tour the Wiesbaden facility. He had found the storehouse fully renovated. Doors had been hung, windows replaced, the roof repaired, the heating system was humming, and Farmer had even placed wet rags over all ducts to maintain proper humidity levels for his masterpieces. While Colonel McBride was pleased with Farmer's ingenuity, he was far more impressed by the beautiful booty stored in his *Landesmuseum*. Upon returning to Washington, McBride recommended to the Roberts Commission, that 202 of the Wiesbaden masterpieces be transferred to the United States, for what was termed as *safekeeping*.[1]

On November 6, 1945, Farmer received a telegram from the Military Government Office in Wiesbaden with an order from higher headquarters to prepare his best paintings for shipment to the United States. He read the wire quickly and in an instant saw his world turn "dark with malevolence and treachery."[2] His own government was about to confiscate German art, and with this action renege on its own policy of trust and respect for the cultural heritage of its vanquished enemy. Farmer, who believed deeply in the ethical mission of the MFA&A, "wept tears of rage and frustration."[3] He found himself trapped between his soldierly duty and his faith in a higher law, a law of fairness and morality.

---

1 Walter I. Farmer, *The Safekeepers: A Memoir of the Arts at the End of World War II.* Revised and prefaced by Klaus Goldmann, with an introduction by Margaret Farmer Planton, Cultural Property Studies (Berlin: de Gruyter, 2000), 64. The proposal to seize German owned art and transfer it to the United States had originated with General Lucius B. Clay in March of 1945. At the Potsdam Conference, on July 19, 1945, Clay had obtained approval from President Truman to send selected German paintings to the United States.

2 Farmer, *The Safekeepers*, 55–6.

3 Walter I. Farmer, "Custody and Controversy at the Wiesbaden Collecting Point," in: *The Spoils of War: World War II and Its Aftermath: The Loss, Reappearance, and Recovery of Cultural Property,* editor Elizabeth Simpson (New York: H.N. Abrams in association with the Bard Graduate Center for Studies in the Decorative Arts, 1977), 133.

Captain Farmer had no choice but to follow orders. He prepared the masterpieces for their perilous December voyage on the high seas. On a rainy day at the end of November, under code-name *Westward Ho, Watteau,*[4] 202 master paintings, packed with great care in forty-five hand-made crates, left for Le Havre and from there for New York. No sooner was this task completed than Farmer, at the risk of being court-martialed, called upon his fellow Monuments Men to join him in a written protest against the immoral conduct of the US Government.[5] His famous letter became known as the Wiesbaden Manifesto. In it the Monuments Men defiantly stated:

> The transportation of these works of art, undertaken by the United States Army, upon direction from the highest authority, establishes a precedent, which is neither morally tenable nor trustworthy.
>
> The Allied Nations are at present preparing to prosecute individuals for crimes of sequestering, under pretext of 'protective custody,' the cultural treasures of German-occupied countries. A major part of the indictment follows upon the reasoning that, even through these individuals were acting under military orders, the dictates of higher ethical law made it incumbent upon them to refuse to take part in, or countenance the fulfillment of these orders. We, the undersigned, feel it is our duty to point out that, though as members of the Armed Forces we will carry out the orders we receive, we are thus put before any candid eyes as no less culpable than those whose prosecution we effect to sanction.
>
> We wish to state that from our own knowledge, no historical grievance will rankle so long, or be the cause of so much justified bitterness, as the removal, for any reason, of a part of the heritage of any nation. ... And though this removal may be done with every intention of Altruism, we are none the less convinced that it is our duty, individually and collectively, to protest against it, and that though our obligations are to the nation to which we owe allegiance, there are yet further obligations to common justice, decency, and the establishment of the power of right, not of expediency of might, among civilized nations.[6]

American newspapers, journals, and leading art magazines got wind of the story.[7] Prominent museum directors and historians signed a protest resolution addressed to President Truman, in which they compared the removal of the Two-O-Two, as the paintings became known, to earlier looting operations carried out by the

---

4 Farmer, *The Safekeepers*, 72.

5 "Walter Farmer – Obituary." *Economist* 344, no. 8031 (1997): 67.

6 Farmer, *The Safekeepers*, 147–52.

7 In her article "The Beautiful Spoils: the Monuments Men," *The New Yorker* 21, no. 40 (1945): 71, author Genêt (pen name for Janet Flanner) wrote: "This export project, casually suggested by American officials at Potsdam, perhaps as a well-meaning attempt to keep the pictures warm this winter in the steam-heated United States, is already regarded in liberated Europe as shockingly similar to the practice of the Einsatzstab Rosenberg, or Minister of Nazi Kultur Rosenberg's Foreign Art Loot Bureau. It has been the task of our Monuments men to undo what we Americans had disdained Rosenberg and his Nazis from doing, and what it was supposedly our policy never to imitate."

Nazis.[8] Congress was deluged with angry protests from curators, artists, educators, and from the public at large. The passionate wording of the Wiesbaden Manifesto expressed everyone's shame over an action that could only be interpreted as greedy and illegal. President Truman and the State Department found themselves on the defensive. And so did the Roberts Commission and its distinguished advisers, who frantically tried to do damage control.[9] Farmer's courageous dissent and the protest storm it ignited quenched any further desire of the US Government for German war booty.[10]

To save face, the paintings were sent on a US grand tour and the proceeds were donated to German children. Millions of visitors across the land marveled at the beauty of canvasses by Rembrandt, Vermeer, Titian, Cranach, Holbein, Raphael, Rubens, Velasquez, Watteau, Dürer, and Botticelli. Thereafter the paintings went into storage. Four years later, the 202 were quietly returned to Germany.[11]

Embroiled in the battle with Washington, Walter Farmer and his curator Friedrich Bleibaum had put the *Hildebrandslied* investigation on the back burner. Wilhelm Hopf, who was unaware of the raging dispute, was deeply frustrated. For months his request for permission to search through the trash in the Goecke cellar had been all but ignored. In January 1946, Hopf decided to step up the pressure. He appealed to the *Landeshauptmann*, the head of the Communal Administration of the District of Kassel, and asked his offices to intervene on his behalf. The *Landeshauptmann* contacted the US Military Government and concurrently alerted the offices of the Governor, the *Regierungspräsident*. On Hopf's

---

[8] Farmer, *The Safekeepers*, 75. The May 9, 1946 petition of ninety-five museum scholars and historians led by Juliana Force and Frederick Clapp said in part: "It is apparent that disinterested and intelligent people believe that this action cannot be justified on technical, political or moral grounds and that many, including the Germans themselves, may find it hard to distinguish between the resultant situation and the 'protective custody' used by the Nazis as camouflage for the sequestration of the artistic treasures of other countries."

[9] *Report of the American Commission for the Protection and Salvage of Artistic and Historic Monuments in War Areas* (Washington: Government Printing Office, 1946), 11: "The Commission accepts without reservations the promise of the United States Government, as voiced by its highest officials, that the works of art belonging to German museums and brought to this country for safekeeping, will be returned to Germany *when conditions there warrant* (our emphasis). The Commission is strongly of the opinion that the resolution sponsored by Dr. Clapp, Mrs. Force, and others is without justification and is to be deplored."

[10] Klaus Goldmann, curator at the *Museum für Vor- und Frühgeschichte* in Berlin, an expert on Second World War trophy-art, is convinced that Farmer's Manifesto was a turning point in the history of the MFA&A, "because it meant that [from then on] nothing further could be moved." See: Farmer, *The Safekeepers*, 109.

[11] "Walter Farmer – Obituary" In 1996, one year before his death, Farmer was awarded Germany's highest civilian honor: the Commander's Cross of the Order of Merit. The medal came with an apology by the German Government for not having recognized sooner his exemplary honesty and extraordinary courage.

behalf, the *Landeshauptmann* reiterated the request for permission to search and inventory the remaining items in the vandalized Goecke war repository. He explained that a written authorization was a condition sine qua non, since US troops still occupied the Bad Wildungen administration building. Finding these unique manuscripts and making them once again accessible to scholars, he wrote, would greatly contribute to the spiritual renewal of the nation.[12]

Hopf's petition, backed up by political clout, was forwarded to the Wiesbaden Monuments Men, administrators of all Hesse art repositories. Under pressure from the highest authority of the Land, the beleaguered Central Collecting Point responded. Regrettably, by then Captain Walter Farmer was no longer in Wiesbaden.[13] US Lieutenant Theodore Heinrich, his successor, informed the *Landeshauptmann* that in the intervening time Hopf's petition had become irrelevant. The Goecke basement had already been vacated and no wooden box with or without manuscripts had been found. In a gesture of good will the Wiesbaden Collecting Point had alerted US Customs Officials, asking that they be on the lookout for the manuscripts at all border points. If spotted, the manuscripts would be seized and returned.[14]

In his personal response to Dr. Hopf, the *Landeshauptmann* suggested that the librarian establish contact with Lieutenant Heinrich, the new director of the Central Collecting Point, and try to engage him in the search for the missing library treasures. Hopf took the advice to heart. He prepared a register of war-repositories used by his library and missing materials and, instead of mailing it out to Heinrich, he delivered his lists in person.[15] He was pleasantly surprised. Lieutenant Heinrich, a man of imposing stature, with an impressive mustache, and an open smile, turned out to be not only gracious, but also helpful and knowledgeable. Far from being an indifferent bureaucrat, Heinrich, an art historian with a doctorate from Cambridge University, was a true-blue Monuments Man, generous with time, ideas, and connections.[16] Backed by Lieutenant Hein-

---

[12] "Hildebrandlied 1," documents from the archives of the Gesamthochschul-Bibliothek Kassel – Landesbibliothek und Murhardsche Bibliothek der Stadt Kassel, deposited with the University of California, Davis, Shields Library, Department of Special Collections. Letter from the offices of the Landeshauptmann to the Regional Officer of the Military Government, Detachment E 4, January 21, 1946.

[13] At the beginning of 1946 Farmer was replaced as Director of the Wiesbaden Central Collecting Point by Captain Judith Standen. Later in the year, Lieutenant Theodore A. Heinrich replaced Captain Standen.

[14] "Hildebrandlied 1," documents from the archives ... Letter of the *Regierungspräsident*, Kassel to counselor Selbert, January 26, 1946 and transmitted to Hopf by the Landeshauptmann, January 30, 1946.

[15] "Hildebrandlied 1," documents from the archives. ... Letter of W. Hopf, February 6, 1946 and disposition of the Landeshauptmann, June 7, 1946.

[16] "Notes for Theodore Allen Heinrich: June 15, 1910 – January 27, 1981," *Artscanada* 38–39,

rich, Hopf obtained permission to reopen the criminal investigation, this time under the aegis of the local Bad Wildungen police. By now, an entire year had passed. Troops had come and gone, leads had run dry, memories had faded. The Bad Wildungen officers interviewed vigorously all witnesses and searched once more through the Goecke debris but in the end came up empty.[17]

Together with Lieutenant Heinrich, Hopf revisited all plausible scenarios and even the most far-fetched theft theories. Topping their list was the strong probability that a US soldier had stolen the manuscripts. If the codices had slipped undetected through Customs checkpoints, they could resurface on the art market. Under this assumption Heinrich told Hopf to send facsimiles to the National Gallery of Art in Washington DC, a central place for information on war-displaced treasures. Reputable dealers were said to check with the National Gallery before committing to any questionable merchandise.[18]

There was also a remote possibility that the box had ended up in Wanfried, east of the Werra River, and had fallen into Soviet hands. Dr. Hopf checked with museum director Pusch, who refuted the idea. Nothing had been moved out of Bad Wildungen before the day of surrender, of that he was certain.[19] Finally, there was a strained hypothesis. A high-ranking, fanatical Nazi could have stolen the manuscripts. The Nazis revered the old warrior ballad and regarded the *Hildebrandslied* as an affirmation of Nordic racial superiority.[20] Lieutenant Heinrich's very short list of suspects included two names: that of former library director Hans Peter des Coudres[21] and the name of the last *Gauleiter* of Hesse, Karl Gerland. Hopf must have rejected the des Coudres suspicion as totally absurd. Des Coudres had put his own position on the line to keep the codices safe. As to Gerland, there was not one single shred of evidence indicating that he had made a detour through Bad Wildungen before fleeing Kassel. While unconvincing, the *Gauleiter* scenario was worth a second look. Hopf petitioned the court and

no. 240/41 (1981): 1. In this obituary, Franz, Prince Sayn-Wittgenstein writes: "Everybody in Germany who knew Theodore A. Heinrich will mourn him. He arrived as enemy and parted as friend. His work as Director of the Central Collecting Points in Wiesbaden and Munich is well known, but what he did for Germany herself was even more and should not be forgotten. Whenever he could help, be it privately or publicly, he did his best, and he did it with a warm heart and quite inconspicuously. He was a real and true friend."

17 "Hildebrandlied 1," documents from the archives. ... Disposition of June 6, 1946. The actual May 15, 1946 report was lost. Indirect evidence indicates that there were no new leads.

18 Ibid., Letter of F. Bleibaum to the Landeshauptmann, November 13, 1948.

19 Ibid., Letter of W. Hopf to the Landeshauptmann, March 6, 1946.

20 Alfred Rosenberg, *The Myth of the Twentieth Century: An Evaluation of the Spiritual-Intellectual Confrontations of Our Age,* translation by Vivian Bird (Newport Beach, California: Noontide Press, 1993), 254–5.

21 "Hildebrandlied 4," documents from the archives. ... Letter of D. Hennig to H-O Weber, October 9, 1972.

obtained a search warrant. He procured a car and, escorted by police, drove to Gottsbüren, in the district of Hofgeismar, to search the home of the dead Gauleiter.[22] As expected, this turned out to be another blind alley.

With this desperate attempt, Dr. Hopf and Lieutenant Heinrich had exhausted all imaginable theories. The offices of the *Landeshauptmann* advised that the time had come to declare the manuscripts irrevocably lost. Since there was no proof of theft, there could be no claim for compensation. The *Landeshauptmann* recommended that the file on the *Hildebrandslied* be closed without publicity.[23]

---

[22] "Hildebrandlied 1," documents from the archives. ... Communication between W. Hopf and the Court in Hofgeismar, July 30, 1948 and search warrant of August 4, 1948.

[23] Ibid. Disposition, June 7, 1946.

Chapter 8: Going, Going, Gone!

"I have known men to hazard their fortunes, go long journeys halfway about the world, forget friendship, even lie, cheat, and steal, all for the gain of a book." [1]

A. S. W. Rosenbach

It was a pewter-gray November afternoon[2] when the officer came calling. Manhattan was festive, preparing for its first Thanksgiving after V-E Day. The officer had an appointment with the Rosenbach Company, a rare bookstore, on Fifteen East Fifty-First Street, off Fifth Avenue, across from Saint Patrick's Cathedral. Oddly, number fifteen did not look anything like a bookstore. There were no beckoning window-displays showcasing opulent volumes with elegant bindings, no shield proudly proclaiming the name of the establishment. This building looked more like a private four-story patrician home.[3] A lacy wrought iron fence with slender lampposts segregated the house from the busy sidewalk. The lacy motif was echoed in the ironwork of the second floor balcony railing. Decorative Corinthian pilasters framed the grand French windows, and the classical entrance was haughtily forbidding. He rang the doorbell and an officious butler answered. Was Dr. Rosenbach in? So very sorry, the Doctor was unavailable. Could perhaps someone else be of service? The officer hesitated. He had brought two beautiful old books for the Doctor to examine. Won't the officer come in? The door swung open and he followed the butler into the elegant foyer.

Clearly, this was not a place of business. There were no library shelves buckling under dusty volumes, as one would have expected, no files spilling out of half-open drawers. Instead, well-worn Persian carpets hushed the step, antique furnishings graced the anteroom, and the etchings on the walls added a touch of artistic refinement. Through connecting French doors, left casually ajar, the officer could see the rich glow of the dining room, complete with its glittering crystal chandelier.[4] This had to be the home of a wealthy scholar, who had

1 A.S.W. Rosenbach, *Books and Bidders: The Adventures of a Bibliophile* (London: Allen & Unwin, 1928), 37.

2 According to the date on the sales invoice, the *Hildebrandslied* and the *Willehalm* codices were sold on November 10, 1945. The weather on that day was cold, cloudy, and rainy, with highs reaching only the mid 40s, and brisk northerly winds. See [Weather] *The New York Times*, Saturday, November 10, 1945, p. 25 L.

3 E. Millicent Sowerby, *Rare People and Rare Books* (London: Constable, 1967), 126–27: "This house was where the Rosenbachs stayed when they were in New York, and their private rooms occupied the whole of the third floor."

4 Ibid., 222: "Some of the pieces used to furnish No. 15 were both beautiful and historic, and gave an air of luxury to the place which was more than pleasant. The grandfather clock in the hall, for instance, had been the property of Empress Josephine, and over the mantelpiece

nothing to do with mundane transactions such as buying or selling.[5] Would the officer mind waiting? Mr. Fleming, the manager, would be in shortly. A stately railed staircase led from the foyer to the upper floors. In a corner, the Empire grandfather clock chimed the hour. The front door closed. Festive Manhattan and the war-torn nightmare from which he had recently returned were safely left behind. He had entered the private world of Doctor Rosenbach.

At sixty-nine the Doctor was the most successful rare book dealer of all times. In London, Paris, and in New York he had made book-auction history. Through his hands had passed an endless flow of volumes recognized the world over for rarity, beauty, and supreme importance, cherished erstwhile possessions of statesmen, poets, kings, and conquerors. His magnetic personality backed by a seemingly unlimited bank account had turned dull public auctions into high stakes encounters. Guided by an unshakable credo that the passage of time could only enhance the value of a great book, the Doctor had sent book-prices soaring. Time and again, the auctioneer's verdict *Sold to Doctor Rosenbach* reverberated around the world in headline after headline.

His life, as narrated in newspapers and magazine articles, was one of zestful adventures and bibliophile pleasures: transatlantic buying trips, elegant dinner-parties in the company of collectors and literati, and sun filled vacations on the Atlantic coast and aboard his private yacht *First Folio*. Disarmed by his charm and stunned by his unmatched string of successes, the *New Yorker* had bestowed upon him the title *Napoleon of books,*[6] while the less romantic London tabloids had dubbed him *Terror of the Auction Room*. British public opinion, forever

---

in the Book Room was one of the most famous of the paintings of Joseph-Siffrede Duplessis, a beautiful pastel portrait of Benjamin Franklin. ... There were two main rooms one on each floor, and in addition to the reception-room on the ground floor there was the large handsomely furnished dining-room, with a gorgeous crystal chandelier."

5 Edwin Wolf 2nd and John F. Fleming, *Rosenbach: A Biography* (Cleveland: World Publishing Company, 1960), 126: "The house ... was created to impress. ... For the great treasures a steel-door vault was installed, for did it not sound a trifle richer to talk of books in your 'vault'? A dining room and a wine cellar hinted at Lucullan fare. Finally, a real life English butler, who answered the door – one had to ring the doorbell to get in – and ushered the guest (customer) into the library (salesroom) where the collector (dealer) would greet him. ... It was the most seductive trap ever designed, and like every successful trap, it was not what it seemed." This description refers to Rosenbach's first bookstore address, on 273 Madison Avenue, but when in 1929, the firm moved to its new location on 15 East 51st Street, Philip Rosenbach, President of the firm and the Doctor's brother, decorated it in the same opulent style. Again Wolf 2nd, 297: "Philip thought that the Madison Avenue house had become too plain and undistinguished. He was never as happier as when he had a house to alter and to decorate. An ostentatious address just off Fifth Avenue, across the street from St. Patrick's Cathedral, half a block from the projected Rockefeller Center, and around the corner from Cartier's had real possibilities for his kind of money's-no-object remodeling."

6 Avery Starkosch, "Profiles: Napoleon of Books," *New Yorker* 4 (1928): 28, and also Wolf 2nd, 218.

Fig. 13. Dr. Abraham Simon Wolf Rosenbach in his library
(The Rosenbach Museum & Library, Philadelphia – Reproduced by permission)

vacillating between admiration and stunned consternation, had watched helplessly as Rosenbach spirited away one treasure after another. First to go were the ninety-nine bound volumes of the *Battle Abbey Cartularies*, those original Norman deeds and legal documents that marked the dawn of English history.[7] Then came a string of Shakespeare First Folios,[8] Gutenberg Bibles, super-rare editions, and unique manuscripts. Rosenbach was known to acquire only the absolute best, those volumes he liked to call *infernally rare*, so as to avoid saying

7 Wolf 2nd, 186: "Battle Abbey had been founded by William the Conqueror to perpetuate the record of his conquest of England, and the treasures contained in the Rolls were the Abbey's original charters, registers, deeds, and other documents from the time of its foundation forward. It was the greatest series of such records of Norman England in existence."
Note: The Cartularies were purchased for $ 18,000 and sold to Huntington for $ 50,000. See Leslie A Morris, *Rosenbach Abroad: In Pursuit of Books in Private Collections* (Philadelphia: Rosenbach Museum & Library, 1988), 38.

8 The First Folio was the first printed collection of William Shakespeare's comedies, histories, and tragedies. There are 240 known Shakespeare First Folios in existence. The largest collection resides at the Folger Shakespeare Library in Washington, DC.

damn, damn rare.[9] Years of flamboyant victories had cemented his reputation as the biggest spending American dealer. He was the first bookman to use auction duels not only for their ten-percent commission but mostly for their priceless publicity. He had realized early on that media hype opened the doors of old English and Irish country homes with rich, ancestral collections. It was these private deals with very private landed gentry that constantly replenished and increased his legendary book stock and fabulous fortune. Blue-blood collectors were most reluctant to see their names in vulgar print but only too eager to quietly part with dusty family volumes for Rosenbach prices.

Innumerable stories swirled around the deeds of the Doctor, some true, many invented, most exaggerated. One famous story was that of the *Bay Psalm Book*. This 1640 volume held a unique place among the Doctor's trophies, and was indeed worthy of the label *infernally rare*. It was the very first book entirely written and printed in Colonial North America. It was a bibliophile's dream of dream. In the 1930s only ten copies were known to exist.[10]

In summer of 1933, a certain Miss Weatherup of Belfast came calling with what she said was a copy of the *Bay Psalm Book*. Rosenbach thought this was another one of those worthless and tattered reproductions, of which he was offered many. But when the seller opened her humble parcel, he found himself starring at the most coveted of rarities. And while awe and emotion must have filled the Doctor's bibliophile heart, cupidity, the reverse facet of his complex character quickly gained the upper hand.[11] He coldly pointed out to the uninformed Miss Weatherup that her volume was imperfect: it lacked a title page, as well as assorted leaves, and the binding was broken. Would the Doctor still consider buying it for the modest sum £ 150? He would. Seventeen years later, Rosenbach was fortunate to acquire another copy of the *Bay Psalm Book* on behalf of Yale University. This time the price was $ 151,000.[12]

Rosenbach made his home in Philadelphia, on DeLancey Street, and it was there that the *Bay Psalm Book* joined his other treasures, those gems quietly purloined from the stock of his two bookstores, in New York and Philadelphia.[13] This pri-

---

9 Ernest Dawson, *A Visit with Dr. R* (Los Angeles: Privately Published, 1948), [13].

10 Wolf 2nd, 386–87, and also James Gilreath, "History of a Book: Madison Council Told of First Book Printed in America," *Library of Congress Information Bulletin* 54, no. 9 (1995): 201: "It is among the most priced artifacts of our national culture."

11 Sowerby, 133: "As far as I know no one stressed what always seemed to me to be one of the fundamental reasons for his really phenomenal success. This was the unusual combination – which I have never met with such a degree in any one else – of a deep and genuine love and feeling for books, and an equally deep and genuine love and feeling for the profits they brought him."

12 Wolf 2nd, 548: "... the highest price ever paid for a printed book at public auction."

13 The word *purloined* is used here literally. See Sowerby, 135: "Any book that the Doctor could

vate collection boasted an array of unsurpassed Americana: manuscripts of George Washington and Ulysses S. Grant, Ben Franklin's *Work Book*, and the only known copy of the first issue of his *Poor Richard's Almanack*. The Doctor also had an original certified copy of the *Declaration of Independence*, Lincoln's first draft of the *Emancipation Proclamation*, entirely in his autograph, and the notebook of Surgeon C. S. Taft, describing Lincoln's last moments. Aside from his Americana, he also owned a selection of the world's most beautiful love letters, penned by Keats, Robert Burns, Thackeray, or by Mary Godwin.[14] For less than $ 2,000, the Doctor had acquired at auction a little known manuscript, that of James Joyce's *Ulysses*. Seventy years later those scribbled leaves, picked up at auction for a song, were worth the price of a Learjet.[15] But above all, the Doctor was known all around the world as the man *who bought Alice*. He had bid the astronomical price of £ 15,400 on a handwritten children story, *Alice in Wonderland,* and in the process had earned millions in publicity. Bold headlines had proclaimed to the world the news of his conquest. President and Mrs. Coolidge had invited the Doctor to the White House for lunch to see the manuscript and talk about his lovely acquisition.[16]

The Doctor's roster of clients read like a who's who of American oil, banking, manufacturing, and commerce. It was mostly for these mighty tycoons that he

---

not bear to part with – and there were many of these – eventually found its way, if he were lucky, to the shelves of his private library in his home in Delancey (*sic!*) Street. The first time I had the pleasure of dining there I was staggered to see the number of treasures that I had fondly imagined were still in their proper places on the shelves of the safe in Walnut Street [i.e., his bookstore in Philadelphia]. The removal of the books from Walnut to Delancey Street had to be done very quietly and unostentatiously, and the books were carefully concealed, one at a time, in the spacious pockets that had been specially made for the purpose under the coat-tails of the Doctor's overcoat. This was a necessary precaution, so that the removal could be accomplished without the knowledge of brother Philip, who, as President of the firm, naturally had good income-tax reasons for objecting to the Doctor's propensity for removing the treasures from the sales shelves."

14 "Letters that we ought to burn," in: A. S. W. Rosenbach, *A Book Hunter's Holiday: Adventures With Books and Manuscripts* (Boston: Houghton Mifflin, 1936), 1–36.

15 Robert Wernick, "The Bookseller Who Couldn't Stand to Sell his Books," *Smithsonian* 23, no.1 (1992): 112.
Note: In December 2000 an autographed chapter of *Ulysses* sold at a Christie's for $ 1.5 million.
Note: James Joyce, who was promised a percentage of the sale price of his manuscript, never expected to receive a paltry $ 240 dollars. To add insult to injury, the telegram he received in Paris must have misspelled the title of his famous novel. The Doctor's cable address read "Rosebrook, Philadelphia." An angry Joyce immortalized Rosenbach in a cantankerous verse: " Rosy Brook he bought the book / Though he didn't know how to spell it / Such is the lure of literature/To the lad who can buy and sell it." (Wernick, 112).

16 For the story of that dramatic auction of this manuscript and the publicity it generated, see Wolf 2nd, 285–303. In a gesture of good will, Rosenbach later facilitated its return as a gift to the British Museum. See ibid., 538–39.

bid and bought on a grandiose scale. One of his early clients was young Harry Elkins Widener, heir to the Philadelphia trolley-car fortune.[17] The attentive Doctor had nurtured Harry's bibliophile passion since his Harvard undergraduate years. In spring of 1912 in London, after acquiring a rare second edition of Bacon's *Essays,* Harry had joyously boarded the Titanic for his journey home.[18] In his memory his grief-stricken mother, comforted by the Doctor, had continued collecting. Her superb acquisitions were later donated to Harvard University.

A long line of illustrious customers succeeded young Harry Widener. Among them were H. C. Folger, former President of Standard Oil, for whom Rosenbach gathered the crown jewels of the future Shakespeare Library, and Henry E. Huntington, the railroad king, whose San Marino, California art collection and library became one of the nation's premier cultural centers. There was also William A. Clark, heir to a mining fortune, who bequeathed his books to the University of California at Los Angeles, and Countess Edward L. Doheny, wife of the oil millionaire, whose splendid religious *rarissima* graced the shelves of the Saint John's Seminary in Camarillo, California. There were the Harknesses, of railroad fame, the financier J. P. Morgan, and Rosenbach's long-time friend and wealthy client, Lessing J. Rosenwald, son of the founder of *Sears, Roebuck & Co.*, whose exquisite acquisitions, hand-picked by the Doctor, now enhance the collections of the National Gallery of Art and Library of Congress.

Friends, clients and associates described Abraham Simon Wolf Rosenbach, A. S. W. R. or Dr. R for short, as a multifaceted personality, a curious fusion of contemplative erudition and aggressive mercantile speculation. His father, Morris Rosenbach, had immigrated to the United States from Gunzenhausen, Germany, and had married Isabella Polock of Philadelphia, descendant of a well-established Jewish-Dutch family. From Uncle Moses or Mo, his mother's frail and bookish brother, a publisher, dealer and collector, young Rosenbach learned the love and respect for rare books. From two other uncles, Lewis and Barnett Polock, he inherited an irrepressible yearning for risk and adventure. Lewis and Barnett, who had joined the forty-niners, ended up killed in gunfights in California.

The last of seven babies, Rosenbach was adored and spoiled by his mother and sisters. He was a chubby child who blossomed into a short, tubby man with a wobbly walk and a mischievous glint in his eye.[19] He favored a scholarly pince-

---

[17] Harry was the son of George Widener (1861–1912). Harry's grandfather Peter Widener (1834–1915) had started the trolley-car transportation system in Philadelphia. George Widener worked on the development of cable and electric trolleys. At the time of his and his son's death on the Titanic, George Widener was enormously rich and owned the majority of stock in several streetcar companies.

[18] Rosenbach, *Books and Bidders*, 46.

[19] Wolf 2nd, 13: "Abraham Simon Wolf Rosenbach had plump pink cheeks, a twinkle in his

nez and dressed impeccably in dark clothes and snow-white shirts. He was single and sedentary, despising all physical activity with the exception of fishing, a hard drinker, known to polish off daily a bottle of scotch whiskey, and a robust eater, willfully oblivious of all dietary restrictions imposed by his diabetes. He was blessed with a phenomenal memory and a marvelous intellectual virtuosity.

Rosenbach spent his formative years in Uncle Mo's Philadelphia bookshop, a drafty, cluttered place, on the second floor of a decaying redbrick building on Commerce Street. Uncle Mo, a reluctant salesman, was highly respected for his knowledge of rare books and for his flair for Americana. Up and down his rickety staircase came and went the soon-to-be famous, the well-known, and the long forgotten, successful and destitute writers, rich collectors and poor browsers, friends, and once in a while a paying customer. Young Rosenbach listened to magical stories of literary hopes, financial triumphs, and alcohol-laced tragedies. Together with the choking book dust, reputed to insure longevity and rumored to have kept Uncle Mo alive long past his date with the Creator, the boy inhaled the noble vice of bibliomania.[20] From the back of an auction-room, at age eleven, he found himself bidding, with an empty wallet, on an illustrated *Reynard de Fox*. To his misfortune he won the bid, and ended up paying for the book in interminable installments, out of his weekly childhood allowance.[21]

Rosenbach went on to earn a doctorate in English literature from the University of Pennsylvania and worked briefly in its English Department.[22] His academic career came to an abrupt halt when Uncle Mo passed away and the twenty-six-year-old Doctor was named executor of his mildewing treasures. Together with his brother Philip, who dabbled in antiques, A.S.W.R. launched in 1903 the Rosenbach Company.[23] Philip, twelve years his senior, ordained himself company president. With a vigilant eye on the company's finances, Philip made sure that his easy-going, fun-loving brother never slackened on the job. And while Philip's own art dealership floundered, the Doctor's book business kept company and family prosperous. His immense success was due to his unsurpassed knowledge of rare books, to his uncanny understanding of the dynamics of the auction room, and to his unrivaled gift for manipulating the media, and for attracting wealthy customers. Armed with the millions of corporate America, and relentlessly pushed by his brother, the Doctor never failed to bring home the

---

eye, walked – as a friend once said – as a penguin would walk if a penguin would walk like Rosy, puffed everlastingly on a pipe or cigar, drank a bottle of whisky a day, and was the greatest antiquarian bookseller the world has seen."

20 Ibid., 48.

21 Rosenbach, *Books and Bidders*, 11.

22 Rosenbach's dissertation was on the Spanish influence on English drama before the Restoration.

23 Wolf 2nd, 48.

cherished jewels of European and American collections along with substantial monetary rewards.

For the first four decades of the twentieth century, Dr. Rosenbach dominated all aspects of the rare book business on both sides of the ocean. But during the war years, when private fortunes withered and the buying power of scholarly libraries eroded, his name faded from the headlines. With ebbing professional success came a decline in health. The Doctor was often in and out of hospital emergency rooms with bouts of high blood sugar levels, hemorrhages, and drink-induced comas.[24] His chronic diabetes forever ignored and despised, was slowly taking revenge on a system weakened by overindulgence in alcohol and rich foods.

While considerably older, his brother Philip remained energetic and focused on profits. Irked by the Doctor's recurrent health problems, Philip decided to liquidate his failing antiques business and take over the lucrative dealings of the rare book department.[25] Together with the mantle of rare books dealer, Philip usurped his brother's academic title.[26] But the false *Doctor Philip* could only dupe an ignorant few, for there was a world of difference between A. S. W. R.'s scholarly knowledge and true love of books and Philip's practical approach to business. Philip's guiding principle was simple: a dollar in the bank was worth more than a book on the shelf. Volume by volume he set out to dismantle the incomparable Rosenbach stock.[27] By the close of 1945, when the officer came calling, the legendary Doctor was owner of his book-business in name only. Philip used his title and his fame, and, with the adroit help of store manager John Fleming, cashed in on his reputation.

The English butler returned and ushered the officer up the stately staircase, to the second floor book room. The book room was even more impressive than the foyer. Floor to ceiling, the walls were clad in elegant bookcases and packed with handsomely bound volumes. In front of the fireplace, a Renaissance desk, with a matching leather-covered chair, anchored the well-proportioned space. From its vintage point above the mantelpiece the portrait of Benjamin Franklin greeted the visitor with sage eyes and tolerant half-smile.[28]

---

[24] Ibid., 541.

[25] Ibid., 511.

[26] Ibid., 559: "While the Doctor faded, Philip soared. ...It was 'Dr'. Philip Rosenbach this, and 'Dr.' Philip Rosenbach that. Those who met him and had not known the Doctor thought Philip was he. The dazzling coat of fame which Abie was too dispirited to wear Phil picked up and, wrapping himself in its borrowed luster, pranced from Lost Angeles to London."

[27] Ibid., 572: "The atmosphere of the business had become that of a frenzied ball with fiddles playing louder and louder, faster and faster. Fleming spun like a dervish from sale to sale and Philip spun about him chortling with glee. Great books and manuscripts flew into the hands of eager collectors as old Dr. R prices were spiraling down."

[28] Sowerby, 222.
Note: The pastel portrait was by Joseph-Siffrede Duplessis (1725–1802).

John Fleming, the firm's manager, welcomed the guest with professional courtesy. The officer unwrapped his parcel, which still displayed US Customs tags,[29] and revealed his merchandise: two venerable looking leather-bound books. Fleming remembered seeing one of the volumes before. It was a fourteenth-century vellum codex with beautiful illuminations, a folio, bound in blind-tooled calf. It had been left with the Rosenbach Company July past for consideration of purchase.[30] The bookstore had not acted on the offer. The other volume was older looking, unadorned, and much smaller.

Fleming picked up the smaller volume and examined it more closely. It was an early theological compendium, in Latin, with one strange exception: its very first leaf. The script on that leaf was different than the writing used in the rest of the volume, and the language was anything but Latin. It had a deep vertical crease, and assorted holes. Dark blemishes obscured some of the words. Fleming, who was known throughout the trade for having "the eye of an eagle when it came to finding anything wrong,"[31] immediately sensed that there was something odd about this leaf. How did the officer acquire the two manuscripts? He had found them in the rubble of southern Germany. Just out of curiosity, price-wise, what did the officer have in mind? The officer was not sure. He was a soldier, not a book collector. What would be the Rosenbach Company's best offer for the pair?[32]

Fleming, the accomplished businessman, had learned the art of buying and selling from the master himself, from the incomparable Dr. R. When selling, Rosenbach was all enthusiasm and ebullience, touting his ware as unique, like Caesar's wife above suspicion.[33] Conversely, when buying, he played for time, his expression bland, uninterested.[34] Fleming, the well-trained assistant, was not about to venture an offer without further delay and examination. He had to con-

---

[29] Archdiocese of Los Angeles. Archival Center. Estelle Doheny Collection of California. Correspondence. Deposited with the University of California, Davis. Shields Library. Department of Special Collections. Letter of J. Fleming to E. L. Doheny, November 19, 1953.

[30] Rosenbach Museum & Library. Archives, 1945 business records and correspondence, documents deposited with the University of California, Davis. Shields Library. Department of Special Collections. Copy of a memorandum released by the Rosenbach Archives to the author in January of 2002. The memorandum is signed "The Rosenbach Company by: John Fleming" and is dated July 6, 1945. It acknowledges receipt from Lt. Bud Berman of a 14th – century vellum manuscript, comprising three books: part one, pages 1–68 written by Ulrich von dem Türlin, part two, pages 70–163 written by Wolfram von Eschenbach, and part three, pages 163r–394d by Ulrich von Türheim.

[31] Sowerby, 196.

[32] Rosenbach Museum & Library. Archives. ... Letter (undated) signed Bud Berman and addressed to Dr. Rosenbach.

[33] Wolf 2nd, 413.

[34] Ibid., 386.

sult with Miss Mayer, the company's cataloger, and seek her opinion about that strange leaf in an otherwise Latin codex.[35]

The reserved Gretel Mayer was summoned down from her secluded fourth floor cataloging room. The Rosenbach Company had hired her two years earlier, after the abrupt departure of the learned Millicent Sowerby. But as Gretel Mayer was soon to discover, no one could ever replace Miss Sowerby. For seventeen years Emily Millicent Sowerby had been the company's chief bibliographer.[36] British upper crust, Cambridge-educated, University of Grenoble-polished Millicent was far more than a bibliographer. She was a scholar and bibliophile, one of the few women known as rare book specialists. For many years, Sowerby had researched and annotated the Doctor's fine treasures. She knew that Rosenbach always tried to place each book in the most fitting collection, in the hands of the most appreciative collector. Sowerby helped him do so by ghostwriting his seductive catalog descriptions, which invariably reeled in the intended, the perfect buyer.[37] It was Miss Sowerby, who, writing in the shadow of the Rosenbach name,[38] had refined, restructured and edited Dr. R's articles, prefaces and speeches, and had compiled his pioneer bibliographies.[39] For her magnificent body of work, she had been rewarded with low pay, minimal recognition, and repeated humiliations. Brother Philip and the Doctor, demanded complete subordination from all assistants but rarely recompensed, praised, or encouraged them.[40] One day in February of 1942, with no apparent reason or forewarning, Philip had fired Millicent Sowerby.[41] In her stead, the company had hired the reserved Gretel Mayer.

---

35 "File Ms. of Hildebrandslied From Kassel," US Department of State, Records Maintained by the Fine Arts and Monuments Adviser, 1945–61, Ardelia Hall Collection, Record Group 59. Lot 62D4, Box 6, Item 2, National Archives and Records Administration, A. Hall, Memorandum of conversation with G. Mayer, January 27 and July 12, 1961.

36 Wolf 2nd, 175.

37 Sowerby, 191–192: "So long as I knew who was the prospective customer, and what were his or her particular interests, I could generally guarantee to sell the book by the descriptions."

38 Ibid., 175: "During the time I worked with the Rosenbach Company I had the privilege and pleasure of being the Doctor's ghost for a great deal of publishing material to be signed by him. This included one whole bibliography, the Early American Children's Books, a considerable portion of another, The American Jewish Bibliography, lives of several important – and unimportant – Americans for the Dictionary of American Biography, articles published in various magazines, and a number of other matters."

39 Ibid., 183–84: "As far as the book (i.e., the Early American Children's Books) was concerned, the Doctor was extremely kind to me, and made no secret of the fact that I had been responsible for it. All he wanted was his name on the title-page, which was, of course, essential to him, though I must admit I used to think the title-page could have had his name in large letters as the owner of the collection, and mine, in small letters as the compiler of the book."

40 Wolf 2nd, 207.

41 Sowerby, 236–37.
Note: This ultimate disgrace had a happy ending. Soon thereafter the Library of Congress

With apprehension, Gretel Mayer heeded Fleming's summons.[42] Downstairs, in the book-room, she found him in the company of a man in uniform. Definitely not a GI, Mayer thought, more likely a lieutenant or captain.[43] Fleming handed her the Latin codex and asked her to look at its first page. Gretel studied it intently. An early German language and old script,[44] she ventured, tenth century perhaps ... She let silence finish her sentence while turning the page. On the verso, toward the bottom, there was a fairly large oval mark, a library ownership seal: *Ex Bibliotheca Cassellana,* Gretel read, from the shelves of the Kassel Library. "You must have spent time in Kassel." The officer looked startled, uneasy.[45] How did she know? She pointed to the seal.

Fig. 14. Kassel Library ownership stamp (Archives of the Universitätsbibliothek Kassel – Landesbibliothek und Murhardsche Bibliothek der Stadt Kassel. Reproduced by permission)

Fleming asked Gretel to check on the history of the manuscript and report back to him in writing within the next three days. Codex in hand, Gretel retired to her fourth floor hideout. But before embarking on her assignment she made a note of the officer's name.[46] Alone in the library room, Fleming and the seller came to a provisional understanding, pending the Doctor's approval: the firm's best offer for the pair was $ 7,000; $ 6,000 for the folio and $ 1,000 for the quarto.[47]

---

offered Sowerby the position of Bibliographer of the Jefferson Collection, a prestigious responsibility commensurate with her skills and talents.

42 "File Ms. of the Hildebrandslied from Kassel," A. Hall, Memorandum of conversation with G. Mayer, July 12, 1961.

43 "Hildebrandlied 2," documents from the Archives of the Gesamthochschul-Bibliothek Kassel – Landesbibliothek und Murhardsche Bibliothek der Stadt Kassel, deposited with the University of California, Davis, Shields Library, Department of Special Collections. Letter from W. F. Twaddell to D. Hennig, June 19, 1974.

44 "File Ms. of the Hildebrandslied from Kassel," A. Hall, Memorandum of conversation with G. Mayer, July 12, 1961.

45 "Hildebrandlied 2," documents from the archives. ... Travelogue of D. Hennig, March 1, 1972.

46 "File Ms. of the Hildebrandslied from Kassel," A. Hall, Memorandum of Conversation with G. Mayer, January 27, 1961.

47 Rosenbach Museum & Library. Archives. ... Receipt released to the author on January 2002.

Gretel's written report must have been far from illuminating. Unlike the incomparable Sowerby, who was born to research, Mayer was not a seasoned bibliographer. She was a lawyer, a recent refugee from Nazi Germany, who had picked up librarianship as a second career. Had she been more experienced, she would have found out, with little or no effort, all there was to know about the *Liber Sapientiae.* Since the ownership stamp had already revealed the provenance of the codex, a walk to the New York Public Library would have easily yielded information on the Kassel manuscript collection. Without any doubt, she would have found Wilhelm Hopf's 1930 landmark publication *Die Landesbibliothek Kassel*, with a chapter on the codex.[48] Not only did Gretel Mayer fail to discover the significance of the text inscribed on the first leaf, but she also failed to notice and report on the existence of the last page of the codex, with a text written in the same "early German language and old script."

When she submitted her findings, Fleming's secretary whispered that the firm had just sold the large beautiful book with pictures for $ 10,000.[49] Later in the week, when the building was quiet, Gretel ventured downstairs to the library room in search of a pencil. In the drawer of the Renaissance desk she came across a single manuscript leaf. She recognized it instantly. It was the one with the odd writing, the one with the oval Kassel library ownership seal on the verso. The leaf had been cut off the text block[50]. The oval library stamp looked blurred, no longer fully legible. Someone had doused it with acid and had tried scraping it off with a blade.[51]

It is dated November 10, 1945, with an "OK" in the upper left-hand margin initialed by A.S.W.R. (Abraham Simon Wolf Rosenbach). The receipt lists two manuscripts bought from Bud Berman: Eschenbach's Titurell (*sic!*) purchased for $ 6,000, and a Bible manuscript (i.e. the *Liber Sapientiae*) purchased for $ 1,000.

48 Wilhelm Hopf, editor, *Die Landesbibliothek Kassel, 1580–1930* (The Kassel State Library: 1580–1930) (Marburg: N. G. Elwert, 1930), part II by Gustav Struck, 31–36.

49 "File Ms. of the Hildebrandslied from Kassel," A. Hall, Memorandum of conversation with G. Mayer, January 27, 1961.

50 The text block is the body of leaves ready to be bound.

51 "Hildebrandlied 2," documents from the archives. ... Letter of D. Hennig to W. von Both, March 3, 1972 and to W. F. Twaddell, April 23, 1974.

Chapter 9: "Belle of the Books"[1]

In the closing days of November 1945, the New York offices of the Rosenbach Co. submitted the medieval Latin compendium *Liber Sapientiae Solomonis* to the Pierpont Morgan Library for sale.[2] Director Belle da Costa Greene must have found this latest Rosenbach offering very desirable, for she had the entire codex filmed and referred to her manuscript expert for further study.[3]

Belle Greene was widely regarded as the first lady of American librarianship, a distinction that had been uniquely hers for decades.[4] She presided over a splendid library; she was the first woman ever elected Fellow of the Medieval Academy of America and a permanent Fellow of the New York Metropolitan Museum. Her fame extended beyond national borders. France had bestowed upon her *Les Palmes d'Officier de l'Instruction Publique,* followed by *La Medaille d'Or du Grand Officier de l'Instruction Publique*,[5] and Italy and Belgium had also granted her special honors and acknowledgments.[6] Although frail and touched by arthritis,[7] Belle Greene's indomitable spirit was still a force to reckon with. Hans Peter Kraus, the well-known book-dealer, experienced it first hand, when he came calling with an illuminated Spanish manuscript. When the sixty-five years old Belle entered the room, he felt in the presence of royalty. She took one look at his codex and banished it as the work of a forger. Her gimlet eyes and ice coated inflections made the seasoned dealer wince.

> Strong willed, not easily charmed [...she] was fiercely devoted to the library, which her book knowledge and two generations of Morgan money had built. Nobody in the

---

1 "Belle of the Books." *Time* 53, no. 15 (1949): 76–78. Title of an article about Belle da Costa Greene.

2 "File Ms. of Hildebrandslied from Kassel," US Department of State, Records Maintained by the Fine Arts and Monuments Adviser, 1945–61, Ardelia Hall Collection, Record Group 59, Lot 62D4, Box 6, Item 2, National Archives and Records Administration. Letter of J. H. Page, to the Commissioner of Customs, Division of Investigations, Bureau of Customs, June 13, 1952.

3 Ibid., Letter of A. Hall to S. Stephens, May 1, 1952.

4 Hans Peter Kraus, *A Rare Book Saga: The Autobiography of H. P. Kraus* (New York: G. P. Putnam's Sons, 1978), 87.

5 *Les Palmes Académiques*, established in 1850 under Louis Napoléon, awards the coveted title of Officier de l'Instruction Publique to leaders in education.

6 See "Greene, Belle da Costa (1883–1950)," in: *Dictionary of American Library Biography*, edited by Bohdan S. Wynar (Littleton, Colorado: Libraries Unlimited, 1978), 217, and also Cass Canfield, *The Incredible Pierpont Morgan: Financier and Art Collector* (New York: Harper & Row, 1974), 153.

7 Wolf 2nd, 517.

Fig. 15. Belle da Costa Greene · Portrait by Paul Hellau.
(The Pierpont Morgan Library, New York. Bequest of Belle da Costa Greene, 1950, 1950. 12. – Reproduced by permission).

> country handled so many precious books or possessed such vast expertise. Her manner befitted her station: regal, aloof. I trembled.[8]

Four decades earlier, a sprightly Belle had burst onto the scene of the rare book-trade and had forever changed its stance. Before her arrival the world of bibliophiles was inhospitable to women.[9] It was an exclusive male club, with a well-defined hierarchy rooted in tradition, financial firepower, specialized book knowledge, and clever business savvy. Year in and year out important private and public sales brought together the mighty book hunters, flanked by their adroit agents. The auction room was the arena where these tycoons, in person or through intermediaries, sparred for the love of a Caxton,[10] a Shakespeare First Folio, or a Gutenberg Bible. With a brisk rap of the ivory hammer treasures unexcelled changed hands from one continent to another, from one library to another. Most large public or private collectors "had a sage and sober envoy. All but the Morgan, which had Belle da Costa Greene."[11]

Without fail Belle's grand entries in a cloud of perfume[12] sent electrical shivers through the auction room. Petite and dainty, she was all energy and verve. With her luminous green eyes and amber complexion framed in a halo of dark hair, the glamorous Belle was said to exude irresistible sensuality.[13] She was far from beautiful, more likely what the French would call *une jolie laide*.[14] She dressed with flair and elegance, donned exquisite jewels, and for additional dramatic effect accented her wear with silk handkerchiefs and long cigarette holders.[15]

---

8 Kraus, 87–88. In the end, Kraus's illuminated Spanish manuscript, haughtily rejected by Greene as a forgery, turned out to be genuine.

9 E. Millicent Sowerby, *Rare People and Rare Books* (London: Constable, 1967), 4, quotes the famous British dealer Wilfried Michael Voynich who, in his peculiar use of the English language, summarized the role of women in his field: "Only one woman had made success in rare-book field, and she was most remarkable woman in United States of America, Miss Belle da Costa Greene of Mr. Morgan's libraries in New York. No other woman could do what she had done; she was unique."

10 William Caxton (1422?–1491) was the first English printer. He learned the art of printing in Cologne, and set up a printing press in Bruges. In 1474, he translated and published the first book in English: *The Recuyell of the Historyes of Troye*. Of his one hundred books, less than forty are still known to exist.

11 Wesley Towner, *The Elegant Auctioneers* (New York: Hill & Wang, 1970), 272.

12 Canfield, 152.

13 Meryle Secrest, *Being Bernard Berenson: A Biography* (New York: Holt, Rinehart and Winston, 1979), 294. Bernard Berenson, among others, had a torrid love affair with Belle. Secrest described Berenson's encounter with Belle "as being hit by a wandering sun. He did not know what color it was, whether it was dark or purple or, as it seemed to him, a radiant gold. It was a miracle he was still alive."

14 An unconventional beauty. Towner, 274 states: "In truth, all her features slanted in strange directions, and nothing about her seemed to go together in an accepted fashion. But if she was not really beautiful, she made many people think she was."

15 Secrest, *Being Bernard Berenson*, 290.

Known for snappy repartees delivered in a beguiling "whisky tenor",[16] she was once rumored to have contemptuously declared that *just* because she was a librarian, she did not need to dress like one.[17] While abroad, she stayed in the best hotels,[18] enjoyed the best theater seats, dined with the intellectual elite, and occasionally brought her thoroughbred horse along for romantic morning rides.[19] Dominant, self-confident, and backed by Morgan's millions, she was the perfect representative of his taste and social status.

All biographical accounts describe Belle as bright and witty,[20] ruthless in negotiations,[21] fanatically loyal to her master and library, and endowed with unerring flair for the authentic.[22] With her originated the standard known in the rare book world as Morgan Quality, which is said to be neither good nor excellent, but supreme.[23] She had an insatiable hunger for learning and a vivid intellectual curiosity. Painfully conscious of her lack of academic training in a world brimming with distinguished scholars, Belle used every opportunity to acquire know-

---

16 Wolf 2nd, 241.

17 Jean Strouse, *Morgan: American Financier* (New York: Random House, 1999), 510.

18 "Greene, Belle da Costa (Dec. 13, 1883–May 10, 1950)," in: *Notable American Women 1607–1950: A Biographical Dictionary*, editor Edward T. James, vol. 2 (Cambridge, Massachusetts: Belknap Press of Harvard UP, 1971), 83.

19 Canfield, 153.

20 Biographical references to Belle da Costa Greene abound. See, for instance, Ernest Samuels, *Bernard Berenson: The Making of a Legend* (Cambridge, Massachusetts: The Belknap Press, 1987), 73; Secrest, 292; Carol Bleier, "The Pierpont Morgan Library: Changing of the Guard," *Wilson Library Bulletin* 62, no. 8 (1988): 43; Sowerby, 202; Strouse, 509–20; or entries under Belle da Costa Greene, in: *Notable American Women*, v.2, 83–85; *Dictionary of American Library Biography*, 216–18; *American National Biography,* John A. Garraty and Mark C. Carnes, eds., vol. 9 (New York: Oxford UP, 1999), 518–19; *American Book Collectors and Bibliographers, Second Series*, editor Joseph Rosenblum, Dictionary of literary biography, vol. 187 (Detroit: Gale, 1997), 131–36.

21 Louis Auchincloss, *J. P. Morgan: The Financier As Collector* (New York: Harry N. Abrams, 1990), 21, citing Stillwell. Additionally, Curt F Bühler, *Early Books and Manuscripts: Forty Years of Research* (New York: Grolier Club & The Pierpont Morgan Library, 1973), 516, describes her as follows: "Her success in the bookmarts and in the auction places of two Continents is familiar to all: for us of her staff, it was ever a fascinating experience to see Miss Greene in action. Watching her deal with the preliminary mechanics of an auction sale – appeasing the auctioneer, quieting (or, with skillful hand, misleading) the opposition and selecting the proper agent for each special transaction – some of us came to wonder, indeed, how Miss Greene escaped being made a partner in J. P. Morgan & Co. Beyond all else, however, her emphasis on quality made a profound impression on friend and friendly foe alike."

22 "Greene, Belle da Costa (1883–1950)", in: *Dictionary of American Library Biography*, 217, quoting Lawrence Wroth, who said that she was blessed with "... an instinct for the authentic, ... a recognition for quality, which [could] only be likened to the possession of 'absolute pitch' in a musician."

23 *The Pierpont Morgan Library: A Review of Acquisitions 1949–1968* (New York: The Library, 1969), [xi].

ledge, train the eye, and improve critical skills.[24] Art experts of international repute vied to become her adoring companions, lovers, and mentors: Sydney Cockerell,[25], Bernard Berenson,[26] William Ivins, Jr.,[27] among others took turns introducing her to the best minds on two continents, and helping her become an expert in her own right.

Prior to Belle Greene's arrival, J. P. Morgan's collecting impulses were triggered by pleasure[28] and validated by price.[29] Once Belle took over the reins of his library, the era of impetuous buying came to an end. She took an unsystematic collection that reflected the taste of a rich neophyte, and gave it professional shape and direction.[30] She embarked on disciplined collection-building expeditions, adding only those materials that clearly fit within expressed collecting guidelines.[31] The Morgan Library, one of the richest and most celebrated educational institutions in the world, and its unsurpassed illuminated manuscripts, papyri, autographed letters, early printed books, rare bindings, and mezzotints, stands today as testimony to her vision, talent, and knowledge.

Legend has it that it was Junius, Morgan's nephew, who first noticed Belle at Princeton University, where he was a student and she a library cataloger-in-train-

---

24 Strouse, 519: "[She] attached herself intellectually and often romantically to a series of distinguished scholars and experts, ... longing to absorb what these men knew."

25 Sir Sydney Cockerell (1867–1962), long-time director of the Fitzwilliam Museum in Cambridge, was renowned for his bibliographic descriptions of medieval manuscripts and art collections.

26 Bernard Berenson (1865–1959), Lithuanian born art historian, was an authority on Italian Renaissance and premier consultant to wealthy American collectors. While Belle Greene burned all his letters before her death, he kept all of hers.

27 William Mills Ivins, Jr. (1881–1961) was a lawyer, collector, accomplished speaker, and highly respected authority on prints and printmaking processes. He was appointed in 1916 as the first Curator of Prints at the Metropolitan Museum of Art, and held the post for the next thirty years.

28 Harry Miller Lyndenberg, "The Ecology of the Pierpont Morgan Library and its First Director," in: *Studies in Art and Literature for Belle da Costa Greene,* editor Dorothy Eugenia Milner (Princeton, N. J.: Princeton UP, 1954), 7, wrote that Morgan bought mostly for "avocation and recreation; the interest was general and incidental, rather than that of a student or scholar; it showed appreciation of important and significant sources, but was far from the avid pursuit of a certain line."

29 Canfield, 157. Morgan is said to have once declared that the most expensive words in any language were *unique au monde*.

30 William M. Voelkle, electronic correspondence with the author of April 20, 2000, deposited with the University of California, Davis, Shields Library, Department of Special Collections.
Note: William M. Voelkle is Department Head and Curator of Medieval and Renaissance Manuscripts at the Pierpont Morgan Library.

31 "Belle da Costa Greene (13 December 1883–10 May 1950)," in: *American Book Collectors and Bibliographers, Second Series*, 134.

ing. Junius was so impressed with Belle's love of rare books, with her organized mind, and remarkable poise, that he recommended her to his uncle, who was looking for someone to manage his growing book collections. The position of principal librarian at "Mr. Morgan's Library" offered the successful candidate a life of privilege, vast opportunities for intellectual and professional growth, and unique social and business contacts. Young Belle had no formal academic training and limited experience. Surely there must have been others vying for this important post, tried and true librarians, seasoned book-lovers, scholars with extensive knowledge of rare books, manuscripts, or incunabula. But it was Belle who so dazzled the sixty-eight-year-old Morgan that he offered her the position at almost double her Princeton salary[32]. She told him she was twenty-two, of cultured but impoverished background. Her unusual name and origins were Portuguese-Dutch. She intimated that she was born abroad, Portugal some friends guessed,[33] and that she grew up in Alexandria, Virginia without a father. Her mother, "a proud and cultivated lady of old-fashioned dignity," gave music lessons to support her and her sisters.[34] With these scant biographical details on which she steadfastly declined to amplify, Belle stepped into the role of the first lady of the Morgan Library and never looked back.[35] From that day forward, the Morgan Library was her stage, da Costa Greene her stage name, and in this setting of splendor she played the starring role with talent and assurance: that of the incomparable librarian, trusted adviser, and loyal representative of Morgan's quest for eminence.

---

[32] Strouse, 509. She was earning $40 a week at Princeton and Morgan offered her $75.

[33] Belle of the Books, 77.

[34] "Greene, Belle da Costa (Dec. 13, 1883–May 10, 1950)," in: *Notable American Women 1607–1950*, v. 2, 83.

[35] In her 1954 foreword to the volume *Studies in Art and Literature for Belle da Costa Greene*, x–xi, Dorothy Miner comments: "A biography of Belle Greene would be a fascinating and colorful account with a fabulous array of personalities, settings, and incidents. It would move against a backdrop of princely palaces and international playgrounds, austere libraries and remote cloisters, of academic meetings and the world of society. The account would be tense with the excitement of the auction room. It would be full of triumphs and fairy-tale successes, gaiety and humor, irony, sorrow, bravado, and courage. Stories would be told of her loyalty and of her sense of fun, her crushing forthrightness of speech and her surpassing generosity. Through the pages would parade fabulous objects of art and history – paintings, sculptures, books and manuscripts, and other things whose beauty made them immortal beyond the lot of those who created them or the great people of every kind and station – some known to all the world by reason of power and accomplishment, some the most obscure of students. It seems unlikely that this biography will ever be written. Even those who knew Belle Greene best never knew all the facets of her personality or of her career. She herself refused to cooperate with efforts to record her life, scorning such personal history as unimportant and of no concern to anyone. The one history that Belle Greene would desire to serve as hers would be that of the development of the Pierpont Morgan Library."

Belle had good reason to conceal her age, alter her name, place of birth, and ancestry. Her motives had less to do with ambition, vanity, or social climbing and more with intellectual and social survival. Belle was black.[36] As an underprivileged, undereducated African-American woman, her chance to be accepted, let alone succeed in the most influential circles of a white, affluent, and prejudiced America were practically non-existent. Her real name was Belle Marion Greener; her age was not twenty-two but twenty-six. She was not born in sunny Portugal but rather on T Street in Washington DC. Her irrepressible drive to succeed forced her to sacrifice the existence of a father who in any colorblind society would have been a child's hero. She was the daughter of Richard Greener, the first black American to graduate from Harvard University.[37] A brilliant mind, Greener, a lawyer by training, taught Latin, Greek, mathematics, and constitutional law at the University of South Carolina, and in his spare time, organized and cataloged the University's library collections.[38] Light-skinned, (his maternal grandfather was a West Indian of Spanish extraction),[39] he married Genevieve Ida Fleet, a mulatto piano teacher, who could easily pass for white. They had six children. Richard Greener struggled to provide for his large family, first as Treasury clerk and lawyer, and later as professor at the University of South Carolina and dean of Howard University Law School. In spite of valiant efforts, the family always teetered on the brink of poverty. When Greener received consular appointments to Bombay and then to the Russian far-eastern seaport of Vladivostok, the family broke up, and Genevieve Greener moved with her daughters to New Jersey. Protected by the anonymity of her new environment, the fair skinned Genevieve shortened her name from Greener to Greene, declared herself a widow, and "passed,"[40] leaving behind a life of racial prejudice. Young Belle

---

[36] Strouse, 509–20, uncovered Belle Greene's racial background and her connection to Richard Greener. She disclosed this information for the first time in her 1999 *Morgan: American Financier*.

[37] See, among other sources, entries under Richard T. Greener, in: *Notable Black American Men*, editor Jessie Carney Smith (Farmington Hills, Michigan: Gale, 1998), 483–84; *Dictionary of American Negro Biography*, editor Rayford Whittingham Logan (New York: Norton, 1982), 267–68; *Twentieth Century Biographical Dictionary of Notable Americans*, editor Rossiter Johnson (Boston: Biographical Society, 1904), v. 4, s.v. "Greener, Richard Theodore"; *Dictionary of American Biography*, Allen Johnson and Dumas Malone, eds., v. 7 (New York: Charles Scribner's Sons, 1928–1958), 578–79.

[38] Strouse (513) described for the first time this love of books and interest in the organization of knowledge, as a curious link between father and daughter.

[39] "Richard T. Greener (1844–1922), Educator, Lawyer, Government Official," in: *Notable Black American Men*, 483.

[40] The phenomenon of passing, which "refers to a crossing of a line that divides social groups" (see "Passing," in *Encyclopedia of African-American Culture and History*, Jack Salzman, David Lionel Smith and Cornel West, eds., vol. 4 (New York: Macmillan Library Reference, 1996), 2105–9) was fairly widespread at the beginning of the century. *The Encyclopedia* mentions Charles S. Johnson's 1925 unsigned editorial in *Opportunity*, which reported that

found a position in the rare book department of Princeton University Library. There she perfected her metamorphosis: she altered her mother's name from Genevieve Ida Fleet to the Dutch sounding Genevieve da Costa Van Vliet and invented her exotic Portuguese origins. It was a secret she would jealously guard all her life.[41] Spurning all marriage proposals she lived with her mother wedded solely to her work.[42] Before she died of cancer in 1950, she burned all her papers in a last, desperate attempt to keep her life private and her ethnicity a secret.[43]

In the early years of the century, when Belle arrived in New York, J. P. Morgan's books and art objects lay scattered around town.[44] Continuously swelling, the splendid possessions demanded a space of their own, where they could be displayed, nurtured, admired, and studied. It took six years of meticulous sketching, planning, building and decorating, before Morgan's private library was ready to showcase his collections. Created by the renowned architect Charles F. McKim, "Mr. Morgan's Library", on New York's elegant Thirty-Sixth Street, between Madison and Park Avenue, was a simple marble cube of serene beauty.

For the library's façade, McKim selected polished, pale-pink Tennessee marble blocks, cut with such precision that not a whisper could fit between the joints.[45] Two stately lionesses guarded the arched columnar entry.[46] A flight of broad

---

between the 1910 and 1920 US Census, close to four hundred thousand mulattos "faded into the great white multitude." According to Strouse, 512: "the 1850 Washington census lists the [Greener] family as mulattos. Belle's birth certificate identifies her as daughter of Genevieve Fleet and Richard Theodore Greener. Place of birth: 1462 T Street, Washington, DC. Date: November 26, 1879. Color: 'Colored.'"

41 There were many whispers regarding her origins. Some guessed that her family had crossed the color line. Berenson surmised that she was Malay (Secrest, 294, Strouse, 517). Others (Towner, 273) less charitable thought she came from the slums of New Orleans.

42 *The Encyclopedia of African American Culture and History*, 2107, quotes Mary Helen Washington's observations about black women and passing: "The woman who passes is required to deny everything about her past: her girlhood, her family, places with memories, folk customs, folk rhymes, her language, the entire long line of people who have gone before her. She lives in terror of discovery – what if she has a child with a dark complexion, what if she runs into an old school friend, how does she listen placidly to racial slurs? And more, where does the woman who passes find the equanimity to live by the privileged status that is based on the oppression of her own people?"

43 In fact, as Strouse noted (512), biographical reference sources have yet to establish a cross-reference between Belle da Costa Greene and Richard Greener.

44 Stanley Jackson, *J. P. Morgan* (New York: Stein and Day, 1983), 258.

45 Auchincloss, 96: "[McKim] is supposed to have told Morgan: 'When I was in Athens, I tried to insert the blade of a knife between the stones of the Erechtheum, and was unable to do it. I would like to follow the example of the Greeks, but it would cost you a small fortune, and no one would see where the additional money had gone. Yet the building would last through the ages.'"

46 The lionesses are the work of artist Edward Clark Potter, who later created the lions guarding the New York Public Library.

marble steps led to massive Italian bronze doors, which opened onto a vaulted, sky lit rotunda. The rotunda divided the building into an East and West wing. The East Wing housed the library proper, while the West Wing was designed as Morgan's private study. To the North, McKim allowed space for a tiny librarian's office. This was to be the library's brain-center, where Belle da Costa Greene would spend the next forty-three years of her life.

The building's exterior simplicity was offset by the opulence of its interior. The focal point of the Library Room was a massive Renaissance fireplace. Above its mantel, a sixteenth-century Flemish tapestry depicted one of the seven deadly sins, the Triumph of Avarice.[47] Triple-tiered bronze and walnut bookcases lined the walls, displaying rare volumes many bound in gold, enamel or ivory, and festooned with gemstones.

On the West Side, Morgan's private study was adorned with masterpieces attributed to Renaissance painters. Its sixteenth-century ceiling had been acquired in Italy and fitted for the room.[48] Stained glass windows, carved furniture and an Italian marble fireplace completed the sumptuous decor.[49] While impressive, these were not Mr. Morgan's most precious possessions. In a corner, a doorway with bars and braces, opened onto his book vault. Its holdings had been dubbed by Belle the *"Oh, my! Stuff,"*[50] a label born out of the gasps of enraptured admiration uttered by visiting scholars. For what was in that vault was "an achievement almost unequaled in the history of collecting ... a view of Paradise!"[51] Such was Rosenbach's expert pronouncement. And as always with the Doctor, the generous compliment included a kernel of self-promotion, for A. S. W. R. was a longtime contributor to the splendor in the vault.

---

47 Auchincloss, 97. Wayne Andrews is quoted as saying that the tapestry depicts a young man tearing off leaves of a manuscript. This interpretation of the image would have added a strange symbolic note to the story of the *Hildebrandslied*. William M. Voelkle, Curator of Medieval and Renaissance Manuscripts, at the Pierpont Morgan Library, however, dispelled this myth. He directed the author to the work of Rotraud Bauer, *Tapisserien der Renaissance nach Entwürfen von Pieter Coecke van Aelst* (Tapestries of the Renaissance: After sketches by Pieter Coecke Van Aelst) (Eisenstadt: Burgenländische Landesregierung, 1981), 67–68, which gives a complete iconographic account of the tapestry. The figure, supposed to be tearing leaves from a manuscript, represents Simony. He holds a monstrance and a sheaf of leaves, which is not a manuscript but rather a pile of dispensations, sold by the Church. (Author's electronic correspondence with William M. Voelkle, April 20, 2000).

48 Auchincloss, 99. It originally belonged to the palace of Cardinal Ignazio Gigli of Lucca.

49 Strouse, 505–8.

50 John Douglas Forbes, *J. P. Morgan, Jr., 1867–1943* (Charlottesville: UP of Virginia, 1981), 140.

51 A. S. W. Rosenbach, *Books and Bidders: The Adventures of a Bibliophile* (London: Allen & Unwin, 1928), 222.

The Morgan Library was one of the Doctor's earliest and most important clients. Half a century of business transactions and social interactions linked its collections to the rare book dealer.[52] Barely a year in business, the young A. S. W. R. had boldly approached J. Pierpont Morgan with a catalog of books in hand belonging to his late Uncle Mo. The young dealer had offered to put his academic knowledge and business sagacity at the service of the wealthy collector. He first offered Morgan an assortment of superb Americana.[53] Intrigued by the unusual inventory of the departed Moses Polock, Morgan went on testing the new rare-book dealer. Not one known to bungle a golden opportunity, A. S. W. R. executed bid after bid with knowledge and flair. In the process he managed to earn sizable commissions and, more importantly, a seat at the exclusive high roller table of the rare book trade.

Following J. P. Morgan's death in 1913, the future of his Library, and that of Belle Greene, came under a cloud of uncertainty. Morgan's son Jack had little interest in library matters. It was Belle who convinced Jack Morgan to continue his father's legacy. Passionate about her work and proud of her achievements,[54] she sparked in the heart of the millionaire's son the fire to collect and the pride to excel. Over time, a comfortable working relationship developed between librarian and tycoon.[55] When Jack Morgan decided to change the mission of the library from a private sanctuary to a public institution,[56] Belle worked tirelessly to ensure a seamless transition.[57] Jack transferred legal ownership to a Board of Trustees, assumed the responsibilities of chairman, and appointed Belle as his permanent director.

---

52 Wolf 2nd, 50.

53 Rosenbach, *Books and Bidders*, 10. He sold Morgan five volumes once owned by George Washington and a 1781 letter of George Washington to Abraham Skinner, Commissary General of Prisoners, discussing, among other topics, the surrender of Lord Cornwallis.

54 Curt F. Bühler, *Early Books and Manuscripts: Forty Years of Research* (New York: Grolier Club & The Pierpont Morgan Library, 1973), 516, considered the secret of Belle's success to be "in the broad Platonic sense of Phaedrus, eine *gottgesandte Begeisterung.*" (A divine enthusiasm).

55 "Belle da Costa Greene (13 December 1883–10 May 1950)," in: Ame*rican Book Collectors and Bibliographers, Second Series*, 134. An often-quoted exchange between Jack Morgan and Belle Greene helps illustrate her passion for completeness and perfection, and also the comfortable professional relationship that existed between the flamboyant librarian and her wealthy employer. In 1924 the opinionated Belle, who had identified several Tennyson items that the Morgan Library did not yet possess, was advising: "In regard to the Tennyson items, which personally I loathe, it is a question of perfecting your already very large and fine collection of imbecilities." To which Morgan replied, "I reluctantly confirm that we ought to have the Tennyson idiocies."

56 *The Pierpont Morgan Library: Review of the Activities and Major Acquisitions of the Library, 1941–1948* (New York: The Library, 1949), 12.

57 Bühler, *Early Books and Manuscripts*, 516.

Jack Morgan went on using the services of his father's rare book dealer, A. S. W. Rosenbach. One remarkable Rosenbach offering of the time was a 1476 epistle from the quill of Amerigo Vespucci, "the only known letter written by the man who gave his name to two continents,"[58] as the Doctor described it. To this noteworthy find, the resourceful Doctor had added a certain book mentioned in the letter, a volume from the library of Vespucci's uncle, which the Doctor said, he just happened to have in stock. This strange coincidence that brought together two Spanish items separated for centuries, made Belle Greene frown with suspicion. While many a collector would have leaped at the chance to acquire the complementary pair, Belle hesitated, reluctant to risk debasing her superb holdings with a find of uncertain lineage. She quizzed Rosenbach closely on the provenance and authenticity of the two Vespucci items. In the end, the Doctor managed to convince her that both letter and companion book were genuine,[59] and only then did Belle grant them entry into the Paradise vault.

The Doctor was especially fond of Belle, whom he must have met in 1911 at one of the most important American book sales: the dispersal of the Robert Hoe collection.[60] Rosenbach, the consummate broker, was bidding for the Wideners and assorted other wealthy patrons. Belle, the refined buyer, was the exclusive emissary of her powerful master. The shrewd dealer and the glamorous librarian had much in common. Like Rosenbach, Belle was the outsider, an interloper who had gained access to an elitist, exclusive club. They were close in age, they were both single, and from similarly modest social backgrounds. While it must have remained unspoken, their racial and ethnic heritage, which set them apart from those whom they so skillfully served, must have created between them a tacit bond of complicity. By sheer intellectual power and dogged perseverance, both had successfully pierced forbidding social strata and had become recognized experts in their own right. Over time the bond between Belle and the Doctor blossomed beyond a simple business connection. Their mutual affection and social intimacy can be easily traced through a variety of small gestures and deeds, chronicled by contemporaries. For Belle the Doctor was informally "Rosie" and she flattered him with notes and autographed portraits.[61] The Doctor enjoyed having Belle as a frequent dinner guest.[62] He admired her efferves-

---

58 Rosenbach, *Books and Bidders*, 55–7.

59 Wolf 2nd, 117.

60 Ibid., 72.
Note: Robert Hoe III (1832–1909) was heir of a fabulous fortune made in the manufacturing of printing equipment. He was a passionate book collector, and one of the founders of the Grolier Club and of the New York Metropolitan Museum of Art.

61 A. S. W. Rosenbach, "Mighty Women Book Hunters," in: *A Book Hunter's Holiday: Adventures With Books and Manuscripts* (Boston: Houghton Mifflin, 1936), 128

62 Sowerby, 211.

cence, and her vast knowledge of medieval manuscripts,[63] which, he believed, was "excelled by few scholars."[64] Known for his own ribald repartees, the Doctor delighted in Belle's brilliant conversation, tart tongue, and seductive grace.[65]

Belle and A. S. W. R. were often seen together at auctions. At times, when Rosenbach was poised to make the killer bid, Belle would stop him in a sultry whisper, suggesting that he yield the coveted rarity to her, for her own collection. And incredibly, the otherwise fiercely competitive Doctor would graciously comply.[66] Once, when Jack Morgan reprimanded Belle in front of the Doctor, the hard-selling dealer packed his wares and left. For him Belle was a distinguished scholar and not "a rich man's employee".[67] And three decades later, when the Doctor's health began deteriorating, Belle, mindful and compassionate, bought one more incunabulum from his stock. She knew instinctively that the best medicine for Rosenbach was to feel successful again.[68]

The Second World War had a profound effect on bibliophile activities. In the crude flare of artillery fire, the genteel sport of sparring at auction seemed shallow and vain. Buying trips became dangerous, catalog purchases unreliable. Ethics warped. Fraud and deceit became acceptable. Rumors were circulating that even the gallant Dr. Rosenbach had surrendered to the insidious trend. Colleagues whispered that he dismissed matters of private property rights with a shrug, claiming that after all, "*every* important book had been stolen at least once."[69]

For Belle Greene, the bad news outnumbered the good in rapid succession. Her sister, one of the few she could openly acknowledge as a member of her *white* family, followed her mother in death. From the front-line came word that her

---

63 Wolf, 2nd, 197: "Mr. Morgan's librarian, the dark, exotic, husky-voiced Belle, had the knowledge, the appreciation, and the judgment to know, when a great book was something she ought to go after and, what was sometimes disconcerting to the Doctor, when a great book was not so great or not so great that a better would not come along if she waited. Happily, Mr. Morgan had enough money to back up her judgment."

64 Rosenbach, "Mighty Women Book Hunters," 127: "This reference to the Morgan collection must inevitably bring up the name of its distinguished director, Miss Belle da Costa Greene, who has reached a height in the world of books that no other woman has ever attained. Miss Greene, besides possessing a genuine love of books, has a knowledge of customs and manners in the medieval period excelled by few scholars."

65 Sowerby, 211.

66 Towner, 309.

67 Wolf 2nd, 198.

68 Ibid., 408.

69 William Freeman Twaddell, "The Hildebrand Manuscript in the U.S.A, 1945–1972," Twaddell Archives, unpublished. October 1973 version, 5–6, citing Julian P. Boyd, editor of the Jefferson Papers and former Librarian at Princeton University.

nephew, whom Belle had legally adopted, had been killed in action. One by one, the mighty book hunters of yesteryear, her old friends and colleagues, began fading into eternity. She suffered a severe blow when Jack Morgan, with whom she had worked closely for thirty years, died in 1943, leaving her greatly concerned about the library and her own future. She tried to escape her worries by throwing herself into her work, her life-long refuge and solace. Anxious for the safety of the Morgan treasures in times of war, she ordered the evacuation of some of her irreplaceable items to safer inland repositories. Once again a trusted Rosenbach connection proved salutary. The Doctor's friend Lessing J. Rosenwald generously offered to store one thousand of her master drawings at no cost at his Alverthorpe Gallery in Jenkintown, Pennsylvania.[70] It must have been comforting to know that the old ties of camaraderie were still intact, connecting the last surviving bibliophiles.

At the close of 1945, around the time when the Rosenbach Company offered the *Liber Sapientiae* to the Morgan Library for sale, New York was awash in European artwork.[71] Returning veterans were flooding the market with war souvenirs. Alarmed, the Roberts Commission, of which Dr. Rosenbach was a member, issued a call to museums, antique dealers, and auction houses, exhorting them to exercise vigilance and caution:

> This commission has had numerous reports of objects being offered to museums and to the trade by present and former members of the armed forces. ... It is, of course, obvious that no clear title can be passed on objects that have been looted from public and private collection abroad. We believe, therefore, that it is to the advantage of both public institutions and the trade, as well as for the good name of this Government and its armed forces that any specific examples of looting of works of art or cultural materials be brought to light as soon as possible.[72]

Leading professional journals echoed that plea, warning collectors to think twice before acquiring dubious manuscripts from returning servicemen:

> Dealers are again urged to use extreme caution before purchasing books and manuscripts, which show the slightest evidence of having been looted from European libraries (both private and public) and offered for sale in this country by returning veterans. ... Looted books are coming into the country, and the American dealer will do well to check all possibilities before paying cash for an item that may at some future time become a source of embarrassment or argument. ... Ethics aside, the matter can be reduced to ... dollars and cents. The dealer who buys a stolen book may find himself in the sad position of having neither the book nor the investment.[73]

---

70 *The Pierpont Morgan Library, 1941–1948*, 17.

71 Sol Chaneles, "The Great Betrayal," *Art & Antiques*, December (1987): 93–103.

72 "File Ms. of Hildebrandslied from Kassel," ... American Commission for the Protection and Salvage of Artistic and Historic Monuments in War Areas. To Museums, Art and Antique Dealers, and Auction Houses. Undated circular.

73 Jacob Blanck, "News from the Rare Booksellers," *Publisher's Weekly* 150, no. 8 (1946): 837–

THE AMERICAN COMMISSION FOR THE PROTECTION AND SALVAGE OF ARTISTIC AND HISTORIC MONUMENTS IN WAR AREAS

Owen J. Roberts, *Chairman*
David E. Finley, *Vice Chairman*
Huntington Cairns, *Secretary*
Charles H. Sawyer, *Assistant Secretary*
William Bell Dinsmoor
Herbert H. Lehman
Paul J. Sachs
Archbishop F. J. Spellman
Francis Henry Taylor
John Walker, *Special Adviser*
Sumner McK. Crosby, *Special Adviser*

OFFICE OF THE SECRETARY
NATIONAL GALLERY OF ART
WASHINGTON 25, D. C.

TO MUSEUMS, ART AND ANTIQUE DEALERS AND AUCTION HOUSES:

This Commission has had numerous reports of objects being offered to museums and to the trade by present and former members of the armed forces. Where the source or origin of these objects may be obscure or suspicious and where the objects may be of special artistic importance, the Commission would appreciate being informed of the facts with as full and specific information as possible concerning the objects themselves and the circumstances under which they came to your attention.

The above information will be made available to the Customs and the Foreign Funds Control officials in the Treasury Department for their attention and any further investigation that may be required. The source of the information will be treated as confidential.

It is, of course, obvious that no clear title can be passed on objects that have been looted from public or private collections abroad. We believe, therefore, that it is to the advantage of both public institutions and the trade, as well as for the good name of this Government and its armed forces, that any specific examples of looting of works of art or cultural materials be brought to light as soon as possible.

Fig. 8. Circular issued by the Roberts Commission
(The United States National Archives and Records Administration.)

The Office of Strategic Services, the precursor of the Central Intelligence Agency, also expressed alarm[74] but in the end all had to watch helplessly as the illegal tide washed over the country. Those glorious pieces once owned by the enemy were far too tempting to human greed. Unscrupulous buyers and sellers profited handsomely, and turned a blind eye to the fact that many were obviously pilfered.

On a late November afternoon in 1945, Meta Harrsen, the Morgan Library manuscript specialist, was absorbed in the study of a theological codex, which had been offered to the Library by its longtime supplier, the Rosenbach Company. The technicians had just finished filming the codex, and now, bent over the manuscript, Harrsen was examining its physical appearance, script, and contents. A tenth century Latin theological compendium, she surmised, opening with the *Oratio et preces contra obloquentes*, and continuing with selections from the Old Testament, such as the *Liber Sapientiae Salomonis*, and the *Liber Iesu filii Sirach.* But when she came to the end of the volume, the verso of the last leaf presented her with an unexpected puzzle. The language on this page was no longer Latin and the script was unlike any other in the book. The Morgan Library manuscript expert was dumbfounded, unable to figure out what this strange text could represent.

---

838. Again Blanck, 837: "Dr. Luther S. Evans, Librarian of Congress, in a written statement asserted that 'the problem of loot is naturally one of the most difficult problems we are called upon to face. … It is widely discussed by librarians in private conversations throughout the country, and it has been the subject of repeated discussions with members of the Library of Congress Mission and with representatives of the War Department.' In recognition of the situation the Library of Congress notified its staff on August 8, 1945, that 'among materials reaching the Library from. … Continental Europe (especially from Germany) there may occur instances of books bearing marks, which indicate that they belong to libraries or other institutions of recognized standing. Such books are to be segregated and called to the attention 'of the Library's authorities.'"

[74] Walter V. Robinson, "US tracked WWII influx of looted art. Government did little to prevent sale of works here, files suggest," *Boston Globe, (*May 9, 1997): A1: "The US Office of Strategic Services expressed alarm during the chaos that attended the war's end in 1945 and 1946 that stolen art was being moved from Europe to the United States without any monitoring."
Note: The Office of Strategic Services was established under the Joint Chiefs of Staff by Presidential military order, June 13, 1942. It conducted overt and covert intelligence procurement activities in support of the war against the Axis Powers, analyzed raw intelligence and disseminated finished intelligence to appropriate government agencies. It was abolished in October 1945 (Executive Order 9621) and later was succeeded in part by the Central Intelligence Agency (CIA).

Chapter 10: The Professor

The fine autumnal mist intensified the delicate pink veins that lay hidden in the marble walls of the Morgan. Hunter College Professor Carl Selmer[1] had taken the afternoon off and was headed for the library. A scholar of medieval literature, Selmer's interest centered on the legend of Saint Brendan, the sixth-century Irish abbot, patron saint of sailors.[2] He had published extensively on the subject, and the Saint had returned the favor by gently watching over him during his travels over the high seas.

More than two decades earlier, in the early nineteen-twenties, Selmer had been forced to leave his native Bavaria. The enormous reparation payments imposed on his country by the First World War victors had led to huge unemployment and rabid inflation. Selmer's doctorate in the humanities had failed to secure him any teaching position. Jobs went by seniority to older war veterans, and although Selmer boasted a bullet-wound under his arm, a painful souvenir of his own tour of duty, his employment number was never called. With money earned from odd jobs, he managed to buy a ring and proposed to his childhood sweetheart, Rose Baur. For their honeymoon, the young couple biked over the Alps to Italy.

It was at Saint Boniface, a Benedictine monastery where the newlyweds stopped for a meal, that a padre mentioned to Selmer the need for teachers in Brazil, a country with an open immigration policy. That casual comment prompted the Selmers to sell their belongings, ask for Saint Brendan's benediction, and sail to Rio de Janeiro. After a difficult journey at sea, and a two-hundred-mile trek through the jungle, the Selmers arrived in the village of Santa Cruz, on the coffee plantation of Senhor Mario Souza de Queiroz. There, Carl took over the education of the owner's four boys and Rose tutored the younger daughter. Conditions in Santa Cruz were primitive. The Selmers lived in a shed, sharing quarters with a cantankerous donkey. Wages were low and often nonexistent, the food was poor and the water unsanitary. One year later with seventy-five dollars saved for a one way ticket to the United States, Selmer took a mule-taxi to town, boarded a train for Rio, and from there booked a third class passage to New York. Rose remained behind.

---

1 Irene Selmer Griffith, daughter of Professor Carl Selmer, has generously provided the author with biographical information about her father. The details of this chapter are closely based on memoirs written by Professor Selmer for his family just before his death in 1972.

2 Selmer authored a series of articles on the legend of Saint Brendan. The Irish monk is said to have sailed in search of the Land of Promise, accompanied by a historically fluctuating number of followers (some put the number as high as one-hundred and fifty). After seven years the pilgrims are said to have reached their destination. Geographers are uncertain as to where exactly Saint Brendan and his entourage set foot.

On board conditions were dreadful, but the amiable Selmer befriended a group of Irishmen and used the time well to improve his halting English. After seventeen days at sea, Ellis Island beckoned with hope and a first drink of clean water. He had in his breast pocket a list of German names, people who might be persuaded to vouch for a newcomer. Of all contacted, only a New Jersey house painter responded to his appeal. Selmer hurried to the immigration hearing eager to face the judge and meet his sponsor. On his way he lost a heel from his only pair of shoes. Stopping to look for it meant risking his chance for admission. Limping, he forged on.

Beginnings were difficult. In Newark, New Jersey he found a job in a chemical factory. Sundays he played the organ in church and saved the five dollars for Rose's ticket. He lived frugally and in time to amassed the $ 200 needed to bring his wife over in style. Once Rose was at his side his luck turned and he landed a position with Hunter College, as professor of German literature. Research and publishing were as always requirements for retention and advancement. After tutoring in the jungle and working with fetid chemicals, the return to reading and teaching was a divine intellectual joy. At the Morgan Library, his splendid home away from home, he could truly indulge his passion. He had befriended the library's specialist in incunabula, curator Curt Ferdinand Bühler. Their discussions had already resulted in a published article.[3] To Selmer's delight, a second paper, on a secular medieval play, was about to be completed.[4]

That late November afternoon in 1945, Selmer arrived eager to resume work on their article. Curator Bühler and Professor Selmer made a good team. Selmer was forty-nine to Bühler's forty. Selmer was from Bavaria, a region well known to Bühler since he had studied in Munich. Dignified and charmingly polite, Selmer was well liked for his convivial humor and easy-going nature. His friends admired his unusual language skills and encyclopedic knowledge and called him affectionately *The Professor*.[5] In addition to French, Italian, Spanish, Portuguese, Old and Middle High German, he was well versed in Latin, Greek, and Hebrew.

Curator Bühler, in contrast, was quietly reserved, ambitious, and doggedly persistent, traits that had earned him from Belle da Costa Greene the backhanded

---

[3] Curt F. Bühler and Carl Selmer, "An Unpublished Middle High German Banntaidig," *PMLA, Publications of the Modern Language Association* 60, no. 1, part 1 (1945): 325–39.

[4] Curt F. Bühler and Carl Selmer, "The Melk Salbenkrämerspiel. An Unpublished Middle High German Mercator Play," *PMLA, Publications of the Modern Language Association* 63, no. 1 (1948): 21–63.

[5] Irene Selmer Griffith, electronic-mail correspondence with the author of November 10, 2000, deposited with the University of California, Davis, Shields Library, Department of Special Collections.

Fig. 16. Dr. Carl Selmer
(Courtesy of Irene Griffith Selmer)

compliment of "that mule in sheep's clothing."[6] As with Selmer, German classical verses and Greek and Latin locutions rolled off Bühler's tongue with ease. Bühler was well regarded in scholarly circles for his fine work on medieval texts and for his writings on the intellectual activity of the fifteenth and sixteenth century. Dr. Rosenbach, who enjoyed mentoring younger talent, had noticed the scholarly curator and had extended him an invitation to teach under the aegis of his University of Pennsylvania lecture series, the prestigious A. S. W. Rosenbach Fellowship in Bibliography Program.[7] Moreover, Bühler had been invited to contribute to the *Festschrift* prepared in Rosenbach's honor, for his upcoming seventieth birthday. The roster of celebrities honoring the Doctor read like a who's who in the world of bibliophiles.[8] For all this special attention, Bühler must have felt deeply grateful to Dr. Rosenbach, the patriarch of the rare book trade.

But on that late November afternoon, Bühler was somewhat disinclined to resume work with Selmer on their medieval play. He was engrossed in the study of an old codex, the *Liber Sapientiae Solomonis*. It had been offered to the Morgan for $10,000. Manuscripts were not Bühler's forte. He specialized in early printed books. He had been called to assist his colleague Meta Harrsen, who was struggling with the codex's last leaf. The text on that leaf appeared to be completely unrelated to any of the other religious passages of the volume. Fluent in German and experienced in historical linguistics, Harrsen and Bühler had already established that the text was written in an archaic Germanic language. It was most likely inconsequential, a filler of sorts, a deed or some other legal document. They invited Selmer to have a look and venture an opinion.

Intrigued, Selmer sat down to study the odd text.[9] With some difficulty he began deciphering the script on the faded parchment: "*hiltibraht. obana ab hevane dat du neo dana halt mit sus / sippan man dinc ni gileitos. want her do ar arme wuntana / bauga cheisuringu gitan. so imo se der chuning gap / Huneo truhtin. dat ih dir it nu· bi huldi gibu. hadubraht / gimalta hiltibrantes sunu. mit geru scal man geba infa / han ort widar orte.* ... The language was Old High German. It told of a father who was offering golden armbands to his hostile, belligerent son. Hiltibraht, Hadubraht. Selmer knew these verses quite well from his university days in Frei-

---

6 Curt F. Bühler, *Early Books and Manuscripts: Forty Years of Research* (New York: Grolier Club & The Pierpont Morgan Library, 1973), 517.

7 Curt F. Bühler, "Incunabula," in: *Standards of Bibliographical Description,* Curt F. Bühler, James G. McManaway, and Lawrence C. Wroth, eds. (Philadelphia: University of Pennsylvania Press, 1949), 3–51.

8 *To Doctor R. Essays Here Collected and Published in Honor of the Seventieth Birthday of Dr. A. S. W. Rosenbach, July 22, 1946* (Philadelphia: [s.n.], 1946), 55–60.

9 The passage describing the discovery of the *Hildebrandslied* is closely based on Carl Selmer's article "Wie ich das Hildebrandslied in Amerika wiederfand" (How I found the Hildebrandslied in America), *Wirkendes Wort* 6, no. 2 (1955/56): 122–25.

burg. This was the *Hildebrandslied.* Yet Selmer could not imagine that a German library would ever consider selling this "sanctissimum sanctorum." It had to be a forgery, for Selmer remembered distinctly that only one copy of the ballad existed, and that this unique relic of the Germanic past was preserved in a library in Kassel.

What he had before him were the last known lines of the poem. He began looking for the opening verse, the one he had learned by heart as a schoolboy, the familiar *Ik gihorta dat seggen.* ... I once heard it said. ... Leaf by leaf, beginning to end, Selmer examined the codex. The first part of the ballad was missing. Yet as he was turning the pages, the eighth leaf appeared loose. In a gathering, the eighth leaf corresponds to the first.[10] Harrsen, Bühler and Selmer looked closely at the gathering. There at the fold was a precise cut, a visible incision executed by a skilled, steady hand.[11] Now it all became clear. The first leaf of the codex with the opening verses of the *Hildebrandslied* had been identified and removed. The mutilator, however, had been either ignorant, in a hurry, or sloppy for he had not discovered the last leaf. Selmer returned to this text. While he was no expert, codex, vellum, and script appeared genuine. The more he looked, the more convinced he became that this was the original. With reverence he cradled in his arms this precious manuscripts, the song that marked the birth of German literary history, the one he reverently called *das heilige Hildebrandslied*, the sacred Song of Hildebrand.[12]

While Selmer was overcome with emotion, Meta Harrsen and Curt Bühler set out methodically in search of proof of authenticity. Selmer had told them that the codex belonged to a library in Kassel. It was only a matter of time until they located a description of the manuscript holdings of Kassel State Library. From the shelves of their rich reference collection they pulled Wilhelm Hopf's study on the *Landesbibliothek.* The librarian who had watched over the codex in peace and peril was now testifying over space and time to the legitimacy of his stolen ward: "theological compendium ... parchment manuscript. ... Twenty-eight and one half by twenty-one cm. ... leaf 1 (recto) and 76 (verso) display the well-known text of the *Hildebrandslied,* ... continuous in prose. ... Carolingian minuscule with insular influences ... inscribed by two monks. ... The first leaf starts with *Ik*

---

10 Commonly codices were put together in a quaternion, which is a gathering consisting of four vellum sheets folded once. The first and eighth, second and seventh, third and sixth, and fourth and fifth leaves are conjoined.

11 "Hildebrandlied 1," documents from the archives of the Gesamthochschul-Bibliothek Kassel – Landesbibliothek und Murhardsche Bibliothek der Stadt Kassel, deposited with the University of California, Davis, Shields Library, Department of Special Collections. Letter from D. Hennig to J. Kalkbrenner, 25 January 1971 and also Letter from D. Hennig to W. F. Twaddell, May 27, 1974.

12 Selmer, 123.

gihorta and ends with *irmingot quad* … the second begins with *hiltibraht obana ab hevane* and brings the text to its conclusion. …"[13] The description matched the text before them. There could be no doubt. This Rosenbach offering was the famous product of the Fulda scriptorium, the one created more then eleven centuries ago, the one preserved for more than two hundred years in the Kassel State Library.[14] It had been obviously looted and callously mutilated.

Meta Harrsen and Curt Bühler were mystified. It was surprising that the learned Doctor would fail to recognize this well-known codex. It was inconceivable that a man of his fame and stature would trade in stolen merchandise. It was unimaginable that the bibliophile A.S.W.R. would cripple an ancient text. And yet before them was the looted Kassel codex, displaying its ugly scar. Meta Harrsen refused to believe that Dr. Rosenbach would ever deface a manuscript. If anyone, she suspected John Fleming, the bookstore manager, who, in her opinion, was an accomplished businessman, but less than experienced where medieval manuscripts were concerned.[15]

Director Belle da Costa Greene and her two learned librarians had a political, professional, and moral dilemma on their hands. It went without saying that Belle would never consider buying a stolen codex. But what must have made the situation awkward, was that the seller was Belle's ailing, long-time friend and Bühler's influential mentor. The Morgan Library had a responsibility to the dealer, who had placed this precious codex in its trust. However, allegiance and friendship aside, the library had an obligation to protect the codex and assist in its return.

The librarians were looking at four ways to handle this awkward situation, and none of them satisfactory. The first option was for the Morgan Library to impound the codex and alert the authorities. It was the proper thing to do, but it could cause irreparable harm. Seizure and indictment would create an international incident and damage the already tarnished reputation of the rare booktrade, not to mention the standing of the Rosenbach firm. Moreover, it was no secret that Doctor Rosenbach had lent his name to the President's commission on war-displaced books. He was implicitly one of the architects of the US policy

---

13 Wilhelm Hopf, editor, *Die Landesbibliothek Kassel, 1580–1930* (The Kassel State Library: 1580–1930) (Marburg: N. G. Elwert, 1930), part 2, 31–35. Gustav Struck wrote the chapter on the manuscript collection.

14 "File Ms. of Hildebrandslied From Kassel," US Department of State, records maintained by the Fine Arts and Monuments Adviser, 1945–61, Ardelia Hall Collection, Record Group 59. Lot 62D4, Box 6, Item 2, National Archives and Records Administration. Letter of the Supervising Customs Agent at New York to the Commissioner of Customs, Division of Investigations, Bureau of Customs, Washington, DC, June 13, 1952.

15 "Hildebrandlied 1," documents from the archives … File note, 24 February 1956, signed W. von Both.

on restitution of trophy-art, duty and honor-bound to enforce it. Not only was his name and reputation on the line but also the prestige of the Roberts Commission, and by extension that of the United States Government.

A second option was to return the codex to the Rosenbach Company and follow up with a public announcement. There was danger in this strategy as well. To save face, the firm could destroy the codex and, if still in its possession, the severed first leaf as well. Option number three was to forego any public announcement, simply return the codex to the Rosenbach Company, describe the significance of the last leaf, and mention that the codex had been looted. Knowing that the Morgan librarians had identified the book as war-booty might shame the rare-book firm into returning the codex and its severed leaf to Kassel.

Judging by the asking price, a relatively modest $10,000, the Doctor had not recognized the enormous importance of the manuscript. If the Morgan Library were to reject it without mentioning the *Hildebrandslied* leaf at the back of the book, the Rosenbach Company might simply turn around and try placing it with another customer. Once the codex was sold, a notice would most certainly appear in the trade press. Then, knowing that the codex was out of the dealer's hands, the Morgan Library could discreetly contact the buyer and arrange for the return of the volume. This last course of action however ignored the fate of the detached Leaf One.

After serious consideration, the librarians decided to go with this last option: return the codex to the Rosenbach Company without disclosing the existence of the last leaf, and watch for a purchase announcement in the trade press. Selmer was alarmed. He did not want to see the codex vanish again. It was far too risky. But in the end he had no say. He was a non-voting bystander who happened to be in the right place at exactly the right time. Reluctantly he handed over his treasure, knowing full well that it was facing an uncertain future, worried that the *Hildebrandslied* might disappear forever.

The codex was returned to the Rosenbach Company on December 11, 1945, with a crisp business letter signed by Curt Bühler[16] but undoubtedly authorized by director Belle da Costa Greene. In it, Bühler confirmed the receipt of the *Liber Sapientiae Solomonis*, a codex submitted for purchase to the Pierpont Morgan Library by the Rosenbach Company. Intense study of the manuscript had identified it as an early creation of the Fulda scriptorium and as the lawful property of the State Library in Kassel. Methodically Bühler went on citing all reference sources he had used to establish its provenance and legal ownership. In closing he emphasized that this manuscript was of great importance to scholars throughout

---

16 "File Ms. of Hildebrandslied from Kassel." Letter of the Supervising Customs Agent at New York to the Commissioner of Customs, Division of Investigations, Bureau of Customs, Washington, DC, June 13, 1952.

the world and that he, Bühler, felt compelled to share this knowledge with the dealer. The verses of the *Hildebrandslied* written on the back of the last leaf were never mentioned. Nor did Bühler make any reference to a missing Leaf One and a loose leaf eight.[17] The letter sternly warned the House of Rosenbach that this manuscript was very valuable and that it was very hot.

One week later,[18] a laconic retort from the dealer attempted to dispel all suspicions. It claimed that the Rosenbach Company had acquired the manuscript legally in the 1930s. The Nazis had sold it to the firm.[19]

---

17 The missing first leaf, with the opening verses of the *Hildebrandlied*, will be henceforth identified as Leaf One.

18 "File Ms. of Hildebrandslied from Kassel," Letter of A. Hall to S. Stephens, April 29, 1952 and handwritten notes. Ardelia refers to the Rosenbach letter as being dated December 19, 1945.

19 There are several documents referring to Rosenbach's statement that he bought the manuscript in the 1930s from the Nazis. See, for instance: "File Ms. of Hildebrandslied from Kassel," Letter of A. Hall to E. Breitenbach, HICOG, Bonn, February 5, 1952; "Hildebrandlied 1," documents from the archives. ... Reply of E. Breitenbach to A. Hall, February 11, 1952, and Letter of A. Hall to E.H. Schwenk, 24 November 1953.

Chapter 11: The Countess of Camarillo

"But, Mr. Rosenbach," Mrs. Doheny objected gently, "you just wrote me a letter quoting this very manuscript for a third of that figure."[1] Lucille Miller, Countess Doheny's longtime secretary,[2] went off in search of the incriminating quote. Caught red-handed, Philip Rosenbach squirmed uncomfortably in his chair. Surely, he whimpered, there must be a clerical error. The Rosenbach Firm would never ... In a flash he saw his lucrative dealings with the wealthy bibliophile shatter in a million shards of broken trust. John Fleming swallowed noisily, trying to regain his composure. Philip's legendary cupidity had, once again, triumphed over caution. The septuagenarian papal countess[3] might have been blind,[4] but when it came to business, she still had a keen grasp of figures.

It was March 1950, and Number Eight Chester Place, the palatial Doheny residence in Los Angeles, surrounded by flowering gardens, looked more inviting than ever.[5] The twenty-two room Gothic Renaissance mansion,[6] with its round

---

1 The almost farcical scene of the *Liber Sapientiae* sale to Mrs. Doheny is gleaned from Edwin Wolf 2nd and John F. Fleming, *Rosenbach: A Biography* (Cleveland: World Publishing Company, 1960), 570–71.

2 Lucile V. Miller, "Edward and Estelle Doheny," *The Ventura County Historical Society Quarterly* 6, no. 1 (1960): 12.
Note: Lucille Miller, the Countess's secretary and librarian, had been in Mrs. Doheny's service since 1931.

3 Ibid., 9 and 12: "In recognition of their service to the Church, Pope Pius XI conferred on Mr. and Mrs. Doheny the title of Knight and Lady of the Equestrian Order of the Holy Sepulchre. ... In 1939 the Most Reverend John J. Cantwell, then Archbishop of Los Angeles and an old friend of her husband's, called on Mrs. Doheny to tell her that His Holiness Pope Pius XII had elevated her to the rank of Papal Countess." See also Francis J. Weber, *Southern California's First Family: The Dohenys of Los Angeles* (Fullerton, California: Lorson's Books and Prints, 1993), 30: "On June 29, 1939, Pope Pius XII conferred upon Carrie Estelle Doheny the unusual distinction (for an American) of Papal Countess."

4 Ibid., 17–18: "On her birthday, August the second, 1944, while she was kneeling at Mass in her private chapel she suffered a severe hemorrhage of her left eye. The sight of that eye was lost immediately and the right eye began to show symptoms of glaucoma."

5 The date of the transaction remains uncertain. See: "File Ms. of Hildebrandslied from Kassel," US Department of State, records maintained by the Fine Arts and Monuments Adviser, 1945–61, Ardelia Hall Collection, Record Group 59. Lot 62D4, Box 6, Item 2, National Archives and Records Administration. Letter of the Supervising Customs Agent at New York, June 13, 1952 to the Commissioner of Customs, Division of Investigations, Bureau of Customs, Washington, DC. Here Philip Rosenbach remembers the date of the sale as being January 1949, but has no records to substantiate his claim. William Freeman Twaddell, "The Hildebrandlied Manuscript in the U.S.A., 1945–1972," *Journal of English and Germanic Philology* 73, no. 2 (1974): 164, quoting a letter of Mary Gayle, at the time Librarian of the Estelle Doheny Collection of Saint John's Seminary in Camarillo, California, also states that the manuscripts were brought to Los Angeles in January 1949. However, Wolf 2nd, 571, who

solarium, grand ballroom, and private chapel revealed its treasures at every turn: royal porcelain, paintings of old masters, rare oriental rugs, fine old silver, elegant period furniture, each piece a worthy addition to any museum. Philip Rosenbach, the consummate New York antique dealer, must have felt right at home.

Like the swallows of San Juan Capistrano,[7] the Rosenbach envoys had returned to Southern California with the first breath of spring, suitcases laden with tempting rarities. Their target was a most extravagant client: Countess Carrie Estelle, the wealthy and pious widow of oil magnate Edward L. Doheny. This sales trip, however, was unlike all others, for this time the urbane Doctor R was absent. Regrettably, Philip explained, a nearly fatal attack had taken the Doctor out of commission.[8] Philip however, flanked by John Fleming, was at the Countess's service, ready and eager to tempt her with a fresh array of choice books. At eighty-six Brother Philip, or Doctor P as he now preferred to be called, exuded dignity, confidence, and vitality.[9] He was using A. S. W. R.'s academic title, convinced that in this line of work success was determined by nothing more than a flashy scholarly epithet wrapped in clever marketing skills.[10]

Mrs. Doheny had taken up collecting in the 1920s,[11] a fashionable hobby for people in her social circles. Like most amateurs, she had started with an array of pretty books, attractive glass paperweights, and volumes with fore-edge paint-

---

based his Rosenbach biography on invoices from the Rosenbach archives, dates the trip to spring of 1950. In "Hildebrandlied 2," documents from the archives of the Gesamthochschul-Bibliothek Kassel – Landesbibliothek und Murhardsche Bibliothek der Stadt Kassel, deposited with the University of California, Davis, Shields Library, Department of Special Collections, Letter of D. Hennig to W. F. Twaddell, May 27, 1974, Dr. Hennig mentions a penciled note discovered in the codex, which reads *Rosenbach 3/50*. This date, March 1950, is believed to be the actual date of the sale.

6 Weber, Francis J. *Southern California's First Family*, 102.

7 The famous birds leave their eighteenth-century Mission home, at the San Juan Capistrano in California, every October 23 and fly 6000 miles south to Argentina. They return on March 19. Their perfectly timed homecoming is greeted each spring by the sound of peeling bells, and joyous celebrations.

8 Wolf 2nd, 570: "During this period of great activity Dr. Rosenbach spent most of his time in and out of the hospital. After he recovered from his almost fatal attack during the past summer, he returned to the hospital with a severe case of arthritis."

9 Ibid., 572: "Philip was a phoenix rising from the dying embers of his brother's career."

10 Ibid., 573: "Philip Rosenbach was at heart a merchant. He had no conception of the motives that led a collector to overspend. He never had an inner desire for, or a conviction of, the great objects of culture. They were all 'goods of the trade' and payable in due course."

11 Francis J. Weber and Josephine Arlyn Bruccoli, "Carrie Estelle Doheny (2 August 1875–30 October 1958)," in: *American Book Collectors and Bibliographers. First Series.* Editor Joseph Rosenblum, Dictionary of Literary Biography, vol. 140 (Detroit: Gale, 1994), 64.

ings.[12] Forever alert to wealthy novices entering the field, Dr. R had zoomed in on the Countess and had showered her with his unique brand of courteous attention. He had gently introduced her to basic principles of book collecting[13] and had patiently indulged her penchant for religious texts and Catholic classics. The shrewdly accommodating dealer had nursed her along, alerting her to fine copies coming up for sale, advising her on bidding, and luring her with those seductive catalog descriptions composed by Millicent Sowerby with the countess in mind.[14] He was unsurpassed in convincing his occasionally reluctant client that money was completely unimportant compared to the joy of offering a true bibliophile a rare and precious book. Over the years he had helped Mrs. Doheny expand her interests beyond religious texts to Medieval and Renaissance manuscripts, incunabula, Americana, fine bindings, and historical documents of distinction.[15] The resourceful Doctor had succeeded in keeping the Countess's bibliophile interests alive long past her decision to donate all her collections to the Doheny Memorial Library of the Saint John's Seminary in Camarillo, California. This delicate high-wire act of salesmanship, showmanship, and scholarship, this uniquely Rosenbach mixture of skill and magic was now about to explode in Brother Philip's bewildered face.

Five years had passed since Belle da Costa Greene had rejected the Kassel codex and had obliquely alerted the House of Rosenbach that it was dealing in stolen property. Philip must have decided that this was a sufficiently long cooling period for the hot manuscript.[16] But after the mishap at the Morgan Library the new

---

12 Miller, 13: "The term refers to a book with a water-color painting – perhaps a landscape, a cathedral, or even a portrait – on the front, or 'fore-edge' of the leaves, The painting is applied with the leaves spread or 'fanned' to make a solid surface. The edges of the leaves are then gilded so that the painting is invisible, when the book is closed."

13 Wolf 2nd, 361: "... the magic of Doctor Rosenbach and his amazing books taught champagne tastes to one who could well afford champagne, but who, because no one had ever offered it to her before, had been drinking beer."

14 E. Millicent Sowerby, *Rare People and Rare Books* (London: Constable, 1967), 191–92. Sowerby purposely slanted all her descriptions of religious books to match the Countess's predilections and sensibilities: "So long as I knew who was the prospective customer," she wrote, "and what were his or her particular interests, I could generally guarantee to sell the book by the descriptions."

15 Donald C. Dickinson, "Robert O. Schad: A Treasure of a Bookman," *Southern California Quarterly* 81, no. 2 (1999): 225: "A. S. W. Rosenbach continued to supply books in a never ending stream."

16 See Twaddell (1974), 164. In a letter dated January 25, 1972 Professor Twaddell wrote to Mary Gayle, Librarian of the Estelle Doheny Collection suggesting the possibility "that Philip could have been unaware of the earlier correspondence (Note: that is, the rejection letter written by Bühler) about the American history of the codex and the manuscript." In her reply of August 22, 1973 Gayle asserted: "I'd be very much surprised, basing my judgment on written and oral comments of others' memories of the events, if Mr. Philip Rosenbach was unaware of Dr. Rosenbach's attempt to sell the manuscript to the Morgan Library."

client had to be more carefully selected. Philip and Fleming had set their sight on the Countess of Camarillo.

Indeed, for many reasons, Carrie Estelle Doheny appeared to be the perfect buyer. The Countess was partial to block purchases. This enabled Philip to offer the codex within a group of other fine selections, making it less conspicuous. Mrs. Doheny was also known to favor religious works, and this early theological compendium with devout selections suited her taste to perfection. Furthermore, it was less risky to offer the manuscript to an eager amateur than to a punctilious institutional buyer, bent on tracing history and provenance. And finally, all of Mrs. Doheny's new book selections went straight to the Treasure Room of the Doheny Memorial Library at Saint John's Seminary, an establishment without professional curator.[17] Stringent restrictions made that Treasure Room practically inaccessible. Scholars, researchers, and priests were allowed to enter the library only twice a year by appointment, seminary students on Visitor's Day only.[18] One could not have invented a safer place for a potentially embarrassing codex.

On that lovely spring day Philip had brought along a cluster of splendors and had displayed them artistically on the table, before the sightless eyes of the Countess. There were the famous tenth-century *Liesborn Gospels* in polychrome oak covers, the fourteenth-century *Bible Hystoriale* with elegant miniatures, several Dürer woodcuts and rare indulgences, a copy of the 1465 *Lactantius*, one of the earliest dated books printed in Italy, and finally, a venerable German theological codex called *Liber Sapientiae Solomonis*. While Philip and Fleming awaited Lucille's return in mortified silence, Mrs. Doheny cautiously reached out and lightly touched the smooth vellum leaf of one of the open manuscript before her. "The crisp, live texture ... thrilled her, and her face lit up with appreciation."[19]

---

17 Weber, Francis J. *Southern California's First Family*, 73.
Note: Robert O. Schad, "The Estelle Doheny Collection," *The New Colophon: A Book-Collectors' Miscellany* 3, no. 9 (1950): 232, explains that at the time there was a librarian *in situ*. But this librarian was solely responsible for the 35,000-volume reference collections belonging to the Seminary Library proper and had nothing to do with the manuscripts in the Doheny Library. Only years later, in 1958, was Lucille Miller hired as special curator of the Estelle Doheny Collection, which was housed on the second floor of the Doheny Memorial Library, an altogether separate building on the Seminary campus.

18 Weber, Francis J. *Southern California's First Family*, 69, 72–73: "Among the raft of directions handed out to our class upon its arrival at Saint John's Seminary ... was a page about library facilities which concluded with these words: 'The Estelle Doheny Collection may be viewed by students on Sunday afternoons by appointment. Please do not ask for that privilege more than twice each academic year. Students were discouraged, scholars restricted and visitors limited in using or even looking at the treasures."

19 Dickinson, 237–38. This description of tactile beatitude refers to Mrs. Doheny's opening of her newly acquired Gutenberg Bible, as remembered by Lucille V. Miller.

Fig. 17. The Doheny Memorial Library – St. John's Seminary, Camarillo, California. (Photograph taken by the author)

At last Lucille returned brandishing the calamitous letter. But just as the second shoe was about to drop the cloud of suspicion disintegrated. Mrs. Doheny dismissed the incident as an oversight, granted the sinners absolution, and graciously handed Philip a check for $ 81,000.[20] Before taking possession of the lot, the meticulous Lucille annotated the invoice, assigning each item an approximate price. The *Liber Sapientiae* clocked in at $ 9,500.[21] As always, the new basket of rarities was dispatched fifty miles north, to the Treasure Room of the Saint John's Seminary Library. Philip and John Fleming returned to New York in high spirits. They had made a handsome profit on their $ 1,000 investment.

At Saint John's, seminarian Francis J. Weber enjoyed a reputation of clandestine bibliophile and closet historian.[22] Night after night, Francis, in violation of

[20] While Wolf 2nd, 571, quoted the price as $ 85,000, Twaddell, (1974), 164, established that it was, in fact, $ 81,000.

[21] Twaddell (1974), 159 citing a December 20, 1972 letter from Mary Gayle, Librarian of the Estelle Doheny Collection of St. John's Seminary in Camarillo, California: "There is a notation with the invoice [to Mrs. Doheny] indicating that the Sydrach was probably valued at $ 9,500." See also: Archdiocese of Los Angeles, Archival Center, Estelle Doheny Collection, deposited with the University of California, Davis, Shields Library, Department of Special Collections. Letter of Mary Gayle to F. Weber, November 14, 1972.

[22] The author would like to express her gratitude to Monsignor Francis J. Weber, the former rebellious seminarian and nocturnal bibliophile, and current Archivist of the Catholic Arch-

house rules, sought entrance to the Treasure Room of the Doheny Memorial Library. Alone in the quiet twilight of the deserted building, he studied the magnificent books and rare documents, admired the rich European tapestries, and marveled at the assorted art objects donated by the Countess. Francis made copious notes in his diary, dreaming that one day his furtive observations would see the light of print.

> The Treasure Room [he noted] houses one of the finest small collections of rare books and manuscripts in the world. The room itself is paneled in walnut, with recessed shelves, protected by bronze grilles. ... The early manuscripts, chief glory of the Estelle Doheny Collection, are stored in a specially constructed vault. ... There are bibles, gospels, commentaries, liturgical works, and a group of richly ornamented books of hours.[23]

Before Francis had a chance to complete the *opus bibliographicum*, his nocturnal escapades were discovered. The seminarian was called on the carpet, accused of being deceptive, presumptuous and proud, and his notebooks were confiscated. For a while it even looked as if Francis would be clipped from orders.[24] The very idea of publishing a bibliographic essay on the Doheny collections was rejected as mortal heresy. The seminary fathers abhorred publicity, which, in their estimation, resulted in throngs of people walking on the grass and picking the flowers.[25] Fate and the clergy seemed to conspire to keep the Doheny collection shielded from prying eyes.[26]

But only months after Philip and Fleming's return from the West Coast, the hiding place of the *Hildebrandslied* was unexpectedly revealed. The announcement came in the form of a paragraph imbedded in a long, scholarly article, published in the 1950 swan-song edition of an esoteric journal called *The New Colophon.*[27] Written by Robert Oliver Schad, Curator of Rare Books at the Huntington Library, the article highlighted recent additions to the Doheny collection. Thirty-one other contributors were featured in this final issue. One of

---

diocese of Los Angeles, for information regarding the sale and return of the *Liber Sapientiae.*

23 Francis J. Weber, *Southern California's First Family*, 42–45.

24 Ibid., 69–71.

25 Ibid., 71.

26 In her March 1, 2002 telephone conversation with the author, Ms. Rita Faulders, the last Doheny Librarian (1980–1988) explained that during her tenure this restrictive policy was lifted. In the 1980s the collections were opened to all seminarians. The library welcomed scholars and visitors from all over the world.

27 *The New Colophon: A Book-Collector's Miscellany.* Duschnes Crawford published the journal in New York, between 1948 and 1950. For the first two years (issue number one through eight), the journal appeared quarterly. The 1950 last volume, known as number nine, was an annual.

them was Curt F. Bühler, Keeper of Printed Books at the Morgan Library.[28] Did Bühler have advance notice of the smoldering charge embedded in Schad's elegant prose?

Robert Oliver Schad was a friend of Mrs. Doheny's. An orphan at seventeen, he had been forced to drop out of school and work as an apprentice cataloger in the private New York library of Henry E. Huntington.[29] His intelligence, his organizational skills, and pleasant personality had made him indispensable to the wealthy collector.[30] When Huntington moved his library to San Marino in California, Schad followed. For the rest of his life he organized exhibitions and lectures, participated in conservation efforts, compiled bibliographies, and acted as the library's principal liaison to booksellers, researchers, and donors.[31]

One of Schad's important donor friends was Countess Carrie Estelle Doheny. The curator was a frequent guest at Number Eight Chester Place. The Countess had come to rely on his advice regarding book-prices, editions, and auctions. Schad, himself of Catholic faith, had been heavily involved in Mrs. Doheny's decision to deed her rare books to the Archdiocese of Los Angeles and to build a memorial library in the name of her husband on the grounds of the Saint John's Seminary in Camarillo. Occasionally, he helped the Countess showcase her acquisitions, a social affair, which delighted the wealthy collector. On May 6, 1950, the day marking the tenth anniversary of the Doheny Memorial Library, Schad secured permission from the Countess to show her rare books to a group of fellow bibliophiles. Acting as guide, he introduced his learned friends to some of its most dazzling additions. It was a memorable event and the gracious Countess agreed to let Schad publish his scholarly remarks in the bibliophile journal, *The New Colophon.*

Schad's essay opened with a poetic description of the hallowed seminary grounds:

> High on a sunny hilltop overlooking the Pacific Ocean, surrounded by fragrant orange groves and mantled by the serene calm of a religious community stands a small, jewel-like building that contains one of the notable collections of manuscripts and rare books in the United States. ... The Doheny Memorial Library is a quiet oasis in a world of turmoil, a seemly and secure sanctuary for the preservation of worthy books.[32]

---

28 Curt F. Bühler, "A Fifteenth-Century List of Recommended Books", *The New Colophon: A Book-Collector's Miscellany* 9 (1950): 49–54.

29 Biographical details on Robert Oliver Schad are based on Donald C. Dickinson's article.

30 Dickinson, 228, citing a letter of Henry Huntington to Elisabeth Brock (November 21, 1922) in which he calls Schad "a treasure of a book-man. One who would treat books right because he loves them."

31 Ibid., 235 mentions that one of these invited speakers was A. S. W. Rosenbach.

32 Schad, 229–30.

Of the 7,000 early manuscripts, Bibles, gospels, commentaries, liturgical works, and illuminated books of hours housed in the seminary vault,[33] Schad singled out a mere handful, those acquired in recent years, and described them chronologically by their date of creation. First featured was the ninth-century *Moralia of Job*, the earliest writing of Saint Gregory, which, Schad explained, had been lovingly restored with the assistance of Belle da Costa Greene. Next he lingered on a book identified as a Rosenbach offering, the tenth-century *Liesborn Gospels*, bound in uncommon polychrome oak covers. Within that very same paragraph Schad touched lightly on one other rarity:

> Another recent addition is the *Liber Sapientiae Solomonis and Liber Sydrach*, our Books of the Wisdom of Solomon and Ecclesiasticus – also of tenth-century German origin. It has special interest for paleographers, because it is partly written in Irish minuscule, a script rarely encountered in American collections. The remaining part of the text is in Carolingian minuscule.[34]

Only fifty-seven words strung in three sentences were devoted to the codex. The description mimicked the format of a brief bibliographic entry: title and translation, place of origin, presumed date, and script. But there was one glaring omission: there was no contents note, no mention of its most important feature, its very last leaf with the *Hildebrandslied*. Yet Schad's description offered enough detail to make the manuscript instantly recognizable to those looking for it. With no other particulars, the Huntington curator went on highlighting other Doheny treasures.

It remains unclear if the timing of Schad's essay was a fortuitous accident, or the response to a silent alarm sounded by the Belle and her librarians. The homage paid to Belle da Costa Greene and the reference to Rosenbach right before the description of the *Liber Sapientiae* might give a suspicious reader pause. Conceivably, the tightly knit community of rare book lovers was on the lookout for the lost Kassel treasure, and Schad's description was the long-awaited message heralding the resurfacing of the *Hildebrandslied*. Be that as it may, Schad's salvo reverberated from shore to shore. After a hiatus of almost five years, the *Hildebrandslied* had finally come back to light. Across the continent, in a small office at Hunter College, Professor Carl Selmer's heart must have leaped with joy.

---

[33] Miller, 16.

[34] Schad, 233.

Chapter 12: Ardelia

***"Ut Servemus.* That we may be of service."**
Smith College – Motto of the Class of 1922

Mixed in with the daily assortment of State Department correspondence was the much awaited dispatch from Germany: the response to her cable wired a week earlier, on February 5, 1952, to the United States High Commission for Germany, known as HICOG.[1] A new case of trade in looted art had come to Ardelia Hall's attention. This time the alleged war-trophy was an ancient German codex belonging to the *Landesbibliothek* Kassel. She had urgently requested confirmation of loss or theft, and background information on the manuscript.

Responding from the field was Edgar Breitenbach, her colleague of Monuments, Fine Arts and Archives days. This in itself was a good omen. Breitenbach was well regarded in Washington circles for his outstanding intelligence work in Munich and for his strong ties to the German library community. The HICOG dispatch yielded an affidavit in German, marked in capital letters: HILDEBRANDSLIED. It was typed on official library letterhead, signed by two library directors, and authenticated with the seal of the *Landesbibliothek Kassel.* Efficient and considerate, Breitenbach had appended an English translation.

Ardelia Hall had good contacts in Germany, especially among Monuments Officers, her fellow art historians and curators. She had been working closely with them since the waning days of the war.[2] While they struggled to recover Hitler's hidden booty and Germany's evacuated collections she was their voice in Wash-

---

1 "File Ms. of Hildebrandslied from Kassel," US Department of State, records maintained by the Fine Arts and Monument Adviser, 1945–61, Ardelia Hall Collection, Record Group 59. Lot 62D4, Box 6, Item 2, National Archives and Records Administration. Telegram of A. Hall to HICOG-Bonn, February 5, 1952.
Note: The United States High Commission for Germany (HICOG) represented the US Government in post-war Germany. It was established in 1949 by Executive Order 10062. Its predecessor agencies were the US Group Control Council, Germany [USGCC], and The Office of Military Government for Germany [OMGUS], which functioned from October 1945 to September 1949. HICOG was abolished on May 5, 1955. Its successor agency was the Department of State, represented in West Germany by the US Embassy in Bonn.

2 Ely Maurer, "The Role of the State Department Regarding National and Private Claims for the Restitution of Stolen Cultural Property," in: *The Spoils of War: World War II and Its Aftermath: The Loss, Reappearance, and Recovery of Cultural Property,* editor Elizabeth Simpson (New York: H. N. Abrams in association with the Bard Graduate Center for Studies in Decorative Arts, 1997), 142: "Here, I might note that Ardelia Hall, who headed the State Department operation in the early years, was a Monuments, Fine Arts, and Archives adviser to the State Department. She served as an MFA&A officer in Europe and continued in the department, working in close cooperation with her counterparts in Europe."

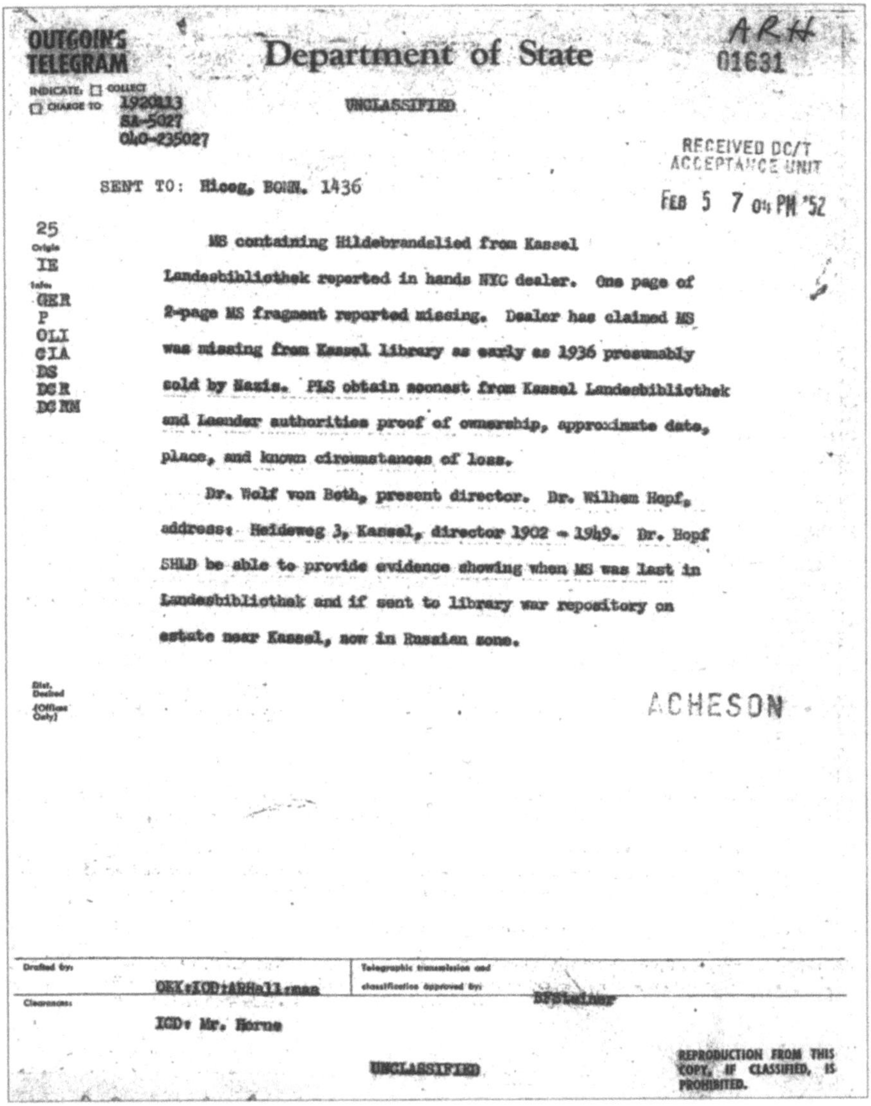

OUTGOING TELEGRAM

Department of State

ARH

01631

INDICATE: ☐ COLLECT
☐ CHARGE TO 1920213
SA-5027
040-235027

UNCLASSIFIED

RECEIVED DC/T
ACCEPTANCE UNIT

FEB 5 7 04 PM '52

SENT TO: Hicog, BONN, 1436

25
Origin
IE
Info
GER
P
OLI
CIA
DS
DCR
DC RM

MS containing Hildebrandslied from Kassel Landesbibliothek reported in hands NYC dealer. One page of 2-page MS fragment reported missing. Dealer has claimed MS was missing from Kassel library as early as 1936 presumably sold by Nazis. PLS obtain soonest from Kassel Landesbibliothek and Laender authorities proof of ownership, approximate date, place, and known circumstances of loss.

Dr. Wolf von Both, present director. Dr. Wilhem Hopf, address: Heideweg 3, Kassel, director 1902 – 1949. Dr. Hopf SHLD be able to provide evidence showing when MS was last in Landesbibliothek and if sent to library war repository on estate near Kassel, now in Russian zone.

ACHESON

Dist. Desired (Offices Only)

Drafted by: OEX:ICD:ARHall:man

Telegraphic transmission and classification approved by: BFSteiner

Clearances: ICD: Mr. Horne

UNCLASSIFIED

REPRODUCTION FROM THIS COPY, IF CLASSIFIED, IS PROHIBITED.

Fig. 18. Telegram to HICOG Bonn, signed Acheson, and bearing Ardelia Hall's initials in the right hand corner
(United States National Archives and Records Administration – Ardelia Hall Collection.)

ington, giving them strong, unwavering support.[3] The massive art restitution operation had ended but many of her colleagues remained in Europe, trapped in the rising tensions of the cold war. Seven years after VE-Day, the political sands had shifted. No longer was there any fear that Germany would rise from its ashes and challenge the Allies. The former enemy had become a political partner while yesterday's brother-in-arms, the Soviet Union, had turned into a dangerous foe. An "iron curtain" had fallen and had divided Europe into two hostile camps, two worlds of irreconcilable ideological differences.

Ardelia's workload as art consultant in the US Department of State's Division of Overseas Information Centers was nothing short of crushing. After the demise of the Roberts Commission in 1946 all its records had been turned over to her unit. The United States policy on the protection of art in times of war, the brain-child of the Commission, had remained virtually unchanged, anchored in its three valiant principles: morality, a sound foreign policy, and compliance with international laws.[4] But it no longer referred exclusively to Hitler's booty. It had been expanded to include search and restitution of trophy-art smuggled into the United States. Ardelia Ripley Hall was the force behind the policy.[5]

The fifty-three-year-old art-historian was an unlikely warrior in an arena that had less to do with art and more with detective work, political negotiations, and bureaucratic savvy. She was petite and slender, with brilliant dark eyes, a high intelligent brow, and strong, confident features. Born and raised in Massachusetts,[6] Ardelia was a graduate of Smith College.[7] The motto chosen by her graduating class, *Ut Servemus*, That we may be of service,[8] must have made an

---

3 *Report of the American Commission for the Protection and Salvage of Artistic and Historic Monuments in War Areas* (Washington: Government Printing Office, 1946), 16 and S. Lane Faison Jr., "Transfer of Custody to the Germans," in: *The Spoils of War: World War II and Its Aftermath: The Loss, Reappearance, and Recovery of Cultural Property,* editor Elizabeth Simpson (New York: H. N. Abrams in association with the Bard Graduate Center for Studies in the Decorative Arts, 1997), 140.

4 Maurer, 142.

5 Ibid., 143: "During the period from 1944 to 1954, the dominant force in the State Department was Ardelia Hall, who was a Monuments, Fine Arts and Archives adviser to the department. She was a persistent, zealous person, passionate in her attempts to recover stolen cultural property, and she succeeded greatly in that effort."

6 *Department of State Biographic Register 1961–62* (Washington: US Department of State, 1962), s. v. "Hall, Ardelia R."

7 Smith College was named after its founder Sophia Smith. The college was established in 1875 in Northampton, Massachusetts, and it remains to this day a private, academically well-regarded, and highly competitive college for women.

8 Details about Ardelia's class motto have been obtained from the Smith College archivist, Nanci A. Young, who in her December 5, 2001 correspondence with the author, (correspondence deposited with the University of California, Davis, Shields Library, Department of Special Collections) explained that each class between 1881 and 1927 had its own motto.

Fig. 19. Ardelia R. Hall
(Archives of Smith College -- Reproduced by permission)

early impression on her, for she seemed destined to become a superb public servant. She went on to earn an advanced degree in art history from Columbia University and worked as museum curator first in New York and then in Boston. In 1943, she made a bold move to Washington, DC as assistant section chief in the Offices of Strategic Services. The Roberts Commission recognized her abilities and recommended her in 1945 for the position of art consultant in the State Department's Office of International Information and Cultural Affairs. A year later, her Office took over the functions of the defunct American Commission for the Protection and Salvage of Artistic and Historic Monuments in War Areas.[9]

Her new assignment was neither charted nor tested. Ardelia's mission was to find, recover, and return war-looted art smuggled into the United States. This was easier said than done, since she had no legal or enforcing authority of her own. While she could investigate and locate trophy-art, Ardelia Hall could not seize, prosecute, or punish.[10] Her funding was meager and her staff non-existent.[11] Yet such bureaucratic adversities never seem to hinder or discourage her.

Her opening shot as Arts and Monuments Advisor was a stern warning published in the *Department of State Bulletin* and addressed to the booming post-war illegitimate art trade.[12] She put all active and aspiring traffickers on notice that dealing in trophy-art was in contravention of United States laws and its international commitments. She followed that warning with an appeal to universities, museums, libraries, art-dealers, and booksellers, potential customers of looted materials. She reminded one and all that it was their duty to watch for infractions and to report to the Secretary of State all suspect artwork offered for sale. Her

---

Between 1920 and 1927 these mottoes were published in the class yearbook. The motto of the class of 1922, "Ut Servemus," is followed by the English translation, "That we may be of service."

9 *Report of the American Commission for the Protection and Salvage of Artistic and Historic Monuments in War Areas*, 16, and "Recovery of Lost European Art Treasures," *The Record* (Department of State, International Exchange) 7, no. 3 (1951): 39.

10 Maurer, 142–43.

11 In the Department of State telephone directories of the time, Ardelia Hall is listed as the only person functioning in the Office of Arts and Monuments, with no other assistant. Dr. Haide Russell, Assistant to the German Cultural Attaché in Washington, confirmed in a letter to W. von Both, dated March 22, 1955, that there was only one lady in charge of lost cultural property within the State Department. See: "Hildebrandlied 1," documents from the archives of the Gesamthochschul-Bibliothek Kassel – Landesbibliothek und Murhardsche Bibliothek der Stadt Kassel, deposited with the University of California, Davis, Shields Library, Department of Special Collections.

12 "Return of Looted Objects of Art to Countries of Origin: Memorandum by the State Department Member of SWNCC (State-War-Navy Coordinating Committee)," *Department of State Bulletin* 16, no. 399 (1947): 358–60. The Roberts Commission originally created this circular. In 1947 it was revised and reissued by A. Hall.

ADDRESS OFFICIAL COMMUNICATIONS TO
THE SECRETARY OF STATE
WASHINGTON 25, D. C.

DEPARTMENT OF STATE
WASHINGTON

To Universities, Museums, Libraries, Art Dealers, and Booksellers.

It is the responsibility and desire of the Government of the United States to recover and return to owner nations those cultural objects, including works of art, archival material and books, looted, stolen or improperly dispersed from public and private collections in war areas and brought to the United States during and following World War II.

This responsibility has been shared by American institutions and American citizens. The response of museums, libraries, and dealers to a circular letter from the American Commission for the Protection and Salvage of Artistic and Historic Monuments in War Areas requesting information about objects without a clear title has led to the recovery by this Government of a number of items of artistic and historic importance. The continued vigilance of American institutions and individuals in identifying cultural objects improperly dispersed during World War II is needed.

Your cooperation in notifying the Secretary of State, Washington 25, D. C., concerning such objects which may come to your attention will be appreciated.

Fig. 7. Circular issued by Ardelia Hall in 1946
(United States National Archives and Records Administration – Ardelia Hall Collection.)

message, widely reprinted in the trade press,[13] yielded spectacular results. Educational and cultural institutions, scholars, dealers, and ordinary citizens responded with valuable information.[14] Eventually over one thousand war-looted objects were recovered and returned to their rightful owners.[15]

With the discipline of a scholar and the tactics of a private eye, Ardelia investigated personally every lead. She worked alone. She researched the history and importance of each alleged war-trophy, tracked down rumors, consulted with specialists, interviewed witnesses, and documented her findings in voluminous file-notes and memoranda. She was masterful in creating alternate ways to compensate for her lack of power and authority. Once culprit and loot were identified, she summoned sister agencies to serve as proxies. She enlisted the Justice Department to prosecute cases that involved stolen objects transported over state lines, Customs to seize smuggled property, Defense to court-martial looters who were members of the armed services, and the all-knowing Internal Revenue Service to look into tax violations.[16] She knew her way around the bureaucracy and navigated with ease the treacherous ways of Washington politics. She was skillful in forging new alliances, and tactful in nurturing old contacts. She focused all her energy, imagination and commitment on one ambitious goal: to locate, recover, and return the illegal spoils of the Second World War.

Some of her cases, such as that of the 1457 *Mainz Psalter,* were relatively simple. This precious book of psalms had resurfaced in New York City in 1950. Ardelia had worked closely with Karl Kup, curator of the New York Public Library, to verify its authenticity.[17] Kup had confirmed that this was the very first vellum book printed in three colors by the renowned German printers Johann Fust and Peter Schoeffer,[18] an item looted from the wartime repository of the State Library of Saxony in Dresden. The Psalter together with a batch of other unlawful souvenirs recovered by Ardelia was promptly returned to the American Zone of Germany.[19]

---

13 "To Museums, Art and Antique Dealers, and Auction Houses," *Department of State Bulletin* 16, no. 399 (1947): 359–60, Appendix B. The letter was reprinted in various journals. See *Magazine of Art* 44, 2 (February 1951): 75, and *College Art Journal* 10, 2 (Winter 1950): 188.

14 Ardelia R. Hall, "The Recovery of Cultural Objects Dispersed during World War II" *Department of State Bulletin* 25, no. 635 (1951): 339, and her "US Program for Return of Historic Objects to Countries of Origin, 1944–1954," *Department of State Bulletin* 31, no. 797 (1954): 496.

15 Hall, "US Program for Return of Historic Objects ...", 496.

16 Maurer, 143.

17 "File Ms. of the Hildebrandslied from Kassel." Letter of A. Hall to K. Kup, January 9, 1952.

18 Printers Johann Fust and Peter Schoeffer published several fine books, including the famous 42-line Bible (1456) and the Mainz Psalter (1457).

19 The 1457 *Mainz Psalter*, of which there are only ten copies still in existence, is a book of

Other cases, such as that of the Petrarch manuscript, taxed her patience and strained her meager resources. At the height of the war, a novice GI had exchanged a fistful of lire and three cartons of cigarettes for an old book, which was later identified as the manuscript of the fourteenth-century Petrarch poem *De Africa*. It had been stolen from a Naples exhibit. The soldier had wrapped his souvenir in oilskins and had stuffed it in his knapsack. With the book on his back, he had made a glider landing in southern France, had shot his way out of the Battle of the Bulge, and had finally returned home to his thread-cutting shop in Union City, New Jersey. Short of cash, the GI had offered his wartime memento to several libraries. One of them had alerted the Department of State.[20] For the past six years Ardelia's attempts to persuade the veteran to surrender his trophy had failed. She had been forced to refer the case to the Justice Department. A protracted legal battle seemed inevitable.[21]

It was during this very same time that news of another looted manuscript reached her desk. This one was said to be of enormous symbolical, literary, and historical importance. Just as the *Mainz Psalter* two years earlier, this war-trophy had been spotted in New York City. Dr. Gerhard Liebers, a librarian at the Murhard Library in Kassel, had seen it mentioned as a footnote in the galley proofs of a journal article written by an American scholar. The footnote implied that the stolen manuscript, which Dr. Liebers called the Kassel *Hildebrandslied*, had been recovered from a New York book dealer and that it was on its way back to Kassel. But when the journal article appeared in print, the footnote was no longer listed. Alarmed, Dr. Liebers had contacted the journal's editor in Urbana, Illinois, who had referred him to the Department of State. Liebers was anxious to know if the US Government was working on the safe return of this most important German manuscript.[22]

---

firsts: it is the first book printed on vellum in red, blue and black, the first to exhibit the names of its printers, the first ever to carry a colophon, and the first to exhibit the day of printing. With the *Mainz Psalter*, Ardelia Hall also returned several tapestries from Bavarian collections, a Dürer engraving, paintings from Bremen, miniatures from Berlin, and a fourteenth-century ivory diptych of the Passion from Kassel. See: "Rare Mainz Psalter of 1457, Looted, Returned to the U. S. Zone in Germany," *Department of State Bulletin* 22, no. 560 (1950): 487; "Mainz Exhibiting Treasured Psalter," *Department of State Bulletin* 23, no. 582 (1950): 349; "Recovery of Lost European Art Treasures," 39–40; and Ardelia R. Hall, "The Recovery of Cultural Objects Dispersed During World War II," 340.

20 "Petrarch Ms. Sought by Trieste is Found in Ex-GI's Jersey Shop," *The New York* Times, *December 22, 1946, p 1, col. 6.*

21 "Rechsteiner Case Petrarch Ms.," US Department of State, records maintained by the Fine Arts and Monuments Adviser, 1946–1961, Ardelia Hall Collection, Record Group 59. Lot 62D-4, Box 6, Item 4, SWNCC 322, National Archives and Records Administration. In December of 1954, after a legal dispute that lasted nine years, ex-GI Walter Rechsteiner returned the manuscript to Italy without compensation.

22 "File Ms. of the Hildebrandslied from Kassel." Handwritten note stating: "Report of ap-

The *Hildebrandslied.* Ardelia jotted down the title and a personal reminder to look it up in a handbook of German literature. She also filled out a library request for a reference book mentioned by Liebers: Wilhelm Hopf's, *Die Landesbibliothek Kassel.*[23] If the *Hildebrandslied* were as important as Liebers professed, Ardelia pondered while doodling on her notepad,[24] it ought to be listed in major English-language encyclopedias. She immediately set out in search of an entry. In the *Encyclopaedia Britannica* she found a first substantive article.[25] The story of the ill-fated father-son encounter must have captivated her, for she copied the full text of the article onto large index cards in her bold, clear handwriting. In the *New International Encyclopaedia* she came across another useful essay. "A fragmentary Old High German poem," Ardelia noted on her cards, "the oldest preserved specimen of German heroic poetry. It is known only through a manuscript preserved in Kassel."[26] She hastened to learn more and discovered that, notwithstanding its disappearance, research on literary, linguistic, and historical aspects of the thousand-year-old ballad was ongoing. She located a book and two scholarly articles,[27] and wrote down their bibliographic citations, planning to request reprints and English translations. Meanwhile, Hopf's book on the history of the Kassel State Library arrived, and Ardelia added new annotations to her growing pile of cards. She chronicled the wanderings of the codex, from its birthplace in Boniface's Fulda, to its rediscovery by the Grimm Brothers. She noted the names of its most recent library trustees: that of former Director Wilhelm Hopf and of his successor, Kassel Library Director Wolf von Both. If director Hopf were alive, his testimony on the loss of the codex would be most valuable. She checked with friends in Bonn and was told

---

pearrance of MS in hands of NYC book dealer. Gerhard Liebers. Murhard Bibliothek, Kassel – Germany. He asked to let him know if any action is taken."
Note: In spite of repeated requests by Dr. Hennig, Gerhard Liebers never left a file note describing this incident (see: "Hildebrandlied 2," documents from the archives. ... Letters of D. Hennig to G. Liebers, March 6, 1975 and June 24, 1975.) The author believes that the elusive footnote appeared in the review "Altdeutsche Handschriften" by Ernst A. Philippson in the *Journal of English and Germanic Philology*, 50 (1951): 248–49. Dr. Helmut Rehder was on the editorial board of the journal.

23 "File Ms. of the Hildebrandslied from Kassel." Handwritten notes.

24 Ibid. Numerous pages of notes in A. Hall's handwriting seem to indicate fleeting thoughts or early options under consideration.

25 "Hildebrand, Lay of," in: *Encyclopaedia Britannica*, vol. 13–14 (Chicago: Encyclopaedia Britannica, 1926), 460–61.

26 "Hildebrandslied," In: *New International Encyclopaedia*, vol. 10 (New York: Dodd, Mead and Co., 1909), 73.

27 Emil T. H. Bunje, *A Reinterpretation of the Expository Verses of the Hildebrandslied*, Berkeley: University of California Press, 1936; H. W. J. Kroes, "Zum Hildebrandslied" (About the Lay of Hildebrand), *Neophilologus* 33, no. 4 (1949): 212–15; and L. L. Hammerich, "Die Trutzreden Hiltibrants und Hadubrants" (The defiant speeches of Hiltibrant and Hadubrant), *Neophilologus* 34, no. 2 (1950): 82–86.

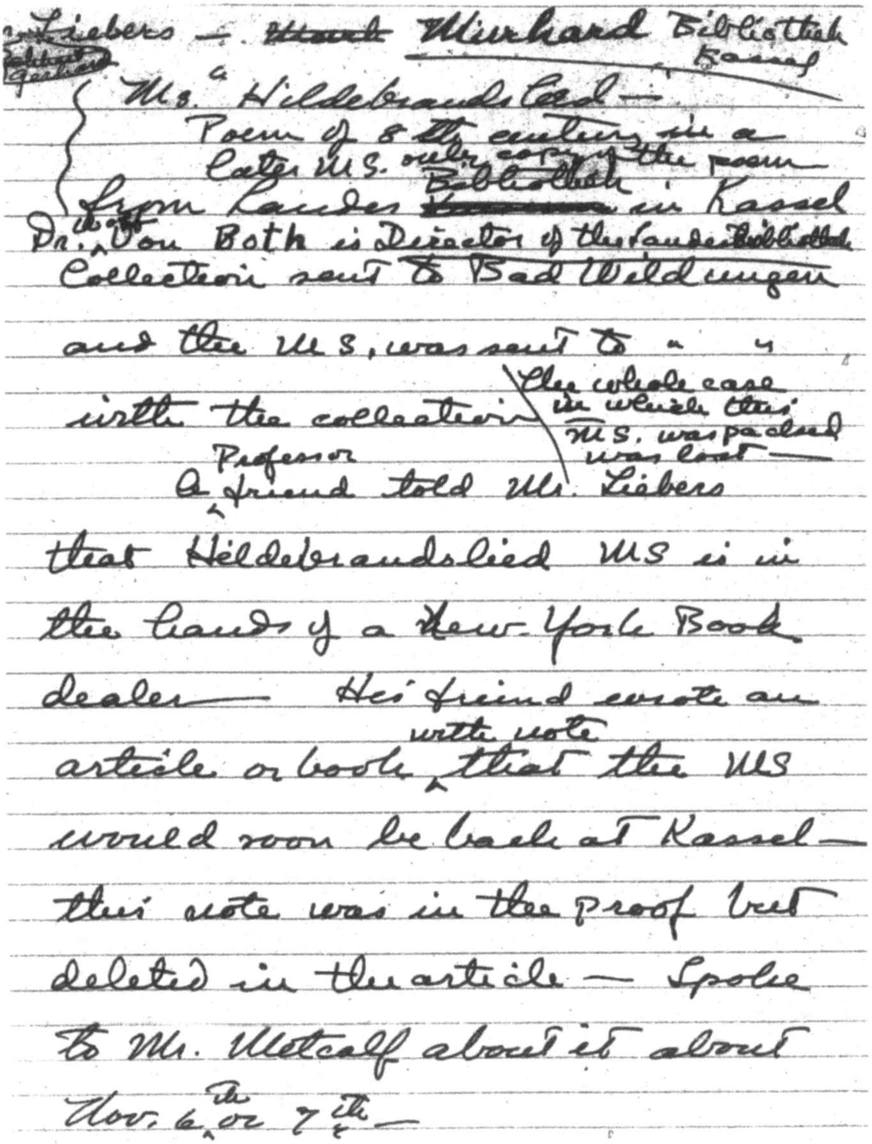
Liebers – Murhard Bibliothek Kassel

Ms. Hildebrandslied –
Poem of 8th century in a later MS. only copy of the poem
from Landes Bibliothek in Kassel
Dr. Wolf Von Both is Director of the Landesbibliothek
Collection sent to Bad Wildungen
and the MS. was sent to " "
with the collection — The whole case in which this MS. was packed was lost —
A Professor friend told Mr. Liebers
that Hildebrandslied MS is in
the hands of a New York Book
dealer — His friend wrote an
article or book with note that the MS
would soon be back at Kassel —
this note was in the proof but
deleted in the article — Spoke
to Mr. Metcalf about it about
Nov. 6th or 7th —

Fig. 20. Ardelia Hall handwritten notes
(United States National Archives and Records Administration – Ardelia Hall Collection.)

that Hopf was still listed in Kassel at Heideweg 3. She appended his address to her swelling documentation.[28]

Now that she had a better understanding of the history of the manuscript and its importance, Ardelia turned to the other lead: the editor in Urbana, Illinois, who had referred Kassel librarian Gerhard Liebers to her office. He was Helmut Rehder, she learned, Chair of the German Department at the University of Illinois, and editor of *The Journal of English and Germanic Philology*, where the footnote on the *Hildebrandslied* had fleetingly appeared. "*My dear Dr. Rehder,*" wrote Ardelia just before Christmas 1951, in her old-fashioned epistolary style. She would very much appreciate it if he would give her whatever information he might have on the reappearance of the *Hildebrandslied* in the United States. Could he perchance remember the name of the New York dealer, who had allegedly purchased the manuscript?[29]

A cordial reply arrived posthaste. Dr. Rehder was most appreciative of the State Department's interest in the case. Alas, his knowledge was merely second-hand. A colleague, Dr. Carl Selmer of Hunter College, had mentioned in passing that the lost *Hildebrandslied* had resurfaced, but he had not revealed the name of the dealer. More recently, Selmer had informed Rehder that the manuscript had been returned to Germany. Rehder was certain that, if contacted, Selmer would assist the Department of State in every respect.[30]

This was Ardelia's first solid lead. She had to find out who Professor Selmer was and how much he knew. And although Rehder had vouched for Selmer's willingness to cooperate, the cautious Ardelia needed a back-up witness, just in case Selmer proved to be less than forthcoming. She let the Christmas holidays go by before approaching the professor, and when she did, her greetings to Selmer were terse and imperious. With very little in the way of an introduction, she demanded that the good professor surrender the name of the dealer, the date the *Hildebrandslied* was in his hands, and any other details that could lead to the recovery of the codex. While she assured Selmer of confidentiality, she also put him on notice that she was addressing this very same inquiry to other scholars who had been helpful to her in the past.[31] Her officious tone and official State Department letterhead were clearly intended to intimidate the witness and melt away any inherent resistance.

True to her word, that very same day, Ardelia fired off a letter to Karl Kup, Curator of Prints at the New York Public Library. She had worked with Kup on

---

28 "File Ms. of the Hildebrandslied from Kassel." Handwritten notes.

29 Ibid. Letter of A. Hall to H. Rehder, December 11, 1951.

30 Ibid. Letter of H. Rehder to A. Hall, December 17, 1951.

31 Ibid. Letter of A. Hall to C. Selmer, January 10, 1952.

the *Mainz Psalter* case. She had learned to trust and respect the curator, whose vast knowledge ranged from ancient Japanese scrolls to medieval illuminated manuscripts.[32] He was well connected in the art world and thus, Ardelia must have concluded, well positioned to tap into the grapevine that linked book dealers, curators, librarians, and bibliophiles. In confidence she asked Kup if he had heard anything about a New York sighting of the *Hildebrandslied*.[33] Once again, Kup did not disappoint her.

Ardelia's letter arrived on the morning of January 16, 1952, as Kup was preparing to leave for Chicago. Born, raised, and educated in Germany, the *Hildebrandslied* must have been an integral part of Kup's cultural formation. The urgent tone of the letter prompted Kup to pick up the phone and dial Ardelia's office in Washington.[34] Yes, he told her, rumor had it that the *Hildebrandslied* was in this country. Years earlier, the renowned rare-book dealer A. S. W. Rosenbach had allegedly offered the codex to the Morgan Library for sale. Kup believed that his colleague, Morgan curator Curt Bühler, still had a cover-to-cover film of that manuscript.[35] Ardelia remembered Bühler. He had assisted her in the Petrarch case, which was still in litigation.[36] Had the Morgan Library purchased the *Hildebrandslied* from Dr. Rosenbach? No, Kup assured her, but someone else had. The buyer was a certain Countess, who had donated her collections to a seminary in California. However, Kup cautioned, he was not entirely convinced that this was a case of plunder. Rumor had it that the codex had gone missing long before the war. Quite possibly the dealer, Dr. Rosenbach, had acquired the manuscript legally.

Ardelia jotted down the information. The amorphous allegations were gradually gaining much needed definition. Still, the facts were second-hand, fragmentary, and in view of Kup's assertions, her entire case of plunder was now suspect. She needed to hear the story directly from Bühler. She pressed Kup to arrange a meeting with the Morgan Library curator. It went without saying that all information would be kept strictly confidential. Kup promised to contact Bühler after his return from Chicago. With time on her hands, Ardelia reviewed and typed her notes. In the margin of her file memorandum, she scribbled one additional detail: John Fleming, Rosenbach Company, 322 East Fifty-Seventh Street, Telephone number: Plaza 5-3242. Later in the investigation, this name and address might come in handy.

---

32 "Karl Kup – Obituary," *The New York Times*, July 7, 1981, sec. A, 21, col. 4.

33 "File Ms. of the Hildebrandslied from Kassel." Letter of A. Hall to K. Kup, January 10, 1952.

34 "File Ms. of the Hildebrandslied from Kassel." Memorandum of telephone conversation of A. Hall with K. Kup, January 16, 1952.

35 Ibid. Letter of A. Hall to E. Schwenk, November 24, 1953.

36 "Rechsteiner Case Petrarch Ms." Handwritten notes.

On Friday afternoon, January 25, 1952, Ardelia met with the two curators in the New York Public Library. The meeting yielded a bonanza of new leads. Bühler had brought along prints of the cover-to-cover film, and pre-war facsimile copies of the two pages of the ballad.[37] He told Ardelia the story of his encounter with the manuscript. Indeed, six years earlier, in November of 1945, the Rosenbach Company had offered the volume to the Morgan for sale, and Professor Selmer, who happened to be in the library that afternoon, had recognized the ballad. Bühler and his colleague, curator Meta Harrsen, had verified its authenticity by comparing the codex to a description found in Hopf's history of the *Landesbibliothek* Kassel. The Morgan Library had filmed the entire book and the film revealed that at that time only the second leaf of the ballad was present. The first leaf with the opening verses was already missing. The late director Belle da Costa Greene had rejected Rosenbach's offer and Bühler had returned the codex to the dealer. In his rejection letter, he had alerted Rosenbach to the book's provenance but had intentionally omitted any mention of the *Hildebrandslied.* He showed Ardelia his letter and Rosenbach's reply.[38] It was useless to contact Dr. Rosenbach, Bühler advised. He was no longer active. His brother Philip had taken over the business. As to Countess Doheny, Bühler described her devotion and generous bequests to the Catholic Church. He also gave Ardelia a copy of Schad's probing article published in the *New Colophon.*[39]

While enormously important, Bühler's story left gaping holes in the weave of her investigation. Had the Nazis really sold the manuscript to Rosenbach, or was this an act of larceny and illegal trade? Ardelia was leery of the *Nazis-have-sold it-to me* defense. She had heard it before. Traffickers caught red-handed had used it once too often.[40] Personal suspicions aside, Ardelia needed irrefutable evidence that the manuscript truly belonged to Kassel, and that it had been looted and not sold. She cabled her colleagues at HICOG and told them in confidence that she had picked up the trail of the lost *Liber Sapientiae* with one of the two pages of the *Hildebrandslied.* She asked them to obtain from the *Landesbibliothek* proof of ownership, and approximate date, place and known circumstances of the loss. To help expedite matters, she sent along the name and address of the retired library director, Dr. Wilhelm Hopf, and that of current director Dr. Wolf von Both. It was incumbent upon those two librarians, she insisted, to certify when and where the manuscript was last seen. She ended her cable with the authoritative signa-

---

[37] "File Ms. of the Hildebrandslied from Kassel." Handwritten notes and letter of A. Hall to S. Stephens, May 1, 1952.

[38] Ibid. Letter of A. Hall to S. Stephens, May 1, 1952.

[39] Ibid. Handwritten notes.

[40] Ibid. Letter of A. Hall to E. Schwenk, November 24, 1953.

ture *Acheson*, a strong reminder to all that she was speaking on behalf of the powerful US Secretary of State.[41]

To launch a formal investigation Ardelia needed more than an affidavit of ownership from Kassel. She had to establish that the Doheny *Liber Sapientiae* volume described in Schad's article was one and the same with the missing Kassel manuscript. In other words, one of Bühler's pre-war facsimile pages of the *Hildebrandslied* had to match the last leaf of the codex shelved in the Doheny Memorial Library. For that, she had to gain access to the seminary book-vault in Camarillo, California. She evaluated her options.[42] First, she toyed with the idea of enlisting the services of Professor Archer Taylor, a California academic. Taylor, who taught German Medieval Literature at the University of California, Berkeley, had the proper credentials, and thus a good excuse to ask for admittance to the Doheny Library. He was also within reasonable geographic proximity to the seminary. She scribbled on her notepad, musing if this were indeed the right approach. But then she thought of a better choice. In vintage Ardelia style, she went straight to the top, to the Archbishop of Los Angeles, the Most Reverend J. Francis L. McIntyre, DD, local overseer of all things Catholic, including the holdings of the Saint John's Seminary, Doheny Memorial Library.

Her letter was a model of respect and diplomacy. She began by reminding *her dear Archbishop* of the important role played by his mentor and brother in Christ, Cardinal Spellman, in 1944. Indeed, it was Cardinal Spellman who had brought to the attention of the Roberts Commission the problem of illegal importation of art and the need for government controls.[43] The recovery pro-

---

41 Faison, Jr., 140.
Note: Dean Acheson was US Secretary of State between 1949 and 1953. For the telegram see: "File Ms. of the Hildebrandslied from Kassel," Telegram of A. Hall to HICOG-Bonn, February 5, 1952. It says in part: "Dr. Hopf SHLD be able to provide evidence showing when MS was last in Landesbibliothek and if sent to library war repository on estate near Kassel, now in Russian zone. Acheson." Obviously, Ardelia Hall was still hoping that the spoilers were Soviet and not American soldiers.

42 "File Ms. of the Hildebrandslied from Kassel." Handwritten notes.

43 *Report of the American Commission for the Protection and Salvage of Artistic and Historic Monuments in War Areas* (Washington: Government Printing Office, 1946), 23: "At the meeting of the Commission in September 1944 Monsignor Griffiths, representing Archbishop Spellman, had called the attention of the American Commission to numerous reports of importation of objects of artistic and religious importance by members of the armed forces. ... Military Government Law 52, established during the period of the Supreme Commander's control in Europe and continued during the period of our Allied military government control in Germany and Italy, prohibited the exportation of works of art or other objects of cultural importance from the Theater. In June 1945 Mr. John A. Gilmore, then Assistant Secretary of the Commission, conferred in New York with representatives of the Bureau of Customs regarding the Treasury Department controls under T.D. 51072 with special relation to possible importations by the armed forces. The Customs authorities admitted that the extent of importation by members of the armed forces was considerable ..."

gram inspired by the Cardinal, she continued, was now in full swing and the return of lost treasures was deeply appreciated by recipient governments. Once again, she wrote, the US Department of State needed the Church's intercession. This time it was with regard to a priceless literary document, which had found its way into the Doheny Memorial Library, an institution under the Archbishop's direction. Ardelia painted a riveting story of theft, greed, and the need for justice. She appended photostat copies of the last leaf of the codex to assist the California Seminary in identification efforts. If this were indeed the right manuscript, she insisted in closing, no action should be taken until the unsuspecting Mrs. Doheny was compensated and the interests of the Seminary were fully protected.[44]

Less than a week later, a first response had arrived by priority air pouch from HICOG Germany. Edgar Breitenbach was unabashedly enthusiastic about the news on the *Hildebrandslied.* What strange coincidence that Ardelia would be looking into this matter precisely when he himself was about to explore leads on this other end. Indeed demands to investigate the Bad Wildungen looting had been mounting on his side of the ocean. American scholars working on various aspects of the *Hildebrandslied* had come to Kassel to study the manuscript. They had been very disappointed to hear that the codex was gone. As to the statement that the Nazis had sold the *Hildebrandslied* to Rosenbach, Breitenbach scoffed, rejecting it as utterly absurd.[45] The Nazis worshipped the ballad.[46] It was ridiculous to even think that they would consider hawking a piece of their cultural heritage to an agent of the enemy.

Ardelia turned to the translation of the sworn affidavit marked in bold letters *HILDEBRANDSLIED*, and immersed herself in the wartime story of the Kassel *Landesbibliothek*. Retired director Wilhelm Hopf and his successor Wolf von Both, the two co-signers, confirmed Breitenbach's view that the codex had not been sold. It had always been the library's most cherished and prized possession. They described the British bombing raid of 1941 and the disastrous loss of their collection. Mercifully, before to the attack, the *Hildebrandslied* together with the *Willehalm Codex*, packed in a simple wooden box, had been evacuated to a midtown bank-vault. In 1943, one month before the complete destruction of Kassel, the chest with the two codices had been moved once again, this time to the resort town of Bad Wildungen. There, the box had been stored in a cellar, under a protective wall spur. Director Hopf had inspected the evacuation site several times,

---

[44] Ibid. Letter of A. Hall to J. F. McIntyre, February 6, 1952.

[45] Ibid. Letter of E. Breitenbach to A. Hall, February 11, 1952.

[46] Alfred Rosenberg, *The Myth of the Twentieth Century: An Evaluation of the Spiritual-Intellectual Confrontations of Our Age*, translation by Vivian Bird (Newport Beach, CA: Noontide Press, 1993), 254–55. Alfred Rosenberg, the Nazi Party ideologist, had postulated that the Teutonic soul had found its heroic Aryan expression in the tragedy of Hildebrand.

alternating with curator Rudolf Helm of the Kassel *Landesmuseum*. Daily security details were the responsibility of Hubert Vonhoff of the Hesse Home Guard. He, and later his wife, had checked the temperature of the cellar no fewer than three times daily. In January of 1945, curator Helm had been called to the *Volkssturm*, and the hidden artwork had come under the supervision of the *Oberpräsident*, the Governor of Hesse. The *Oberpräsident* had failed to inform the US Monuments Officers about the Bad Wildungen evacuation sites in a misguided attempt to protect the art from looters. On the day of surrender, the area around Bad Wildungen had been sealed off. Weeks later Hopf had learn that the box with the two manuscripts had disappeared. An extensive search conducted with the assistance of the US Monuments Officers had failed to find any trace of the manuscripts.

Ardelia was pleased with the detailed report but puzzled to read about the loss of yet another codex, the *Willehalm*, which, according to the two library directors, had vanished from the same box and bunker. This was the first time that she had seen the title mentioned. She immersed herself into her customary background investigations. She copied the *Willehalm* chapter from Hopf's book on the *Landesbibliothek* and ordered a translation.[47] She searched for additional references, and obtained from the Library of Congress a treatise written by Robert Freyhan on the *Willehalm* miniatures.[48] She went to New York and made confidential inquiries among curators, bibliophiles, and former Monuments Men.[49] But this time no matter how wide she cast her net, she could not haul in any shred of information.[50] The *Willehalm* seemed to have vanished without a trace.

After a bright and promising start, clouds of concern had begun gathering on the horizon of her investigation. From HICOG in Frankfurt there was pressure to keep all information confidential until the three items, the *Liber Sapientiae,* its cut-off first leaf, and the *Willehalm,* were safely recovered. HICOG insisted that all three be returned together at the same time. Breitenbach cautioned that American prestige was on the line. Inquiring scholars had been led to believe that the manuscripts had been stolen by refugees and smuggled into the Soviet Zone.[51]

---

47 "File Ms. of the Hildebrandslied from Kassel," Department of State, Division of Language Services, TC Job 48822, March 10, 1952. Translation by Mrs. Mantz.

48 "File Ms. of the Hildebrandslied from Kassel." Handwritten notes on the Kassel *Landesbibliothek*. Ardelia refers here to the treatise by Robert Freyhan, *Die Illustrationen zum Casseler Willehalm-Codex: ein Beispiel englischen Einflusses in der rheinischen Malerei des XIV. Jahrhunderts* (The Illustrations to the Willehalm Codex from Kassel; An example of English influence on Rhennish painting style in the fourteenth-century) (Marburg: Verlag des Kunstgeschichtlichen Seminars, 1927).

49 Ibid. Request of Approval of Official Travel to New York. Confidential memorandum of A. Hall to Mr. Hodge, February 26, 1952.

50 Ibid. Letter of A. Hall to S. Stephens, May 1, 1952.

51 Ibid. Letter of E. Breitenbach to A. Hall, March 18, 1952.

Revelations about a New York book-dealer pointed an accusing finger at US military personnel. Americans, Breitenbach wrote, could be held responsible for the theft and such accusations would be hard to repudiate. Due to the immense importance of the manuscripts, a news embargo was not only desirable but mandatory until the case was successfully resolved. Ardelia was annoyed. A blackout was no longer an option and for that she blamed Professor Carl Selmer.

Seven years earlier at Bühler's request Selmer had reluctantly agreed to keep his discovery secret and allow the *Liber Sapientiae* to go under. Ever since, he had been haunted by his decision, blaming himself for the codex's uncertain fate. Year-in and year-out he had pored over all sales announcements, domestic and foreign, hoping to find a trace of the lost manuscript. When five years later, Schad had made his Camarillo discovery public Selmer had felt released of his onerous covenant.[52] Convinced that the codex was practically on its way back to Kassel, the Professor had begun sharing his story with colleagues and friends.

But to his dismay month had succeeded month and no one had seized and returned the codex. One-and-a-half years later, with the codex still in Camarillo, Professor Selmer had become convinced that fate was offering him a second chance to assist the wayward *Hildebrandslied.* This time he had to act quickly and decisively. And act he did. He used the platform of the sixty-sixth annual meeting of the Modern Language Association, held in Detroit in December of 1951, to call on his scholarly colleagues for help. A groundswell of righteous academic indignation could force the US Government or the Camarillo fathers into action. As it turned out, he was right.

Selmer's story spread like wildfire throughout the convention halls. Professor Ernst Rose of New York University made a public announcement expressing hope that the *Hildebrandslied* would be soon returned to the world of scholarship.[53] One medievalist rushed to include the happy news in a footnote, and when that footnote was deleted, Kassel librarian Dr. Gerhard Liebers alerted the US Department of State. Ardelia was utterly annoyed by the widespread publicity caused by Selmer's disclosure.

A winter chill had settled over Washington when Ardelia received a reply from Professor Selmer to her January letter of inquiry. The specter of an official investigation, the icy tone of her epistle, and the ominous governmental letterhead, must have greatly alarmed the German immigrant, for he had asked his boss, Hunter College President Dr. George N. Shuster, to respond on his behalf. Arde-

---

52 Carl Selmer, "Wie ich das Hildebrandslied in Amerika wiederfand," (How I found the Hildebrandslied in America), *Wirkendes Wort* 6, no. 2 (1955/56): 124.

53 "Hildebrandslied wiedergefunden" (The Hildebrandslied found), *Kasseler Post,* May 30, 1952.

lia was irritated. True, George Shuster enjoyed impeccable credentials. He had just returned from Germany, where he had served with great distinction as Land Commissioner for Bavaria.[54] But did Selmer really need such lofty representation? As to contents, there was nothing new in Shuster's letter that Ardelia did not already know from either Kup or Bühler. Furthermore, Shuster steadfastly referred to the New York dealer as *Rosenthal* instead of Rosenbach. Ardelia bristled, annoyed with the error.[55] In a polite but frigid response she rejected Shuster's offer to have Selmer travel to California and identify the manuscript.[56] Archbishop J. Francis McIntyre was a far better choice.

She was also dissatisfied with the tempo of her investigation, which had slowed down to a crawl. For months her persistent probing had turned up no leads on the *Willehalm* and no new information on the severed Leaf One. The fact that HICOG continued to insist on secrecy and on the simultaneous return of all three manuscripts made her task more difficult. One silver lining was the knowledge that the *Liber Sapientiae* codex with the surviving second leaf was safely shelved in a California Seminary Library vault. Ardelia believed that she could easily reach out and recover it any time she so desired.

The bloom was off the Capital's cherry trees, when Ardelia decided to take a new course of action. Since her personal search efforts had reached an impasse, she called for an Federal investigation of the Rosenbach Company. The *Liber Sapientiae*, a codex looted from a war repository in Germany, had passed through the hands of the Doctor. It seemed reasonable to assume that it was Dr. Rosenbach, or one of his employees, who had removed the first leaf of the codex. It was also conceivable that in 1945, the Doctor had acquired not only the *Liber Sapientiae* but also its companion volume, the *Willehalm*. Since the *Liber Sapientiae* had been brought into the United States illegally, an investigation by the US Bureau of Customs was an appropriate course of action.[57] Supportive, the Bureau responded by assigning Agent J. H. Page to the case.

Her battle plan set in motion Ardelia prepared to leave for Germany with a batch of newly recovered trophy-art. The Kassel codices were but one of many cases

---

[54] *The National Cyclopedia of American Biography*, vol. 61 (Clifton, New Jersey: James T. White, 1982), 71: "Shuster was on leave of absence from Hunter from June, 1950, to December, 1951, at which time he was in government service assigned to the Office of the U.S. High Commissioner for Germany as land commissioner for Bavaria with offices in Munich. He served as representative of the high commissioner to the Bavarian government and was responsible for the promotion of U.S. policies in the fields of politics, economics, education, and jurisprudence."

[55] "File Ms. of the Hildebrandslied from Kassel." Letter of A. Hall to S. Stephens, May 1, 1952.

[56] Ibid. Letter of A. Hall to G. Shuster, February 1, 1952.

[57] Ibid. Letter of A. Hall to S. Stephens, May 1, 1952.

vying simultaneously for her attention. She had been more successful in solving others. In the name of the United States Government Ardelia Hall handed over to the German Foreign Office in Bonn a painting by Rubens, a first-century Egyptian gold ring, a manuscript of Frederick the Great, and a collection of rare books stolen from the Prussian Meteorological Institute.[58] These were not the first, nor indeed would they be the last stolen artworks returned to their rightful owners, vowed Ardelia in her presentation address.[59]

By the closing days of spring, Customs Agent Page, armed with names, dates, and supporting evidence,[60] called on the Rosenbach Company and asked to see the Doctor. The firm's New York offices had moved from their stately address on Fifteen East Fifty-First Street to an elegant tenth floor suite on 322 East Fifty-Seventh Street. The new quarters, originally owned by a lawyer to the stars, had been once again decorated in Philip Rosenbach's take on baronial splendor.[61] Alas, the Doctor was unable to meet with the Customs Agent, Brother Philip explained. He was under twenty-four hour medical supervision, having suffered a complete physical and mental breakdown. Agent Page was given to understand that his condition was irreversible.[62] Nonetheless, Philip, President of the Rosenbach Company, assisted by General Manager John Fleming, would be happy to meet with the agent.

After customary introductions, Agent Page broached the subject of a looted theological compendium known as the *Liber Sapientiae Solomonis.* He inquired who among them had purchased it in 1945. It was most definitely the Doctor, of this both Philip and Fleming were certain. They also remembered that Dr. R had paid a fairly modest sum, about $2,000 dollars for it. Agent Page must have quietly noted that there was no longer any mention of a pre-war purchase from the Nazis. He asked to see the sales slip. Regrettably those records were no lon-

---

58 The Rubens painting of St. Katherine was recovered with the help of the Los Angeles County Museum from J. P. Frary, a US Army officer, who had purchased it in Germany. One other painting, a landscape of the Rhine by B. C. Koekkoek, was recovered at the same time. Both paintings had been stolen from their Bad Wildungen repository. The Koekkoek landscape turned out to be looted by the Nazis from the Netherlands. For more information, see "Paintings from Bad Wildungen Repository – Koekkoek and Maes." US Department of State. Records Maintained by the Fine Arts and Monuments Adviser, 1944–61, Ardelia Hall Collection, Record Group 59. Lot 62D-4, Box 9, Item 5, National Archives and Records Administration.

59 "Cultural Articles Returned," *Information Bulletin: A Monthly Magazine of the Office of US High Commissioner for Germany* (July 1952): 18.

60 "File Ms. of the Hildebrandslied from Kassel." Report of J. H. Page to the Commissioner of Customs, Division of Investigations, Bureau of Customs, June 13, 1952.

61 Wolf, 2nd, 559: "It was still the grandest bookstore in the world ..."

62 Ibid., 587. The condition was indeed irreversible. Less than one month later A. S. W. Rosenbach passed away.

ger available. Surely, Agent Page was aware of the fact that the firm was under no legal obligation to keep business records beyond the latest five years. All 1945 account-books had been destroyed. Could they remember the name of the seller? He was some returning US army officer but neither Philip nor Fleming could recall his name. Had Dr. Rosenbach purchased any other item from the officer? No, he had only acquired the one book, the *Liber Sapientiae*. Shortly thereafter, the codex had been submitted for sale to the Morgan, but the library had declined the offer. Did the Doctor know that inscribed on the end flyleaf of the codex were the last known verses of the famous *Hildebrandslied*? Stunned silence. Neither Philip nor Fleming had ever heard of the *Hildebrandslied*. Was there a loose leaf in the volume? No, not at all, the codex was in good condition. Was the manuscript eventually sold? Once again there was silence. When Agent Page produced a copy of Schad's article in the *New Colophon*, both Philip Rosenbach and John Fleming remembered selling the *Liber Sapientiae* to Countess Estelle Doheny of Los Angeles. Yes indeed, that codex had been part of an $ 80,000 block sale. What was the unit price allotted to the *Liber Sapientiae*? Well, there were no individual prices ascribed to any item in the lot, but once again, if they were to guess, the price of the codex could not have exceeded $ 4,000.

There was no point in continuing the interview. The 1945 sales records were no longer available, the name of the army officer had been conveniently forgotten, the price of the looted codex sold in California was quoted below the $ 5,000 value-threshold established by Federal law,[63] and the alleged offender, Dr. Rosenbach, was on his deathbed. Agent Page lowered the flag and sounded the retreat. He filed a detailed report, and his superiors agreed with his conclusions: without the name of the officer, without witnesses, without evidence of transgression, the Customs Bureau had no legal basis to continue the investigation. Upon returning from Bonn, Ardelia stoically received the news of the failed offensive. With the dog days of summer around the corner, her options had withered and her leads had run dry.

[63] The Bureau of Customs is subordinated to the US Department of Justice, which oversees the National Stolen Property Act, (U.S. Code Title 18, Crimes and Criminal Procedure, Sections 2314 and 2315). The Act makes it a crime for a person to transport in international commerce or over state borders objects worth $ 5,000 or more that are known to be stolen.

Chapter 13: From the Ashes of the Phoenix

Seven years after the Hour Zero, Kassel, the once proud capital of the Prussian province of Hesse-Nassau and heart of the homeland, remained a shattered border-town. Neighboring Frankfurt and Wiesbaden had taken over most of its former economic and administrative functions.[1] With the partition of Germany, the bustling pre-war railroad hub had become terminus for eastbound trains. Right across the Werra River loomed the chasm that ripped farm and family apart, the border that separated the free world from a communist dictatorship.

Border town or capital, war-torn Kassel was determined to resume its thousand-year-old existence. With every passing day, the swelling cacophony of revival pushed back the silence of despair. Twisted skeletal buildings donned veils of scaffolding. Abandoned rows of ruins gave way to busy construction sites. Choked-up thoroughfares re-emerged, blasted out of rubble. Heaps of smashed brick conceded to green spaces festooned with colorful flowerbeds.[2] Kassel's city fathers abandoned the idea of rebuilding the historic town center in favor of a more functional contemporary urban master plan. The newly carved pedestrian zones sprouted shops, offices, and banks, pulsating with people. Around the blackened ruins of the library on Friedrich Square a modern metropolis was slowly rising from its ashes.[3] Day in, day out, the beat of the hammer and the sing-song of the handsaw proclaimed a throbbing rhythm of life, a frenzy to forget, an urgency to live and start anew.

The city's two research libraries, the *Landesbibliothek* and the Murhard Library, were also caught in this renaissance fever. While waiting for the Museum Fridericianum to be rebuilt, Dr. Hopf had opened on the Ständeplatz number eight a modest reading room with twenty-one workstations, and had endowed it with 2,000 reference books and 200 journal subscriptions. To everyone's delight, the library's manuscript collection returned safely from its evacuation site in Marburg. Once again, loan requests and research questions began streaming in from

---

1 The State of Greater Hesse, later simply called Hesse, was created on September 19, 1945 by Proclamation No. 2 of the Military Government in Germany, American Zone. The new state incorporated the former provinces of Kurhesse and Nassau, Hesse-Starkenburg, Ober-Hesse, and portions of Rhein-Hesse. All administrative and political functions were concentrated in the new capital at Wiesbaden, which soon blossomed into an active center for the publishing, insurance, and film industry. Frankfurt developed into an important financial and business center.

2 Kurt Kersten, "Das auferstandene Kassel" (Kassel resurrected), *Sonntagsblatt Staats-Zeitung und Herold – New York,* October 17, 1954, 20C.

3 Wolfgang Bangert, "Kassel – Reconstruction of the City Center," *Town Planning Review* 29, no. 2 (1958): 99–102.

cities across the land and places across the ocean.[4] In the first year alone, more than 6,000 readers returned to the library. But this joyful revival was also marked by a rite of passage. At the age of seventy-three, after thirty-seven years of service, Dr. Wilhelm Hopf was preparing to step down. The Kassel *Landesbibliothek* had been his life. He had nurtured its collections during the best of times and had fiercely protected them during the worst. He had brought the library back from the brink of dissolution and now he was ready to transfer the awesome responsibility of leadership to a new generation. Hopf had chosen a successor in Dr. Wolf von Both, a native of Kassel, a scholar of philology, art, and history. For the past two years they had worked side by side to insure an orderly transition.[5]

In February of 1952, Wolf von Both, the new director of the *Landesbibliothek*, received an unexpected telephone call from an old library colleague of pre-war times, Dr. Edgar Breitenbach.[6] The former Munich sleuth had been transferred to the Frankfurt office of HICOG, the US High Commissioner for Germany, successor agency of the US Military Government. He was now working in its Division of Cultural Affairs on aspects of reeducation, professional exchanges, and German cultural revival. Breitenbach had great news. He told von Both that the US Department of State had picked up the trail of the lost *Liber Sapientiae*. The first leaf with the beginning verses of the *Hildebrandslied*, however, appeared to be missing. While still vague on details, he assured the library director that the codex was practically on its way home. He had it on good authority, from Ardelia Hall, the person in charge of art restitution in Washington, DC. She had asked that von Both and former director Hopf prepare an affidavit of ownership and explain the loss of the manuscript. In high spirits, Breitenbach proposed to celebrate the return of the codex with proper panache at the upcoming meeting of the German Library Association, scheduled for early June in Mainz, the city of Gutenberg.[7] Due to the sensitive nature of the investigation,

---

4 Gerhard Liebers, "Die Bibliotheksverhältnisse in Kassel nach dem Kriege" (Library conditions in Kassel after the war), *Zentralblatt für Bibliothekswesen* 65, no. 9/10 (1951): 384–85. Note: The Lending Section reopened on February 8, 1948 in the *Neue Galerie*, and was relocated to the Haus Ständeplatz 8 on December 12, 1948. The Reading Room became functional one year later, on March 19, 1949.

5 *Ex Bibliotheca Cassellana: 400 Jahre Landesbibliothek, 20.11.1580–20.11.1980* (From the Kassel Library: 400 years of State Library, 11/20/1580–11/20/1980), editor Hans-Jürgen Kahlfuß ([Kassel]: Gesamthochschul-Bibliothek-Kassel, Landesbibliothek und Murhardsche Bibliothek der Stadt Kassel, 1980), 46, 96.

6 "Hildebrandlied 1," documents from the archives of the Gesamthochschul-Bibliothek Kassel – Landesbibliothek und Murhardsche Bibliothek der Stadt Kassel, deposited with the University of California, Davis, Shields Library, Department of Special Collections. Letter from W. von Both to the Minister for Education and Culture, Wiesbaden, June 25, 1954.

7 "File Ms. of the Hildebrandslied from Kassel," US Department of State, Records Maintained by the Fine Arts and Monuments Adviser, 1945–61, Ardelia Hall Collection, Record

however, he advised that von Both refrain from giving the matter any premature publicity.

Not quite a month later, von Both received another communication, this time in the form of an effusive message signed by a New York academic, a certain Dr. Carl Selmer. "Esteemed Archivist," wrote the affable Professor, "by now you must have heard that Master Hildebrand has been apprehended on his flight over the Vandal Sea in the Land of Almerich. He will soon return to you. I cannot tell you how delighted I was to assist the old gentleman on his homeward journey." And the Professor closed with a Latin adage: "*Habent fata sua – heroes!*" Heroes have a fate of their own![8] Alarmed by Selmer's allusions, and worried that the unintended indiscretion might jeopardize negotiations, von Both forwarded a copy of the letter to Breitenbach, who sent it to Ardelia.[9] She was not pleased.[10]

Winter faded into a cool spring and spring melted into a radiant summer without any other news from Washington. True to his pledge, von Both kept a tight lid on the story. But whispers and rumors can never be fully controlled. To his distress he learned that at a scholarly meeting in Detroit that very same professor had made a public announcement about the discovery of the lost *Hildebrandslied* and suddenly the international scholarly community was abuzz with excitement. A frenzy of interest ripped through the German press. The looting in Bad Wildungen, the dark years of wanderings, and the impending happy ending, made excellent copy. The *Kasseler Post,*[11] the *Hessische Nachrichten,*[12] *Die Lesestunde,*[13] came out with clamorous headlines and romanticized versions of heist

---

Group 59. Lot 62D4, Box 6, Item 2, National Archives and Records Administration, Letter of E. Breitenbach to A. Hall, February 11, 1952.

8 "Hildebrandlied 1." documents from the archives. ... Letter of C. Selmer to the administration of the *Landesbibliothek* Kassel, March 6, 1952: "Sehr geehrter Herr Archivar! Sie werden wohl inzwischen erfahren haben, daß Meister Hildebrand bei seiner Flucht über das Wendelmeer in Almerichs Lande aufgegriffen wurde. Er wird sich wohl wieder bald bei Ihnen einfinden. Daß es mich freute, mehr als ich sagen kann, dem alten Herrn zu seinem Heimweg verholfen zu haben, brauche ich Ihnen nicht zu versichern. Habent fata sua – heroes! Ergebens Ihr, Carl Selmer." (Reproduced with the permission of Mrs. Irene Griffith Selmer).
Note: The name Amerigo (as in Vespucci) is derived from the old Gothic name of Amalrich or Almerich. Selmer was trying to force a historical connection between the name of the United States (the Land of Almerich or Amerigo, i.e. America) and the warrior Hildebrand.

9 "File Ms. of the Hildebrandlied from Kassel." Letter of A. Hall to S. Stephens, May 1st, 1952.

10 Ibid. Letter of A. Hall to S. Stephens, April 29, 1952.

11 "Hildebrandslied wiedergefunden" (The Hildebrandslied has been found), *Kasseler Post,* May 30, 1952.

12 "Das Hildebrandslied wurde jetzt in den Vereinigten Staaten gefunden" (The Song of Hildebrand has just now been found in the United States), *Hessische Nachrichten,* May 31, 1952.

13 Erich Kaiser, "Das Schicksal des Hildebrandsliedes: Eine moderne Odyssee" (The Fate of

and search.[14] Von Both was besieged with letters of inquiry and telephone calls.[15] How did the *Hildebrandslied* disappear? Who stole it? Was it truly seized at gunpoint? The harassed director was as much in the dark as his tormentors.

Selmer's prophecy of an imminent return did not come to pass. One month after another went by without any news and von Both began worrying that something had gone awry. He had no direct contact with the US Department of State, his lifeline was Breitenbach, and thus he turned once more to his colleague for advice. Was there anything his library, his *Landeshauptmann*, or his government could do to expedite the return process? Breitenbach had few suggestions. Patience, he advised. American authorities were no doubt engaged in delicate negotiations. Quite possibly the State Department was trying to recover not only the codex, but also the missing Leaf One and the *Willehalm*. Convoluted legal maneuvers were as always time-consuming. Diplomatic pressure could achieve little and might even end up hindering the investigation.[16] Reluctantly, von Both agreed to wait some more.

After yet another hundred days of silence, the director's anxiety level reached a new high. Two fresh letters from Professor Selmer cast serious doubt on the progress of the investigation. Selmer was distressed that Master Hildebrand con-

---

the Hildebrandslied: A modern odyssey), *Die Lesestunde: Zeitschrift der deutschen Buch-Gemeinschaft* 28, no. 7 (1952): 5.

14 The article in *Hessische Nachrichten*, "Das Hildebrandlied wurde jetzt in den Vereinigten Staaten gefunden," for instance, claimed that, when the manuscripts were reported missing, all local garbage cans as well as the Bad Wildungen city dump were thoroughly searched. "Das Schicksal des Hildebrandsliedes" by Erich Kaiser published in *Die Lesestunde* alleged that the manuscripts were first hidden in the cellar of castle Friedrichstein, atop a hill overlooking Bad Wildungen, and then at the hour of surrender moved frantically from bunker to bunker. A circulating urban legend implied that an American officer had forced curator Dr. Israël at gunpoint to hand over both manuscripts. (This rumor also resurfaced in a letter of H. Rosenfeld to H. Bahlow, November 7, 1955. See: "Hildebrandlied 1," documents from the archives ...).

15 "Hildebrandlied 6, Anfragen," documents from the archives ... lists a collection of requests for information. For instance: May 17, 1952, Professor Wolfgang Krause from the University of Göttingen, who lectured on Old High German literature, needed updated information for his seminars. *Deutsche Presse-Agentur* asked on May 30, 1952 for additional details on news circulating about the manuscript's return. Dr. Willy Krogmann, who on October 14, 1952 was preparing an article, asked for an update on the manuscript's whereabouts. Gg. Alms from Bad Segeberg inquired April 2, 1953, if the codex was indeed on its way back to Kassel. G. Hafner, who was preparing the fourth edition of the Vogelpohl-Hafner *Geschichte der deutschen Dichtung*, requested clarifications on April 14, 1953. Professor Dr. Werner Betz, who was preparing a new edition of the *Reallexikon der deutshen Literaturgeschichte*, needed an update on July 12, 1953. Professor Werner Kluge wrote a letter on November 27, 1953, and in the name of his entire class requested details on the theft.

16 "Hildebrandlied 1," documents from the archives. ... Letter of W. von Both to the *Landeshauptmann*, August 16, 1952.

tinued to remain at large. He had given Washington the location of the Seminary library, the name of the librarian, and even the floor on which the manuscript was shelved.[17] Surely even bureaucrats could follow such simple directions. Selmer had put together an article on his New York encounter with the codex, a matter of great interest to scholars of German literary history.[18] He was worried that some bureaucratic snafu or even worse, a political blunder was now blocking the return.

Selmer's letters must have had a demoralizing effect on the Kassel library director for he turned again to Breitenbach, this time insisting on an update.[19] Caught between the guarded Ardelia and the apprehensive von Both, Breitenbach tried to walk a fine political line. The delay did not necessarily mean that no progress had been made, he argued. In three weeks time he would be in Washington, and would personally call on Ardelia Hall to discuss the status of the investigation. Meanwhile, von Both might be well advised to begin exerting some diplomatic pressure on the US Department of State via the German Chargé d' Affaires in Washington.[20]

A green light from HICOG was all the encouragement von Both needed to activate the German political machine. He immediately appealed to the Lord Mayor of Kassel and to the *Landeshauptmann*, the Head of the Communal Administration of the district. The *Landeshauptmann* contacted State Secretary Dr. Walter Hallstein, at the Foreign Office in Bonn.[21] Dr. Hallstein followed up with an official address to the German diplomatic representation in Washington, DC requesting an update on the matter of the lost Kassel codex.[22] And the German diplomats in Washington leaned on the US Secretary of State.

At the State Department, Ardelia Hall was neither ready nor willing to show her hand. She was not intimidated by pressure, domestic or foreign, she was merely annoyed. She had nothing to report since she did not have the *Liber Sapientiae* codex in hand or any lead on the two other missing items. The visit of Agent Page to the House of Rosenbach had ended in failure. But since that unsuccessful episode, there had been some changes: both Doctor Rosenbach and his brot-

---

17 Ibid. Letter of C. Selmer to W. von Both, November 21, 1952.

18 Ibid. October 3, 1952.

19 Ibid. Letter of W. von Both to E. Breitenbach, December 16, 1952.

20 Ibid. Letter of E. Breitenbach to W. von Both, January 5, 1953.

21 Dr. Walter Hallstein (1902–1982), Professor of Law and Rector of the University in Frankfurt am Main (1946–1948), was Secretary of State (1951–1957), close adviser to Konrad Adenauer, and one of the architects of the integration of post-war Germany into the European community and Western alliance.

22 "Hildebrandlied 1," documents from the archives. ... See: Letters of von Both to Mayor Weismann and to the *Landeshauptmann*, and letter of *Landeshauptmann* to Dr. Hallstein, all of January 20, 1953.

her Philip had passed away.[23] Their Philadelphia home and splendid collections had been turned into a public institution for the advancement of fine art and scholarship. There was now an outside chance that the trustees of the newly established Rosenbach Foundation[24] would prove more inclined to cooperate with the Department of State. The tenacious Ardelia was planning to pay them a personal visit in Philadelphia.[25]

The other reason for her protracted silence was due to the fact that James Francis Louis Cardinal McIntyre DD, Archbishop of Los Angeles, had so far ignored her request for assistance. It was high time to send him a gentle reminder. Insofar as she could determine, Ardelia wrote to the prelate with dulcet diplomacy, the Department of State had received no reply to its letter in more than one year. In the intervening time her office had gathered a considerable amount of new information, and she was anxious for a chance to *update her dear Cardinal* on the matter of that lost German manuscript.[26]

She must have said a special prayer while placing the letter in the mail for this time His Eminence replied without delay. He had no recollection of any earlier correspondence. If Ardelia could send him a new batch of photostats, he would be more than happy to have them compared to the alleged stolen codex.[27] New copies and descriptions were sent to California posthaste. Ardelia assured His Eminence that, if indeed this turned out to be the codex in question, the Rosenbach Foundation would have to reimburse Mrs. Doheny for the full amount paid.[28] If there were any perceived *hesitation* on the part of the Foundation,

---

23 Edwin Wolf 2nd and John F. Fleming, *Rosenbach: A Biography* (Cleveland: World Publishing Company, 1960), 587. The Doctor had passed away on July 1, 1952, three weeks short of his seventy-sixth birthday. Eight months later, on March 5, 1953 Philip Rosenbach died of a heart attack at the age of eighty-nine.

24 Ibid., 568–569. Before their deaths, the Rosenbach brothers created the Rosenbach Foundation (April 1950), and endowed it with substantive funds and with their most valuable books and works of art.

25 "1945 Missal From Würzburg," US Department of State. Records Maintained by the Fine Arts and Monuments Adviser, 1945–61, Ardelia Hall Collection, Record Group 59 Lot 62D4, Box 6, National Archives and Records Administration. Letter of A. Hall to E. H. Schwenk, November 10, 1953.

26 "File Ms. of the Hildebrandslied from, Kassel." Letter of A. Hall to Cardinal McIntyre, March 6, 1953.

27 Ibid. Letter of Cardinal McIntyre to A. Hall, April 7, 1953.

28 William Freeman Twaddell, "The Hildebrandlied Manuscript in the U.S.A., 1945–1972," *Journal of English and Germanic Philology* 73, no. 2 (1974): 164. Estelle Doheny was fully reimbursed: "A letter dated December 17, 1953, over the signature of John Fleming indicated that Rosenbach refunded the $9,500 to Mrs. Doheny, and receipt of the check is acknowledged in a letter to Mr. Fleming dated January 8, 1954, and signed by Olin Wellborn III."
Note: Correspondence between Mary Gayle and F. Weber, dated November 14, 1972, released to the author by the Archdiocese of Los Angeles, the Archival Center, Estelle Doheny Collection of California, and deposited with the University of California, Davis, Shields

Ardelia would immediately seek *guidance* from the Department of Justice. With the assistance of the prelate she was hoping to wrap up this case without further delays.[29] The impatient frown on Ardelia's brow was clearly visible between the lines.

His Eminence was expeditious. The good fathers at the Saint John's Seminary compared Ardelia's photocopy to the last page of the codex on their shelf and confirmed that they were indeed identical. Countess Doheny and the Seminary declared themselves ready to surrender the *Liber Sapientiae*.[30] Ardelia was delighted. Her next step was to arrange for a safe transfer of the manuscript to Washington DC. This was easier said that done. Obviously, the irreplaceable codex could not be sent cross-country via regular mail. The fact that her first letter to the Cardinal had gone astray gave her justifiably pause. She consulted with curators of the National Gallery of Art, who were experienced in the transfer of valuables, and was advised to use a reliable messenger service.[31]

While Ardelia was busy with the minutiae of authentication and retrieval, Selmer, perplexed by the news blackout, sounded once again the alarm. Twelve months had passed since he had last heard from the Department of State, he complained in a letter to von Both. His article on the New World adventures of Master Hildebrand was ready for print. He was eager to share his story with the *Landesbibliothek* and the rest of the academic world. It was his dogged pursuit that had brought back to light this unique vestige of German literature. Without his knowledge and perseverance the ballad would have disappeared forever. He had earned, after all, a legitimate right to claim a bit of recognition for himself.[32] Rest assured, Selmer wrote to von Both, he would only speak of personal experiences. He did not intend to embarrass or accuse anyone. His article was written in German, addressed to a scholarly audience. This in itself was fairly restrictive. And he had taken additional precautions. All details pertaining to theft, sale and recovery had been intentionally scrambled. All place names had been obscured, all identities veiled, and all dates distorted so as to detract any would-be scan-

---

Library, Department of Special Collections, speaks of a rider, which was attached to Mrs. Doheny's 1953 Personal Income Tax Return. In this rider Mrs. Doheny indicates the need to amend her 1950 Tax Form relative to gifts given to St. John's Seminary in the amount of $9,500.

29 "File Ms. of the Hildebrandslied from Kassel." Letter of A. Hall to Cardinal McIntyre, May 5, 1953.

30 Ibid. Letter of A. Hall to S. Stephens, June 4, 1953. It mentions a letter received from the Cardinal dated May 19, 1953 agreeing to the release of the manuscript by the Saint John's Seminary. This letter is missing from the *Ardelia Hall Collection*.

31 Ibid. Letter of A. Hall to S. Stephens, May 5, 1953.

32 "Hildebrandlied 1," documents from the archives. ... Letter of C. Selmer to W. von Both, April 17, 1953.

dalmonger. This was a true *article-à-clef*, an encoded essay, he vowed. Von Both implored Selmer to delay publication until the codex was safely home.[33]

But nagging suspicions began raising their ugly heads. Were there truly nefarious forces at play in the United States that blocked the return of the codex, as Selmer seemed to imply?[34] Once again von Both turned to the offices of the *Landeshauptmann*. And once again the Hesse Minister of the Interior appealed to the Consul General of the German Diplomatic Representation in Washington, DC.[35] Cultural Attaché Dr. Bruno E. Werner called on the US Department of State demanding an update on the investigation. And once again Ardelia stonewalled.[36]

While Kassel was going through convulsions, Breitenbach, true to his promise, called on Ardelia Hall in Washington. She was busy with transfer arrangements, and unwilling to issue any communiqué. Breitenbach tried in vain to impress upon her that it was vital to keep the *Landesbibliothek* apprised of all developments. He explained that von Both was understandably anxious and warned that the prolonged news blackout could now backfire, resulting in negative publicity in Germany.[37] But no amount of direct or indirect exhortation could move the cautious Ardelia. She was determined to release no information until she had the codex in hand. Too many things could still go wrong.[38] While she sympathized with Breitenbach's mission of mercy, she had no time for explanations. She was about to launch the first phase of her transfer operation.

Her opening move was a letter to the fathers at the Saint John's Seminary Library citing chapter and verse on the infractions caused by the illegal removal and subsequent sale of the codex.[39] The theft in Bad Wildungen, she wrote, violated articles 47 and 56 of the Annex of the Hague Convention (IV) of 1907, as well as articles 318 and 329 of the Rules of Land Warfare (War Department Field Manual FM27-10, 1 October 1940). The codex was exported and sold in violation of Military Government Law 52, article II, paragraph 3(d) and of the November, 21 1944 directive known as *Prohibition of Sale and Export of Works*

---

33 Ibid. Letter of W. von Both to C. Selmer, April 24, 1953.

34 Ibid. Letter of W. von Both to E. Breitenbach, April 24, 1953.

35 Ibid. Letter of the *Landeshauptmann* to Dr. Krekeler, April 24, 1953.

36 "File Ms. of the Hildebrandslied from Kassel." Letter of Secretary of State to the Chargé d'Affaires of the Federal Republic of Germany, June 9, 1953. Although the final letter was transmitted under the signature of the Secretary of State, the draft reveals at the bottom the initials of its real author, Ardelia Hall.

37 "Hildebrandlied 1," documents from the archives. ... Letter of E. Breitenbach to W. von Both, May 9, 1953.

38 "File Ms. of the Hildebrandslied from Kassel." Letter of A. Hall to E. H. Schwenk, September 10, 1953.

39 Ibid. Letter of A. Hall to Saint John's Seminary, June 5, 1953.

of Art in Germany of the Supreme Headquarters of the Allied Expeditionary Force (SHAEF). Finally, the manuscript was transported in interstate and foreign commerce in contravention of Federal Law[40], of United States Customs regulations, and of Treasury Decision 51072. It was these violations that now authorized her in the name of the US Department of State to impound the looted volume. The return of the codex to its rightful owner was mandated under the general policies of the United States Government and under procedures laid down in the statement of policy *Return of Looted Objects to Countries of Origin*, (SWNC/322) approved by the State-War-Navy Coordinating Committee on January 28, 1947.

After issuing her multi-count indictment, Ardelia summoned a sister agency to redress the violations. On behalf of the US Department of State, the Head of Penalties of the Washington Customs Bureau, Shirley Stephens, dispatched Colonel Carl F. White, Collector of Customs, to Los Angeles to secure the codex. On June 26, 1953, after exchanging proper receipts and assurances, a representative of Cardinal McIntyre handed over to Colonel White a bound Latin codex called *Liber Sapientiae* with the second page of the *Hildebrandlied*.[41] With this, phase one of the transfer operation was successfully concluded.

Phase two was aimed at bringing the codex safely to Washington, DC. Once again Ardelia attended personally to all transfer details. She first tried to find a pilot who could act as her personal messenger, only to learn that union contracts prohibited airline personnel from transporting valuable property on board.[42] Next she inquired if the courier division of the Armed Services could retrieve and deliver the codex. Yes, she was told, it could be done. She obtained a Top Secret classification and researched optimal airline connections to and from Los Angeles. On August 11, 1953, with all arrangements in place, Ardelia issued her final instructions. In the cropped phrasing of a telegram, she laid down directives for the courier, listing flight numbers, routes, contact people, and hand-over procedures. Her wire ended in an order: "Secure movement manuscript paramount."[43] There was to be no press release. Until she had the manuscript in hand, she was not willing to take any chances.

On August 13, 1953 Edward Blaisdell Fenstermacher, Diplomatic Courier of the United States, acknowledged in writing the receipt of one bound volume known

---

[40] National Stolen Property Act, U.S. Code Title 18, Crimes and Criminal Procedure, Sections 2314 and 2315.

[41] "File Ms. of the Hildebrandslied from Kassel." Letter of S. Stephens to A. Hall, June 15, 1953 and letter of C. F. White to Commissioner of Customs, Washington, June 26, 1953.

[42] Ibid. A. Hall personal handwritten notes, not dated.

[43] Ibid. A. Hall teletyped instructions to the courier, August 11, 1953.

as the *Liber Sapientiae Solomonis*, and containing one page of the heroic ballad known as the *Hildebrandslied*. Traveling east under a Top Secret classification, he landed safely in Washington, DC and delivered the codex in person to Ardelia Hall at the US Department of State.[44] After eighteen months of searching, strategizing, and planning, Ardelia finally held in her hand the eleven hundred-year-old treasure of the Kassel *Landesbibliothek*.

There remained one final phase in her return operation: the transfer of the manuscript to Bonn and from there to its home library in Kassel. Only then could Ardelia claim at least partial victory and celebrate with a splashy public relations campaign. She signaled HICOG that she was ready to send the *Liber Sapientiae* to Germany within the week. The restitution of this manuscript of enormous importance was bound to generate widespread interest, she cautioned. To parry any potentially embarrassing questions, she offered to craft a press release for distribution to German radio, television, and newspapers, in which she reiterated the US State Department's pledge to spare no effort in the continued search for the still-missing Leaf One and for the *Willehalm*.[45] Convinced that in a matter of days the return operation would be concluded, Ardelia arranged for the *Liber Sapientiae* to be sent to Bonn via Pentagon Army Courier, once again under a Top Secret classification, and began drafting her Public Information Statement.[46]

The confidential injunction received from Bonn six days later must have been utterly disappointing. HICOG reiterated its former directive that the codex could not be returned without its missing leaf and without the *Willehalm*. Rumors were swirling in Bonn that the severed page of the *Hildebrandslied* had been sold to a high-ranking American. The repatriation of the mangled codex alone could set off bitter recriminations, which could seriously affect the prestige of the United States.[47]

What HICOG had failed to understand, was that Ardelia's investigation had come to a dead end. For months her informers had found no new lead. After the failed investigation of Agent Page, Ardelia had little reason to believe that a second visit to the new Rosenbach Foundation would prove more productive. Her very last recourse was an appeal to the general public, but even that was a

---

[44] Ibid. Receipt signed by E. B. Fenstermacher, August 13, 1953; Office memorandum of the Collector of Customs, Los Angeles, California to the Commissioner of Customs, Washington, DC, August 14, 1953 and letter of S. Stephens to A. Hall, August 20, 1953.

[45] Ibid. Letter of A. Hall to E. H. Schwenk, September 10, 1953.

[46] Ibid. Handwritten notes. The very professional and reserved Ardelia Hall must have been utterly annoyed by this politically motivated injunction, for she coarsely refers to her canceled *Public Information Statement* by its initials (PIS), marked in big letters and highlighted in bold black pen.

[47] Ibid. Letter of E. H. Schwenk to A. Hall, September 16, 1953.

very long shot.[48] However an order is an order, and as a good soldier she could only shrug her shoulders and obey. Ardelia understood all too well that the search for the Kassel codices was a politically charged issue. She had no choice but to lock up the mutilated *Liber Sapientiae* in her departmental safe, cancel all outstanding transfer arrangements, tear up her Public Information Statement, and pursue her petering investigation to its very last gasp.

48 Ibid. Letter of A. Hall to E. H. Schwenk, October 26, 1953.

Chapter 14: Return of the Wounded Warrior

Before launching a public appeal, Ardelia called the Rosenbach Foundation in Philadelphia to set up an appointment with its trustees. Regrettably, she was told, a meeting could not be arranged since all trustees were traveling abroad.[1] Undaunted, Ardelia took down their names,[2] and zeroed in on the most prominent of all: Lessing J. Rosenwald, President of the Rosenbach Foundation, her best hope for insider information.

A. S. W. Rosenbach and his wealthy client Lessing J. Rosenwald had been friends forever. The Doctor had nurtured Lessing Rosenwald's budding love for early-illustrated books and had groomed him to become one of the greatest private collectors the country had ever seen. So ardent was Rosenwald's passion that, at the early age of forty-eight, he had resigned his position as Chairman of the Board of Directors of Sears Roebuck and Co. in order to devote the rest of his life to his bibliophile pursuits. He now lived in Jenkintown, outside Philadelphia, on a 150-acre estate called Alverthorpe. His Georgian manor had a built-in gallery especially designed to house his extraordinary collections created with the expert help of the Doctor.

On the telephone, Elizabeth Mongan, Rosenwald's personal curator, was less than engaging. Her employer was not available, she told Ardelia. Questions regarding Doctor R were best addressed to the Foundation or to Edwin Wolf 2nd, Rosenbach's nephew and former manager of the Philadelphia bookstore. Ardelia must have insisted, for Mongan agreed to arrange a meeting between Ardelia and Edwin Wolf at the Alverthorpe Gallery, sometime before Christmas.[3] Ahead of the meeting date, Ardelia sent to Jenkintown photostats of the missing Leaf One and copies of several miniatures from the *Willehalm Codex*.[4]

No sooner had Ardelia hung up, than Elizabeth Mongan called the Rosenbach Foundation, asking to speak with its Executive Director, John F. Fle-

---

1 "File Ms. of the Hildebrandlied from Kassel," US Department of State, Records Maintained by the Fine Arts and Monuments Adviser, 1945–61, Ardelia Hall Collection, Record Group 59. Lot 62D4, Box 6, Item 2, National Archives and Records Administration, Letter of A. Hall to E. H. Schwenk, October 26, 1953.

2 Ibid. Handwritten notes.

3 Ibid. Handwritten notes dated October 28, 1953. Letter of A. Hall to E. Mongan, November 6, 1953.
Note: Elizabeth Mongan and Edwin Wolf 2nd had collaborated on two catalogues: in 1939 they had published together a descriptive catalogue of the works of William Blake, and in 1940 they had co-edited another catalogue commemorating the five-hundredth anniversary of the invention of printing.

4 Ibid. Letter of H. Hall to E. Mongan, November 6, 1953.

Fig. 21. John F. Fleming, Dr. A. S. W. Rosenbach, and Lessing J. Rosenwald (Archives of the Rosenbach Foundation – Reproduced by permission)

ming.[5] She let Fleming know that the Department of State had recovered the looted *Liber Sapientiae* from the Doheny Library in California, and that art consultant Ardelia Hall was on the warpath, trying to retrace the history of that sale. Alarmed, Fleming called Lucille Miller, Mrs. Doheny's secretary, with explanations and apologies, and followed up with a letter to the Countess. The Rosenbach Company, he explained with obvious chagrin, had purchased the *Liber Sapientiae* – a tenth century codex of little distinction – in good faith from a returning US Army officer, who had found it in the rubble of southern Germany. At the time, there had been no reason to doubt the legitimacy of the business transaction. The story of the soldier sounded very convincing. He had obtained the permission of his commanding officer to send the ownerless manuscript home. The package had passed US Customs without incident, for Fleming remembered seeing the postal wrappings with the official tags still on. What made this awkward situation even more deplorable, he wrote to the Countess with embarrassment, was that the Rosenbach Company had failed to notice the last page of the manuscript. Had they recognized the *Hildebrandslied* they would have immediately placed the codex under protective custody. Now, that

[5] Archdiocese of Los Angeles, Archival Center, Estelle Doheny Collection of California correspodence deposited with the University of California, Davis, Shields Library, Department of Special Collections. Letter of J. F. Fleming to E. L. Doheny, November 19, 1953.

the error had come to light, Fleming and the Rosenbach Foundation trustees were ready to reimburse Mrs. Doheny for the cost of the codex. The Countess accepted the compensation, but treated Fleming's explanations with a healthy dose of skepticism.[6]

Elizabeth Mongan's discouraging tone of voice and defensive demeanor must have dashed Ardelia's last hope for new information. Thus, on December 10, 1953, after properly notifying HICOG, she contacted the German Cultural Attaché, and informed him that the *Liber Sapientiae* with Leaf Two of the *Hildebrandslied* had been recovered and that it was securely locked up in her safe at the State Department. She assured the diplomat that she would not rest until the other two manuscripts were found and returned.[7] For Kassel, the Advent season had opened with a miracle. The *Landesbibliothek* could not have wished for a better Christmas present.[8]

Despite her misgivings, Ardelia did not cancel her Alverthorpe meeting. She remained determined to pursue all leads, no matter how tenuous. On Tuesday morning, December 15, 1953, she traveled to Jenkintown. As expected, the encounter was less than productive. Curator Mongan had no direct knowledge of the *Hildebrandslied*-affair and offered no further suggestions. And neither did Dr. Rosenbach's nephew, Edwin Wolf 2nd. Ardelia quizzed him on his wartime activities and learned that in spring of 1945 he had served under G-2, Intelligence in the Fulda District, close to Bad Wildungen. Wolf explained that at the time he was investigating the art dealings of Philip von Hesse and Hermann Goering, and promised to send her his final report.[9] This was very interesting, but had nothing to do with the *Hildebrandslied* case and Ardelia left Alverthorpe empty handed.

There was one last arrow left in her quiver, an appeal to the general public. Her call for help appeared in the October 1954 issue of the *Department of State Bulletin*, the official record of US foreign policy.[10] Ardelia told her readers about the

---

[6] Letters at the Archival Center of the Archdiocese of Los Angeles attest to the fact that Mrs. Doheny and her librarian considered the role of the Rosenbach Company in the purchase and subsequent sale of the *Liber Sapientiae* open to question. See, for example, letter of M. Gayle to F.J. Weber, November 14, 1972; letter to F. J. Weber to B. G. Hawkes, November 15, 1972; as well as letter to B. G. Hawkes to M. Gayle, November 20, 1972.

[7] "Hildebrandlied 1," documents from the archives of the Gesamthochschul-Bibliothek Kassel – Landesbibliothek und Murhardsche Bibliothek der Stadt Kassel, deposited with the University of California, Davis, Shields Library, Department of Special Collections. Letter of B. E. Werner to W. von Both, December 10, 1953.

[8] Ibid. Letter of W. von Both to B. E. Werner, December 23, 1953.

[9] "File Ms. of the Hildebrandslied from Kassel." Handwritten notes.

[10] *The Bulletin* was published weekly from 1939 to 1989, and included information on US foreign relations and on the work of the Department of State and Foreign Service.

looting in Bad Wildungen, about the history of the ballad, and about its importance to history, literature, and the cultural identity of the German people. "The two surviving pages owned by the Kassel Library, are among the most valuable manuscripts of world literature," she wrote with thinly veiled emotion. The severed leaf was "probably the greatest single loss to literature resulting from World War II." She appended full-page illustrations of Leaf One and of miniatures from the *Willehalm*. If the manuscripts were found she asked her readers to return them to the nearest public library with a request for safe transfer to the US Department of State in Washington, DC. She ended her solicitation with a credo that echoed the voice of the Monuments Officers, of whom she was one of the last active members.

> The protection of cultural property and respect for its ownership are based upon the traditional principles upheld by the United States Government. ... By returning the dispersed objects, which have passed from public collections in Europe to private hands in the United States, the US Government has performed a great public service. It is a service not only to the nations, which have regained precious symbols of their cultural heritage, but to all lovers of art and literature ...[11]

By summer's end, Ardelia had gathered in her departmental safe another choice harvest of US war-trophies. On the morning of September 10, 1954, in a formal ceremony, she handed over to German Cultural Attaché Dr. Bruno E. Werner the precious *Liber Sapientiae Solomonis*. Her other war-mementos included a 1495 *Würzburg Missal*, the fifteenth- and seventeenth-century archives of the town of Grebenstein in Hesse, a group of assorted Munich gems and Weimar coins, a Düsseldorf painting, and an Aachen banner.[12] The return of these war-displaced objects received no coverage in the US press.

In contrast, European radio, television and newspapers had a field day. The story of the *Hildebrandslied* was carried throughout the German-speaking world and beyond. Bold headlines sprinkled with uninhibited superlatives heralded the return of one of the most important manuscript of the Middle Ages.[13] In Kassel, letters of congratulation from literati, historians, medievalists, professors, students, and ordinary citizens poured in. In the midst of visits, telephone calls, telegrams, and interviews, a sober message from the Foreign Office in Bonn reminded Director von Both that he had to insure the codex for its upcoming

---

[11] Ardelia R. Hall, "U.S. Program for Return of Historic Objects to Countries of Origin, 1944–1954," *Department of State Bulletin* 31, no. 797 (1954): 495, 497.

[12] "File Ms. of the Hildebrandslied from Kassel," Department of State Press Release, no. 502, September 10, 1954 and Receipt for cultural objects signed by B. E. Werner and A. Hall, September 10, 1954 and Schedule A of the same date.

[13] Articles appeared, among others, in the *Kasseler Zeitung* of September 11, 1954; *Kasseler Post* of September 11/12, 1954; *Hessische Nachrichten*, September 9, 1954, a second article in the *Kasseler Post* of September 18/19, 1954, and in *Deutscher Kurier*, October 10, 1954.

RECEIPT FOR CULTURAL OBJECTS

The undersigned, Dr. Bruno E. Werner,

duly accredited by the German Government,

hereby acknowledges the receipt on behalf of the said government, from the Secretary of State on behalf of the UNITED STATES GOVERNMENT for the items described in Schedule "A" attached hereto.

The delivery of these items is subject to the following conditions:

1. The receiving government hereby certifies that the items described in Schedule "A" attached are the property of that government or of a national of that government.

2. The receiving government undertakes to restore any object delivered to it by mistake to the Secretary of State of the United States of America for restitution to the government of the rightful owner.

3. The receiving government agrees that the United States Government and all its agents, representatives, and xxxxxxx shall be saved harmless from any claim for loss, damage, or deterioration suffered by any item from the time of its removal from the jurisdiction of the country receiving restitution until its return thereto.

Ardelia R. Hall	Bruno E. Werner
Witness	Signature
September 10, 1954	Bruno E. Werner
Date	Signature typed
Washington, D. C.	Cultural Counselor
Place	Title or Capacity of Signer

Fig. 22a. Official return receipt for the mutilated *Liber Sapientiae*
(United States National Archives and Records Administration – Ardelia Hall Collection.)

Page 1 of 3 pages

SCHEDULE "A" Date September 10, 1954.

ITEM	DESCRIPTION (including statement of condition of object)
Hildebrandslied Codex of the Kassel Landesbibliothek. 1 Item	The text of the Hildebrandslied, dating from about the year 800 A. D., on two pages: leaf 1 <u>recto</u> and leaf 76 <u>verso</u> of a 10th century bound manuscript: "Liber Sapientiae"; originally 76 leaves, with 1 MS. page glued to back cover, parchment, size 28.5 x 21 cm; bound in leather, rebacked. Blue leather box to hold MS. <u>Leaf 1: one of the two pages of text of the Hildebrandslied has been removed and is missing.</u> Manuscript now contains only 75 leaves. The pages are numbered in pencil from 1 -75. The manuscript is loose from the binding. Page 8, now numbered 7, from which page 1 was torn is loose. On back cover, written in ink "6362" and in pencil "Rosenbach 3/50".

Fig. 22b.

voyage home. Its material value was inestimable and the suggested coverage of 1 to 5 million marks, or $ 300,000 to $ 1.5 million, bore no relation to its real worth. After some serious number crunching, von Both declared that the codex would return to Germany the same way it had left, completely uninsured.[14] Furthermore, he decided that it would journey by sea, and not by air.[15] Planes, in the library director's opinion, had a nasty habit of crashing, and this could prove quite discomforting to Master Hildebrand, an aging warrior in armor.[16] It took another six months before Cultural Attaché Bruno Werner found time and opportunity to chaperone the manuscript on its maritime voyage home.[17]

In the closing days of March 1955, almost five years after the discovery of the codex in California, von Both received word from the Cultural Division of the Bonn Foreign Ministry that his *Liber Sapientiae* was back on German soil. He was asked to come and retrieve it without delay since the ministerial vault was not secure. The unexpected urgency put the director and his library in a financial bind. It was the last week of the budget cycle, and under the heading "Travel Expenses" the treasury showed a positive balance of fifteen marks, the equivalent of five dollars. The cost of a second-class round trip train ticket to Bonn was sixty-one marks and the library director needed at least another twelve for ground transportation and sundry expenses. With obvious difficulty, Director von Both succeeded in covering the travel costs out of pocket. His meager librarian salary must have left a very narrow margin for unexpected expenses. He remained cautiously optimistic that the Ministry of Education would eventually reimburse him for the trip.[18]

On Friday, March 25, von Both arrived in Bonn on the 12:44 afternoon train and called on the Foreign Ministry to pick up his treasure.[19] He had brought along a leather briefcase in which he planned to carry the fragile codex home. The thought of packing a gun to defend the *Hildebrandslied* in case of attack crossed his mind more than once.[20] In the end, unarmed and unescorted, he boarded his second-class train compartment for the trip home, and placed the $ 1.5 million

---

14 "Hildebrandlied 1," documents from the archives. ... File memorandum of W. von Both, not dated, possibly October 11, 1954.

15 Ibid. Letter of W. von Both to Dr. von Beyme, February 11, 1955.

16 "Ritter Hildebrand von langer Irrfahrt zurück" (Knight Hildebrand back from long odyssey), *Kasseler Post,* July 16 1955.

17 "Hildebrandlied 1," documents from the archives. ... Letter of H. Russell to W. von Both, March 22, 1955.

18 Ibid. Letter of W. von Both to Dr. von Bila, March 22, 1955.

19 Ibid. Receipt signed by W. von Both for Dr. von Beyme, March 31, 1955.

20 "Ritter Hildebrand von langer Irrfahrt zurück." Also: "Nach 10jähriger Odyssee: Hildebrandslied zum Teil wieder daheim" (After a ten year journey, part of the Hildebrandslied is back home), *Hessische Nachrichten,* July 19, 1955.

briefcase on his knee, arms linked protectively across it. His amicable travel companions had no inkling that an eleven-hundred-year-old passenger had hitched along for the ride. As soon as he arrived in Kassel, von Both deposited the codex in the vault of the city bank.[21] Then he set out to organize the official festive return of Master Hildebrand.

* * *

"With reverence, gratitude and longing, I now hold in my hand this document of old," a document, which embodies "the spirit and identity of the German people." With these emotional words the Minister of Education and Culture of Hesse, Arno Hennig, officially returned the *Liber Sapientiae Codex* to its home library.[22] In the temporary reading room at the Ständeplatz, cheerfully decorated with sprays of red and white gladiola, some one hundred festively attired patrons, politicians, press representatives, and library friends had gathered on Saturday, July 16, 1955 to celebrate the homecoming of the wounded warrior. Director Wolf von Both raised his glass to toast those who had spared no effort in the search for his *Lieblingskind*, his favorite child: his colleague Edgar Breitenbach, the indefatigable Ardelia Hall, and the doting chaperon, diplomat Bruno E. Werner. On a lighter note, just for the Minister of Education and Culture, von Both theatrically recited the perennial lament of the librarian, which opened with demure demands for more funds, more books, more space, more people. It was a well-timed masterpiece of library promotion. To everyone's delight the dramatic lament extracted from the softened-up politician the promise of a new library building.[23] Present among well-wishers were two witnesses to the codex's tumultuous existence: the recently rehabilitated Hans Peter des Coudres, now head of the Library of the Max-Planck Institute for Foreign and International Civil Law in Hamburg[24] and Wilhelm Hopf, the soul of the *Landesbibliothek*. For them the day was a mixture of sunshine and shadow, for the joyful return of the *Liber Sapientiae* brought into sharp focus the loss of the glorious *Willehalm Codex* and the absence of the first half of the heroic warrior ballad.

---

21 "Hildebrandslied hinter dicken Panzertüren" (The Hildebrandslied behind heavy steel doors), *Kasseler Post*, July 16, 1955.

22 "Hildebrand wieder daheim" (Hildebrand is back home), *Hessische Nachrichten*, July 18, 1955.

23 Ibid.

24 According to Michael Labach, des Coudres's biography is a prime example of the rehabilitation of former Nazis in post-war West Germany and of their return to library leadership positions. See: His "Der Verein deutscher Bibliothekare während des Nationalsozialismus" (The German Library Association during National Socialism), in: *Bibliotheken während des Nationalsozialismus*, part 2, Peter Vodosek and Michael Komorowski, eds. (Wiesbaden: Harrassowitz, 1992), 167, footnote 41.

Chapter 15: Eyewitness

It was on a Friday, in late January of 1961, long past the season of miracles, when Edgar Breitenbach called on Ardelia Hall with stunning news. He had chanced upon an eyewitness, a person who had seen the *Liber Sapientiae* change hands in New York, right after the war. Back from Germany, Breitenbach was now Chief of the Prints and Photograph Division at the Library of Congress. His eyewitness was a library colleague, a cataloger. Her name was Gretel Mayer, a woman in her mid-fifties, a former German judge. Like Breitenbach, Mayer had been forced to flee her homeland, and had wandered around Europe before immigrating to the United States.[1] Fate had brought them together under one roof, at the Library of Congress. One day they had struck up a conversation and this was how Breitenbach discovered that Mayer had been Rosenbach's cataloger. And yes, late in 1945 she had witnessed the sale of the *Liber Sapientiae*. She was right there in the room when Fleming bought the book.[2]

Breitenbach went methodically over his conversation with Gretel Mayer earlier that day. At the close of 1945, a returning US officer had brought two books to the store, hoping for a quick and profitable sale. One was large, with colorful illustrations, the other unadorned and much smaller. Gretel Mayer remembered seeing a seal of ownership in the smaller book, the one she called the *Liber Sapientiae*. Days later, purely by accident, in a desk drawer, Mayer had come across a single vellum leaf. It was the one with the ownership mark. Someone had cut the leaf out of the codex. She also remembered one other detail: the bookstore secretary had mentioned that Rosenbach had sold the other manuscript, the one with illuminations, for many times the amount originally paid by the firm.

A breakthrough. After seven years of silence, finally there seemed to be a breakthrough. Ardelia's public appeal had gone unheeded. Not one single soul had stepped forward with information. She had come to believe that only a miracle could breathe life into her unsolved case. This *Mayer ex machina* was perhaps her seven-year wonder. The eyewitness seemed to validate Ardelia's long held suspicion that the codex was whole at the time of purchase, that in 1945 the first leaf

---

1 Ben R. Tucker, Gretel Mayer's colleague at the Library of Congress, generously provided the author with biographical data. See: Ben R. Tucker, correspondence with the author, deposited with the University of California, Davis, Shields Library, Department of Special Collections.

2 "File Ms. of Hildebrandlied from Kassel," US Department of State. Records Maintained by the Fine Arts and Monuments Adviser, 1945–61, Ardelia Hall Collection, Record Group 59. Lot 62D4, Box 6, Item 2, National Archives and Records Administration. Memorandum of Conversation: E. Breitenbach and A. Hall, January 27, 1961.

Fig. 23. Gretel Mayer
(Library of Congress Gazette, October 20, 1995. US Government illustration.)

with the beginning of the ballad was part and parcel of the book. More than that, now there also seemed to be a reference to the *Willehalm*, a book with beautiful illustrations, which had commanded a handsome price. Gretel Mayer's testimony could blow the case wide open. Ardelia had to talk to her in person, as soon as possible, preferably on Monday.

Breitenbach hastily arranged a meeting between Ardelia, Gretel Mayer and Gretel's supervisor, Jane Hall. Monday morning January 30, Ardelia headed for the Library of Congress, directions in hand: second floor of the Annex, center room at the rear.[3] Miss Mayer was waiting. She was a middle-aged woman, with frank, probing eyes. After customary introductions, Ardelia asked Mayer to describe the incident. She obliged. She remembered John Fleming, manager of the Rosenbach New York store, calling her downstairs to the book-room one November day in 1945 because he could not figure out the text on the first page of an other-

[3] Ibid. Undated. Handwritten note by Ardelia.

Ardelia R. Hall - CU/AM
(Drafting Office and Officer)

OFFICIAL USE ONLY

DEPARTMENT OF STATE

Memorandum of Conversation

DATE: July 12, 1961

SUBJECT: Missing Hildebrandslied Page and Willehalm Codex

PARTICIPANTS: ARHall
Miss Gretel Mayer, Descriptive Catalogue Division
Library of Congress
Tel. L. C. Code 173, Ext. 609
Home address: 215 C St. S.E.
Washington 3, D. C.

COPIES TO:

Miss Mayer said she wanted to explain that when the American brought the 10th century "Liber Sapientiae" to Rosenbach she was called from her desk to the Reception Room to look at the MS. and on the front page was an oval mark of the Kassel Library, in Latin, reading "Bibliotheca Kastelana." She was called in because Mr. John F. Fleming was not able to read the early German language in an old script (A.R.H. comment, this would mean the Hildebrandslied).

Miss Mayer said to the American, who was offering the MS for sale, so you were in Kassel. He seemed surprised and asked her how she knew and she pointed out the stamp of the Kassel Library. She said, she was given the Liber Sapientiae to study for three days and wrote a report for Mr. Fleming on it.

She said it was a book without its cover, just the MS.

Sometime later, she opened the drawer of a Renaissance table in the vault, looking for a pencil and saw the page with the Kassel Library mark, that had been cut from its binding.

Miss Mayer

OFFICIAL USE ONLY

GPO 885971

Fig. 23. Ardelia Hall's memorandum of conversation with Gretel Mayer
(United States National Archives and Records Administration – Ardelia Hall Collection.)

wise Latin codex. Gretel thought the text was written in an early German language. On the verso, she noticed a fairly large oval library ownership stamp which read *Ex Bibliotheca Cassellana*. This prompted her to ask the seller if he had spent time in Kassel during the war. The seller was puzzled, a bit disconcerted. Fleming had given Gretel three days to study the codex and write a report. And yes, later in the week she had come across that very same page, the one with the odd text on one side and the library stamp on the other, casually thrown in a desk drawer. This time, the leaf was detached[4] and the stamp blurry.

The identity of the GI was of utmost importance and Ardelia asked if Miss Mayer could recall his name. He was not a GI, Mayer corrected her. He was an officer. No, she could not remember his name offhand, but she had it written down on a piece of paper. The note had to be somewhere in her files at home. Ardelia made Mayer promise to call as soon as she found her note.[5] To put her witness at ease and gain her confidence, Ardelia offered to send her a copy of her appeal for the return of the missing Kassel manuscripts. If Gretel understood the immense historical and cultural importance of the lost items, she might be more inclined to testify, should it ever become necessary.

Ardelia was very pleased with this initial meeting. Back in her office, after mailing off the article, she looked up the name and address of the curator of the Rosenbach Museum. Armed with this new ammunition, the time had finally come to pay him and his Foundation an official governmental visit. "Mr. William H. McCarthy, Jr.," Ardelia wrote down in her clear, bold handwriting, "the Philip H. and A. S. W. Rosenbach Foundation, on 2010 DeLancey Place in Philadelphia." She underlined the phrase five times, as if to strengthen her resolve to go once more on the attack.[6]

But no word came from Gretel Mayer. As winter turned to spring, and spring to summer, Ardelia called the Library of Congress and arranged a follow-up meeting. This time, Mayer was no longer cooperative. She huffily remarked that both Edgar Breitenbach and Ardelia Hall had completely misunderstood her. What she had seen in 1945 was most definitely not the *Hildebrandslied*. It was a page from a Latin codex called the *Liber Sapientiae*. Patiently Ardelia explained that there was no misunderstanding, they were talking about one and the same thing. But her explanations had no effect. The more she insisted, the more refractory Mayer became. No, there was nothing more to add about those two codices or about her former employer. Could she at least explain why she had resigned from the Rosenbach Company? She had to, Mayer blurted out, because of such deal-

---

4 Ibid. Memorandum of Conversation, A. Hall and G. Mayer, July 12, 1961.

5 Ibid. Memorandum of Conversation, E. Breitenbach and A. Hall, January 27, 1961.

6 Ibid. Undated handwritten note.

ings![7] This said, she did not want to further implicate Philip Rosenbach or John Fleming.[8] And no, she had not found her note with the officer's name.

Ardelia was puzzled. Gretel Mayer appeared frightened. She changed tactics from pressure to reassurance. For many years, Ardelia explained, librarians in leading research institutions, had voluntarily assisted the Department of State in its search for war-looted art. This close cooperation had led to the return of more than one thousand objects. Their information and testimony had always been held in strict confidence. Miss Mayer had nothing to fear, for her statements would also remain confidential. But no amount of eloquence could dispel Mayer's panic attack. She did not want to be interviewed again, she declared, not unless it was cleared in advance with Jane Hall, her supervisor. And with that she abruptly broke off the meeting.[9]

From the Library of Congress Ardelia went straight to her friend and confidant, the Chief of the Customs Bureau. Was Mayer's confused testimony enough to reopen the investigation? They analyzed their meager information and discussed the reliability of their star witness. There was not enough to work with.[10] Customs needed at least the name of the officer and a strong commitment from Gretel Mayer that she would remain firm on her facts under cross-examination. Ardelia was doubtful that she could deliver either.

---

7 Ibid. Memorandum of Conversation, A. Hall and G. Mayer, July 12, 1961.
Note: In his June 21, 2000 letter to the author, Ben R. Tucker, Gretel Mayer's long-time colleague, commented on Gretel Mayer's probity: "If Ms. Mayer had witnessed dishonesty and had at the time testified to the same, I would believe her. She was not a timid person. That later she feared ... Mr. Fleming doesn't necessarily alter this picture of her not only of being honest but forthright. ... What can be averred confidently is that such fearful timidity was never an element in her character as known to her Library of Congress colleagues." (Quote reproduced by permission)

8 "Hildebrandlied 2," documents from the Archives of the Gesamthochschul-Bibliothek Kassel – Landesbibliothek und Murhardsche Bibliothek der Stadt Kassel, deposited with the University of California, Davis, Shields Library, Department of Special Collections. Travelogue of D. Hennig, March 1, 1972. While in Washington, Dr. Hennig was given the Embassy's *Hildebrandslied File* to study. It included an interview conducted by Diplomat Karl J. Maes, of the German Embassy, with Gretel Mayer. During the interview, Gretel Mayer had alleged that it was Fleming who had tried to obliterate the ownership stamp. Gretel was described as an elderly lady, reluctant to be drawn into a legal battle and seemingly uncomfortable to implicate her former employer.

9 "File Ms. of Hildebrandslied from Kassel." Memorandum of Conversation, A. Hall and G. Mayer, July 12, 1961.
Note: This reaction of fear and panic was most unusual. Again Ben R. Tucker: "The courage she showed [on many occasions when facing pressures from people in power] makes it difficult to see her as a timid person apt to be 'terrorized' for no reason at all." (Quote reproduced by permission)

10 Ibid. Memorandum of Conversation, A. Hall and J. Hall, July 13, 1961.

Unwilling to concede, Ardelia returned the next day to the second floor of the Annex, center room in the rear, determined to question Mayer one last time, albeit in the presence of her supervisor. Before calling Mayer in, Ardelia had a private conversation with Jane Hall. She explained that the Kassel codices were enormously important, high among the most precious cultural items lost during the war. Surely catalogers and book lovers like Jean Hall and Gretel Mayer could empathize with such tragic loss. The information known to Miss Mayer was of utmost importance to the Department of State, for without her testimony there could be no further investigation. Jane Hall was supportive, but there were definite limits to what she could do. She called Gretel Mayer once again to her office.[11]

A downright hostile Mayer entered the room. No, for the last time, she did not remember the name of the seller, and she did not find her note. Could she at least describe the officer? Stubbornly, Gretel refused. Ardelia showed her the 1954 signed receipt for the mutilated *Liber Sapientiae.* The returned manuscript had only seventy-five leaves, and historical descriptions listed it with seventy-six. One leaf was missing, and that leaf was the one Gretel had seen in the drawer, the first page with the *Hildebrandslied.* But neither logic, nor pressure could move Gretel to disclose anything more. Vehemently she declared that if she were brought before Mr. Fleming, she would not utter one other word. She had visualized the confrontation and had decided to avoid it at all costs.[12] The interview was over.

Ardelia was left with one minor lead to pursue. Gretel had mentioned a beautiful manuscript, a second book purchased by Fleming from the same returning soldier. It had sold for many times the amount paid, Mayer remembered hearing. This could well be the *Willehalm.* The high price pointed to a wealthy collector or well-endowed institution. Ardelia called her friend Karl Kup at the New York Public Library. Was there a way to know if in the mid-to-late 1940s a leading library had acquired the *Willehalm*? Yes, Kup confirmed, there was a way. His colleague Bill Bond at Harvard had just completed a census of medieval manuscripts held in US library collections.[13] It covered the years 1936–1950, precisely the time frame in question.[14] And there was one other rumor. Edward S. Peck, a California art professor, had recently seen at the Saint John's Seminary

---

[11] Ibid.

[12] Ibid.

[13] William Henry Bond, curator of manuscripts at the Houghton Library Harvard (1948–1964), was the editor of the "Supplement to the Census of Medieval and Renaissance Manuscripts in the United States and Canada" (New York: Bibliographical Society of America, 1962).

[14] "File Ms. of Hildebrandslied from Kassel." Memorandum of Conversation, A. Hall and K. Kup, July 14, 1961.

Library in Camarillo, a manuscript with brilliant miniatures. Judging by its description, it sounded like the *Willehalm*.

Ardelia immediately contacted William Bond at Harvard. Four days later the curator responded. His census of manuscripts was at the printer's but the galley proofs were due back within the week. He promised to check for an entry under *Willehalm*. While waiting, Ardelia followed up on the other lead. Ted Peck was a former Monuments Man, now on the faculty of the University of Southern California. Ardelia asked him to describe the illuminated codex he had just seen at the Saint John's Seminary Library, in the Doheny Wing.

In the closing days of September 1961 two letters arrived on Ardelia's desk. One was from Harvard, the other from the University of Southern California. Regrettably, Bill Bond reported, his census featured no entry under *Willehalm*. Ted Peck wrote that the manuscript he had seen in the Doheny collection was most certainly not the *Willehalm* either. In an effort to assist Ardelia, he had checked with the Clark Memorial Library in Los Angeles and with the Department of Special Collections at the University of California at Los Angeles. Neither had any information on the splendid Kassel codex.[15]

Peck's response was the very last entry in the *Ardelia Hall File on the Hildebrandslied from Kassel*. Ardelia Hall retired in 1964, after twenty years of loyal service in the hunt for war-displaced art. Her voluminous files were closed and sent to the regional offices of the National Archives and Records Administration in St. Louis, Missouri. Fifteen years later a brief note in the *Washington Post* mentioned her name one more time. It was a Superior Court notice in which the brilliant Ardelia Hall was declared incompetent. The court had ordered the sale of her estate.[16] The art historian, who had handled inestimable riches, had no treasure of her own. On Tuesday, September 4, 1979, Ardelia died alone in a nursing home.[17] Did anyone ever tell her how the *Hildebrandslied*-saga ended? Did anyone ever thank for her unwavering service?

---

[15] Ibid. Letter of E. S. Peck to A. Hall, September 25, 1961.

[16] Superior Court of the District of Columbia in re: Ardelia R. Hall, Fiduciary No. F-22–79 Adult Ward, *The Washington Post*, August 9, 1979, Section Style; Legal Notice: D. 19. Her earthly possessions amounted to proceeds from the sale of her home.

[17] "Ardelia Hall – Obituary," *The Washington Post*, September 10, 1979, Metro, C4.

Chapter 16: Ten Years Later ... Proof, Proof and More Proof

Esteemed Doctor Hennig. The message, dated November 19, 1970, bore the imprint of the West German Embassy in Washington, DC. Recently appointed Cultural Attaché Jürgen Kalkbrenner was eager to touch base with Dieter Hennig, the new director of the Murhard Library of the City of Kassel and State Library, formerly known as *Landesbibliothek Kassel.*[1] He had news.

After ten years of inertia,[2] the US Department of State appeared to be showing renewed signs of interest in the unsolved case of the lost Kassel manuscripts.[3] Two weeks earlier, Kalkbrenner wrote, State Department officials had called for

---

1 *Ex Bibliotheca Cassellana: 400 Jahre Landesbibliothek, 20.11.1580–20.11.1980* (From the Kassel Library: 400 years of State Library, 11/20/1580–11/20/1980), editor Hans-Jürgen Kahlfuß, ([Kassel]: Gesamthochschul-Bibliothek-Kassel, Landesbibliothek und Murhardsche Bibliothek der Stadt Kassel, 1980), 53.
Note: On November 11, 1957 the two research libraries, the *Murhardsche Bibliothek* and the *Landesbibliothek* converged to form the *Murhardsche Bibliothek der Stadt Kassel und Landesbibliothek*. Later, in 1976, the name of the library would change once more when the libraries were absorbed into the Kassel University Library to become *Gesamthochschul-Bibliothek Kassel – Landesbibliothek und Murhardsche Bibliothek der Stadt Kassel.* Now it calls itself *Universitätsbibliothek Kassel Landesbibliothek und Murhardsche Bibliothek der Stadt Kassel.* Although knowingly incorrect, for reasons of brevity, we will continue to refer to the former *Landesbibliothek Kassel* as the Kassel Library.

2 The case of the lost Kassel codices may have been dormant but it was not forgotten. One after another, a succession of Kassel Library directors pursued every available lead. Library Director Wolf von Both used all conceivable venues to keep the search for the manuscripts alive. In addition to numerous letters of inquiry addressed to German public officials and US scholars, in June of 1955 he helped place an appeal in *The Rotarian,* calling on American Rotarians to search for the *Hildebrandslied.* (See "Search for a Missing Page," *The Rotarian* 86, no. 6 (June 1955): 44). His successor, Dr. Ludwig Denecke, library director between April 1959 and April 1968, continued the search efforts. Fifteen letters to various German political and administrative entities attest to Denecke's persistent involvement with the case. And as soon as he assumed the leadership of the Kassel Library, Dr. Dieter Hennig contacted the West German Embassy in Washington, DC and expressed hope that the diplomats would persevere in their search for the missing Kassel heirlooms. If the manuscripts were found, Dr. Hennig, an expert in paleography and codicology, offered to help in the authentication process.
Note: Paleography refers to the study of ancient written documents. Codicology is the science that looks at the writing surface of bound manuscripts, i.e., it examines the preparation of parchment, its gatherings, linings, layout, and binding.

3 "Hildebrandlied 1," documents from the Archives of the Gesamthochschul-Bibliothek Kassel – Landesbibliothek und Murhardsche Bibliothek der Stadt Kassel, deposited with the University of California, Davis, Shields Library, Department of Special Collections. Letter of J. Kalkbrenner to D. Hennig, November 19, 1970.

a meeting with representatives of the West German Embassy.[4] Unfortunately, neither the Americans nor the Germans were conversant with the details of this quarter-century-old larceny case. The last promising lead in the search for the lost *Hildebrandslied* fragment and *Willehalm* had withered a decade earlier. Meanwhile diplomats and bureaucrats had come and gone, memories had faded, and to make matters worse the Embassy's documentation on the case had been destroyed.[5] The officers of the US State Department fared no better: their knowledge of the case was sketchy and their file on war-displaced art, the so-called *Ardelia Hall Collection*, was no longer at hand. It had been sent to the regional offices of the National Archives in St. Louis, Missouri. John Kornblum,[6] of the State Department's German Desk, was trying to recall the documents, but to date he had not succeeded.

Their collective knowledge hinged upon information obtained from Edgar Breitenbach of the Library of Congress, one of the few people who remembered events and places long left behind.[7] Breitenbach had provided them with an out-

---

4 Ibid. Memorandum signed by K. J. Maes, November 12, 1970. Present at the meeting were Karl J. Maes of the German Embassy and three representatives of the US Department of State: Charles N. Brower, Assistant Legal Advisor, and Elwood Williams III, and William Newlin from the German Desk.

5 Ibid. Memoranda of November 14, 1968 and March 18, 1969, signed K. J. Maes. The German Embassy files on cultural matters covering the years to the mid-1950s were destroyed, as attested by Embassy archivist Tscherner. In a letter to the author dated January 27, 1999, Dr. Franz-Josef Kos of the German Foreign Office (*Auswärtiges Amt*) in Bonn confirmed that after a review of all relevant documents of the Cultural and Legal Section, no files where found on the search and return of the *Hildebrandslied* fragment. He added that this might be due in part to the fact that a majority of documents contained in dossier 605 of the Cultural Section, covering the years up to 1955, were destroyed.

6 John Christian Kornblum's career with the State Department, which began in 1964, was capped by his appointment in 1997 as US Ambassador to the Federal Republic of Germany. He served until 2001.

7 In his correspondence of May 6 and May 31, 2002 with the author (Letters deposited with the University of California, Davis, Shields Library, Department of Special Collections), Dr. Arnold Price explained how the State Department decided to revisit the case of the lost Kassel manuscripts. After Ardelia Hall retired in 1964, all inquiries on the status of the search were redirected to Elwood Williams III, resident expert on US-German relations at the State Department's German Desk. Williams was wheelchair bound and he enlisted Dr. Arnold Price, a former State Department specialist on German issues, to help him find background information on the case. Dr. Price had left the State Department and was working as a specialist in Central European Affairs at the Library of Congress. After reading Carl Selmer's encrypted article, Price turned to his library colleague Edgar Breitenbach asking for clarification. Breitenbach convinced Price that the two missing manuscripts were still in the Rosenbach vault. Years later, during an official trip to Germany, Price shared his Rosenbach theory with First Secretary of the US Embassy in Bonn, Jonathan Dean. Fascinated by the story, Jonathan Dean contacted Washington and urged Elwood Williams III of the German Desk to reopen the investigation. Williams then called for a meeting with German Embassy diplomats.

line of the story and with a cast of characters: the Rosenbach brothers, Fleming, Selmer, Harrsen, Doheny. He had referred them for additional details to the Pierpont Morgan Library and to the rare book cataloger Gretel Mayer.[8] The information so gathered was still inconclusive but the story was so compelling, that the US Department of State was willing to revisit the case.

The US officials were looking at two possible approaches to revive the investigation: one approach was to open a dialogue with John F. Fleming, former general manager of the Rosenbach Company. Fleming had purchased the leftover book stock of the Rosenbach brothers for a whopping two million dollars. Along with the books, he had acquired the right to be called "formerly associated with Dr. A. S. W. Rosenbach," in other words he was Dr. R's legitimate business successor.[9] It was conceivable that now, so many years after the death of the Rosenbach brothers Fleming might feel more inclined to cooperate. The other approach was for Kassel to consider bringing a lawsuit against the Rosenbach Foundation and the John F. Fleming Company.

As in all legal procedures, a first crucial step was the provision of evidence. Director Hennig was asked to submit proof of title to the lost manuscripts in the form of a dated library inventory or a dated catalog entry. Equally important were sworn testimonies from witnesses, people who could corroborate dates and places where the manuscripts were seen. Furthermore, it was essential to obtain an affidavit attesting that the wooden chest with the manuscripts was locked at the time of the evacuation, and when and where that chest had been last seen with its locks still intact. Without detailed, irrefutable proof, this new initiative was doomed to fail or even worse, to backfire.[10]

The diplomat's message contained a peculiar blend of hope and hazard. On the one hand, the inherent risks of a costly lawsuit were bound to cast a chilling shadow on anyone's budding temerity. On the other, the cogent approach suggested by the US Department of State and the implied offer of assistance from the West German Embassy could only be viewed as a welcome development.

Dr. Hennig had been director of the merged *Murhard* and *Kassel State Library*, for a scant thirty months.[11] Together with the heavy responsibility of managing a complex institution with manifold needs and resurgent collections, he had also

---

[8] The State Department officials and the German diplomats re-interviewed Gretel Mayer, who declined to sign a deposition against her former employer. See: "Hildebrandlied 2," documents from the archives ...Travelogue of H. Hennig, March 1, 1972.

[9] John T. Winterich, "Dr. Rosenbach: the Tycoon of Rare Books," *Harper's Magazine* 212, no. 1270 (1956): 88.

[10] "Hildebrandlied 1," documents from the archives. ... Memorandum signed by K. J. Maes, November 12, 1970.

[11] Dr. Hennig was appointed library director on May 1, 1968.

inherited the mandate to carry on the search for the missing Leaf One and the *Willehalm*. The history of the manuscripts was well documented in a file left behind by his four predecessors: Hans Peter des Coudres, Wilhelm Hopf, Wolf von Both, and Ludwig Denecke. Hennig was well acquainted with the events and names mentioned in Kalkbrenner's letter.[12] Among the memos, correspondence, and affidavits, Hennig had come across a note describing Meta Harrsen's visit to Kassel.

While on a business trip to Germany in February of 1956, Meta Harrsen, Keeper of Manuscripts at the Morgan Library, had stopped by the *Landesbibliothek*.[13] She had given Director von Both a gripping first-hand account of Rosenbach's failed attempt to sell the *Liber Sapientiae* to Belle da Costa Greene. Miss Harrsen was no longer sure of her dates, but she distinctly remembered holding the codex in hand and seeing both pages of the *Hildebrandslied* bound in it. As proof, she promised to send photocopies from a film made by her library. Harrsen did not mince words when it came to John Fleming. She suspected him in the mutilation of the codex. If the first leaf of the ballad had survived, it could still be in the Rosenbach vault. Months later, when the film copies arrived, von Both did not find any trace of Leaf One.[14] Obviously, Miss Harrsen was wrong. And as far as director Hennig could determine fourteen-years later, no attempt had ever been made to follow up on Harrsen's suggestion and search the Rosenbach vault.[15]

Washington's renewed interest in the manuscripts and the sensible game plan suggested by the West-German Embassy galvanized the Kassel library director into action. Days later, Hennig sent off dozens of letters seeking information and testimony. He understood all too well that the fate of the manuscripts was now hanging from the rapidly fraying thread of memory and time. Wilhelm Hopf was no longer alive, but he had left behind an affidavit describing the transfer of the codices to Bad Wildungen, which Hennig intended to submit as evidence. The two other wartime directors, Hans Peter des Coudres and Hermann Baldewein, were next on his roster of witnesses, and Hennig hastened to contact them.

For years des Coudres had lived under a cloud of suspicion. Malicious gossip implied that he was somehow responsible for the loss of the manuscripts. Some

---

[12] "Hildebrandlied 1," documents from the archives. ... Letter of D. Hennig to J. W. von Buddenbrock, March 25, 1969 and April 14, 1969.

[13] "Hildebrandlied 1," documents from the archives ... Memorandum signed by W. von Both, February 24, 1956.

[14] Ibid. Letter of W. von Both to M. Harrsen, June 12, 1956.

[15] The Kassel librarians had no way of knowing that the US Customs Bureau had already attempted, albeit unsuccessfully, to investigate the Rosenbach Company.

Fig. 25. Dr. Dieter Hennig – 1999
(Courtesy of Dr. Dieter Hennig)

even went so far as to suggest that he was the Bad Wildungen thief.[16] Hennig's appeal reached him in Hamburg, at his post as head of the library of the Max-Planck Institute for Foreign and International Civil Law. Des Coudres was only too eager for a chance to provide testimony and clear his name.[17] In April of 1939, when he became director of the *Landesbibliothek*, des Coudres wrote in a sworn affidavit, both codices were kept under lock and key in a safe on the first floor of the building. He was the only one with access to that safe. Insinuations that the *Liber Sapientiae* had been sold before the war were pure fantasy. The codex had never left the library, not even for legitimate scholarly exhibits. In 1939, des Coudres had authorized the transfer of twenty of his most important manuscripts to the underground vault of the State Credit Bank in Kassel. The *Hildebrandslied* and the *Willehalm Codex* were among the twenty, carefully packed in a gray wooden chest. A note in his diary validated his recollection that at the time of transfer the wooden chest was securely locked.

Des Coudres's sworn statement confirmed two crucial points: that in 1939 both codices were whole and extant, part of the *Landesbibliothek* manuscript collection, and that their container was sealed at the time of transfer. Wilhelm Hopf's written testimony brought the story forward to the years 1943–1944, when the box was moved once again, this time to the Bad Wildungen war repository. It corroborated des Coudres's statement that the chest was locked when it left Kassel and was still locked in July of 1944, when Hopf last visited Bad Wildungen. The two concurring affidavits were a promising start. They gave director Hennig good reason to hope that future statements would further clarify the timeline and amplify the findings.

Hennig's request for information reached Hermann Baldewein, the former wartime deputy director, at the princely library in Burgsteinfurt.[18] But instead of validating des Coudres's testimony, Baldewein's recollections undermined several established facts. Baldewein claimed to have seen the codices in early April of 1940, seven months after their evacuation to the midtown bank vault. He wrote that he remembered showing his bride the *Willehalm Codex* and the two pages of the *Hildebrandslied* displayed side by side in the glass cabinet of the catalog room. He further volunteered that he had been opposed to the transfer of the manuscripts to Bad Wildungen. In his opinion, the State Archive in Marburg would have provided far better protection. The relocation to Bad Wildungen had

---

16 "Hildebrandlied 4," documents from the archives. ... Letter of D. Hennig to H-O Weber, October 9, 1972.

17 "Hildebrandlied 1," documents from the archives. ... Letter and draft of sworn testimony of H. P. des Coudres, December 7, 1970.

18 "Hildebrandlied 1," documents from the archives. ... Letter of D. Hennig to H. Baldewein, January 12, 1971.

been des Coudres's idea, for des Coudres had remained heavily involved in library decisions, even during his military conscription.[19]

Baldewein's letter was not only an attack on des Coudres's credibility but also a damaging invalidation of the previously established timeline. One rather embarrassing explanation was that the former deputy director could not tell an original manuscript from a reproduction.[20] For indeed, in 1940 there had been facsimiles exhibited in the display cases of the catalog room. A hint of irritation crept into Hennig's reply. Could it be that Director Baldewein had proudly shown his bride a replica rather than the original? In a two-sentence answer, Baldewein admitted tersely that he could not rule it out.[21]

It was mid-December when the mayor of Bad Wildungen Dr. Lückhoff responded.[22] He had searched through the city's archive but had been unable to locate the 1945 police reports on the looting of war repositories. The mayor had contacted the Vonhoffs, the couple who had kept watch over the Goecke cellar. Frau Vonhoff was unable to recall much of anything, but her husband Hubert remembered returning from the war in September of 1945, and being interrogated by two local detectives, Karl Müller and Rudolf Hörchner. Müller was still in town, could speak generally about the looting, but with no relevant details.[23] Hörchner had moved to Herten where he was living on his governmental pension. The mayor promised to track him down through administrative channels.

In a shaky handwriting, the elderly Hörchner replied directly to Hennig. The Goecke cellar had been ransacked sometime before his arrival in Bad Wildungen, which happened at the very end of April 1945.[24] Hörchner's note was brief and his hand obviously uncertain, but the date mentioned was important. Since US troops had entered Bad Wildungen on March 31, Hennig could now narrow down the time of robbery to the thirty days of April. His instincts must have been truly piqued, for he immediately wrote to the archives in Marburg requesting copies of records dated March, April or May 1945, which mentioned police investigations in the Bad Wildungen area. Disappointingly, in spite of extensive searches, none were found.[25]

---

[19] Ibid. Letter of H. Baldewein to D. Hennig, January 18, 1971.

[20] Ibid. Letter of D. Hennig to H. Baldewein, January 20, 1971.

[21] Ibid. Letter of H. Baldewein to D. Hennig, January 31, 1971.

[22] Ibid. Letter of Dr. Lückhoff to D. Hennig, December 16, 1970.

[23] Ibid. Letter of Dr. Lückhoff to D. Hennig, February 12, 1971 and letter of K. Müller to D. Hennig, February 26, 1971.

[24] Ibid. Letter of R. Hörchner to D. Hennig, January 18, 1971.

[25] Ibid. Letter addressed to the library and signed Sieburg, January 29, 1971.

Throughout the next couple of weeks, bits of useful information continued trickling in. From the Governor's archives Hennig secured a copy of the 1945 report of the Criminal Investigations Division of the US Seventh Army and its decision to close the case on the Bad Wildungen larceny due to lack of evidence. He also tracked down the deposition of Felix Pusch, the local museum director, who had evacuated the shattered remnants of the Kassel art collection. Was Dr. Pusch still around?[26] The mayor of Bad Wildungen replied that Pusch had died in 1948.[27] But Frau Riza Pusch, his widow, and the neighbor, who had loaned him his horse-drawn wagon, were both alive. The frail Frau Pusch and the elderly Herr Schleiermacher remembered with surprising clarity an Easter Sunday long ago and a city gripped in the agony of surrender. They told the story of a fearful Pusch waving his evacuation permit, of hostile US soldiers, and of a quick getaway with the scraps of the Kassel art collection.[28] However, neither Frau Pusch nor Herr Schleiermacher remembered anything about a wooden chest with manuscripts.

By mid-spring, Hennig's methodical investigation had brought back to life a panorama of people, places, and events from the time of surrender in Bad Wildungen, but hardly anything on the robbery and not one shred of evidence on the identity of the thief.[29] To cover all bases, Hennig decided to visit the crime-scene: he called and asked permission to see the Goecke cellar. The resort hotel had remained structurally unaffected since the day of surrender. Administrator Ewald Härtel, who had been working in the building since April of 1945, offered to show Hennig around. He explained that during the occupation, the cellar had been used by American troops as a telecommunication center. He took Hennig down a flight of stairs to the basement. At the bottom, a double steel door opened onto the wartime evacuation site.

Except for recently added wooden shelving, the cellar had remained virtually unchanged. Steel bars still secured its windows. Hennig looked carefully around,

---

26 "Hildebrandlied 2," documents from the archives. ... Letter of Dr. Koolman to Dr. Lückhoff, March 13, 1972.

27 Ibid. Letter of Dr. Lückhoff to the Library, March 16, 1972.

28 "Hildebrandlied 3," documents from the archives. ... Report on the evacuation of the *Hildebrandslied* manuscript and of the *Willehalm-Codex* to Bad Wildungen, signed Koolman, April 15, 1972 and countersigned by R. Lorenz.

29 Among the people interviewed by Dr. Hennig was a former US officer named Warren Meyerhoff, a German immigrant, who in 1972 was vacationing in Bad Wildungen. In June of 1945 US Officer Meyerhoff had been stationed in Bad Wildungen. He remembered people and events with great clarity. He gave Dr. Hennig a list of names and potential witnesses, and also mentioned a fellow officer named Bud or Buddy (he did not remember his last name), who was active in requisition work. Meyerhoff, however, did not have any direct knowledge of the looting at Hotel Goecke. See: ibid. File note signed by D. Hennig, May 17, 1972 and correspondence of D. Hennig with the author of November 27, 2001. Letters deposited with the University of California, Davis, Shields Library, Department of Special Collections.

trying to locate the ledge, that protective wall spur mentioned repeatedly by Dr. Hopf, the nook in which he had placed the gray wooden chest. The space was simple and severe, the walls straight and bare, with no ledge or wall spur anywhere. Hennig checked again with the building administrator but was assured that structurally nothing had been altered since the war days. As he was turning to leave, he noticed outside the steel door under the stairs a ridge masking a dark recess. The wall spur? Could Hopf have left his treasure-chest outside the reinforced entrance, at the mercy of the first spoiler? If this were true, then even if the chest had survived the April looting, it could have easily been overlooked at the time of Pusch's evacuation.[30] A troubling, disheartening thought.

Hennig returned to Kassel and brought out the crippled *Liber Sapientiae*. At the fold of the first gathering, the codex displayed a clean incision. The precise surgical cut denoted assurance, a hand deft with a scalpel and familiar with the quivers of vellum. The vandal had realized that the top page with its large oval library stamp had to be eliminated, since it revealed the manuscript's home. This could not have been the work of a simple soldier, for the mutilator was not only skillful with the blade but also fully cognizant of the threatening significance of that imprint.[31]

Hennig collated all the strands of his findings, and wove them into an informative report, designed to keep Washington's interest alive.[32] He appended des Coudres's sworn affidavit, copies of the original statement made by Wilhelm Hopf and the file-memo on Meta Harrsen's visit. So far as he could determine, he wrote to Cultural Attaché Kalkbrenner, all evidence pointed to the House of Rosenbach. The *Liber Sapientiae* had passed through the hands of the Doctor. The two missing manuscripts could still be in his library. US investigators had to find a way to gain access to the Rosenbach vault.

Month succeeded month in disappointing silence. One morning, toward the end of September 1971, Hennig received an unexpected telephone call.[33] The man on the phone introduced himself as Dr. Götz Fehr, managing director of the organization *Inter Nationes*.[34] He was privy to an exclusive scoop. A high-ranking US diplomat had informed him that Leaf One of the *Hildebrandslied* had survived

---

30 "Hildebrandlied 3," documents from the archives. ... File note signed by D. Hennig, May 17, 1972.

31 "Hildebrandlied 1," documents from the archives. ... Letter of D. Hennig to J. Kalkbrenner, January 25, 1971.

32 Ibid.

33 "Hildebrandlied 1," documents from the archives. ... File note signed by D. Hennig, September 22, 1971.

34 Inter Nationes e. V. is an organization created in 1952, with the expressed purpose of advancing international relations, establishing international contacts, overseeing German libraries and exhibits abroad, and offering information on political, economic, and cultural issues.

the war and was now in the hands of a well-known American collector. The holder was willing to return it on two conditions. One, that the restitution be handled with utmost discretion, no inquiries could ever be made as to where it had been since 1945. Two, that the return not be publicized. The US diplomat was given to understand that while the mysterious owner was embarrassed by his possession, he was nonetheless not adverse to a financial reward. Dr. Fehr had already contacted the *Bundesministerium des Innern (BDI)*, the Federal Ministry of the Interior, and had discreetly inquired whether the government would be willing to put up the ransom. Yes, he was told, the Ministry would consider underwriting the reward. Would Dr. Hennig be free to meet in Bad Godesberg with Dr. Götz Fehr and with his friend, the American diplomat?

On Wednesday morning, September 29, 1971, director Hennig hastened up to Bad Godesberg near Bonn, anxious to learn more about this mysterious restitution offer. First impressions were encouraging. The high-ranking diplomat, Dr. Fehr's connection, was a bona-fide US official, Jonathan Dean, First Secretary of the US Embassy in Bonn. Dean was supposedly on professional leave and thus the meeting took place in his home, on Martin-Luther-King-Straße. A pretext, Hennig suspected, to keep the conversation out of the public arena.

What First Secretary Dean had to say was highly confidential. He started out by reassuring Dr. Hennig that Leaf One was well cared for, in the hands of a distinguished US collector. The holder was working through an intermediary, an American, Dr. Arnold Price. He had contacted Dr. Price with the plea to find a way to return the leaf without publicity. Indeed the holder was said to be very embarrassed by his war-trophy. He had purchased it in good faith, without realizing its enormous importance and value. If he were to return it, however, he expected to be compensated for the loss. The dollar amount was not specified. Dr. Price, the alleged middleman, had contacted US Embassy Secretary Jonathan Dean in West Berlin to discuss the offer.[35] The diplomat had called the

[35] "Hildebrandlied 1," documents from the archives. ... File note signed by D. Hennig, September 30, 1971.
Note: According to Dr. A. Price (Correspondence with the author, deposited with the University of California, Davis, Shields Library, Department of Special Collections, letter of May 31, 2001), at the time, US Embassy First Secretary Jonathan Dean was working with US Ambassador to Germany Kenneth Rush, on the status of Berlin. Arnold Price, who happened to be in Berlin on official business, had classified information regarding the US right to occupy the Berlin suburb of Düppel, in the American Sector. Dr. Price met with First Secretary Jonathan Dean prior to the start of the US-Soviet negotiations to give him information on the Düppel issue. Jonathan Dean, Dr. Arnold Price points out in his letter to the author, confuses this meeting with an earlier discussion they had, while on a Rhine cruise. It was during that cruise that Dr. Price mentioned A. S. W. Rosenbach as the probable holder of the Kassel manuscripts, an assumption he was making based on information received from his friend and colleague Edgar Breitenbach. In his letters to the author, Dr. Price emphatically denied any other knowledge regarding the *Hildebrandslied* leaf.

Fig. 26. Dr. Arnold H. Price
(Courtesy of Arnold Price)

Department of State's German Desk in Washington, DC, asking for guidance. He had spoken to Elwood Williams III, the mainstay of the office, and had been counseled to treat Dr. Price's information seriously and with the utmost secrecy.

For now, Dr. Hennig had little choice but to accede in principal to all stipulations. He insisted however that additional inquiries be made on the whereabouts of the *Willehalm Codex*. It was premature to discuss the size of the reward or the authenticity of that manuscript. He told First Secretary Dean to contact the middleman, and ask that he engage the unnamed collector in discreet and serious negotiations. The very last thing Hennig wanted was to provoke a panic reaction and with it the retraction of the offer. The holder was said to be very nervous.

Upon returning to Kassel, Hennig pondered whether or not he should inform Cultural Attaché Kalkbrenner about this latest twist. He did not particularly want to broaden the circle of people in the know.[36] Nonetheless, since Jonathan Dean had already discussed the offer with the German Desk at the State Department, it seemed appropriate to keep the West German Embassy also informed. Hennig put pen to paper and shared the latest developments with Kalkbrenner. He asked if Kalkbrenner could find out if this middleman, this Dr. Arnold Price, were indeed an honest broker. But first he swore the diplomat to secrecy.[37]

The German diplomat found this new development most astonishing, for he was well acquainted with the alleged middleman. Born and raised in Germany Dr. Arnold Price, a former officer of the State Department, was now a specialist in Central European studies at the Library of Congress. And not only did Kalkbrenner know Price well, but coincidentally he was scheduled to meet with him to discuss bilateral cultural issues, since Price had just returned from a tour of German libraries. Kalkbrenner considered Arnold Price a man of honor, who would most certainly do his best to see the *Hildebrandslied* returned. It went without saying that he would abide by Hennig's request for strict confidentiality. Nonetheless, if Price were to bring up the subject of the lost manuscript, Kalkbrenner thought it would be wise to strike while the iron was hot.[38]

This last statement was a bit disconcerting. It was far to early in the process for Kalkbrenner to interject himself into the negotiations. Well intentioned as he might be, he could easily scare away both intermediary and collector. Alas, it did not take long for Hennig's apprehensions to be proven right. The very next letter from Washington shattered all hope for a connection with the alleged holder. Kalkbrenner reported that, when the subject of the manuscript came up, Arnold Price was taken aback. Jonathan Dean of the US Embassy in Bonn was sorely mistaken, for Price knew nothing on the whereabouts of the *Hildebrandslied*, nothing on the true identity of the collector, and most certainly nothing about any brokered deal.[39] While on official business in Germany, he had mentioned to

---

36 Ibid. Letter of D. Hennig to J. Kalkbrenner, November 9, 1971.

37 Ibid. Letter of D. Hennig to J. Kalkbrenner, September 30, 1971.

38 Ibid. Letter of J. Kalkbrenner to D. Hennig, October 6, 1971.

39 In his letter to the author of May 6, 2001 Dr. A. Price stated: "Sometime in the sixties Elwood William III of the State Department called me, saying he had an inquiry from the Germans (the German Embassy?) asking for the location of the still missing *Hildebrand* page. Elwood had a distinguished Air Force career in WWII, but was wheelchair-bound, and the mainstay of the Department's German Desk. So, I took on the task by first reading up on the postwar fate of the manuscript (by the way the *Willehalm* is included in this narra-

Jonathan Dean an unsubstantiated theory advanced years earlier by his friend and colleague Edgar Breitenbach.

The disheartening letter ended in an odd way. While there were no guarantees, Kalkbrenner wrote, there might still be a chance to make contact with the mysterious US collector. Hennig would be well advised to make arrangements and fly over for a visit. The Embassy was prepared to back him up on legal matters. Psychological pressure coupled with the promise of a financial reward might still lead to a positive outcome.[40]

Dr. Hennig set aside the bad news of the illusory deal and grasped at the fresh blades of straw tossed his way. A personally financed trip to the United States was out of the question, he wrote back to the Washington diplomat. It was far too expensive. However, he would be willing to apply for a professional travel-grant. But if he were to put forward a request for funding, there had to be some assurance that the manuscript truly existed. Furthermore, there was also the thorny issue of the financial reward. Before any money changed hands, Hennig had to make sure that what was offered was the genuine *Hildebrandslied* and not some clever facsimile. As a chemical analysis on vellum and ink was impractical, he would be forced to bring with him the defaced *Liber Sapientiae* and compare it to the offering.[41] And this in itself presented a great risk.

---

tive). I had some misgivings about the account of the return of the first section of the *Hildebrandlied*, so I turned to my friend and colleague, Dr. Edgar Breitenbach, Chief of the Library of Congress' Prints and Photographs Division. He said: There is nothing wrong with the article (N.B. Dr. Price means Selmer's article), but the still missing page is held by a certain book-dealer. (I no longer remember his name). Gretel Mayer, who had worked in the store, had told him so. She had seen the manuscripts and recognized them. So I reported back to Elwood, who thanked me, but after a few days called back saying that the Department would not act on this information, as they were afraid that the dealer may be alarmed and do away with the manuscripts. There was not much I could do for various reasons: I had to respect my source's privacy, as a Federal officer I could not act against government policy, and honestly I saw no way for me to go about this matter. But in 1971 when I was in Germany on official business I was able to convey to the brilliant Foreign Service officer Jonathan (Josh) Dean my concerns about the manuscripts. That was the last I heard of it until I was invited by the German Embassy to be present when the manuscripts were returned." (Quote reproduced by permission).

40 "Hildebrandlied 1," documents from the archives. ... Letter of J. Kalkbrenner to D. Hennig, October 22, 1971.
Note: In his letter to the author of May 31, 2002, Dr. Arnold H. Price surmises that First Embassy Secretary Jonathan Dean might have received permission from the State Department (i.e. from Elwood Williams III) to suggest to Cultural Attaché Kalkbrenner, that the missing Leaf One was kept in the vault of the Rosenbach Museum & Library. This explains why Kalkbrenner urged Dr. Hennig to travel to the US for a meeting with the unnamed holder of the manuscript.

41 Ibid. Letter of D. Hennig to J. Kalkbrenner, November 9, 1971.

The year 1971, which had started in hope, ended in dejection. Dr. Götz Fehr and Embassy First Secretary Jonathan Dean voiced displeasure upon hearing that Hennig had confided in Kalkbrenner,[42] a disclosure that in their estimation had doomed the alleged Arnold Price connection. And to top it off, after a thorough review of the Ardelia Hall File, finally retrieved from St. Louis, Missouri by John Kornblum, the US Department of State concluded that the evidence was insufficient to warrant a law suit. While in theory the US government remained committed to the return of the Kassel manuscripts, in practice it was unable to suggest any new course of action.[43] With this pronouncement the US Department of State officially closed its investigation into the case of the looted *Hildebrandslied* and the *Willehalm Codex*.

---

[42] Ibid. Letter of D. Hennig to J. Kalkbrenner, January 24, 1972.

[43] Ibid. Letter of the State Department to the German Embassy, December 30, 1971: "In the review which the Department has just concluded, efforts were made to locate persons who were thought to have knowledge of the missing page. These efforts have failed to produce any evidence, which encourage hope in the pursuit of legal action in recovering the manuscripts. Aside from the public appeal suggested in the Embassy's note of June 9, 1967, the Department is unable to suggest any other feasible course the Embassy can undertake. The Department wishes to assure the Embassy, however, that it remains keenly interested in locating the manuscript and returning it to its owner, and will be alert to any possibility for doing so."

Chapter 17: To Err is Human, to Admit, Divine

While disappointing, the Department of State's decision to close its investigation had come hardly unexpected. The trail was cold. Since Gretel Mayer in the early sixties no other evidence had come to light. Yet neither director Hennig nor diplomat Kalkbrenner were about to give up, not when all signs still pointed in one singular direction. Testimony after testimony repeated the same allegation. How could anyone discount the scathing remarks of Meta Harrsen, the nervous recollections of Gretel Mayer, the speculations of Edgar Breitenbach, the conjectures of Agent Page, the professional intuition of Ardelia Hall, and of late the educated guess of Arnold Price, all chanting in a tired *ritornello* one familiar name: Rosenbach. True, there was no real proof that the two missing items had ever passed through the Doctor's hands, no factual evidence of wrongdoing. Not even the tenacious Ardelia and her valiant Customs Agent had succeeded in laying blame at the Rosenbach door. However, according to Gretel Mayer, Leaf One and the *Willehalm* were last seen in the Rosenbach library. Unlike the *Liber Sapientiae*, the two had never resurfaced on the US or international book market. They could very well still be in the Rosenbach vault.

As often, when one star wanes, another brightens. Left with no other recourse, the German diplomat turned for advice to a long-time friend of the Embassy. Attorney Kennedy C. Watkins[1] was a respected Washington insider, who had recently retired as Assistant Director and General Counsel of the National Gallery of Art. Over the years, he had repeatedly assisted the West German Embassy, most notably in the recovery of a group of sixteenth century woodcuts belonging to the University Library in Heidelberg.[2] While working on this and on other cases of war-displaced art, the German diplomat and the American attorney had learned to trust and respect one other. Their conversations had occasionally returned to

---

1 Karl J. Maes, First Secretary of the Embassy of the Federal Republic of Germany in Washington, was the diplomat who initially made contact with attorney Kennedy C. Watkins. In consultation with the State Department, Maes had asked Watkins in 1968 to conduct two searches for the missing *Hildebrandslied* leaf through the collections of the National Gallery of Art. The searches were unsuccessful. Over time Maes and Watkins had become friends. In February 1972, Maes was transferred to a diplomatic post in South America. Cultural Attaché Jürgen Kalkbrenner was Maes's successor. (See "Hildebrandlied 2," documents from the archives of the Gesamthochschul-Bibliothek Kassel – Landesbibliothek und Murhardsche Bibliothek der Stadt Kassel, deposited with the University of California, Davis, Shields Library, Department of Special Collections. Cultural report signed by Karl J. Maes, February 14, 1972). Details on Kennedy C. Watkins's role in the recovery of the *Hildebrandslied* are gleaned from his letter to W. F. Twaddell. (See "Hildebrandlied 3," documents from the archives. ... Letter of K. C. Watkins to W. F. Twaddell, September 8, 1973).

2 "Hildebrandlied 2", documents from the archives. ... Cultural report signed by Karl J. Maes, February 14, 1972.

the unsolved Kassel case and, at the behest of the State Department, Watkins had ordered two separate searches for the manuscripts through the vast collections of the National Gallery. Both searches had turned up empty.

At Kalkbrenner's request Watkins reviewed the Embassy's *Hildebrandslied File* and Dr. Hennig's recommendation to revisit the Rosenbach connection.[3] The suggestion of the library director was certainly valid, but there was no legal justification to reopen an official inquest. There had to be another way to gain access to the Rosenbach vault. Watkins was one of few, who could still remember the days when Dr. Rosenbach's exploits dominated the headlines. He also recalled a peculiar tendency of Rosenbach's, which others, younger or less observant, had missed or had not fully appreciated. He knew that the Doctor never sold a rare book solely for profit, but that he always tried to place it in the best collection, matching each peerless find with the most appreciative owner.[4] If Watkins could figure out, which collection Rosenbach would have considered worthy of the Kassel treasures, he would know where to start looking. Of all libraries blessed by the Doctor's magic touch, one stood out as a superb achievement: Alverthorpe, the gallery of Lessing J. Rosenwald.

Alverthorpe was unquestionably a splendid home, worthy of the Kassel manuscripts, but there was one caveat: Lessing Rosenwald was mostly interested in early-illustrated printed books, and to a far lesser extent in medieval manuscripts. However, one obvious argument put the Alverthorpe Gallery at the very top of Watkins's search list: Lessing J. Rosenwald was President of the Rosenbach Foundation, that research center and museum established after the death of the brothers. In other words, he was the keeper of the mythical key to the Rosenbach vault.

Lessing J. Rosenwald was universally praised for his knowledge of rare books and revered for his unmatched generosity. Years earlier, he had donated his magnificent collections to the nation. During his lifetime his artwork remained at Alverthorpe Gallery but already 25,000 rare prints and more than 2,000 rare books had been earmarked for the National Gallery of Art and the Library of Congress.[5] The philanthropist served on numerous governing boards of cultural

---

3 "Hildebrandlied 1," documents from the archives. ... Letter of D. Hennig to J. Kalkbrenner, January 25, 1971.

4 *Rosenwald and Rosenbach: Two Philadelphia Bookmen. Catalogue of an Exhibition at the Rosenbach Museum & Library from the Lessing J. Rosenwald Collection at the Library of Congress, April 30 to July 31, 1983* (Philadelphia: Rosenbach Museum Library, 1983), xx: "Dr. Rosenbach knew his books well, understood his collectors and had a vision for each of their collections. If he felt that a book belonged in a certain collection, he tried to place it there."

5 Meryle Secrest, "Lessing Rosenwald, Collector of Great Prints, Rare Books," *Smithsonian* 2, no. 12 (1972): 51.

institutions, most notably as a Trustee of the National Gallery of Art. Kennedy C. Watkins, former Assistant Director and General Counsel of the National Gallery had been privileged to work with Lessing Rosenwald.

A simple letter of inquiry addressed to the Alverthorpe Gallery might stir up new leads. But before discussing his idea with diplomat Kalkbrenner and before contacting the Gallery, Watkins sought guidance from the US Department of State. As an American citizen, he did not want to become involved in an international dispute, nor did he want to place the US Department of State or the West-German Embassy in an awkward position. Once the State Department confirmed that it had closed its investigation, and that the search for the *Hildebrandslied* was now a private matter in which the US Government had no further interest,[6] Watkins felt free to share his Rosenwald-idea with Cultural Attaché Jürgen Kalkbrenner. The diplomat thought the plan had real merit.

Watkins did not want to raise any adverse implications and thus he addressed his inquiry to the Alverthorpe curator, J. Frederick Cain, Jr., and not to Lessing Rosenwald personally. Tactfully he explained that in late 1945 Dr. Rosenbach had acquired a stolen codex of inestimable value, called the *Liber Sapientiae*. Years later the codex, lacking its first leaf, had been returned to Germany. He asked if curator Cain, perhaps in consultation with his boss Lessing Rosenwald, could suggest any venue or lead, which would assist the Embassy in its search for that missing leaf. He assured the curator that he had no personal financial stake in the matter and that his inquiry was motivated solely by public interest.[7] The letter was postmarked January 18, 1972.

* * *

DeLancey Place is a narrow, tree-lined street, between Spruce and Pine, not far from Rittenhouse Square, in one of the most fashionable residential areas of historic Philadelphia. While the twenty-first century roars by in the distance, this tranquil lane festooned with red-stone buildings conjures old post-card images of affluence and gentility. Twenty-ten, a three-story townhouse wedged in the middle of the block, was home to the legendary doctor. Back in 1950, Philip had purchased this late-nineteenth century dwelling, with its well-proportioned rooms and serene garden, and had remodeled it to suit Dr. R's growing infirmities. It was to be the brothers' last residence.

> 2010 DeLancey Street [noted Dr. R's biographer] was Philip Rosenbach's masterpiece and survives today as his personal monument. All the best and showiest of the once large stock of antiques and objects d'art were assembled to decorate drawing room, sitting rooms, bedrooms, dining rooms, and libraries. ... The second floor,

---

6 "Hildebrandlied 3", documents from the archives. ... Letter of K. C. Watkins to W. Twaddell, September 8, 1973.

7 Ibid.

> complete with gold-plated bathroom fixtures, was his suite. The third floor was turned over to the Doctor, and it was there that the most valuable treasures of the house were gathered. The front was fixed up as a library, ... to hold Dr. Rosenbach's own collection, that amazing hoard of fabulous volumes quietly purloined from his major purchases, and ranging from the Dublin *Bay Psalm Book* to the original manuscript of *Ulysses* ...[8]

Slouched in his armchair, his diabetes-corroded leg propped up on a footstool, the incomparable Dr. R had spent his final hours in his third-floor library, gazing nervously upon his *infernally rare* masterpieces. He was a "dying pharaoh, already immured in his tomb," suffering from recurrent visions of future grave robbers.[9] After his death and that of his brother Philip, the townhouse was turned into a public research institution.

Twenty years later, on a quiet wintry morning at the end of January 1972, Clive Driver, the Rosenbach Library curator was about to become the Doctor's prophetic grave robber.[10] As he was tending to his books and manuscripts, Driver received a telephone call from the new Foundation President, Dr. Werner L. Gundersheimer. The caller asked if the curator knew of a manuscript leaf called the *Hildebrandslied*, an item not featured in the museum's catalog but nonetheless rumored to be in the library.

---

8 Edwin Wolf 2nd and John F. Fleming, *Rosenbach: A Biography* (Cleveland: World Publishing Company, 1960), 574–75.

9 Ibid., 575: "And Dr. R was worried about grave robbers. The business that he had built slipped and was taken from his hands; the collection which he had culled from it with love and care and uncanny discrimination was all that remained to him. Fearful that his less sentimental brother would be tempted to turn these objects of his lifetime of bibliophily into dollars and cents, the Doctor, ... spent his waning energy compiling a check list ..."

10 While Driver was only a participant in the removal of the Kassel manuscripts from the Rosenbach collection, he later initiated his own string of pickings. During his conversation of April 12, 2000 with the author, Dr. Werner Gundersheimer commented on Clive Driver's legal misfortunes: "Driver served as full time curator until the late seventies, I believe. He asked to be relieved of his full time responsibility because he wanted to move from the Philadelphia area up to a house that he had bought on Cape Cod. But he did want to retain a connection with the institution ... The Board agreed to name him part-time curator. ... When Driver was working in Philadelphia, one week a month, since he no longer had a residence, he was permitted to reside in the Museum. He actually lived in the house. It was discovered subsequently that a number of very important manuscripts had gone missing. And these were ultimately traced to Mr. Driver, who had removed them from the collection, had attempted to eradicate their presence in the catalog, and had consigned them to various dealers and auction houses." See: Werner L. Gundersheimer, tape-recorded telephone conversation of April 12, 2000, deposited with the University of California, Davis, Shields Library, Department of Special Collections (Quote reproduced by permission).
The April 22, 1987 *The New York Times*, Section C, 23, carried an article on the civil complaint filed by the Rosenbach Museum against its former curator. Driver was alleged to have removed from the museum's archives thirty rare letters worth a quarter of a million dollars. In 1991 (see "Museum Director Fined in Theft Case," *Boston Globe*, 4 December 1991, p. 40). Driver pleaded *nolo contendere*, was fined, and sentenced to three years' probation.

Driver knew exactly which leaf Gundersheimer was referring to. It was the one, which he had been sternly counseled never to catalog, never to display, and never to mention.[11] The ironclad interdiction had been issued by one of the Foundation trustees on Driver's very first day on the job. That trustee had recently passed away. Obviously with his death the emphatic adverb *never* had lost its absolute value. Driver reluctantly acknowledged that the leaf existed, tucked away in one of his locked bookcases.[12]

Watkins's letter had spurred a ripple, and that ripple had billowed into a wave, and the wave had washed ashore a secret jealously guarded for more than a quarter century. As suggested by Watkins, Alverthorpe curator Cain had shown the letter to his boss Lessing J. Rosenwald. The eighty-one year old philanthropist, who had just stepped down as President of the Rosenbach Foundation, had never heard of the lost Kassel leaf. He was unfamiliar with the heroic ballad,

---

[11] Dr. Gundersheimer stated in his conversation with the author of April 12, 2000: "As best I recall, I got a telephone call ... asking whether I knew anything about the manuscripts, as it was believed that they had come in the possession of Dr. Rosenbach and they may be still in his possession or in the possession of the Foundation, that had become a public institution. I had never heard of that and told the caller (N.B. it must have been Lessing J. Rosenwald) that I would be looking into it. So I called the curator of the Rosenbach Museum, Clive Driver, now deceased, [and asked] if he knew anything about the two German manuscripts in the Rosenbach, and he said that indeed he did. And he said that when he had taken the position of curator, a member of the Board had advised him that there were two such documents in the museum and that they were not to be accessioned or made a permanent part of the collection. And that they should be kept in safekeeping. So that is what he did." (Quote reproduced by permission).
This statement is independently corroborated by Twaddell, who learned from an undisclosed source inside the Rosenbach Foundation that Clive Driver had been aware of the existence of the two manuscripts since 1968. (See: "Hildebrandlied 2," documents from the archives. ... Letter of W. F. Twaddell to D. Hennig, February 3, 1975). Clive Driver's sister, Dr. Beverley Eddy also confirmed in her September 16, 2002 electronic-mail correspondece with the author, that Driver knew about the existence of the manuscripts but that he was sworn to secrecy. See: Beverley D. Eddy, electronic-mail correspondence with the author, deposited with the University of California, Davis, Shields Library, Department of Special Collections.
According to Wolf 2nd, 569, the original members of the Board of Trustees of the Philip H. and A. S. W. Rosenbach Foundation were: "those friends in whom they [i.e., the brothers] had implicit trust – Dr. I. S. Ravdin, Lessing J. Rosenwald, Morris Wolf, Edwin Weisl, and D. Hays Solis-Cohen. ..." Twaddell states in the above mentioned letter of February 3, 1975, that the Board member who had issued the gag-order had passed away just prior to the disclosure made by Driver. The one Board member who had passed away on January 13, 1972 was Edwin Weisl. Later in the interview Dr. Gundersheimer told the author: "He (i.e., Clive Driver) had been specifically requested to keep it secret, years before, when he first came. Someone took him aside and told him that we had those things, and, *sub rosa*, not to talk about it. They did not know what to do with them." (Quote reproduced by permission)

[12] Details regarding Clive Driver's knowledge about the existence of the missing Leaf One are culled from the April 12, 2000, telephone conversation of Dr. Gundersheimer with the author.

which he insisted on calling *The Hildebrandsleid* – Hildebrand's Sorrow.[13] But since Watkins mentioned his friend Dr. Rosenbach in the same breath with a stolen codex, Lessing Rosenwald felt compelled to look more closely into the allegation. He called Edwin Wolf 2nd, the Doctor's nephew, store-manager, and biographer. Wolf had spent years working with the Rosenbach archives. Had he come across any reference to this looted manuscript leaf? He most certainly had. The leaf was in the Rosenbach Library and it had been there for as long as Wolf could remember.[14] Ardelia, who had grilled Wolf earlier on this very same topic, would have been dumbfounded to hear the spontaneous confession.

Deeply concerned, Lessing Rosenwald asked the new Foundation President Dr. Gundersheimer to double check with the curator. And this is when Clive Driver turned grave robber. For decades, the Doctor, brother Philip, general-manager John Fleming, curator Clive Driver, and at least one trustee of the Rosenbach Foundation, had observed a conspiracy of silence.[15] It must have been easier to deny the existence of the ill-gotten treasure than to admit to the guilt of possession.[16] A simple, direct question had suddenly forced the secret out in the open.

Lessing Rosenwald immediately contacted Kennedy C. Watkins and owned up to the embarrassing discovery. It went without saying that neither he nor the Foundation wished to have any property to which they were not entitled.[17] Rosenwald's disclosure seemed to imply a willingness to surrender the *Hildebrandslied* fragment. The admission exceeded Watkins and Kalkbrenner's wildest expectations. In an earlier note to Hennig, Kalkbrenner had cautiously intimated that psychological pressure coupled with the promise of a financial reward might convince the unnamed holder to relinquish his trophy. He was struggling to find

---

13 "Hildebrandlied 2," documents from the archives. ... Letter of L. J. Rosenwald to K. C. Watkins, February 3, 1972.

14 William Freeman Twaddell, "The Hildebrandlied Manuscript in the U.S.A., 1945–1972," *Journal of English and Germanic Philology* 73, no. 2 (1974): 165 footnote 16. He quotes a letter received on February 1, 1973 from Edwin Wolf 2nd: "When Mr. Rosenwald asked me what I knew about it [N.B. the Hildebrandlied sheet], I told him it was in the Rosenbach Museum. Why it was never catalogued I have no idea."

15 "Hildebrandlied 2," documents from the archives. ... Letter of W. F. Twaddell to D. Hennig, June 19, 1974. Twaddell states that besides Edwin Wolf 2nd others also knew about the existence of manuscripts.

16 In his conversation of April 12, 2000 with the author, Dr. Gundersheimer mentioned that the Rosenbach Foundation Trustees did not know what to do with the ill-gotten manuscripts.

17 "Hildebrandlied 2," documents from the archives. ... Letter of L. J. Rosenwald to K. C. Watkins, February 3, 1972.
Note: Dr. Gundersheimer remembers: "When it came to my notice and I ascertained from Driver that these things were actually in the building, I of course discussed it with the Trustees at the Rosenbach and we all agreed that we wanted to act in a way that was totally consistent with United States policy on restitution of looted objects." (Telephone conversation with the author, April 12, 2000. Quote reproduced by permission).

a way to gain access to Rosenbach's secret cache. But he had never envisioned such a swift and happy turn of events.

Like an answer to a thousand prayers, the extraordinary news was greeted in Kassel with unbridled joy.[18] In a personal message, Rolf Pauls, Ambassador of the Federal Republic of Germany to the United States urged director Hennig to attend at once to the complex procedures of restitution. As legal representative of the owner library, as a scholar of Old German, and a specialist in paleography and codicology, his presence in Philadelphia was not only appropriate but also necessary. It was incumbent upon Hennig to demonstrate that this Rosenbach leaf was one and the same with the lost leaf of the *Hildebrandslied*, and that the fragment truly belonged to the Kassel Library.[19]

Hasty travel arrangements were made and on February 24, 1972, the library director was on a transatlantic flight to Washington, DC. This was his very first visit to the United States.[20] Together with a powerful magnifying glass, Hennig brought along an arsenal of legal and evidentiary material: an official statement attesting that he was the director of the Murhard Library of the City of Kassel and State Library, the rightful owner of the *Hildebrandslied*, a formal claim authorizing him to sign a restitution agreement, a scholarly description of the manuscript, Hopf's 1937 reproduction of Leaf One, and, just in case, photocopies of *Willehalm* miniatures. In a special folder, Hennig carefully placed his star witness: the loose eighth leaf of the *Liber Sapientiae*,[21] that twinleaf, which in a gathering corresponds to the first. Unlike the novice Hennig, this thousand-year-old calfskin was crossing the Atlantic for a third time.

He arrived mid-afternoon in Washington and was welcomed by Jürgen Kalkbrenner and by Counselor Nöbel, representing the Ambassador, who was out of town.[22] Hennig checked into the comfortable Windsor Park Hotel. Later in the day he was briefed by the Embassy on protocol and politics. He was cautioned not to exercise any undue pressure on the Rosenbach Foundation. Early next morning, February 25, 1972, director Hennig accompanied by attorney Watkins and diplomat Kalkbrenner, set out for their ten o'clock meeting in Philadelphia. At 2010 DeLancey Place they were greeted by four representatives of the Rosenbach Foundation: Lessing J. Rosenwald, immediate past-president, attorneys

---

18 Ibid. Letter of D. Hennig to J. Kalkbrenner, March 3, 1972.

19 Ibid. Letter from the Ambassador of the German Federal Republic R. Pauls to D. Hennig, February 9, 1972.

20 Ibid. Letter of D. Hennig to J. Kalkbrenner, March 3, 1972.

21 "Hildebrandlied 3," documents from the archives. ... Letter of J. Kalkbrenner to S. Levy, May 9, 1972.

22 "Hildebrandlied 2," documents from the archives. ... Details of the trip are, unless otherwise noted, culled from D. Hennig's travelogue of March 1, 1972.

and trustees Samuel H. Levy and Morris Wolf, Edwin's father, and by Clive Driver, the museum curator. They were shown into the elegant conference room, and were seated around the highly polished table with coruscating crystal chandeliers.[23]

Kennedy C. Watkins opened the meeting with an explanation of the importance of the *Hildebrandslied* to history, world literature, and to the cultural identity of the German people. In the name of the Federal Republic of Germany, Cultural Attaché Kalkbrenner formally requested the full cooperation of the Foundation in the return of the recently discovered leaf. After these preliminaries it was Library Director Hennig's turn. As representative of the owner library, he requested permission to examine the manuscript. The tension in the meeting-room became palpable. There on the table, in a simple, transparent sleeve, was the ancient ballad, the object of a long and intense search, the vellum leaf with its shadows and creases, and with its well-known opening verse: *Ik gihorta dat seggen* ... I once heard it said ...

Armed with his powerful magnifying glass Hennig began the analysis.[24] He checked the leaf for size, lines, holes, stains, and color. He studied the writing, the absorbency of the vellum around the inked letters, and the stylus markings in the margins, those notations made by scribes while testing the tip of their writing tool, and then compared all findings to historical descriptions, and to the 1937 facsimile. Then he turned the leaf over and compared the Latin text on its verso with the description found in Hopf's *Landesbibliothek Kassel*. So far, everything matched. Until its disappearance in 1945, the first page of the *Hildebrandslied* had been part of the *Liber Sapientiae Codex*. This was confirmed by Hopf and repeated in the appeal published by Ardelia Hall. Since the Kassel State Library was the owner of the full codex, it was implicitly owner of the severed leaf. To validate this claim, at some point in the nineteenth century, the library had applied its ownership stamp onto the verso of the first leaf. Hennig now looked for that mark. What he found was a faded, barely visible outline of the stamp's oval imprint. The three-tiered letter-block, *Ex Bibliotheca Cassellana*, was blurred, hardly legible. Someone had used a razor blade and chemicals in a clumsy, albeit vain attempt to remove the incriminating inscription. The excellent ink had resisted the impudent assault.

Then Hennig picked up the ancient leaf, and walked over to the window. From its folder, he pulled its twin, the eighth, the one brought from Kassel, and held both leaves up to the light, matching wound against wound. The serration in the margins melted into one. On each side, the crescent-shaped stitching holes,

---

23 Wolf 2nd, 574.

24 "Hildebrandlied 2," documents from the archives. ... Statement of authentication, signed by D. Hennig, March 1, 1972.

where a sewing cord once laced the leaves together, returned to form a circle. It was a perfect match. This was the precious first leaf of the *Hildebrandslied*.[25] The hands of the eighty-one-year-old Lessing Rosenwald trembled, as he repeated the test, only to reach the same inevitable conclusion. The wealthy collector sighed heavily, bowed his head, and whispered: "Oh, Rosenbach – and you were my friend. ..."[26] A pained hush fell around the table.

The silence was broken by the voice of Samuel Levy, trustee and attorney for the Foundation, who tersely informed Hennig that there could be no immediate restitution. The Kassel Library had to wait for the full Board of Trustees to vote on the issue. In advance of the Board's meeting, director Hennig had to submit a written brief supporting his claim and a complete bound replica of the *Liber Sapientiae* codex. The trustees, Levy insisted, would be hard pressed to grasp how the beginning of a ballad could appear on the *recto* of the first leaf of a book and its conclusion on the *verso* of the last. Such explanations were, to say the least, confusing, and a three-dimensional model was an absolute necessity. Concerned Hennig turned to the fair-minded Lessing Rosenwald, silently pleading for reason. But the elderly patriarch looked drained and despondent.[27] It

---

25 Gustav Süßmann, *Das Hildebrandlied – Gefälscht?: Eine Untersuchung* (The Hildebrandlied – a forgery?: An appraisal), (Staufenberg: Gustav Süßmann, 1988), 233, citing Kalkbrenner's letter of March 12, 1987: "Aus den drei Treffen mit den Vorstandsmitgliedern haben sich folgende Szenen mir deutlich eingeprägt: Bei der Indentifizierung als Dr. Hennig mit von Ergriffenheit zitternden Händen an ein Fenster im Sitzungszimmer des Rosenbach-Museums trat, das 1. Blatt und das durch dessen Herausreißen in der Mitte des Codex gelockerte, von ihm aus Kassel mitgebrachte Blatt zusammengefügt und die beiden Rißstellen zusammenpaßten, eine Bewegung, die dann der Vorsitzende des Aufsichtsrats der Stiftung, der über 80jährige Sammler und Philanthrop Lessing Rosenwald, mit vor Alter zitternden Händen wiederholte. ..." (Of the three meetings with the Trustees, I can clearly remember the following scenes: When Dr. Hennig, his hands trembling with emotion, stepped to a window of the meeting room in the Rosenbach Museum, and joined Leaf One to the leaf from the middle of the codex, which had become loose when the first one was torn away, and which he had brought with him from Kassel, the two tear-wounds fit together. This motion was repeated by the Chairman of the Board of Trustees, the more than eighty-year-old collector and philanthropist Lessing Rosenwald, whose hands also trembled due to advanced age.")
See also "Hildebrandlied 3," documents from the archives. ... The letter of K. C. Watkins to W. F Twaddell, September 3, 1973, only remarks that the situation was tense with emotional excitement. The reserved Dr. Hennig (see: "Hildebrandlied 2," documents from the archives. ... Statement of authentication, March 1, 1972), simply notes that the scientific analysis confirmed the identify of the first leaf of the *Hildebrandslied*.

26 Dieter Hennig, correspondence with the author of July 4, 2002, deposited with the University of California, Davis, Shields Library, Department of Special Collections. (Quote reproduced by permission).

27 "Hildebrandlied 2," documents from the archives. ... Travelogue of D. Hennig, March 1, 1972.

must have been too painful for him to acknowledge that his idol, his friend, the incomparable Dr. R, had feet of clay. Mindful of the Embassy's plea for Solomonic restraint, Hennig acceded quietly to Levy's demands.

Before the meeting ended, Hennig asked the trustees if they could suggest any approach in the search for his other missing manuscript, the *Willehalm Codex*. He showed them the reproductions brought along from Kassel. The trustees had no advice to give. Yet the eyes of the museum curator remained riveted on the miniatures. It was obvious to the perceptive Hennig that Clive Driver had seen those miniatures before.[28] Driver returned the copies and casually remarked that only a well-endowed library could have purchased such a beautifully illustrated book. Three came readily to mind: on the West Coast, the Huntington, and on the East Coast, the New York Public and the Morgan Library. Hennig would be well advised to contact all three. And in the unlikely case that the *Willehalm* had ended up in the hands of a wealthy bibliophile, it would be wise to place an appeal in *The Book Collector*.

Driver's offhand remarks were replete with insinuations. Without naming a culprit, the curator appeared to be saying that he knew where the *Willehalm* was. He had identified three libraries by name and then, as an afterthought, he had mentioned a wealthy private collector. Was he perchance referring to Dr. Rosenbach? If the *Willehalm* were shelved in the Rosenbach Library, Hennig could easily spot the opulent, oversize volume. The library director made a split-second decision. He delayed his departure and asked for a tour of the Rosenbach Library. Obligingly, curator Clive Driver took the guests up to the third floor, and showed them a dazzling array of manuscripts, early printed books, and historical documents. Emboldened by his cordiality, Hennig requested to see the catalog or, lacking one, a business ledger, showing when and how the precious items had entered the collection. There was no catalog, Driver retorted, and neither was there a business ledger. The US Tax Code required retention of business records for the latest five years only. Earlier receipts of purchases were routinely discarded. Hennig perused all volumes shelved in plain view, but none resembled the grand old codex.

Upon returning to Kassel on February 29, Hennig went into high gear. The recovery process was at a critical juncture and he was determined to do everything in his power to help the trustees reach the right decision. He commissioned a high quality, full-scale photo-facsimile of the *Liber Sapientiae*. He asked his bindery unit to study the medieval binding technique of the codex and replicate it with the utmost of care.[29] He put together a travelogue to keep friends and higher-ups

---

28 Ibid.

29 Ibid. Letter of D. Hennig to J. Kalkbrenner, March 3, 1972.

apprised of developments, and filed a report on the methods used to authenticate the *Hildebrandslied* leaf.[30] He requested from the Hesse Minister of Culture an official restitution claim to be submitted to the Foundation, once the vote of the Board of Trustees became final. Together with manuscript curator Dr. Erika Kunz, he prepared a paleographical and codicological description of the *Willehalm,* which he intended to file with the Huntington, the New York Public and the Morgan Library, just as Clive Driver had suggested. He asked Kalkbrenner to contact all three libraries on his behalf and follow up with an appeal to bibliophiles in *The Book Collector*. Thoughtful and considerate, he also wrote to the three former library directors: Wolf von Both in Marburg, Hans Peter des Coudres in Hamburg, and Ludwig Denecke locally in Kassel.[31] All three had earned the right to share in the hope of the moment.

Early morning on March 3, 1972 a telegram arrived from Washington, DC. While rummaging through the armoire drawers of the townhouse, Clive Driver, the Rosenbach Museum curator, had accidentally stumbled across the long-lost *Willehalm Codex.*[32]

---

30 Ibid. Statement of authentication, signed by D. Hennig, March 1, 1972.

31 Ibid. Letter of D. Hennig to W. von Both and H-P des Coudres, March 3, 1972.

32 Ibid. Telegram of J. Kalkbrenner to D. Hennig, March 3, 1972.

Chapter 18: The Owl of Minerva

With the symbolic opening of an armoire drawer, a twenty-seven-year search spanning two continents, involving two governments, and countless institutions, scholars, and collectors had come to its anticlimactic conclusion. And although a decision to return the *Willehalm* had not been articulated, the restitution of both manuscripts appeared to be only a matter of time and formality.[1] Once again, the Rosenbach Foundation demanded that Kassel provide proof of ownership, authentication, and a detailed history of the loss. While time-consuming and wearing, these requirements were not entirely unjustified. As a public research institution the Foundation had a right to proceed in a systematic and judicial manner.[2]

To save Kassel the inconvenience of a second transatlantic journey, Kalkbrenner offered to stand in for Hennig at the follow-up conference with the Rosenbach Foundation trustees, set for May 12, 1972. The German side had been asked to present supplementary information on the *Hildebrandslied* page and authenticate the Rosenbach codex believed to be the Kassel *Willehalm*. Two weeks prior to that meeting, Kalkbrenner received from Hennig, via the Hesse Ministry of Culture an impressive packet with evidentiary materials.[3] It yielded a superb replica of the *Liber Sapientiae*, as stipulated by Foundation attorney Samuel H. Levy. Skilled craftsmen had created a near perfect facsimile, all but undistinguishable to the naked eye from its famous original.[4]

To that volume, Hennig had added a summary of his codicological analysis performed in Philadelphia, and two important new findings regarding foliation and chain of custody. Historical records ascribed to the *Liber Sapientiae* seventy-six leaves. Yet the manuscript recovered in 1954 numbered only seventy-five. To disguise the removal of Leaf One, the mutilator had attempted to alter the leaf numbers. While working on the facsimile, the library specialists had uncovered the original foliation, partially erased and partially crossed-out. Even more revealing was a pencil annotation discovered on the inside back cover of the codex,

---

1 "Hildebrandlied 3," documents from the archives of the Gesamthochschul-Bibliothek Kassel – Landesbibliothek und Murhardsche Bibliothek der Stadt Kassel, deposited with the University of California, Davis, Shields Library, Department of Special Collections. Letter of J. Kalkbrenner to D. Hennig, May 5, 1972.

2 Werner L. Gundersheimer, tape-recorded telephone conversation of April 12, 2000. Deposited with the University of California, Davis, Shields Library, Department of Special Collections.

3 "Hildebrandlied 3," documents from the archives... Letter of J. Kalkbrenner to D. Hennig, May 5, 1972.

4 Kalkbrenner in the above letter to Hennig calls the binding a masterpiece.

in the lower left-hand corner. It read *Rosenbach* and displayed the numbers *3/50* underneath, in all probability the date of the Doheny sale.[5] Hennig had also appended reports on the theft in Bad Wildungen, and the name and address of a material witness: Carl Selmer, the Hunter College professor who had identified the *Hildebrandslied* in November of 1945.

The next group of documents in the packet focused on the *Willehalm*. There was a detailed description of the codex,[6] with a reference to its Kassel catalog number, 2° Ms. 1, inscribed inside the front cover, and to ownership statement on the verso of leaf 395:

> In the year of our Lord one thousand three-hundred and thirty-four, the illustrious Heinrich, Landgrave and Lord of the Land of Hesse, had this [codex] written at his court in honor of Saint William Marchionis; never to be transferred but to remain forever in the possession of his heirs.

The Kassel *Willehalm* was famous for its sixty-two fully or partially completed miniatures. As no facsimile edition existed, Hennig had sent along reproductions from the 1927 treatise *Die Illustrationen zum Casseler Willehalm-Codex,* by art-historian Robert Freyhan.

The last item in the Kassel evidence packet was a linen folder fashioned to the exact dimensions of Leaf One and lined with genuine, hand-made Japanese papers.[7] The *Hildebrandslied* page had apparently been kept in a transparent sleeve of unknown chemical properties, potentially damaging to the vellum.[8] To minimize any harmful effects, Hennig urged the diplomat to place the leaf in the green linen folder the moment he had it in hand.

Kalkbrenner pored over the reports and documents with the intensity of a doctoral student facing qualifying exams. Worried that the mountain of information could still prove insufficient, he borrowed from the Library of Congress, courtesy of Edgar Breitenbach, the complete Freyhan treatise and studied the *Willehalm* miniatures and descriptions cover-to-cover.[9] On the morning of May 12, 1972, a fairly confident Kalkbrenner, flanked by his Embassy colleague Dr. Barbara Jaschke, returned to the Rosenbach Museum & Library.[10] This time, the

---

5 "Hildebrandlied 2," documents from the archives. ... Beweismittel zum Hildebrandlied-Kodex (2° Ms teol. 54), signed by D. Hennig, March 16, 1972.

6 Ibid. Beweismittel zum Willehalm-Kodex (2° Ms poet. et roman.1), signed by D. Hennig, March 16, 1972.

7 Japanese paper is used in archival conservation. It is hand-made, neutral, very strong, and allows air to circulate.

8 "Hildebrandlied 3," documents from the archives. ... Letter of D. Hennig to J. Kalkbrenner, July 28, 1972.

9 Ibid. Letter of J. Kalkbrenner to D. Hennig, May 5, and June 19, 1972.

10 Ibid. *Kulturreferat* signed by J. Kalkbrenner, May 12, 1970. Details of the meeting are based on Kalkbrenner's report.

new Foundation President Dr. Werner Gundersheimer was in attendance. The German diplomats were ushered into the elegant conference room, where Lessing Rosenwald, Morris Wolf, Samuel Levy, and museum curator Clive Driver were waiting. They were seated around the highly polished grand table adorned with glittering candelabra, and all eyes turned to Kalkbrenner.

The diplomat opened with an overview of the post-war saga of the *Liber Sapientiae* codex, starting with its disappearance, sale and mutilation, and ending with its recovery by the US Department of State. He never once mentioned Abraham Simon Wolf Rosenbach, Philip H. Rosenbach, or John F. Fleming by name. Using Hennig's facsimile as a teaching tool, he demonstrated how the text of the ballad appeared on its first and last page, and how the first leaf in the gathering was conjoined to the eighth. When the codex was recovered, he explained with tactful ambiguity, its first leaf was absent and the eighth was loose. For decades the US Department of State searched for that severed first leaf. Three months earlier in this very room Director Hennig had identified it beyond any doubt. On behalf of the Government of the Federal Republic of Germany, representing the State of Hesse, and on behalf of the State of Hesse representing the Kassel Library, Kalkbrenner formally asked the trustees to allow the *Hildebrandslied* to return home.

There was a tension-filled silence, and then suddenly a barrage of questions. Deeply troubled, the trustees, who were hearing the story of the *Hildebrandslied* for the very first time, demanded to know more. They wanted details on the plunder in Bad Wildungen, particulars on that appalling act of defacement, and above all, they wanted the name of the person who had offered the codex to the Morgan Library and who had later sold it to Countess Doheny. Here the evidence assembled by Hennig and Kalkbrenner's diplomatic skills proved salutary. Kalkbrenner showed them the report on the looting in Bad Wildungen. Specifics on the attempted sale to the Morgan Library and final sale to Mrs. Doheny were irrelevant, he added with thoughtful consideration. The Rosenbach name had been intentionally omitted from his presentation and from all written claims. After so many years, there seemed to be no reason to cast aspersion on the memory of an illustrious bibliophile. Nonetheless, there were clear indications that the codex had passed through the Doctor's hands. Kalkbrenner directed their attention to the pencil annotation on the inside cover of the codex: *Rosenbach 3150*. He also showed them the report of Customs Agent Page and Ardelia Hall's public appeal for the return of the missing leaf, which had remained unheeded.[11] His measured remarks, conciliatory tone, and convincing evidence seemed to appease some of the misgivings.

---

[11] Ibid. Letter of J. Kalkbrenner to D. Hennig, May 5, 1972 and *Kulturreferat* of May 12, 1972, signed by J. Kalkbrenner.

Next on the agenda was the authentication of the codex believed to be the Kassel *Willehalm*. The diplomat launched into a well-rehearsed explanation of its genesis, history, and of the circumstances that linked its fate to that of the *Hildebrandslied*. As he paused, curator Clive Driver directed his attention to a sumptuous, oversize volume, resting on an adjacent table. This was the moment, for which Kalkbrenner had been so ardently preparing. Methodically, like Hennig before him, he checked the physical characteristics of the codex against descriptions received from Kassel. Aside for one missing upper buckle, the binding was intact. He then compared the miniatures with those reproduced by Freyhan. Together with Barbara Jaschke, he counted the vellum leaves out loud, giving everyone a chance to follow along.[12] He compared the final number to historical descriptions. It was identical. Vellum leaves and miniatures displayed no sign of damage.[13] Inside the front cover he found the old Kassel catalog number: 2° Ms. 1, and on the verso of leaf 395, the famous ownership statement of Landgrave Heinrich. As he concluded his analysis, he sensed no resistance and no enmity around the table.

After a brief conference with the trustees, Dr. Gundersheimer declared the evidence fully convincing. As private individuals, he told Kalkbrenner, they would not hesitate to hand over the manuscripts right then and there. But as officers of the Foundation they were duty-bound to follow a strict set of procedures, and for that he asked for additional time and patience. The entire Board had to vote on restitution, and their next conference was scheduled for the second half of July.[14] With this, the meeting was adjourned.

As Kalkbrenner was about to leave, Gundersheimer quietly stopped him with a very personal remark.[15] He was born in Germany, he told the diplomat, in Frankfurt am Main. His father was director of the Rothschild Museum. On *Kristallnacht*, November 9, 1938, the museum was brutally attacked and looted. He remembered vividly that "night of broken glass and shattered lives," relived over and over again through his parents' memories. Its anniversary was for him the most painful time of the year. Except for a handful of objects, all of his father's exhibits, those precious items reflecting a millennium of Jewish life on German soil, had vanished forever.[16] As a child, he had seen first hand the violence inflicted on cultural objects, an image impossible to forget. The restitution of the Kassel heirlooms was the right thing, the ethical thing, and the only thing to do.[17]

---

[12] Ibid. Letter of J. Kalkbrenner to D. Hennig, June 6, 1972.

[13] Ibid. Letter of J. Kalkbrenner to S. H. Levy, May 12, 1972.

[14] Ibid. *Kukturreferat* of May 12, 1972, signed by J. Kalkbrenner.

[15] Ibid.

[16] Werner Gundersheimer, "Kristallnacht Revisited: A Nightmare, a Legacy," *Washington Post*, 9 November 1988, A15.

[17] Author's telephone conversation with Werner Gundersheimer, April 12, 2000.

History had come full circle. An act of hatred had brought forth a credo of justice and fairness. Kassel, the birthplace of *Kristallnacht,* was about to reap the benefits of a painful memory, seared in the heart of a child.[18] Across the ocean, night had fallen. Still under the powerful impressions of the day, Kalkbrenner placed a telephone call to the home of Dr. Hennig in Kassel. There was so much to be thankful for, he told the library director. He had seen the *Willehalm*. It was safe, unharmed. The Foundation trustees were men of honor and integrity, motivated by generosity and good will. A favorable decision of the Board was now only a matter of time.

A note of sadness tempered the joyous news. In the closing days of June, a headline in the New York *Staats-Zeitung und Herold* announced the death of Carl Selmer.[19] The distinguished scholar, who had so valiantly fought for the return of the ballad, did not live to see its first leaf returned. Liselotte Suschke, Dr. Hennig's assistant, filed the obituary in the library's *Hildebrandslied* archive.

For years the efficient Frau Suschke had attended to all matters pertaining to the lost manuscripts. Day in and day out she had typed all correspondence, had tended to files and dossiers, and had answered one phone call after another. Together with the Kassel librarians, who had struggled to keep the faith, Frau Suschke had trusted and despaired, had prayed and maledicted, and had hoped against hope to see the codices return. It was only fitting for fate to choose her as its ultimate messenger.

On the evening on July 27, 1972, as Frau Suschke was about to leave the office, there was one last telephone call. So very sorry, Dr. Hennig was tied up in a meeting with University officials. But then she recognized the voice at the end of the line. It was Dr. Kalkbrenner from Washington. The Rosenbach Board of Trustees had concluded their meeting, Kalkbrenner told her, and had unanimously voted to return both manuscripts without preconditions or demands for compensation. Dr. Hennig was invited to attend the formal return ceremony scheduled for mid-September.[20] When Frau Suschke recovered from the jolt of the news, she rushed over to the conference room and interrupted the long-winded discussions. For once she knew that the reserved Dr. Hennig would not mind in the slightest this improper outburst of emotion.[21]

* * *

---

18 "Hildebrandlied 3," documents from the archives. ... Kalkbrenner recorded this conversation in his cultural report, filed on May 12, 1972.

19 "Carl Selmer – Obituary," *Staats-Zeitung und Herold – New York,* June 26, 1972.

20 "Hildebrandlied 3," documents from the archives. ... File note signed S [for Suschke], time 17:45, July 27, 1972.

21 Ibid. Letter of D. Hennig to J. Kalkbrenner, July 28, 1972.

"Die Eule der Minerva beginnt erst mit der einbrechenden Dämmerung ihren Flug" – The Owl of Minerva takes wing only with the onset of dusk.[22] Two months later, Hegel's prophetic words echoed in the elegant conference room at 2010 DeLancey Place. It was the morning of September 22, 1972 and Americans and Germans had gathered one last time in the Rosenbach Museum, around the highly polished grand table, with its silver candelabra, crafted for Ernest Augustus, Duke of Cumberland and King of Hanover.[23] Kassel Library Director Hennig was present, and so were Cultural Attaché Kalkbrenner, German Consul General Weil, and Embassy officer Jaschke. The formal return ceremony was hosted by Foundation President Gundersheimer and by distinguished members of its Board of Trustees. The ailing Lessing Rosenwald was absent.

In a gesture of gracious hospitality, Dr. Gundersheimer addressed his guests in German. Hegel's beautiful analogy conveys the notion that historical meanings only become apparent at the very end of a chain of events. But as Hegel's owl does not fly every single night, many questions on the presence of the Kassel manuscripts in the hands of an eminent book-lover will remain a mystery.[24] Over six hundred years earlier, the illustrious Heinrich, Landgrave and Lord of the Land of Hesse and first owner of the *Willehalm* ordained that his precious codex never leave his library. It was time to honor his command. And with these words, Dr. Gundersheimer formally handed over the *Willehalm Codex* and the severed leaf of the *Hildebrandslied* to Dr. Jürgen Kalkbrenner, who returned them to their legal guardian, Kassel Library Director Dr. Dieter Hennig.

Hennig had brought along a leather-bound facsimile of the second page of the *Hildebrandslied*, a special edition issued only in twenty-five copies. He offered it to the Foundation as a sincere gesture of gratitude. Deeply moved, he thanked the trustees for their decision to return the manuscripts without preconditions, an unprecedented gesture in the history of libraries.[25] Since it was only midmorning, the participants toasted each other with coffee, posed for the local newspaper and, in a flurry of sound bites parted ways.[26] An Embassy car whisked Hennig and the diplomats back to Washington, DC where the codices were once again the center of attention. Members of the press, officials of the State

---

[22] The famous Hegel phrase is from the Preface of his *Grundlinien der Philosophie des Rechts*, 1820.

[23] Art Milner, "Philadelphia's Rosenbach Museum: A Visit to DeLancey Place," *Wilson Library Bulletin* 60, no. 3 (1985): 15.

[24] "Hildebrandlied 3," documents from the archives. ... Remarks of W. L. Gundersheimer, September 22, 1972.

[25] Ibid. Remarks of D. Hennig, September 22, 1972.

[26] Adolf Katz, "Search for 2 Ancient German Literary Works Ends in Phila.," *Philadelphia Sunday Bulletin*, September 24, 1972, sec. I, XB5.

Fig. 27. Return ceremony at the Rosenbach Museum and Library, September 22, 1972
From left to right: Mrs. Gundersheimer (from the back), Dr. Dieter Hennig, standing Dr. Kalkbrenner, Dr. Werner L. Gundersheimer, and Mr. Levy.
(Archives of the Universitätsbibliothek Kassel – Landesbibliothek und Murhardsche Bibliothek der Stadt Kassel – photographer unknown)

Department and of the German Embassy, Washington area students and scholars attended a reception, and listened to a story that began in misery and ended in cooperation and good will.[27]

After an action-packed week, it was time to say good-bye. Hennig and his two protégés had secured permission to return home on a German military air-

[27] "Hildebrandlied 3," documents from the archives. ... Press Release of the West-German Embassy in Washington, September 21, 1972 and "Hildebrandlied 4", letter of D. Hennig to L. von Friedeburg, Hesse Minister of Culture and to the Lord Mayor of Kassel, October 3, 1972.

Fig. 28. ... and the world exploded in headline after headline
(Montage by Claudia Graham, IET Mediaworks, University of California, Davis)

plane.[28] There was one other well-known passenger on that flight: Helmut Schmidt, German Minister of Economies and Finance, and future Chancellor, who had been in Washington for currency negotiations.[29] All through the night, all through the flight, the watchful Hennig kept vigil over his codices.[30] His predecessor Wolf von Both had set the example years earlier, albeit under much humbler circumstances. After an uneventful journey, manuscripts, library director, and high dignitary landed safely at the military airport Cologne-Wahn, where director Hennig was met by police officers and escorted back to Kassel.[31]

---

28 "Hildebrandlied 4," documents from the archives. ... Letter of H. Hennig to L. von Friedeburg, Hesse Minister of Culture, and to the Lord Mayor of Kassel, October 3, 1972. Hennig explained that if he were to send the manuscripts home via air courier, they would end up in the cargo bin. Due to their irreplaceable nature, he insisted to accompany the manuscripts during the crossover flight. This request could only be accommodated on a special military airplane.

29 William Freeman Twaddell, "The Hildebrandlied Manuscript in the U.S.A., 1945–1972," *Journal of English and Germanic Philology* 73, no. 2 (1974): 168.

30 "Hildebrandlied 4," documents from the archives. ... Letter of H. Hennig to L. von Friedeburg, Hesse Minister of Culture, October 3, 1972 and author's telephone conversation with W. Gundersheimer, April 12, 2000. Hennig told Gundersheimer that during the flight he would keep the manuscripts on his lap.

31 "Hildebrandlied 4," documents from the archives. ... Letter of H. Hennig to L. von Friedeburg, Hesse Minister of Culture, and to the Lord Mayor of Kassel, October 3, 1972.

While the manuscripts were traveling toward sunrise across the Atlantic, the German-speaking world exploded in headlines,[32] greeting the final return of the *Hildebrandslied* and that of the most lavishly illustrated secular manuscript of the Middle Ages, the *Willehalm Codex*. Surely, out there in the great beyond, the incomparable Dr. R was smiling approvingly. He so loved publicity.

[32] Other European newspapers also heralded the return of the manuscripts. *The Times* of London, for instance, carried the news on page one. See: "Books – Hildebrandlied: Manuscript Found in U.S." *Times* (London) September 28, 1972, p. 1, col. G.

Chapter 19: "The Last, the Worst, Dull Spoiler, Who Was He?"

***Childe Harold* - Lord Byron**

Once the media frenzy tapered off, the flowery speeches ended, the applause faded, and the last dignitary departed, it was time to turn to the difficult issues of restoration and preservation. As with all unique documents a balance had to be struck between pent-up research demands and archival protection. For while the *Hildebrandslied* and *Willehalm* remain irreplaceable resources to which scholars must have access,[1] they also represent priceless heirlooms with distinctive conservation needs.

The *Liber Sapientiae* codex was showing alarming signs of deterioration.[2] Its leather binding was worn and its four clasps were missing. The detached text block was resting loosely between the boards of its all too narrow binding. The spine sewing was weak, the pages warped and slightly cockled. The condition of Leaf One raised the most serious concerns. Chemicals applied by mid-nineteenth century scholars attempting to make illegible words fleetingly discernible had left deep shadows on the vellum surface.[3] A side-by-side comparison with the fac-

---

1 The *Hildebrandslied* remains one of the most analyzed literary ballads. Since its return to Kassel, research interest has intensified. "After the rediscovery of the two parchment leaves in American archives ... the *Hildebrandslied* has provoked a constant stream of publication." (See: Albrecht Classen, "Why do their words fail? Communicative strategies in the Hildebrandlied," *Modern Philology* 93, no. 1(1995): 8). In fact, between 1955 and 2003, major English language indexing sources alone list over eighty articles and book chapters, and some forty books dedicated to various aspects of the *Hildebrandslied.*

2 The signs of deterioration and the measures taken for the restoration of the manuscript are gleaned from the final report of the Bavarian State Library, Institute for Book Restoration. See Gustav Süßmann, *Das Hildebrandlied – Gefälscht?: Eine Untersuchung* (The Hildebrandlied – a forgery?: An appraisal) (Staufenberg: Gustav Süßmann, 1988), 30.

3 Hartmut Broszinski in *Kasseler Handschriftenschätze* (Kassel manuscript treasures), Pretiosa Cassellana (Kassel: Johannes Stauda, 1985), 145, explains these experiments as follows: "Das unrühmlichste Kapitel in der Geschichte der Handschrift bleibt noch zu vermelden: Der damalige Kasseler Bibliothekar und später hochbedeutende Altgermanist und -anglist Christian Wilhelm Michael Grein, 'wandte das Reagens an', behandelte 1855 einige Textstellen mit Gallusstinktur, um schwer Lesbares für Augenblicke lesbarer zu machen. Unbegreifliche Respektlosigkeit dieser Zeit vor einem einzigartigen Zeugen hoher Kunst." (An infamous chapter in the history of the manuscript still needs to be cited: Christian Wilhelm Michael Grein, at the time librarian in Kassel and later renowned scholar of Old German and English studies, 'applied the reagent'. In 1855 he used gallic tincture to make hard to read words fleetingly visible. Unimaginable disrespect of that time for a unique witness of high art.)
In his article "Handschriftenrestaurierung in Kassel (2)" (Restoration of manuscripts in Kassel. 2), published in *Informationen. Theater und Musik, Kunst und Wissenschaft in Kassel*

simile of 1937 revealed a conspicuous darkening of those stains. It seemed as if the writing underneath was slowly vanishing.[4]

There was one additional worry. The leaf had apparently been preserved in a transparent sleeve. A harmful reaction between cover and vellum could not be ruled out. Results of initial testing showed no apparent threat of acidity. For a conclusive analysis, Hennig forwarded a sample of the see-through sleeve to the best laboratory in Germany, the Institute of Macromolecular Chemistry of the Technical University in Darmstadt. To everyone's relief this second test also turned out negative.[5]

Director Hennig made arrangements to send the *Liber Sapientiae* and its cut-off leaf for a complete evaluation and treatment to the Institute for Book Restoration at the Bavarian State Library. The Institute was known the world over for its distinguished specialists and cutting-edge laboratory equipment.[6] There the codex underwent a thorough rehabilitation.[7] Respectful of the manuscript's recent history, Hennig allowed Leaf One to remain detached from its original text block, a mute testimony to the violence it had suffered. In consultation with experts, he also decided to forego treatment of the stained areas. Test tube experiments suggested that bleaching the stains might adversely affect whatever writing remained concealed underneath. Until better laboratory methods and technologies were perfected, it was prudent to leave well enough alone. The leaf was simply cleaned, pressed, expanded with a vellum strip, and set in its own

---

6 (1982): 10, Broszinski states: "Vermutlich Jacob Grimm selbst wandte das Reagens an – zumindest fand er es völlig normal, daß man es anwandte –, um Verschwundenes wieder lesbar zu machen." (Presumably Jacob Grimm himself applied the reagent – at least he found the method fully acceptable to make the vanished letters visible again.)

4 Broszinski, "Handschriftenrestaurierung in Kassel (*2*)", 10.

5 "Hildebrandlied 4," documents from the archives of the Gesamthochschul-Bibliothek Kassel – Landesbibliothek und Murhardsche Bibliothek der Stadt Kassel, deposited with the University of California, Davis, Shields Library, Department of Special Collections. Letter of D. Hennig to J. Kalkbrenner, December 5, 1972. Also: Süßmann, 29, citing the final report of the Bavarian State Library, Institute for Book Restoration.

6 Broszinski, "Handschriftenrestaurierung in Kassel (2)", 10.

7 According to the final report of the Bavarian State Library, Institute for Book Restoration, reproduced in Süßmann, 28–31, the text block and the covers were taken apart. The original binding was made out of narrow oak boards covered in leather. The leather was pealed off the wood, cleaned and reused. The narrow boards were expanded with strips of oak. Spine and corners were redone in new leather. Two facsimile clasps instead of the original four were fashioned and reattached. A narrow piece of vellum, an extension to the inner margin, was added to the loose eighth leaf. When the leaf was reinserted, this strip acted as a placeholder, marking the original location of the now separately bound Leaf One. All leaves were cleaned and flattened and the codex was reassembled. A dark-blue leather slipcase with moleskin lining was fashioned to house both mother codex and its separately bound Leaf One. Restoration work began on July 4, 1973 and was completed on September 6, 1973; Arnold Wensky performed the work under the supervision of Karl Jäckel.

leather-covered boards. After eight weeks of intense treatment, a rejuvenated *Hildebrandslied* went on public display in Munich to the delight of unending lines of visitors. Meanwhile, the *Willehalm Codex* spent time in the Herzog August Library in Wolfenbüttel where it too received care and attention.[8] Once restored, the codices returned to Kassel, and eventually took residence in the library's state-of-the-art underground treasure chamber.

The war and hostage years of the Kassel codices left many questions unanswered. Voices in the media clamored to know more about the circumstances surrounding their disappearance and wanderings.[9] While such demands were understandable and perhaps even justified, neither Hennig nor Kalkbrenner were eager to revisit the past. Thankful to the Rosenbach Foundation trustees for their cooperation and good will, they did not want to repay generosity with a salvo of allegations.[10] In fact, when asked by reporters how the codices had found their way into the Rosenbach collection, Kalkbrenner bluntly retorted: "Nobody knows and nobody is really interested. What matters is that they were found."[11]

Across the Atlantic, Brown University Professor William Freeman Twaddell thought otherwise. Upon reading in the *Philadelphia Sunday Bulletin* about the startling discovery of the *Hildebrandslied* in a small American library,[12] Twaddell contacted the Department of State and then the German Consulate in Boston, hoping to learn additional details. Both offices warily referred him to Kalkbrenner in Washington, DC. Unwilling to reopen old wounds, Kalkbrenner tried to dissuade Twaddell from digging into the past.[13] But the Brown University professor would not be easily discouraged. For him the significance of the poem far transcended "the dilemma of a burly Goth some fifteen hundred years

---

8 Nineteenth-century restorers had used chemically tanned leather strips to mend the original oak tanned binding. As a result the codex had developed red rot along the spine. It had to be taken apart and rebound. Red rot is a deterioration of leather bookbinding, leading to a hardening of the leather, which can be so severe as to destroy it completely. See: "Hildebrandlied 4," documents from the archives. ... Letter of D. Hennig to J. Kalkbrenner, December 5, 1972.

9 See for instance Marlene Manthey, "Hildebrandlied heimgekehrt" (Hildebrandlied returned home), *Die Presse*, 17 September 1972, p. 5, and also her "Ende einer literarischen Odyssee" (The end of a literary odyssey), *Wiesbadener Tagblatt*, 27 September 1973.

10 "Hildebrandlied 4," documents from the archives. ... Letter of J. Kalkbrenner to D. Hennig, February 21, 1973.

11 Adolf Katz, "Search for 2 Ancient German Literary Works Ends in Phila.," *Philadelphia Sunday Bulletin*, September 24, 1972, section 1, XB5.

12 Ibid. The *Philadelphia Sunday Bulletin* was the only US newspaper, which covered the story of the return of the manuscripts.

13 "Hildebrandlied 4," documents from the archives. ... Letter of J. Kalkbrenner to D. Hennig, February 21, 1973.

Fig. 29. William F. Twaddell around 1975
(Courtesy of the Twaddell Family)

ago."[14] The ballad was one of the greatest poems of world literature and as such it had earned the right to have its history fully explained. As an American he believed that American scholarship had to carry the investigation as far as possible. It was, in his view, a matter of propriety and obligation.[15] It was imperative to gather all details without delay, he told a defensive Kalkbrenner, for time was not on their side. The deaths of director Wilhelm Hopf, of the Rosenbach brothers, and that of Professor Carl Selmer were poignant reminders that memories of events were becoming ever more difficult to retrieve.[16]

Brushing aside all objections, Twaddell started his inquiry with Selmer's 1955 encoded article, the only published history of the post-war US odyssey of the *Hildebrandslied*. Stumped by its string of enigmatic allusions, Twaddell turned to

---

[14] William Freeman Twaddell "Hildebrandlied," lecture to the *Brunonische Gelehrtenrepublik* of Brown University, October 16, 1972, p. 22. Manuscript. Twaddell Family Archives. Deposited with the University of California, Davis. Shields Library. Department of special Collections.

[15] "Hildebrandlied 4," documents from the archives. ... Letter of W. F. Twaddell to J. Kalkbrenner, January 22, 1973.

[16] Ibid., February 3, 1973.

Rose, Professor Selmer's widow.[17] It was Rose Selmer who gave Twaddell the answers to the riddles. From her, he learned, and later made public, the identity of the unnamed New York book dealer, Dr. Rosenbach, of the pious countess, Mrs. Doheny, of the large research library, the Morgan, and that of the sunny California village, Camarillo.

From the pages of the Rosenbach's biography by Edwin Wolf 2nd and John Fleming, Twaddell gleaned another important detail: the farcical scene describing Philip Rosenbach and John Fleming in the process of selling the *Liber Sapientiae* to Countess Doheny.[18] He contacted the Doheny Memorial Library and obtained a copy of the Rosenbach reimbursement check. The check, bearing the signature of John Fleming was not for $ 4,000, as Philip once told Agent Page, but rather for more than double that amount: $ 9,500.[19]

In 1954, after the official return of the *Liber Sapientiae*, the Department of State had issued a public appeal with full-page illustrations featuring the missing leaf

---

[17] In the October 1973 manuscript version of his article, Twaddell acknowledges the assistance received from Mrs. Carl Selmer. See: William Freeman Twaddell, "The Hildebrandlied Manuscript in the U.S.A., 1945–1972," October 1973 version, Twaddell Archives. Unpublished. Deposited with the University of California, Davis, Shields Library, Department of Special Collections.

[18] "Hildebrandlied 4," documents from the archives. ... Letter of W. F. Twaddell to J. Kalkbrenner, January 22, 1973.

[19] W. F. Twaddell, "The Hildebrandlied Manuscript in the USA, 1945–1972," *Journal of English and Germanic Philology* 73, no. 2, (April 1974): 164.
Note: The $ 9,500 price of the codex may have been in violation of the provisions of The National Stolen Property Act of 1934. Created as part of the United States Code, Title 18 (Crimes and Criminal Procedure), Chapter 113 (Stolen Property), it lists provisions regarding transportation, sale, or receipt of stolen property. It states that whoever transports, transmits, or transfers in interstate or foreign commerce any goods, wares, or merchandise valued at $ 5,000 or more, *with the knowledge that the goods were stolen* (emphasis added), shall be fined and/or imprisoned for not more than ten years (Section 2314). Whoever receives, possesses... or sells any goods of the value of $ 5,000 or more, *that have crossed a State or United States boundary after being stolen, knowing the goods to have been stolen* (emphasis added), shall be fined and/or imprisoned for not more than ten years (Section 2315).
Even if the A. S. W. Rosenbach, Philip Rosenbach, and/or John Fleming had bought the manuscripts in good faith – which seems unlikely, since both codices displayed prominently the Kassel ownership stamp – only weeks later, the clear rejection letter received from Morgan Curator Curt Bühler, ought to have changed their view on the legality of the transaction. For those unfamiliar with the law, there were many reminders in the press. A stern warning, for instance, was issued by the Department of State in its 1947 *Bulletin*, three years prior to the Doheny sale. It said in part: "The introduction of looted objects of art into this country is contrary to the general policy of the United States and to the commitments of the United States under The Hague Convention of 1907, and in case of objects of value of $ 5,000 or more is a contravention of Federal law." ("Return of Looted Objects of Art to Countries of Origin: Memorandum by the State Department Member of SWNCC," *Department of State Bulletin* 16, no. 399 (1947): 358).

and *Willehalm* miniatures.[20] It seemed highly improbable to Professor Twaddell that John Fleming and the Rosenbach Foundation officers would have remained unaware of the continuing search, and incognizant of the two war-trophies hidden in their library. He set out to prove his conjecture, and discovered that indeed several members of the Rosenbach entourage were in on the secret. Among them Edwin Wolf 2nd, who, when asked, candidly admitted knowing,[21] Clive Driver, the museum curator, sworn to secrecy and rumored to have known since 1968,[22] and at least one of the Rosenbach Foundation trustees, the one who had issued the gag-order.[23] Once the State Department had launched its public appeal, the least embarrassing solution for the Foundation was to silence its museum curator and keep the manuscripts hidden.[24]

Emboldened by his findings, Twaddell pressed on, intent to expose the name of the spoiler and, if different, that of the seller. He combed through military archives determined to find out which units had been stationed in Bad Wildungen in April of 1945. He did not succeed.[25] Unable to uncover the identity of the thief, Twaddell turned his attention to the seller. He interviewed Edgar Breiten-

---

20 Ardelia R. Hall, "U.S. Program for Return of Historic Objects to Countries of Origin, 1944–1954," *Department of State Bulletin* 31, no. 797 (1954): 493. "The two surviving pages owned by the Kassel Library are among the most valuable manuscripts of world literature. ... For one thousand years these two parchment pages have survived. They were bound with a 10th century manuscript on religious subjects, 'Liber Sapientiae,' where they were apparently reused as the end-pages of the latter manuscript. ... Unfortunately the bound manuscript, which has been now found, contains only the second page of the Hildebrandlied. The first page... had been removed from the manuscript and is missing. ... Its removal from the codex is probably the greatest single loss to literature resulting from World War II."

21 Twaddell (1974), 165, footnote 16.

22 "Hildebrandlied 2," documents from the archives. ... Letter of W.F. Twaddell to D. Hennig, June 19, 1974.

23 Werner L. Gundersheimer, tape-recorded telephone conversation of April 12, 2000. Deposited with the University of California, Davis, Shields Library, Department of Special Collections.

24 When the author asked Dr. Gundersheimer, where the *Willehalm Codex* had been between 1945 and 1972, he explained: "It had just been in a cabinet in the Rosenbach Library. The Rosenbach is a townhouse. It must have been, all along, in one of the armoires. They have a lot of these armoires there with shelves connected with cabinets at the bottom. I think it must have been in one of those. It is possible that Driver was not altogether candid with me. But to the best of my knowledge, it was there all the time. (...) It had not been sold." (Quoted by permission.)

25 Twaddell (1974), 158.
Note: Two requests (December 2001 and January 2002) by the author to the National Archives and Records Administration, Military Personnel Records, St. Louis, Missouri remained unanswered. On a third attempt (in July 2002) the National Personnel Records Center finally replied, that a major portion of their records regarding Army military personnel of the period 1912 through 1959 had been lost in a fire, and that no other information was available to researchers without expressed permission of the soldier's next of kin.

bach and then Gretel Mayer. As Mayer refused to surrender the officer's name, Twaddell contacted the only other known survivor of the 1945 sales transaction in New York, John Fleming. But in spite of repeated and insistent requests, Fleming remained silent and uncooperative.[26] Reluctantly, Twaddell had to acknowledge that the pillage in Bad Wildungen and the sale in New York were not matters of public record.

Finally, Twaddell filed a petition with the Department of State requesting access to the *Ardelia Hall File*. Inexplicably, after a considerable delay, the National Archives notified him in writing, that no records on the *Hildebrandslied* or the *Willehalm* could be found.[27] Frustrated, the Brown University professor went public with what he had learned, and highlighted what continued to remain a mystery. His informative article "The Hildebrandlied Manuscript in the USA, 1945–1972," appeared in the April 1974 issue of the *Journal of English and Germanic Philology*. For over a quarter century Twaddell's paper remained the only factual account on the hunt for the Kassel treasures.[28]

Twenty-six years later, in December of 2001, as work on this book was entering its final stages, the author appealed to the Rosenbach Museum & Library requesting information on the 1945 purchase of the Kassel codices. One paragraph in the Wolf and Fleming biography of Dr. Rosenbach seemed to contradict the claim that all business records were routinely destroyed every five years. That paragraph read:

> The brothers hoarded paper as misers do gold. In dozens of filing cabinets, cartons, ledgers, scrapbooks, salesbooks, and piles merely bound with string they kept the important with the inconsequential – ... personal and business letters sent and received, newspaper clippings, invoices of merchandise bought, and sales slips – a vast, unsorted accumulation of over fifty years.[29]

"Invoices of merchandise bought, and sales slips ... of over fifty years ..." The wording suggested that in spite of repeated denials, the invoices of 1945 could still be on file. The response received on January 3, 2002 confirmed the assumption. The brown manila envelope bearing the imprint of the Rosenbach Museum

---

26 Ibid., 159. Twaddell wrote seven times to John Fleming. The only answer he received was an evasive redirect to the Rosenbach archive.

27 Ibid., 158, footnote 4: "Mr. Harry W. John, General Archives Division of the National Archives and Records Service, has informed me, in a letter of 2 August 1973, that 'we have completed a search among the records in our custody known as the 'Ardelia Hall Collection,' but we have been unable to locate any information concerning the Hildebrandlied manuscript or the Willehalm Codex.'"

28 There is one other brief article titled "Through diplomatic Efforts Stolen Historic Manuscripts Recovered" by James S. Sutterlin, which appeared in *Department of State Newsletter* 2, no.142 (1973): 27.

29 Edwin Wolf 2nd and John F. Fleming, *Rosenbach: A Biography* (Cleveland: World Publishing Company, 1960), 8.

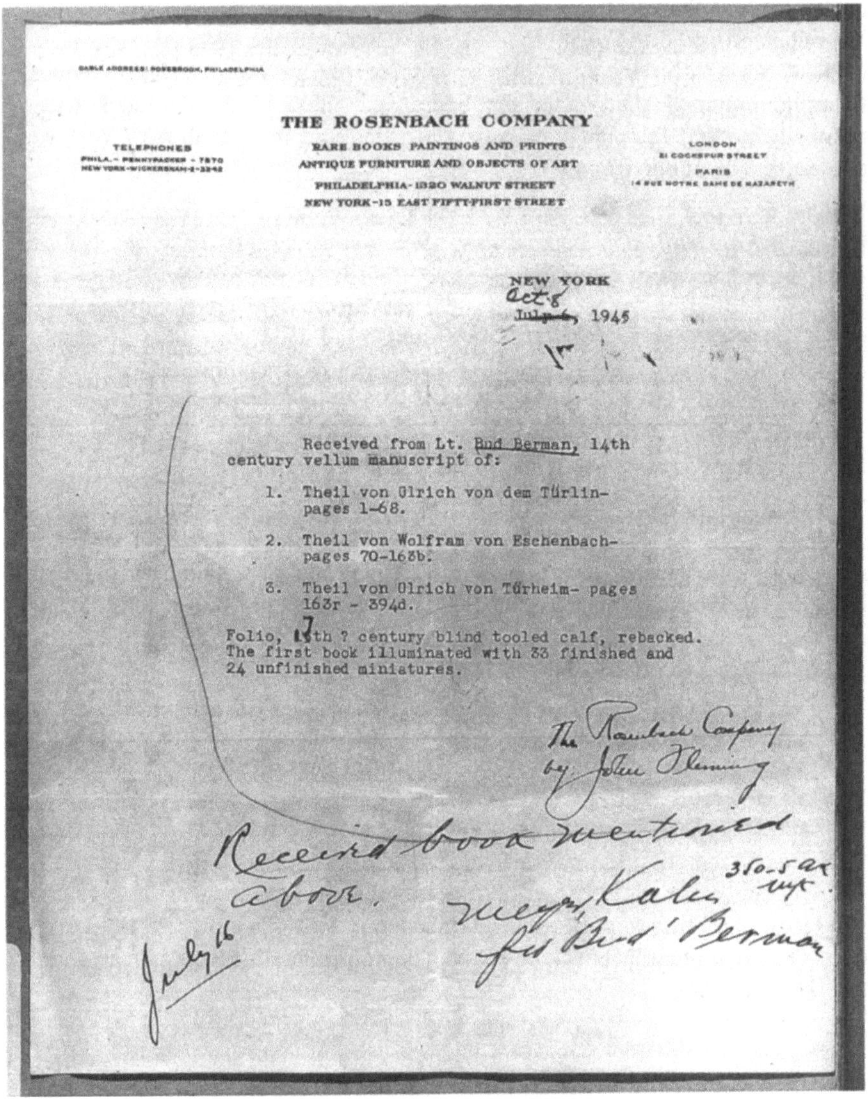

CABLE ADDRESS: ROSEBROOK, PHILADELPHIA

THE ROSENBACH COMPANY
RARE BOOKS PAINTINGS AND PRINTS
ANTIQUE FURNITURE AND OBJECTS OF ART
PHILADELPHIA - 1320 WALNUT STREET
NEW YORK - 15 EAST FIFTY-FIRST STREET

TELEPHONES
PHILA. - PENNYPACKER - 7570
NEW YORK - WICKERSHAM - 2 - 3242

LONDON
21 COCKSPUR STREET
PARIS
14 RUE NOTRE DAME DE NAZARETH

NEW YORK
Oct 8
~~July 6~~, 1945

Received from Lt. Bud Berman, 14th century vellum manuscript of:

1. Theil von Olrich von dem Türlin- pages 1–68.

2. Theil von Wolfram von Eschenbach- pages 70–163b.

3. Theil von Olrich von Türheim- pages 163r - 394d.

Folio, 17th ? century blind tooled calf, rebacked. The first book illuminated with 33 finished and 24 unfinished miniatures.

The Rosenbach Company
by John Fleming

Received book mentioned above.
Meyer Kahn
for 'Bud' Berman

July 16

Fig. 30. Rosenbach Company Archives. Deposit receipt signed by John Fleming. (The Rosenbach Museum & Library, Philadelphia – Reproduced by permission.)

& Library yielded a cache of four business records retrieved from the now open archives of the Rosenbach Foundation. These were the proverbial "smoking gun" documents, disclosing for the very first time the date, the price, the name, and the intentions of the seller.[30]

The earliest of the four was a deposit receipt, issued on official Rosenbach letterhead, and signed by bookstore manager John Fleming. It revealed that on July 6, 1945, a scant three months after the looting in Bad Wildungen, US Army Lieutenant Bud Berman had deposited with the Rosenbach Company an illuminated codex, bound in blind-tooled calf. According to the description, the codex, with thirty-three completed and twenty-four (*sic*) unfinished miniatures, consisted of three interlocking stories written by Ulrich von dem Türlin, Wolfram von Eschenbach, and by Ulrich von Türheim. Without a doubt, this was Kassel *Willehalm*.

For some reason, the Rosenbach Company did not act on the offer. Ten days later, a friend of the seller's, a man named Mayer Kahn residing at 350 Fifth Avenue, New York City, came by to retrieve the codex.[31] Three months passed, and on October 8, 1945, the seller returned and resubmitted the codex. The original deposit receipt was simply amended in longhand to reflect the new date, and the name of the seller was underlined, to indicate that it was one and the same.

The second document was a neatly penned, three-page letter, addressed to Dr. Rosenbach and signed by the "owner" of the manuscripts, US Army Lieutenant Bud Berman. The writer was pleading for a swift decision regarding the two books he had picked up in Germany. The matter was urgent, for within the next sixty days he was scheduled to return to civilian life. But before talking price, Lieutenant Berman wanted to make his intentions perfectly clear: if they were to come to an understanding, the sale of "his manuscripts" would be final. Should the US Government rule at some later date that books picked up in Germany had to be returned he would not be willing to refund the money. He had already received several good offers, and had come to realize that at least one of "his" volumes was very desirable. But being neither an art-expert nor a book-collector,

---

30 The four documents (the memorandum of deposit, the Berman letter, the voucher, and an itemized sales slip) were received on January 3, 2002 from Dr. Derick Dreher, Director of the Rosenbach Museum & Library, upon written request by the author. In his letter, Dr. Dreher informed the author, that the Rosenbach Board of Trustees had adopted a policy of open Archives to scholars. See: Rosenbach Museum & Library, Archives, 1945 business records and correspondence, deposited with the University of California, Davis, Shields Library, Department of Special Collections.

31 This information comes from the handwritten annotation found at the bottom of the memorandum of deposit, which identifies the date as July 16, and the person retrieving the codex as Mayer Kahn. It appears that, at the time, the Rosenbach Company had either rejected the offer or postponed a purchase decision. In his letter to Dr. Rosenbach, Berman refers to Mayer as "a friend".

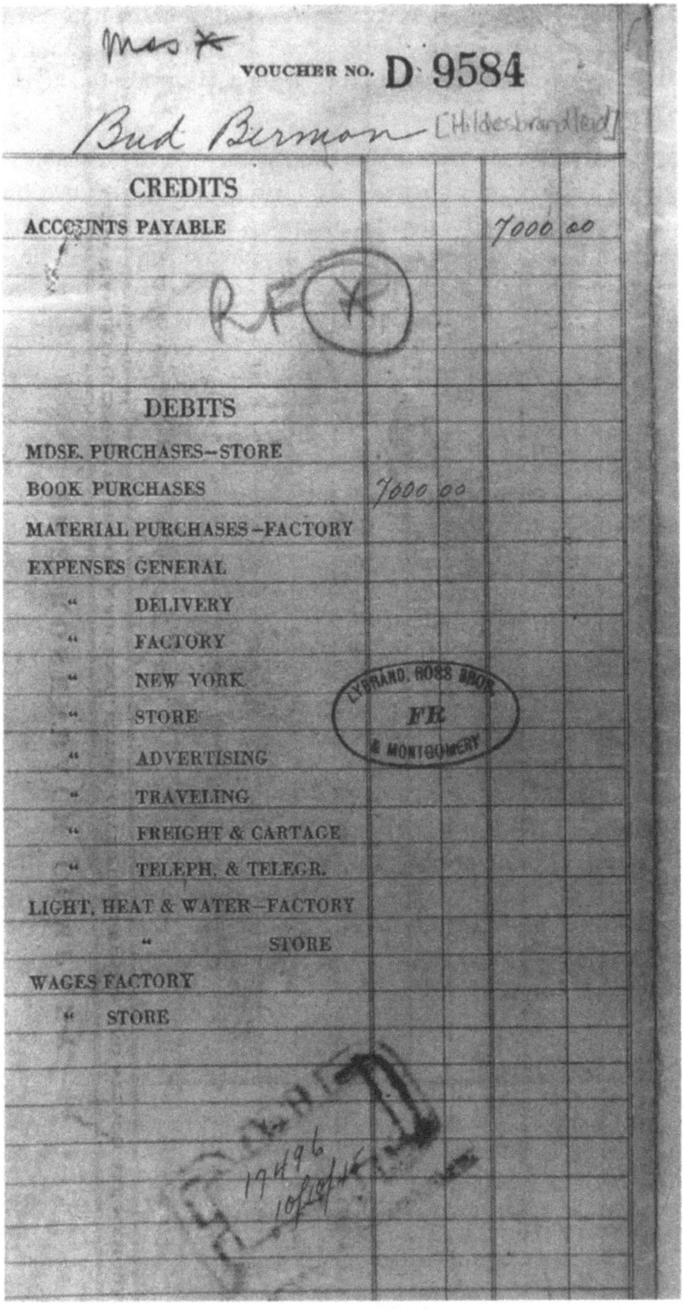

Mas *

VOUCHER NO. D 9584

Bud Berman [Hildesbrandlied]

CREDITS				
ACCOUNTS PAYABLE			7000	00
RF (*)				
DEBITS				
MDSE. PURCHASES–STORE				
BOOK PURCHASES	7000	00		
MATERIAL PURCHASES–FACTORY				
EXPENSES GENERAL				
" DELIVERY				
" FACTORY				
" NEW YORK				
" STORE				
" ADVERTISING				
" TRAVELING				
" FREIGHT & CARTAGE				
" TELEPH. & TELEGR.				
LIGHT, HEAT & WATER–FACTORY				
" STORE				
WAGES FACTORY				
" STORE				

LYBRAND, ROSS BROS. & MONTGOMERY
FR

17496
10/10/16

Fig. 31. Rosenbach Company Archives. Purchase voucher D 9584.
(The Rosenbach Museum & Library, Philadelphia Reproduced by permission.)

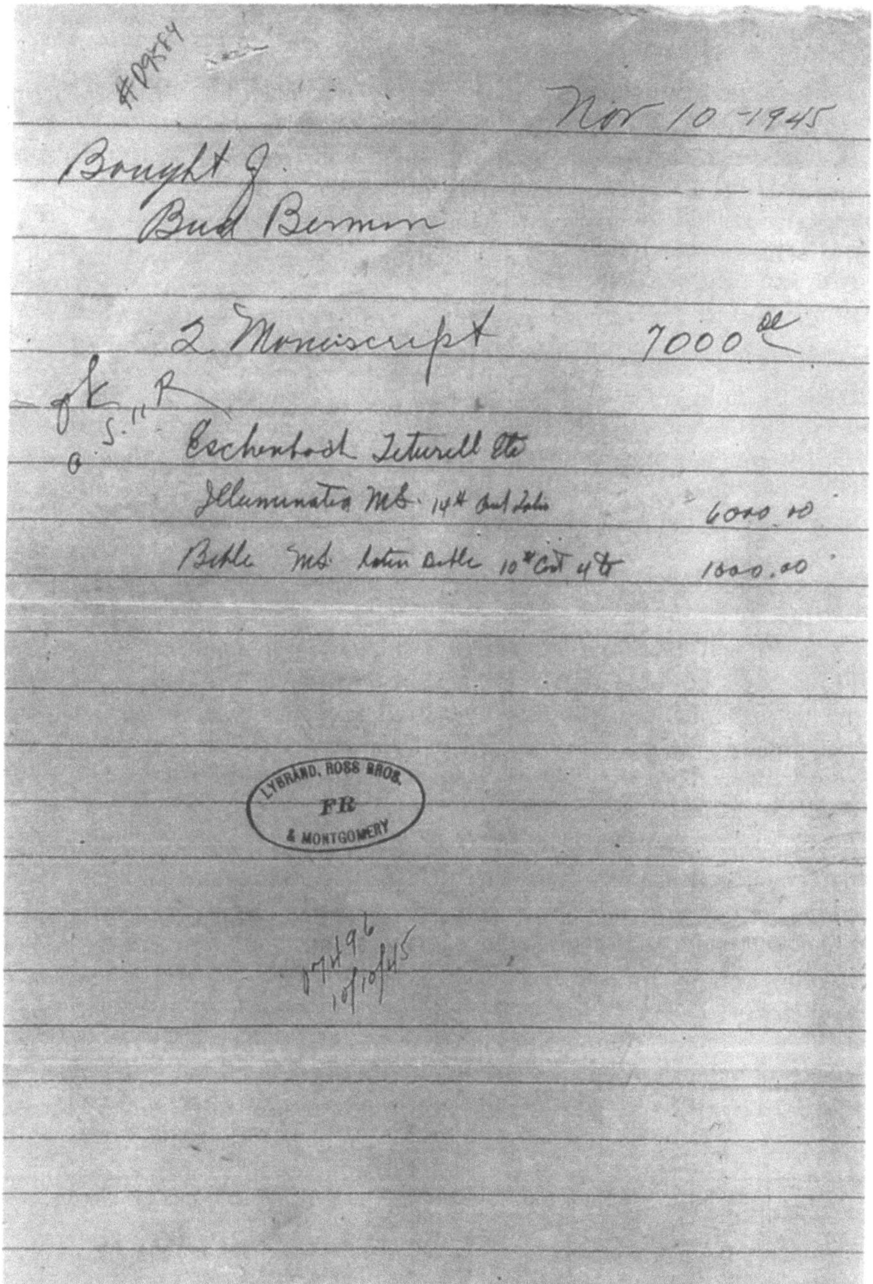
Nov 10-1945
Bought of
Bud Berman
2 Manuscript 7000.00
Eschenbach Titurell etc
Illuminated MS. 14th Cent folio 6000.00
Bible MS. Latin Bible 10th Cent 4to 1000.00

07496
10/10/45

Fig. 32. Rosenbach Company Archives. Descriptive sales slip, November 10, 1945. (The Rosenbach Museum & Library, Philadelphia — Reproduced by permission.)

he wanted the Doctor to handle the sale. Berman "honestly" believed that in this manner the highest market price would be obtained.

Lieutenant Berman's eloquence must have persuaded the House of Rosenbach to take another look at his merchandise. Thereupon, seller and buyer had come to an understanding. The third document in the group, Voucher No. D 9584, confirms the sale of the two manuscripts for the sum of $ 7,000. On the attached itemized sales slip, the last of the four documents, Berman's volumes are identified as *Eschenbach Titurell* [sic], etc., Illuminated MS., 14th century, folio, valued at $ 6,000, and a Bible MS., Latin Bible, 10th century, 4to, valued at $ 1,000. In the left-hand corner the transaction is authorized by none other than A. S. W. R. – Abraham Simon Wolf Rosenbach.

While the identity of the spoiler remains to this day a mystery, for there is no indication that seller and thief are one and the same, all questions pertaining to the disposition of the manuscripts can be finally put to rest. In spring of 1945, somewhere in occupied Germany, US Army Lieutenant Bud Berman *picked up* two valuable-looking books. Berman's choice of words might prompt a charitable soul to grant him the benefit of doubt. Napoleon would have certainly dismissed the deed as a simple search-and-rescue operation: "Voler, c'est malhonête, le soldat trouve!" The verb *to pick up* is rather ambiguous and can refer to a range of activities, from bartering to buying, from obtaining to finding. John Fleming was not a charitable soul. In a 1974 letter to Dr. Hennig, his office bluntly stated that the *Liber Sapientiae* was purchased from a returning US soldier, who had *looted it* in Germany.[32] And in an earlier letter to Mrs. Doheny, the same Fleming, borrowing a phrase from Napoleon, explained that the officer *had found* the manuscript in the rubble of southern Germany.[33] Perhaps that pile of rubble was at the bottom of a stairwell, in the basement of a Bad Wildungen inn.

Indifferent to the frailty of the ancient codices, and certainly unaware of their inestimable value, Lieutenant Berman allegedly obtained permission from his commanding officer to mail "his" two manuscripts home. The package passed Customs without incident, for Fleming remembered seeing the original mail wrappings, complete with US Customs' tags.[34] The practice of sending stolen artwork unprotected through regular mail was, unfortunately, not uncommon. Joe Meador, the Quedlinburg thief, used the Army Post Office to send home to Texas the irreplaceable treasures of a thousand-year-old cathedral. "If they get

---

32 "Hildebrandlied 2," documents from the archives. ... Letter of B. Langstaff to D. Hennig, April 30, 1974.

33 Archdiocese of Los Angeles. Archival Center. Estelle Doheny Collection of California. Letters deposited with the University of California, Davis. Shields Library. Department of Special Collections. Letter of J. Fleming to E. L. Doheny, November 19, 1953. Released to the author in March 2002.

34 Ibid.

there, they get there," a fellow soldier recalled him saying, "and if they don't, they don't."[35]

Three months later, while director Wilhelm Hopf and US Monuments Officer Ted Heinrich were moving heaven and earth in search of the manuscripts, while Bad Wildungen museum director Felix Pusch was sifting though mountains of debris looking for a scrap of vellum or wood, Lieutenant Bud Berman was already in New York, intent to turn a profit on his unlawful souvenirs. When bookstore manager Fleming deferred a decision, Berman brazenly sidestepped the office-help, and went straight to the owner insisting on a swift resolution, since he was about to be out of uniform.

Rosenbach, the accomplished rare-book dealer, must have been well acquainted with the work of Wolfram von Eschenbach. In 1913 he had sold the Johann Mentelin 1477 first edition of Wolfram's *Titurel* and *Parzival*[36] to John B. Stetson, Jr.[37] And in 1935, only ten years prior to the Berman transaction, that very same 1477 volume had passed through the Doctor's hands once more, when the Stetson collection was dispersed. This time, the Doctor sold the volume to John H. Scheide.[38] This might perhaps explain why on the itemized sales slip, the Doctor identified the codex not as the three-part *Willehalm*, as originally described by the punctilious Fleming, but erroneously as *Eschenbach's Titurell* [sic], a work with which he was more familiar. When it came to the *Liber Sapientiae*, the Doctor, relying on Gretel Mayer's deficient report, failed to recognize the Kassel codex altogether, and listed it as a tenth-century Latin Bible valued at a modest $ 1,000.

It seems unlikely that seller and buyer were unaware of the illegal nature of their transaction. Both books displayed prominently the large, five-centimeter ownership seal of the Kassel *Landesbibliothek*. Bud Berman was apprehensive: he was unwilling to return the money, if the Government were to declare the deal null and void. The Doctor, as a member of the Roberts Commission, a group dedicated to the preservation and return of cultural objects dispersed in times of war, ought to have been fully conversant with the policies of the US government regarding trophy-art, and very much aware of the booming illegal art trade of the time. To his defense, one might argue that at the time of the transaction, the Doctor was not in the best of health.

---

35 "T as in Treasure, Texas – and Theft," *The New York Times*, 20 July 1990, Section A, 26, 1: "The soldier had mailed the artwork home, wrapped in plain brown paper."

36 Wolf 2nd, 83.

37 John B. Stetson, Jr. (1884–1952), heir to a hat fortune, was an avid bibliophile. His father was John B. Stetson, creator of the "Hat of the West" or "Boss of the Plains" a style of hats popular with cowboys and gold miners.

38 Wolf 2nd, 410.
Note: John Hinsdale Scheide (1875–1942), son of William T. Scheide, pioneer in the oil business in Pennsylvania, was an omnivorous reader and avid book collector.

The newly released documents allow us to speculate as to why Philip Rosenbach and John Fleming, in their interview with Customs Agent Page, and later Clive Driver in his 1972 conversation with library director Hennig, repeatedly denied the existence of the 1945 business records. It was not to protect the identity of the seller, as one might have suspected, but more likely because both Kassel manuscripts were listed on one and the same voucher. To release that voucher was to admit to the purchase of not one, but two war-trophies, with the *Willehalm* listed at $ 6,000, a value exceeding the legal $ 5,000 threshold established under Federal law.

As to the *Willehalm*, Dr. R must have fallen in love with the illuminated codex (or he must have considered it too risky to unload), for he never sold it. Dr. Gundersheimer stated that between 1945 and 1972 the codex had remained in Dr. Rosenbach's Philadelphia library.[39] At the end of December 2002, Professor Beverley Eddy,[40] sister of curator Clive Driver, corroborated Dr. Gundersheimer's assertion. She remembered a Thanksgiving holiday visit to the Rosenbach Museum & Library in the late 1960s. At the time she was a doctoral student in German Literature. Clive Driver secretly showed his sister the severed leaf of the *Hildebrandslied,* which he kept tucked between the leaves of the *Willehalm Codex*.[41]

There remains perhaps one last question to be asked and answered. If it had not been for Professor Selmer's chance encounter with the *Liber Sapientiae* at the Morgan and later for his dogged perseverance to see the codex returned, would the mutilated manuscript have remained forever sequestered in the Seminary, lost among the many artifacts of the Doheny Memorial Library? The answer to this question is a qualified no.

On December 2, 1987, forty-three years after the war, in the London chambers of Christie's, Estelle Doheny's splendid manuscript collections were put on the auction block. The Seminary's Theologate Board of Directors had come to the sober realization that maintaining and insuring the collection rather than investing its cash value in the market resulted in a daily loss of $ 10,000 to the seminary endowment fund.[42] Strapped for cash, the Seminary fathers voted for dispersal. Cardinal Mahony's liaison with Christie's was none other than the

39 Werner L. Gundersheimer, tape-recorded telephone conversation of April 12, 2000, deposited with the University of California, Davis, Shields Library, Department of Special Collections.

40 Dr. Eddy is Professor of German on the faculty of Dickinson College in Pennsylvania. Her 1970 doctorate degree in German Literature is from Indiana University. Her current teaching interests include medieval literature.

41 Beverley D. Eddy, Electronic-mail correspondence of September 16, 2002, deposited with the University of California, Davis, Shields Library, Department of Special Collections.

42 Francis J. Weber, *Southern California's First Family: The Dohenys of Los Angeles* (Fullerton, CA: Lorson's Books and Prints, 1993), 74.

once insubordinate seminarian and secret bibliophile, Monsignor Francis J. Weber. That December day, if Kassel were still listening, it would have heard the rap of the ivory hammer marking the sale of one, ninth century Latin codex known as the *Liber Sapientiae*.

In 1978, after extensive remodeling, the Kassel Library inaugurated its state-of-the-art, underground treasure chamber.[43] From behind shatterproof glass, in climate controlled display cases, the fragile *Hildebrandslied* and the radiant *Willehalm* serenely greet the occasional visitor. At first glance, nothing in this sanctuary of soft light and cool silence betrays their tumultuous past. Only to the compassionate observer does the *Hildebrandslied* reveal its stigmata. And only to the initiated does it whisper a story that opens with the magical words: *Ik gihorta dat seggen* ... I once heard it said ...

Fig. 33. The underground Treasure Chamber of the Universitätsbibliothek Kassel – Landesbibliothek und Murhardsche Bibliothek der Stadt Kassel - current home of the *Hildebrandlied*
Left: the separately bound Leaf One. Right: Liber Sapientiae with the last leaf
Front: edition of the *Hildebrandslied* by the Brothers Grimm
(Archives of the Universitätsbibliothek Kassel – Landesbibliothek und Murhardsche Bibliothek der Stadt Kassel – Reproduced by permission)

---

[43] *Ex Bibliotheca Cassellana: 400 Jahre Landesbibliothek, 20.11.1580–20.11.1980* (From the Kassel Library: 400 years of State Library 11/20/1580–11/20/1980), editor Hans-Jürgen Kahlfuß, (Kassel: Gesamthochschul-Bibliothek-Kassel, Landesbibliothek und Murhardsche Bibliothek der Stadt Kassel, 1980), 55.

Appendix

Biographical Sketches

Hermann Baldewein, librarian and priest, was born in 1907 in Oldenburg. He studied theology and law and earned a doctorate with the dissertation "Organ und Stellvertreter als Elemente der allgemeinen Rechtslehre." He accepted a position as researcher with the State Archives of Münster, interned at the Münster University Library and later at the Berlin State Library. After passing his qualifying examinations for librarianship in 1939 he joined the *Landesbibliothek* in Kassel and was named acting director in 1942. Because of his Nazi past, he was dismissed in 1945 without pay. He served as an evangelical priest first in Minden, Soest and later in Aplerbeck/Dortmund. He retired in 1969.

Isaac Bencowitz, chemist and Director of the Offenbach Archival Depot, was born in Unitcha, Russia in 1896. A veteran of World War I, he studied at the University of Chicago and in 1923 earned a doctorate in chemistry from Columbia University with the dissertation "Compound Formation, Specific Conductivity, and Ionization in Fused Salt Mixtures." He worked at New York University between 1925 and 1926 and at the Rockefeller Institute from 1927 until his retirement in 1961. A captain in the army, he directed the Offenbach Collecting Point from April until October 1946 and perfected sorting procedures of recovered looted items. He died in 1972.

Bud Berman, 1945 lieutenant in the US Army. The identity of Bud Berman remains a mystery. A search through biographical indices, obituaries, and US Military Personnel Records proved inconclusive. What is known is that Lt. Berman, an officer in his mid- to late twenties, returned in November 1945 from the European Theater of War. His writing style and composition are clear and logical, his penmanship cultivated, suggestive of a higher-level education. He sold the two Kassel manuscripts, the *Liber Sapientiae* and the *Willehalm Codex* to the Rosenbach Company in 1945.

William Henry Bond, curator of manuscripts, was born in York, Pennsylvania in 1914. He graduated with a Ph.D. in English literature from Harvard University in 1941 with the dissertation "The Reputation and Influence of Sir Philip Sidney." Between 1942–43 he held a civil servant position with the US Navy Department in Washington and served in the US naval reserves until 1946. He was assistant to the director of the Houghton Library at Harvard in 1946 and in 1948 he was appointed curator of manuscripts at Houghton Library. Further biographical details are unknown.

Wolf Rudolf Hans Emanuel von Both, library director, was born in 1901 in Kassel. He studied German philology, history and art history at universities in Breslau, Rostock, and Munich. In 1926 he earned a doctor degree with the dissertation "Luther und die Fabel." After library internships in Breslau and Berlin, he passed his qualifying examinations and was appointed librarian at the State Library in Berlin. Drafted in 1940, he worked as curator for art and education in Prague. He was appointed in 1949 director of the *Landesbibliothek Kassel.* In 1957 he left Kassel to assume the position of assistant director of the State and University Library, Darmstadt. From 1960 to 1966, the year he retired, von Both was director of the University Library in Marburg. He died in 1976.

Edgar Breitenbach, librarian, was born in 1903 in Hamburg, Germany. He studied art history, and German and Nordic philology in Munich and Hamburg. He earned a Ph.D. summa cum laude in 1927, with the dissertation "Speculum Humanae Salvationis: eine typengeschichtliche Untersuchung." After library training in Göttingen and Berlin he passed his qualifying examinations in 1929. He worked at the State Library in Frankfurt am Main, later at the Rothschild Library, and at the Art and Technical Library. In 1933 he was fired, a victim of the Nazi Law for the Restoration of the Professional Civil Service. He found temporary employment in Basel and London and immigrated in 1937 to the United States where he taught art history at Mills College in California, and worked as a migrant in the orchards of the Pacific Northwest. He became a US citizen 1943. He was hired by the Federal Communications Commission and later transferred to the Office of War Information. In 1945 he was assigned to Germany, to work with the Monuments, Fine Arts & Archives Section of OMGUS. While in Germany he helped create the Berlin *Amerika-Gedenkbibliothek* (American Memorial Library), where he functioned between 1953–1955 as the official Library of Congress representative. In 1956 he became curator at the *Germanisches Nationalmuseum* in Nürnberg. The German Government honored him with a citation for meritorious service and with the West German Order for Merit, First Class (1959). From 1956 to the time he retired in 1973 he was Chief of the Prints and Photograph Division of the US Library of Congress. In 1973 he received the Commander's Cross of the Order of Merit of the Federal Republic of Germany "for his work furthering the exchanges between German and American libraries and for his assistance in restoring to Germany materials which disappeared during and following World War II." Among the materials he helped return were the *Weltkriegbücherei* – Stuttgart, confiscated by the US in 1945, the *Hildebrandslied* and the *Willehalm Codex,* and the collections of the German Documentary Film-Library. He died in 1977 near Celle, Germany.

Curt Ferdinand Bühler, curator, authority on incunabula, was born in New York City in 1905. He earned a doctorate from Trinity College of the University of Dublin in 1930. After post-graduate studies in Munich he was appointed as incunabula specialist at the Pierpont Morgan Library in New York, where he worked until his retirement in 1973. He was a Rosenbach Fellow at the University of Pennsylvania in 1947 and again in 1958–59, President of the Bibliographic Society of America for a number of years, and director and chairman of the American Council of Learned Societies. He died in 1985.

J. Frederick Cain, Jr., museum curator, was born in Philadelphia in 1938. He received a Masters of Fine Arts from Temple University and continued his studies at Laval, Harvard, and the University of Pennsylvania. Before joining the Alverthorpe Gallery in Jenkintown, Pennsylvania as curator of the Lessing J. Rosenwald Collection, he worked in leading national museums. Between 1972 and 1976 he taught art history at the Smithsonian in Washington, DC. He organized important collections, contributed to a number of scholarly publications and received various national and international awards.

Hans Peter des Coudres, library director, was born in 1905 in Berlin-Spandau. He studied law and earned a doctorate with the dissertation "Die Durchführung des Kinderarbeitsschutzrechtes." He interned in Leipzig and passed his librarianship qualifying examinations in 1935. During the same year, he was appointed Library Director of the SS Academy in Wewelsburg, Westfalen. In 1939 he became the director of the *Landesbibliothek* Kassel. He served in the Second World War. After the war, he worked as a librarian at the Federal Court of Justice in Karlsruhe (1950). In 1953 he was appointed as a librarian and later as the director of the library of the Max-Planck Institute for Foreign and International Civil Law in Tübingen (1952) and Hamburg (1953). He retired in 1972 and died in 1977.

Jonathan Dean, diplomat, was born in 1924 in Canada. He served in the Second World War with the infantry from Normandy to the Elbe. In 1950 he joined the Foreign Service in Bonn, was desk officer for East Germany in the Department of State, and First Secretary of the American Embassy in Prague. In the 1960s he served in Africa. In 1968 he returned to the American Embassy in Bonn and was deputy US negotiator for the 1971 quadripartite agreement on Berlin. In 1973 he earned a Ph.D. in political sciences from George Washington University with the dissertation "National Elites and the Political Culture." Between 1973 and 1981 he was US representative to the NATO-Warsaw Pact Force Reduction Negotiations in Vienna. He lives in active retirement.

Ludwig Denecke, library director and Grimm scholar, was born in Hameln in 1905. He studied classical philology at Leipzig University, where he earned a Ph.D. with the 1929 dissertation "Ritterdichter und Heidegötter (1150–1220)." In 1930 he joined the Berlin working group on the German Dictionary of the Grimm Brothers. He passed his librarian qualifying examination in 1935. In 1949 he worked as librarian in Göttingen. In 1959 he succeeded Wolf von Both as library director of the *Landesbibliothek* Kassel where he remained until 1968. While in Kassel he worked on the creation of a Grimm Brothers Museum and served as its first director. He traveled often to East Berlin to continue his work on the Grimm Brothers, last in 1995, a few months before his ninetieth birthday. He died in 1996.

Carrie Estelle Doheny, collector and philanthropist, was born in 1875 in Philadelphia. She was the daughter of German immigrants. After high school, she found employment as a telephone operator. Legend has it that oil magnate Edward Laurence Doheny was charmed by her melodious phone-voice and married her. The Dohenys gave liberally to charitable causes. In 1931, in recognition of their service to the Church, Pope Pius XI conferred on them the title of Knight and Lady of the Equestrian Order of the Holy Sepulchre. In 1939 Pope Pius XII elevated Mrs. Doheny to the rank of Papal Countess. She began collecting books in the 1920s and founded the Doheny Memorial Library in 1939. She continued collecting for the library until her death in 1958.

Clive Driver, curator, was born in 1935. He earned a Master's Degree in Library Science from Columbia University. After graduation he worked at the City College of New York and in 1965 was hired as director of the Rosenbach Museum & Library in Philadelphia. In 1978 he moved to Truro, Massachusetts, but continued working for the Rosenbach Museum on a part-time basis. In 1987 he was appointed director of the Pilgrim Monument & Museum in Truro. In April of that year, the Rosenbach Museum & Library sued Driver for illegally removing important documents. He was fined and sentenced to three years' probation. He died in 1999, at age 63.

Johann Georg von Eckhardt, German philologist and historian, was born in 1664. He studied history and philology in Leipzig and found a position as secretary to Graf Flemming. In 1694 he left for Hanover, where he worked for years as Leibniz's assistant. He later accepted a position as professor of history at the University in Helmstädt. Unhappy with his professional situation and hoping for support from the Catholic establishment, Eckhardt embraced Catholicism in 1723 and was appointed court and university librarian in Würzburg and later councilor. He made major contributions to the fields of history, genealogy, and German philology. In 1729 he issued a Latin translation of the *Hildebrandslied* and a reproduction of its first fourteen lines. He died in 1730.

Walter Ings Farmer, art professor and Director of the Wiesbaden Collecting Point, was born in 1911 in Alliance, Ohio. He studied architecture and mathematics at Miami University, Ohio and went to work for the designer firm A. B. Closson, Jr. in Cincinnati. In 1942 he joined the US Army and in 1945 became a member of the Monuments, Fine Arts & Archives Commission and Director of the Wiesbaden Central Collecting Point (1945–1946). On November 7, 1945, he protested the shipment of 202 paintings to the US in a famous letter known as The Wiesbaden Manifesto. The paintings were later returned to Germany. He lectured at the University of Cincinnati and was one of the founders of the Contemporary Art Museum in Houston, Texas and of the Miami University Art Museum in Oxford, Ohio. In 1996, he was awarded the German medal *Das Große Verdienstkreuz* and in 1997, although not a Mason, the Humanitarian

Prize of the Year of the Grand Lodge of Ancient Free and Accepted Masons of Germany. He died in 1997.

John F. Fleming, book dealer and collector, was born in New York City in 1910. At the age of fifteen he joined the Rosenbach Company, where he worked his way up from packing clerk to general manager of the New York branch, and to vice-president in 1948. After Rosenbach's death in 1954, Fleming purchased two million dollars' worth of Rosenbach stock and opened his own business: The John F. Fleming Rare Book Company in New York. He became a dominant force in the antiquarian and manuscript market. He was a member of the Grolier Club, the Philobiblon Club, the Bibliographic Society, and the Shakespeare Society of America. He died in 1987. His archives, maintained by the Grolier Club, New York, will be accessible in 2008.

Karl Gerland, *Gauleiter*, was born in Gottesbüren, Hesse in 1905. He studied mechanical engineering at the Technical College in Hanover. In 1929 he became a member of the National Socialist German Workers' Party. In 1930 he was appointed *Kreisleiter* in Hofgeismar and *Bezirksleiter* in Hofgeismar-Wolfhagen. He moved quickly up the ranks and in 1932 he became head of the propaganda unit of the Gau Hesse-Nassau-North. In 1937, after various positions with the Nazi Party and a brief service in the army, he joined the SS and after one year was elevated to *SS-Standartenführer* (Colonel). In 1938 he became deputy *Gauleiter* in Niederdonau. He was wounded in the war, decorated (EK II) and discharged with the rank of officer. In 1944 he was appointed *Gauleiter* of Hesse and *Oberpräsident* (Governor) of Kurhesse. On April 1, 1945, after US troops occupied Hesse, Gerland fled to Berlin and tried to contact Hitler. Bormann blocked his audience with the Führer. He fought against the Soviets and was killed in battle on or around April 21, 1945.

Belle da Costa Greene, librarian, was born in 1880 in Washington, DC as one of seven children of Richard Greener, a lawyer, and Genevieve Ida Fleet, a music teacher. After her parents separated, mother and daughters moved to Princeton, New Jersey, where Belle worked as apprentice cataloger at Princeton University and later as assistant in the rare books department. In 1905 J. P. Morgan hired her as his private librarian. She built the superb collections of the Morgan Library and administered them for decades with talent and vision. She retired in 1948 and died in New York in 1950.

Richard Theodore Greener, educator, lawyer, government official, father of Belle da Costa Greene, was born in 1844 in Philadelphia. The family moved to Cambridge, Massachusetts where he attended racially mixed schools. He went to college first at Oberlin and then at the Philips Academy, Andover, and in 1865 was admitted to Harvard. In 1870 he became its first black graduate. For the next two years he taught school. After unsuccessful attempts to establish a black newspaper, he accepted a position as professor and University Librarian at the University of South Carolina. He studied law and was admitted to the bar in South

Carolina in 1876. In 1877, he passed the bar in the District of Columbia and taught at Howard University, where he later became dean. He joined the Foreign Service and accepted diplomatic positions in Bombay and Vladivostock, first as consul and than as commercial agent. He was awarded the order of the Double Dragon from the Chinese Government for work on famine relief. He returned in 1906 to Chicago and was active in politics. He died in 1922.

The Grimm Brothers were born in Hanau, Jacob Ludwig Carl in 1785 and his brother Wilhelm Carl in 1786. The brothers studied law at the University of Marburg and accepted positions as librarians in Kassel. In 1812 they published their famous collection of stories, *Kinder- und Hausmärchen*, followed by *Deutsche Sagen*. In 1819 they received honorary doctorate degrees from the University of Marburg for their work on linguistics, folklore, and medieval studies. They left Kassel, worked in Göttingen and Berlin, and dedicated their lives to research and to their monumental German Dictionary. Wilhelm Grimm died in 1859 and Jacob Grimm in 1863.

Herman Samuel Gundersheimer, art historian, father of Werner Leonard, was born in Würzburg, Germany in 1903. He studied art history and earned a Ph.D. from the University of Leipzig in 1930 with the dissertation "Matthäus Günther: die Freskomalerei im süddeutschen Kirchenbau des 18. Jahrhunderts." He was museum curator in Ulm and director of the Rothschild Museum in Frankfurt am Main. He immigrated to the United States in 1940, became a naturalized citizen, and taught art history at Temple University. In 1984 he was invited back to Frankfurt am Main to help create a museum of Jewish history and culture. Four years later he was present at its dedication. Dr. Gundersheimer lives in center city Philadelphia, and still visits his friends at the Tyler School of Art, Temple University.

Werner Leonard Gundersheimer, historian, son of Herman Samuel, was born in 1937 in Frankfurt am Main, Germany. He studied history and earned a Ph.D. from Harvard University in 1963 with the dissertation "Vicissitude and Variety: the Life and Works of Louis Leroy." He taught at the University of Wisconsin, Johns Hopkins University, Swarthmore College, Tel Aviv University, and the University of Pennsylvania, where he was chairman of the History Department and Director of the Center for Italian Studies. He served as trustee and Chairman of the Rosenbach Foundation & Museum between 1969 and 1989. In 1984 he became director of the Folger Shakespeare Library in Washington, DC. He retired in 2001.

Ardelia Ripley Hall, art historian, was born in East Weymouth, Massachusetts in 1899. She received Master's degree in art history in 1927 from Columbia University, and worked as research assistant at the Metropolitan Museum of Art and later on the curatorial staff of the Museum of Fine Arts in Boston. In 1943 she moved to Washington and worked in the Office of Strategic Services. Following the war, she joined the Department of State as consultant on issues of reclamation of war stolen art works. She retired in 1964 and died in Greenfield, MA in 1979.

Jane Sarah Hawkins Hall, cataloger, was born in Elmhurst, New York in 1905. She received a Master of Sciences from Columbia University, School of Library Service in 1941. She worked as a cataloger in various universities and taught cataloging at Syracuse University, Columbia, and Queens College. In the early 1960s she was Assistant Head, Department of Descriptive Cataloging at the Library of Congress. She died in 2000(?).

Chief Marshall Sir Arthur T. Harris, a.k.a. Bomber Harris, was born in 1892 in England. At the age of sixteen he immigrated to Rhodesia and during the First World War served in German South-West Africa. He returned to England and joined the Royal Flying Corps, the predecessor of the RAF. In 1939, after various stints in Egypt, Palestine, Transjordania, and the USA, Harris was promoted to Air Vice-Marshall and in 1941 he became acting Air Marshall and was appointed to run Bomber Command. Harris believed that intense incendiary bomb attacks would bring Germany to its knees. Successful raids on Lübeck, Rostock, Hamburg, and in the Ruhr Valley earned him the nickname *Bomber Harris*. However, the mounting losses suffered during repeated attacks on Berlin and the infamous attack on Dresden turned public and professional opinion against him. He was ignored in the 1946 victory honors list and resigned a year later. He died in 1984.

Meta Philippine Harrsen, librarian, keeper of manuscripts, was born in St. Louis in 1891. In 1923 she joined the Pierpont Morgan Library where she worked as a manuscript specialist. She died in 1977.

Theodore Allen Heinrich, art curator, professor of art history and Monuments Officer was born in 1910. He studied philosophy, art, and art history at the University of California, Berkeley and earned a Ph.D. from Cambridge University in 1936 with the dissertation "The Apostles of the Picturesque: Richard Payne Knight and Sir Uvedale Price." During the war he served as a junior officer on the intelligence staff of General Eisenhower. At the conclusion of hostilities he joined the Monuments, Fine Arts & Archives Branch of the US Military Government and served in Hesse while simultaneously working as director of several collecting points. In 1951 he was appointed Curator and Senior Fellow for Art History at the Henry E. Huntington Library and Art Gallery in San Marino, California. Between 1953 and 1955 he was Associate Director of Painting and Curator-in-charge of Drawings at the Metropolitan Museum of Art in New York. Later he became Director of the Royal Ontario Museum in Toronto and, from 1965 to his death in 1981, professor of art history at York University in Toronto, Ontario. His archives are deposited with the University of Saskatchewan, Regina campus.

Dieter Hennig, library director, was born in 1924. He studied English at the interpreter school in Regensburg, and then German philology at the Georg August

University of Göttingen, where, between 1953 and 1958, he also was a contributor to the German Dictionary of the Grimm Brothers. He earned a doctorate in 1957 with the dissertation "Studium zum Subjekt impersonal gebrauchter Verben im Althochdeutschen und Altniederdeutschen unter Berücksichtigung gotischer und altwestnordischer Zeugnisse." After qualifying examinations in library science, he worked as librarian at the University in Freiburg. On May 1, 1968, Hennig was appointed director of the merged Murhard Library and Kassel State Library, and later Director of the Grimm Brothers Museum succeeding Ludwig Denecke. He mounted a vigorous search for the two lost manuscripts and assembled an archive that reflects the history of the massive search effort. In 1972 he successfully identified in Philadelphia the lost first leaf of the *Hildebrandslied.* His efforts culminated in the return of Leaf One and of the *Willehalm Codex* in September of 1972. Since 1989 Hennig has been living in active retirement in Zierenberg, near Kassel.

Wilhelm Hopf, library director, was born in 1876 in Herborn. He studied history, German philology and theology in Tübingen and Marburg and earned a Ph.D. with the dissertation "Landgraf Wilhelm VIII von Hessen und England während der Jahre 1758 und 1759." He worked as an intern at the University Library in Freiburg and at the University Library in Rostock. In 1912 he was hired as librarian at the *Landesbibliothek* in Kassel. He was a member of the *Historical Commission for Hesse and Waldeck.* He fought during the First World War and was decorated. In 1920 he returned to work as curator in the *Landesbibliothek* and one year later was named director. At the same time he continued working for the history association and was elected President in 1924. Unfavorably regarded by the Nazis, he was forced to retire as director and to step down from the leadership of the historical association in 1938, but was allowed to continue as a bibliographer in the *Landesbibliothek.* In 1944 he was reinstated as director. He was decorated with the *Bundesverdienstkreuz* in 1960. He died in 1962.

Henry Edwards Huntington, railroad-king and book collector, was born in 1850 in Oneonta, New York, where his father owned a general store. His uncle Collis P. Huntington, a man of ruthless ambition and drive, founded the Southern Pacific railroad and amassed immense wealth. Collis Huntington mentored his nephew, and later made him his heir. In 1898 Henry E. Huntington embarked on the reorganization of the street railway system in Los Angeles, and in 1902 he launched the "Big Red Car" of the Pacific Electric Railway, a transportation system, which linked cities and towns in Southern California. His San Marino mansion, gardens, art collections, and superb private library were donated to the nation. He died in 1927 at the age of 77.

Jürgen Kalkbrenner, diplomat, studied law and political sciences and received a Ph.D. from the University of Kiel in 1951 with the dissertation "Die Tötung von Einwohnern kriegsgemäß besetzter Gebiete durch die Besatzungmacht als Gegenmaßnahme gegen Widerstandshandlungen, an denen sie nicht beteiligt gewesen sind." He was named Cultural Attaché of the Embassy of the Federal Republic of Germany in Bonn and later was Consul General in Boston. He lives in active retirement in Germany.

John Christian Kornblum, ambassador, was born in Detroit, Michigan in 1943. Shortly after graduation from Michigan State University he embarked on a career with the US Foreign Service and served in Hamburg, Bonn, and Berlin. In 1973 he returned to Washington, DC and worked in the government. He returned to Berlin in 1985 and worked in Brussels as US Deputy Permanent Representative to NATO. Important assignments in various European capitals followed. On May 21, 1997 President Clinton nominated him Ambassador to the Federal Republic of Germany, where he served until 2001.

Karl Kup, library curator, was born in Berlin in 1903. He studied art history at universities in Munich, Berlin, and Paris and worked for the University of Oxford Press in London, Leipzig, and New York as book designer. In 1934 he joined the New York Public Library and for more than three decades worked as Chief of the Spencer Collection of illustrated books, manuscripts and fine bindings. He was also curator of prints and chief of the art and architecture division. Kup retired from the library in 1968 and continued lecturing on art history, book production, and graphic arts at universities around the world. He died in 1981.

Gerhard Liebers, librarian, was born in 1914 in Radebeul bei Dresden. He studied classical philology, German language and literature, and philosophy at the Leipzig University and received his doctorate in 1944 with the dissertation "Virtus bei Cicero." After the war, he completed the requirements of librarianship and worked in Frankfurt am Main. In 1952 he accepted a position in the administration of Murhard Library in Kassel, where he was active until 1958. He left Kassel to become assistant director of the University Library in Göttingen and in 1962 director of the University Library in Münster. He retired in 1979 and died in 2000.

Harry Alexander McBride, Administrator at the National Gallery of Art, was born in 1887 in Flint, Michigan. He studied in Dresden, Germany and held various consular positions in Europe and around the world. From 1940 to 1953 he was Administrator at the National Gallery of Art in Washington, DC and member of the Foreign Buildings Committee at the Department of State. During the war he held the rank of Lieutenant Colonel, US Army (1942), Colonel (1943), and was decorated with the Legion of Merit (1943). He died in 1961.

James Francis Louis Cardinal McIntyre, archbishop of Los Angeles, was born in New York City 1886. Until the age of 29 he was a runner for the old Curb Exchange and an office manager for a firm at the New York Stock Exchange. He was ordained priest in 1921, Bishop in 1941 and Archbishop in 1946. He was appointed Archbishop of Los Angeles in 1948 and was elevated to Cardinal in 1953. He retired in 1970 and died in 1979 at the age of 93.

Charles Follen McKim, architect, was born in 1847 in southeastern Pennsylvania. He studied at the Harvard Lawrence Scientific School and at the *Ecole des Beaux-Arts* in Paris. He returned to the United States and worked for Henry Hobson Richardson in New York and partnered with Mead and White to form one of the most successful architectural firms of the time. Among their best-known works are the American Academy in Rome, the Boston Public Library, the Morgan Library, Pennsylvania Station in New York, and the Rhode Island State Capitol in Providence. He died in 1909.

Gretel Mayer, judge and later librarian, was born 1906 in Darmstadt, Germany. Her father, Ludwig Mayer, was a prominent physician. She graduated with a law degree and won an appointment in 1932 as a state junior judge, one of the youngest women to hold such a position in Germany. In 1933 she was fired, a victim of the Law for the Restoration of the Professional Civil Service. She fled to France and in 1936 immigrated to the United States. She enrolled at Columbia University and obtained a master's degree in library science. She became an American citizen in 1942. The Rosenbach Company hired her in 1943 as a bibliographer. She left in 1946 and worked as a cataloger for Yale University. In 1950 she accepted a position with the Library of Congress working as cataloger for German imprints. In 1967 Gretel Mayer was named director of the Library of Congress Field Office at the Austrian National Library in Vienna. She returned to the US in 1970 to become principal cataloger for rare books at the Library of Congress. She retired in 1972 and died in 1995.

Lucille V. Miller, librarian, was born in 1901 and began working for Carrie Estelle Doheny in summer of 1931 as a typist for catalog cards. Lucille learned to appreciate and catalog rare books on the job and authored the "Catalogue of Books & Manuscripts in the Estelle Doheny Collection, 1940–55." After Mrs. Doheny's death in 1958, she became the first curator of the Estelle Doheny Collection at Saint John's Seminary Library, Camarillo, California. She retired to San Buenaventura, California and died in 1989.

Elizabeth Mongan, curator and art historian, was born in 1910, as the daughter of a family physician. She graduated from Bryn Mawr College and studied at the Paul Sachs's training school for museum curators. From 1937 to 1963 Mongan worked as curator of the private print collection of Lessing J. Rosenwald. When the collection moved to the National Gallery of Art, she went with it as curator. Mongan compiled catalogs on Klee, Fragonard, Morisot, Daumier, Gaugin. She retired from the National Gallery in 1963, and taught art history at Smith College until 1975. She died in 2002 at age 92.

John Pierpont Morgan, collector and banker, was born in 1837 in Hartford. He went to school in Switzerland and Germany and joined his father's business as a banker. He had four children, three girls and one son, John Pierpont Morgan, Jr. or Jack, who was born in 1867 in Irvington, New York. Morgan began collecting in 1851 and amassed one of the best art collections in the United States. He died in Rome in 1913 and Jack succeeded him as head of the Morgan Empire and master of all collections. In 1924 Jack changed the character of the Pierpont Morgan Library from of a private library to a public research institution. He died in 1943.

Edward Peck, art historian, was born in Colorado Springs, Colorado. He studied at the American School of Classical Studies in Athens and later earned a doctorate from Harvard. After service with the Monuments, Fine Arts, & Archives during the war, he returned to teaching. He held various faculty positions in Virginia and Ohio. In 1950, he accepted a position as Professor of Art History and Director of the University Galleries at the University of Southern California. He died in 1970.

Moses (Mo) Polock, rare book dealer, was born in 1817. At a young age he went to work for McCarty & Davis, publishers and booksellers. When Davis died, he left Mo Polock a sum of money, with which he bought the business. A reluctant bookseller and avid collector, Mo Polock instilled in his young nephew Abraham Simon Wolf Rosenbach the passion of collecting. When he died in 1903, Rosenbach purchased most of his uncle Mo's rare finds. It marked the beginning of an illustrious career and established the nucleus of an incomparable collection.

Arnold Hereward Price, historian and librarian, was born in 1912 in Bonn as the son of Hereward T. Price, a British Shakespeare scholar, and of Elisabeth Prym Price, a German national. He studied at the University of Michigan and earned a doctorate with the dissertation "The Evolution of the Zollverein, a Study of the Ideas and Institutions Leading to German Economic Unification Between 1851 and 1833." He served in the military in 1943–1946, worked in the Office of Strategic Services in its research and analysis branch, and later in the State Department as specialist in German area studies. In 1960, he joined the Library of Congress as specialist in Central European studies. He retired in the early nineteen eighties and leads an active intellectual life.

Felix Pusch, museum director, was a physical sciences scholar of national reputation. His research centered on the fauna of the ice age. In 1943 he was named director of the *Heimatmuseum* in Bad Wildungen. During the war, he was responsible for art repositories in the city, with the exception of the bunker at Hotel Goecke. In the aftermath of the devastating bombardments of Kassel, his own *Heimatmuseum* was turned into a refugee shelter. He died in 1948.

Helmut Rehder, Professor of German Literature and Language, was born in 1905 in Bergedorf-Hamburg, Germany. After a two-year apprenticeship in banking, he enrolled at the Universities of Berlin and Heidelberg and in 1929 earned a Ph.D. in German with the dissertation "Die Philosophie der unendlichen Landschaft. Ein Beitrag zur Geschichte der romantischen Weltanschauung." He immigrated to the United States and in 1937, became a naturalized citizen. He taught at the

Universities of Missouri, Wisconsin, and Illinois, where he was Head of the Department, and later at the University of Texas at Austin. In 1955 and again 1959 he was awarded the Schiller Medal of the Federal Republic of Germany and in 1972 he received the Order of Merit First Class. He collaborated extensively with Professor W.F. Twaddell. He died in 1977.

Owen J. Roberts, Chief Justice, was born in Germantown, Pennsylvania in 1875. He graduated from the University of Pennsylvania and received a law degree in 1889. For the next twenty years he taught, worked as a lawyer, and held various public offices. As a Special United States Attorney he investigated between 1924 and 1930 alleged wrongdoing in the Harding Administration. In 1930 President Hoover appointed him to the Supreme Court. He resigned from the Court in 1945 and died in 1955.

Abraham Samuel Wolf Rosenbach, book-dealer and collector, was born in 1876 in Philadelphia and spent a good portion of his childhood in Moses Polock's bookstore. He studied English literature at the University of Pennsylvania and earned a Ph.D. in 1901 with the dissertation "Spanish Influence in the English Drama before Restoration." He went into business with his brother Philip. Rosenbach's erudition combined with savvy salesmanship, and a penchant for high drama, attracted wealthy customers. Together with his brother, he established in 1950 the Philip H. and A. S. W. Rosenbach Foundation. He died in 1952 and left his superb collections to the Rosenbach Museum and Library.

Philip Hyman Rosenbach, art-dealer, was born in 1863. A businessman at heart, he began by opening a restaurant in Philadelphia, then a gift-shop, and then in 1903, together with brother Abraham, he founded the Rosenbach Company. He ordained himself president and remained to the end of his life in charge of finances. He died in 1953 and left the bulk of his estate to the Rosenbach Foundation.

Lessing Julius Rosenwald, collector and philanthropist, was born in Chicago in 1891. His father, Julius, was the founder of Sears, Roebuck, and Co. He studied at Cornell University for two years, and then returned to work for his father. At the age twenty-five, he left for Philadelphia to establish the East Coast branch of Sears. He succeeded his father as Chairman of the Board of Trustees and took early retirement in 1939 to indulge his passion: collecting rare prints and early-illustrated printed books. He moved to Alverthorpe, a 150-acre estate in Jenkintown, Pennsylvania. In 1943 he donated his works of art to the nation but continued collecting until late in life. He played an important role in philanthropic and community service, and received a great number of distinctions. He was Member of the Board of Directors of the Philadelphia Museum of Art, Trustee of the Free Library of Philadelphia, President of the Rosenbach Foundation, Trustee of the National Gallery of Art, member of the Royal Society of Art. He died in 1979.

Margarita Ivanova Rudomino, librarian, was born in 1900 in Bialystock, today Poland. Orphaned at fifteen, she was raised by relatives. She studied librarianship in Saratov and worked locally as a librarian. She was invited to Moscow to help develop the library of the newly established Institute for Modern Philology. Rudomino continued her studies in Romance Languages, German Literature and Language, and Marxism-Leninism at the University of Moscow. Between 1945 and 1947 she held the rank of lieutenant and was President of the Cultural Committee of the Red Army in occupied Berlin, in charge of library needs for the Red Army and East German acquisitions for her own Moscow institution. After the war she brought home from occupied East Germany hundreds of rail cars of trophy-books. For years she reigned unchallenged as director of the State Library of Foreign Literature in Moscow. She was active in international library organizations and was honored for her role in East-West relations. She died in Moscow in 1990.

Robert Oliver Schad, library curator, was born in 1900 in New York City. His father died when he was six, his mother when he was seventeen. He dropped out of school and went to work full time for the New York Public Library. At the age of eighteen he was hired as assistant cataloger for Henry E. Huntington's private collection in New York. In 1920, he followed Huntington to San Marino, California, where the collector was building a new library. In 1926, he was named curator of rare books. In December 1952 he was diagnosed with a brain tumor, was operated on but never fully recovered. He died in 1961.

Helmut Schmidt, Chancellor of the Federal Republic of Germany, 1974–1982, was born in Hamburg in 1918. He was a lieutenant during the Second World War, was captured by the British Army, and detained in Belgium. He became Member of the Bundestag in 1953. In 1969 he became Minister of Defense under Willi Brandt and in 1972 Minister of Economies and Finance. When Willy Brandt resigned in 1974, Helmut Schmidt was elected *Bundeskanzler* and served until 1982. Since October 1985 he is co-publisher of the weekly newspaper *Die Zeit*.

Johann Hermann Schmincke, librarian and educator, was born in 1684 in Kassel. He studied philosophy, mathematics, Greek, and Latin in Marburg and later theology, church history, Jewish antiquity, and physics. In 1708 he was hired as tutor to the offspring of a rich Kassel family. He traveled extensively with his pupil. In 1722 he became president of the University in Marburg, and librarian in Kassel. He discovered the *Hildebrandslied*. He wrote extensively on the history of Hesse. He died in 1743.

Carl Selmer, Professor of German Language and Literature, was born in 1896 in Esting, Bavaria. His parents died when he was in his early teens and his uncle Rupert sent him to a Catholic boarding school in Scheyern, where he learned Latin, Greek, and Hebrew. Selmer studied music, played the piano and cello, sang in the choir and learned fundamentals of composition and conducting. He continued his education at the University of Munich where he studied language history, world history, philosophy, logic, psychology, education and paleography.

He earned a Ph.D. in 1922 in German philology from the University of Freiburg im Breisgau with the dissertation "Studien zu den älteren mittelhochdeutschen Benediktinerregeln." He was drafted in the First World War, served in communications and was wounded. After the war he married Rose Baur, daughter of a Munich architect. The Selmers sailed to Rio de Janeiro in search of work. From the Brazilian coast, they traveled 200 miles inland toward the Paraguayan border to Limeira, and from there to the village of Santa Cruz and the coffee plantation of their employer, Senhor Mario Souza de Queiroz, where they worked as tutors. Financial and health problems forced the Selmers to leave the plantation and move to Sao Paulo. Selmer taught for a year at the Mariann School and Rose opened a kindergarten. In 1924, after getting proper documents and visas, Selmer sailed to the United States. He arrived in New York on September 17, 1924 and was processed through Ellis Island. He settled in New Jersey, accepted odd jobs, worked in a chemical factory, played the organ in church, and amassed the necessary funds to bring his wife over. After repeated rejections, the Head of the German Department of Hunter College, New York, Dr. Adolf Busse, hired him for two thousand dollars a year. During the Second World War, as students no longer enrolled in German classes, Selmer taught music appreciation, medieval poetry, and Portuguese. The fear of anti-German sentiment played an important role in Selmer's decision not to challenge publicly the return of the *Hildebrandlied* to Rosenbach. He retired in 1966 at the age of 70, after forty years of teaching. In 1968 he was decorated with the *Verdienst-Kreuz*, the German Merit Cross. He died in 1972 of lymphosarcoma.

Georg Nauman Shuster, Hunter College President, journalist, and author was born in 1884 in Lancaster, Wisconsin. He graduated from Notre Dame in 1920. He studied at the University of Poitiers and at the *Hochschule für Politik* in Berlin. During the First World War he served in the Intelligence Section, US Army. He returned as Head of the English Department at the University of Notre Dame. He earned a Ph.D. in comparative literature from Columbia University. In 1939, he was appointed dean of Hunter College, New York and one year later president. He remained in office until 1960. On leave from Hunter College between 1950 and 1951, he served as Land Commissioner for Bavaria in Munich. In1960 he accepted a position as assistant to the president of the University of Notre Dame and director of the Center for the Study of Man in Contemporary Society. He died in 1977.

Emily Millicent Sowerby, bibliographer and bibliophile, was born in 1883 in England and studied at Girton College, Cambridge University and at the University of Grenoble, France. She began her career in London as a cataloger for the renowned rare book dealer Wilfrid Michael Voynich, and then for Sotheby's. In 1923 she booked a passage to the United States for what she believed to be a one-year educational trip. The sojourn lasted a lifetime. She worked in the New York Public Library and later as a bibliographer and rare-book specialist for the

Rosenbach Company in Philadelphia and New York. In February of 1942 Philip Rosenbach fired her without apparent reason. Five months later the Library of Congress hired her as the bibliographer of the Jefferson Collection. She authored the five-volume catalogue of the papers of Thomas Jefferson. She retired in the mid-1950s but continued working for the Library of Congress as a consultant. She died in 1977 in Muncie, Indiana.

Bernard Taper, Art Intelligence Offer with the Monuments, Fine Arts & Archives corps of the US Military Government in Germany between 1946 and 1948. He studied at the University of California, Berkeley and Stanford University and earned a degree in journalism. A prolific writer, he was a contributor to the *New Yorker*, *The Nation* and *Harper's*, a reporter for the *San Francisco Chronicle*, and a professor of journalism at UC Berkeley. He lives in active retirement in Berkeley, California.

William Freeman Twaddell, Professor of German and Linguistics, was born in Rye, New York in 1906. He received a Bachelor's Degree in 1926 from Duke University and a Ph.D. from Harvard in 1930 with the dissertation "The Morphology and Syntax of the Periphrastic Passive in the German Works of Notker III." He taught German at the University of Wisconsin, where he was Chairman of the German Department and Chairman of the Division of the Humanities. In 1946 he left Wisconsin for Brown University, where once again he was Chairman of the Department of German and Linguistics. He retired in 1971. He died after a brief illness in 1982.

Kennedy Campbell Watkins, General Counsel at the National Gallery of Art, was born in 1911 in Washington DC. He received a master's degree in law from Harvard University in 1937. He entered Federal service in the Treasury Department's Bureau of Internal Affairs, and during the Second World War served as attorney in the Office of Chief of Ordnance with the rank of major. In 1948 he was appointed assistant to the Assistant Secretary of Treasury and lectured on taxation at George Washington University. In 1953 he left government service to become a tax attorney with the Association of American Railroads. He joined the National Gallery of Art as deputy secretary in 1965 and was elected Secretary in 1970. He retired in 1971. For his contributions to the return of the Kassel codices, Watkins was honored with the German Order of Merit First Class and with the Medal of the City of Kassel. He died in 1998.

Francis J. Weber, priest, archivist and museum director, was born in Indianapolis in 1933. He received a bachelor's degree at Saint John's College, Camarillo, California in 1955, where he continued as a seminarian and was ordained in 1959. He went on to receive a Masters of Art from the Catholic University of America (1962) and a certificate in archival administration. In the same year he was appointed archivist at the Catholic Archdiocese of Los Angeles. Weber is a prolific writer on topics ranging from biographical accounts to the history of California missions.

Philipp Wehner, librarian, was born in 1780 in Fulda. He was a priest and professor at the local Gymnasium and Lyceum. In 1825 he became librarian at the *Fulda Landesbibliothek*. He retired in 1842. He is said to have forged the complete text of the *Hildebrandslied* on a parchment roll, which he destroyed before his death in 1856.

Karl Weinrich, *Gauleiter*, was born in 1887 in the Harz. He studied mining and opted for a career in military administration. In 1922 he became a member of the NSDAP. He moved to Kassel in 1924 and was appointed *Gauleiter* of Hesse-Nassau-North in 1928. Goebbels demoted him in 1944 after the devastating bombardment that destroyed Kassel. In 1945 he was arrested, and in 1949 sentenced to ten years political incarceration of which he served seven. He died in 1973.

Bruno Erich Werner, diplomat, publicist, and art critic, was born in 1896. Between 1926 and 1938 he worked as a journalist for the *Deutsche Allgemeine Zeitung*, and later for *Neue Linie.* He was captain during the Second World War and was decorated with the Iron Cross. After the war, he was one of the founders of *Norddeutscher Rundfunk* and during 1949–52 editor of the *Neue Zeitung*. He wrote novels, among them the 1949 bestseller *Die Galeere*. In 1953 he came to Washington as cultural counselor at the German Diplomatic Mission, where he remained until 1961. He died of a heart attack in Davos, Switzerland in 1964.

Elwood Williams III, international relations officer, was born in 1914 in New York City. He studied in Germany, and later received a Bachelor Degree from Georgetown University, Washington DC. In 1940 he joined the Foreign Service and during the war fought as a Navy officer in the Atlantic and Pacific. After the war he was assigned to the Bureau of German Affairs as an expert in US-German relations. He retired in 1974 and died of multiple sclerosis in Washington in 1982.

Edwin Wolf 2nd, book dealer and librarian, was born in Philadelphia in 1911. He was the son of Morris Wolf, friend and lawyer of the Rosenbach brothers. Edwin skipped several grades at William Penn Charter School and graduated at age fifteen. He traveled to England, spent time at Bedale's studying Latin, Greek, and bookbinding and, at age 18 returned to the United States to work for his uncle, A. S. W. Rosenbach. He volunteered for duty during the Second World War (1943) and served in the Military Intelligence Service as a German and French interpreter, and counterintelligence agent. He returned to manage the Philadelphia branch of the Rosenbach firm. In 1953 he left the firm after an argument with Philip Rosenbach and became curator of the Library Company of Philadelphia, a subscription library founded in 1731 by Benjamin Franklin, where he worked for the next 32 years. He retired in 1984 and died of lung cancer in 1991.

Works Cited

Archival Documents, Correspondence, Dissertations, Interviews, Manuscripts.

Title entries:

Archdiosese of Los Angeles. Archival Center. Estelle Doheny Collection of California. Correspondence. Deposited with the University of California, Davis, Shields Library, Department of Special Collections.

"Besitzgeschichte der Handschrift 4° MS. Math. 50 Gebetbuch Herzogs Johann Albrecht Von Mecklenburg." (History of ownership of the manuscript 4° MS. Math. 50 Book of Prayers of Prince Johann Albrecht of Mecklenburg). Documents from the Archives of the Gesamthochschul-Bibliothek Kassel – Landesbibliothek und Murhardsche Bibliothek der Stadt Kassel. Deposited with the University of California, Davis, Shields Library, Department of Special Collections.

"Cicero. Rückführung des Manuscripts." (Cicero. Return of the manuscript). Documents from the Archives of the Gesamthochschul-Bibliothek Kassel – Landesbibliothek und Murhardsche Bibliothek der Stadt Kassel. Deposited with the University of California, Davis, Shields Library, Department of Special Collections.

"File MS of Hildebrandslied from Kassel." US Department of State. Records Maintained by the Fine Arts and Monument Adviser, 1945–61, Ardelia Hall Collection, Record Group 59. Lot 62D4, Box 6, Item 2, National Archives and Records Administration.

"Hildebrandlied (Dossiers 1–6)." Documents from the Archives of the Gesamthochschul-Bibliothek Kassel – Landesbibliothek und Murhardsche Bibliothek der Stadt Kassel. Deposited with the University of California, Davis, Shields Library, Department of Special Collections.

"1945 Missal From Würzburg." US Department of State. Records Maintained by the Fine Arts and Monument Adviser, 1945–61, Ardelia Hall Collection, Record Group 59, Lot 62D4, Box 6, National Archives and Records Administration.

"Paintings from the Bad Wildungen Repository – Koekkoek and Maes." US Department of State. Records Maintained by the Fine Arts and Monument Adviser, 1944–61, Ardelia Hall Collection, Record Group 59. Lot 62D4, Box 9, Item 5, National Archives and Records Administration. Deposited with the University of California, Davis, Shields Library, Department of Special Collections.

"Rechsteiner Case Petrarch Ms." US Department of State. Records Maintained by the Fine Arts and Monument Adviser, 1946–1961, Ardelia Hall Collection, Record Group 59. Lot 62D4, Box 6, Item 4, SWNCC 322, National Archives and Records Administration.

Rosenbach Museum & Library. Archives. 1945 business records and correspondence. Deposited with the University of California, Davis, Shields Library, Department of Special Collections.

Author entries:

Eddy, Beverley D. Electronic-mail correspondence with the author. Deposited with the University of California, Davis, Shields Library, Department of Special Collections.

Faulders, Rita, last Doheny Librarian (1980-1988). Telephone communication with the author of March 1, 2002.

Gundersheimer, Werner L. Tape-recorded telephone conversation with the author of April 12, 2000. Deposited with the University of California, Davis, Shields Library, Department of Special Collections.

Hennig, Dieter. Correspondence with the author. Deposited with the University of California, Davis, Shields Library, Department of Special Collections.

Poste, Leslie I. "The Development of U.S. Protection of Libraries and Archives in Europe During World War II." Dissertation, University of Chicago, 1958.

Price, Arnold H. Correspondence with the author. Deposited with the University of California, Davis, Shields Library, Department of Special Collections.

Rosenbach, A. S. W. "Spanish Influence in the English Drama before the Restoration." Dissertation, University of Pennsylvania, 1901.

Selmer-Griffith, Irene. Electronic-mail correspondence with the author. Deposited with the University of California, Davis, Shields Library, Department of Special Collections.

Tucker, Ben R. Correspondence with the author. Deposited with the University of California, Davis, Shields Library, Department of Special Collections.

Twaddell, William Freeman. "The Hildebrandlied Manuscript in the U.S.A., 1945–1972." October 1973 version. Twaddell Archives. Unpublished. Deposited with the University of California, Davis, Shields Library, Department of Special Collections.

–. "Hildebrandlied." Paper presented at the meeting of the Brunonische Gelehrtenrepublik of Brown University, October 16, 1972. Twaddell Archives. Unpublished. Deposited with the University of California, Davis, Shields Library, Department of Special Collections.

Voelkle, William M. Electronic correspondence with the author. Deposited with the University of California, Davis, Shields Library, Department of Special Collections.

Young, Nanci A. Electronic correspondence with the author. Deposited with the University of California, Davis, Shields Library, Department of Special Collections.

Monographs, Chapters, and Journal Articles

Title entries:

American Book Collectors and Bibliographers. Second Series. Editor Joseph Rosenblum. Dictionary of literary biography. Vol. 187. Detroit: Gale, 1997.

American National Biography. Editors John A. Garraty, Mark C. Carnes. Vol. 9. New York: Oxford University Press, 1999.

"Belle of the Books." *Time* 53, no. 15 (1949): 76–78.

"Bis 5 Minuten nach Zwölf: Letzte Kriegstage 1945 in Kassel in Tagebüchern und anderen zeitgenössischen Quellen." (Five minutes past midnight: The last days of the war in 1945 in Kassel reflected in diaries and other contemporary sources). Editor Frank-Roland Klaube. Kasseler Quellen und Studien. Kleine Reihe, Band 5. Marburg: Jonas, 1995.

Civil Affairs and Military Government Activities in Connection With Monuments, Fine Arts, and Archives – The General Board, United States, Army, Forces in the European Theater [The General Board, USFET], [Bad Nauheim, Germany], [1945 or 1946].

"Cultural Articles Returned." *Information Bulletin: A Monthly Magazine of the Office of US High Commissioner for Germany* (July 1952): 18.

Department of State Biographic Register 1961–62. Washington, D.C.: US Department of State, 1962.

Dictionary of American Biography. Editors Allen Johnson, and Dumas Malone. Vol. 7. New York: Charles Scribner's Sons, 1928–1958.

Dictionary of American Library Biography. Editor Bohdan S. Wynar. Littleton, Colorado: Libraries Unlimited, 1978.

Dictionary of American Negro Biography. Editor Rayford Whittingham Logan. New York: Norton, 1982.

Dictionary of the Middle Ages. Editor Joseph R. Strayer. New York: Charles Scribner's Sons, 1982–1989.

Der Dom zu Fulda (The Fulda Cathedral). 22nd ed. Fulda: Parzeller, 1997.

Encyclopedia of African-American Culture and History. Editors Jack Salzman, David Lionel Smith, and Cornel West. New York: Macmillan Library Reference, 1996.

The European Recovery Program: US/UK Occupied Areas of Germany, 1. April 1948–30. September 1948. Joint Report of the United States and United Kingdom Military Governors. s.l.: Office of the Military Government for Germany (U.S.) and Control Commission for Germany (British Element), 1948.

Ex Bibliotheca Cassellana: 400 Jahre Landesbibliothek, 20.11.1580–20.11.1980 (From the Kassel Library: 400 years of State Library, 11/20/1580–11/20/1980). Editor Hans-Jürgen Kahlfuß. [Kassel]: Gesamthochschul-Bibliothek-Kassel, Landesbibliothek und Murhardsche Bibliothek der Stadt Kassel, 1980.

Fuldische Handschriften aus Hessen mit weiteren Leihgaben aus Basel, Oslo, dem Vatikan und Wolfenbüttel. Katalog zur Ausstellung anläßlich des Jubiläums '1250 Jahre Fulda.' Hessische Landesbibliothek Fulda, 19. April bis 31. May 1994. (Fulda manuscripts from Hesse with additional loans from Basel, Oslo, the Vatican, and Wolfenbüttel. Catalog of the Exhibit of the Jubilee '1250 Years of Fulda' Hesse State Library, April 19 to May 31, 1994). Editors Hartmut Broszinski, and Sirka Heyne. Fulda: Hessische Landesbibliothek, 1994.

Handbuch der historischen Buchbestände in Deutschland. (Handbook of historical book collections in Germany). Editor Bernhard Fabian. Vol. 5. Hildesheim: Olms-Weidmann, 1992.

Handschriftarchiv Bernhard Bischoff (1906–1991) (Manuscript archive Bernhard Bischoff (1906–1991). *(Bibliothek der Monumenta Germaniae Historica, Hs. C 1, C 2).* Editor Arno Mentzel-Reuters. Microfiche Edition. Hs C 1 XLI. Kassel. Landes- und Murhardsche Bibliothek. 1. Korrespondenz. Notizen zu einzelnen Hss. Munich: Bibliothek der Monumenta Germaniae Historica, 1997.

Hessen und Thüringen – Von den Anfängen bis zur Reformation: Eine Ausstellung des Landes Hessen (Hesse and Thuringia – From the beginning to the Reformation: An exhibit of the Province Hesse). Marburg: Historische Kommission für Hessen, 1992.

"Hildebrand, Lay of." In: *Encyclopaedia Britannica*, 460–61, vol. 13–14. Chicago: Encyclopaedia Britannica, 1926.

Das Hildebrandlied: Faksimile der Kasseler Handschrift mit einer Einführung von Hartmut Broszinski (The Song of Hildebrand. Facsimile of the manuscript from Kassel with an introduction by Hartmut Broszinski). Second edition. Pretiosa Cassellana. Kassel: Johannes Stauda, 1985.

"Hildebrandslied." In: *New International Encyclopaedia*, 73, vol. 10. New York: Dodd, Mead and Co., 1909.

Das Hildebrandslied. Kassel: Der Landeshauptmann in Hessen, 1937.

Inter-Allied declaration against acts of dispossession committed in territories under enemy occupation and control – January 5, 1943. In: *The Spoils of War: World War II and Its Aftermath: The Loss, Reappearance, and Recovery of Cultural Property.* Editor Elizabeth Simpson, 287. New York: H. N. Abrams in association with the Bard Graduate Center for Studies in the Decorative Arts, 1997.

Katalog der Drucke des XVI. Jahrhunderts aus den Beständen der VGBIL (Catalog of 16th century imprints in the collection of the Union State Library for Foreign Literature – VGBIL). Compilers E. A. Korkmazova, and A. L. Ponomarev. Moscow: Rudomino, 1996.

"Mainz Exhibiting Treasured Psalter." *Department of State Bulletin* 23, no. 582 (1950): 349.

Manuscripta Theologica: Die Handschriften in Folio (Manuscripta theologica: The folio manuscripts). Editor Konrad Wiedemann. Die Handschriften der Gesamthochschul-Bibliothek Kassel – Landesbibliothek und Murhardsche Bibliothek der Stadt Kassel, 1,1. Wiesbaden: Harrassowitz, 1994.

Monthly Report of the Military Governor US Zone. Monuments, Fine Arts and Archives no. 2 (1945).

Monumenta Germaniae Historica Inde Ab Anno Christi Quingentesimo Usque Ad Annum Millesimum Et Quingentesimum. Poetarum Latinorum Medii Aevii. Leipzig: Hiersemann, 1880 –.

Monumenta Germaniae Historica Inde Ab Anno Christi Quingentesimo Usque Ad Annum Millesimum Et Quingentesimum. Scriptorum. Vol. 13. Hanover: Hahn, 1926–1934.

Namen und Schicksale der Juden Kassels, 1933–1945. Ein Gedenkbuch (Names and fate of Kassel Jews, 1933–1945. A memorial). Editors Beate Kleiner and Wolfgang Prinz. Kassel: Magistrat der Stadt Kassel – Stadtarchiv, 1986.

The National Cyclopedia of American Biography. Vol. 61. Clifton, New Jersey: James T. White, 1982.

Notable American Women 1607–1950: A Biographical Dictionary. Editor Edward T. James. Vol. 2. Cambridge, Massachusetts: Belknap Press of Harvard University Press, 1971.

Notable Black American Men, Editor Jessie Carney Smith. Farmington Hills, Michigan: Gale, 1998.

"Notes for Theodore Allen Heinrich. June 15, 1910–January 27, 1981." *Artscanada* 38–39, no. 240/41 (1981): xvi-2.

The Papers of Dwight David Eisenhower. The War Years: III. Editor Alfred D. Chandler, Jr. Baltimore: Johns Hopkins Press, 1970.

The Pierpont Morgan Library: A Review of Acquisitions 1949–1968. New York: The Library, 1969.

The Pierpont Morgan Library: Review of the Activities and Major Acquisitions of the Library, 1941–1948. New York: The Library, 1949.

Public Opinion in Occupied Germany: The OMGUS Surveys, 1945–1949. Editors Anna J. Merritt, and Richard L. Merritt. Urbana: University of Illinois Press, 1970.

Der Quedlinburger Schatz wieder vereint (The Quedlinburg treasure together again). Editor Dieter Kötzsche. Berlin: Kulturstiftung der Länder: Ars Nicolai, 1992.

"Rare Mainz Psalter of 1457, Looted, Returned to U.S. Zone in Germany." *Department of State Bulletin* 22, no. 560 (1950): 487.

"Recovery of Lost European Art Treasures." *The Record* (Department of State, International Exchange) 7, no. 3 (1951): 39–42.

Report of the American Commission for the Protection and Salvage of Artistic and Historic Monuments in War Areas. Washington, D.C.: Government Printing Office, 1946.

"Return of Looted Objects of Art to Countries of Origin: Memorandum by the State Department Member of SWNCC (State-War-Navy Coordinating Committee)." *Department of State Bulletin* 16, no. 399 (1947): 358–60.

Rosenwald and Rosenbach: Two Philadelphia Bookmen. Catalogue of an Exhibition at the Rosenbach Museum & Library from the Lessing J. Rosenwald Collection at the Library of Congress, April 30 to July 31, 1983. Philadelphia: Rosenbach Museum Library, 1983.

Supplement to the Census of Medieval and Renaissance Manuscripts in the United States and Canada. Originated by C. U. Faye, continued and edited by W. H. Bond. New York: The Bibliographical Society of America, 1962.

"Search for a Missing Page," *The Rotarian* 86, no. 6 (June 1955): 44.

To Doctor R. Essays Here Collected and Published in Honor of the Seventieth Birthday of Dr. A. S. W. Rosenbach, July 22, 1946. Philadelphia: [s.n.], 1946.

"To Museums, Art and Antique Dealers, and Auction Houses." *Department of State Bulletin* 16, no. 399 (1947): 359–60, Appendix B.

Twentieth Century Biographical Dictionary of Notable Americans. Editor Rossiter Johnson. Boston: Biographical Society, 1904.

"U.S. Seeks to Replace Cultural Property Displaced During World War II." *Department of State Bulletin* 25, no. 635 (1951): 345.

Volksgemeinschaft und Volksfeinde: Kassel 1933–1945. Eine Dokumentation (Folk community and folk enemies: Kassel 1933–1945. A documentation). Editors Jörg Kammler, Dietfried Krause-Vilmar, Siegfried Kujawski, Wolfgang Prinz, and Robert Wilmsmeier. Fuldabrück: Hesse, 1984.

"Walter Farmer – Obituary." *Economist* 344, no. 8031 (1997): 67.

Author entries:

Akinsha, Konstantin, and Grigorii Kozlov. *Beautiful Loot: The Soviet Plunder of Europe's Art Treasures*. New York: Random House, 1995.

Alford, Kenneth D. *The Spoils of World War II: The American Military's Role in the Stealing of Europe's Treasures*. New York: Birch Lane, 1994.

Auchincloss, Louis. *J. P. Morgan: The Financier as Collector*. New York: Harry N. Abrams, 1990.

Bangert, Wolfgang. "Kassel – Reconstruction of the City Center." *Town Planning Review* 29, no. 2 (1958): 99–102.

Barker, Ralph. *The RAF at War*. Alexandria, VA: Time-Life Books, 1981.

Bauer, Rotraud. *Tapisserien der Renaissance: Nach Entwürfen von Pieter Coecke Van Aelst* (Tapestries of the Renaissance: After Sketches by Pieter Coecke Van Aelst). Eisenstadt: Burgenländische Landesregierung, 1981.

Baumann, Carl-Friedrich. *175 Jahre Henschel: Der ständige Weg in die Zukunft; 1810–1985* (175 years of Henschel: The persistent path toward the future: 1810-1985). Moers: Steiger, 1985.

Berenson, Bernard. *Seeing and Knowing*. London: Chapman & Hall, 1953.

Blanck, Jacob. "News from the Rare Booksellers." *Publisher's Weekly* 150, no. 8 (1946): 837–38.

Bleier, Carol. "The Pierpont Morgan Library: Changing of the Guard." *Wilson Library Bulletin* 62, no. 8 (1988): 41–44.

Böhm, Elga. "Der Central Collecting Point – München: Erste Kunstsammelstelle nach Kriegsende." (The Central Collecting Point in Munich: First Collecting Point for art after the end of the war in 1945). *Kölner Museum Bulletin*, no. 4 (1987): 24–29.

Botting, Douglas. *In the Ruins of the Reich*. London: Allen & Unwin, 1985.

Brackmann, Karl-Heinz. *NS-Deutsch: "Selbstverständliche" Begriffe und Schlagwörter aus der Zeit des Nationalsozialismus* (Nazi-German: Common concepts and expressions of the National Socialist era). Straelen/Niederrhein: Straelener Manuskripte, 1988.

Brauns, Eduard. "Wilhelm Hopf: Verzeichnis seiner Schriften." (Wilhelm Hopf: A bibliography). *Zeitschrift des Vereins für Hessische Geschichte und Landeskunde* 63 (1952): 128–34.

Breitenbach, Edgar. "Erinnerungen." (Recollections). In: *Bibliothek '76 International: Rückschau und Ausblick. Freundesgabe für Werner Mevissen zu seinem 65. Geburtstag am 16. April (Library '76 International: Retrospective and Prospective. Tribute to Werner Mevissen on his 65th Birthday on April 16)*, 40–46. Bremen : Stadtbibliothek, 1976.

–. "Historical Survey of the Activities of the Intelligence Department, MFA&A Section, OMGB, 1946–1949." *College Art Journal* 9, no. 2 (1949–1950): 192–198.

–. *Speculum Humanae Salvationis, Eine typengeschichtliche Untersuchung* (Speculum Humanae Salvationis: A historical-typological study). Strassburg: J. H. E. Heitz, 1930.

Broszinski, Hartmut. "Handschriftenrestaurierung in Kassel. 2." (Restoration of manuscripts in Kassel. (2 and 3)). *Informationen. Theater und Musik, Kunst und Wissenschaft in Kassel* 6 (1982): 11–12.

–. *Kasseler Handschriftenschätze* (Kassel manuscript treasures). Pretiosa Cassellana. Kassel: Johannes Stauda, 1985.

Bühler, Curt F. *Early Books and Manuscripts: Forty Years of Research*. New York: Grolier Club & The Pierpont Morgan Library, 1973.

Bühler, Curt F. "A Fifteenth-Century List of Recommended Books." *The New Colophon: A Book-Collector's Miscellany* 9 (1950): 49–54.

–. "Incunabula." In: *Standards of Bibliographical Description*. Curt F. Bühler, James G. McManaway, and Lawrence C. Wroth, 3–60. Philadelphia: University of Pennsylvania Press, 1949.

Bühler, Curt F., and Carl Selmer. "The Melk Salbenkrämerspiel. An Unpublished Middle High German Mercator Play." *PMLA, Publications of the Modern Language Association* 63, no. 1 (1948): 21–63.

–. "An Unpublished Middle High German Banntaiding." *PMLA, Publications of the Modern Language Association* 60, no. 1, part 1 (1945): 325–39.

Bunje, Emil T. H. *A Reinterpretation of the Expository Verses of the Hildebrandslied.* Berkeley: University of California Press, 1936.

Canfield, Cass. *The Incredible Pierpont Morgan: Financier and Art Collector.* New York: Harper & Row, 1974.

Chaneles, Sol. "The Great Betrayal." *Art & Antiques* December (1987): 93–103.

Christ, Karl. *The Handbook of Medieval Library History.* (Translated and edited by Theophil M. Otto). Metuchen: Scarecrow, 1984.

Classen, Albrecht. "Why do their words fail? Communicative strategies in the Hildebrandlied." *Modern Philology* 93, number 1(1995): 1–22.

Coles, Harry L., and Albert K. Weinberg. *Civil Affairs: Soldiers Become Governors.* United States Army in World War II. Special Studies. Vol. 8. Washington, D.C.: Office of the Chief of Military History, Department of the Army, 1964.

Dawidowicz, Lucy S. *From That Place and Time: A Memoir, 1938–1947.* New York: Norton, 1989.

Dawson, Ernest. *A Visit with Dr. R.* Los Angeles: Privately Published, 1948.

Denecke, Ludwig. "Die erste Niederschrift des Hildebrandliedes – Aus mündlicher Überlieferung auf Wachstafeln?" (The first recording of the Hildebrandlied – From oral transmission on wax tables?): 107–107. *Neophilologus: An International Journal of Modern and Mediaeval Language and Literature* 62, no. 1 (1978).

–. "Die zweite Handschrift des Hildebrandliedes." *Anzeiger für deutsches Altertum und deutsche Literatur* 83 (1972): 227–29.

Dettmar, Werner. *Die Zerstörung Kassels im Oktober 1943: Eine Dokumentation* (Destruction of Kassel in October of 1943: A documentation). Fuldabrück: Hesse, 1983.

Dick, Ernst S. "The Grimms' Hildebrandslied." In: *The Grimm Brothers and the Germanic Past.* Editor Elmer H. Antonsen, 71–86. Amsterdam: John Benjamins, 1990.

Dickinson, Donald C. "Robert O. Schad: A Treasure of a Bookman." *Southern California Quarterly* 81, no. 2 (1999): 221–46.

Diefendorf, Jeffry M. *In the Wake of the War: The Reconstruction of German Cities After World War II.* New York: Oxford University Press, 1993.

Edler de Roover, Florence. "The Scriptorium." In: *The Medieval Library.* James Westfall Thompson, 594–612. Chicago: University of Chicago Press, 1939.

Faison Jr., S. Lane. "Transfer of Custody to the Germans." In: *The Spoils of War: World War II and Its Aftermath: The Loss, Reappearance, and Recovery of Cultural Property.* Editor Elizabeth Simpson, 139–41. New York: H. N. Abrams in association with the Bard Graduate Center for Studies in the Decorative Arts, 1997.

Farmer, Walter I. "Custody and Controversy at the Wiesbaden Collecting Point." In: *The Spoils of War: World War II and Its Aftermath: The Loss, Reappearance, and Recovery of Cultural Property.* Editor Elizabeth Simpson, 131–34. New York: H. N. Abrams in association with the Bard Graduate Center for Studies in the Decorative Arts, 1977.

–. *The Safekeepers: a Memoir of the Arts at the End of World War II.* Revised and prefaced by Klaus Goldmann. With an introduction by Margaret Farmer Planton. Cultural Property Studies. Berlin: de Gruyter, 2000.

Fischer, Hanns. *Schrifttafeln zum althochdeutschen Lesebuch* (Facsimiles for the Old High German textbook). Tübingen: Max Nieneyer, 1966.

Forbes, John Douglas. *J. P. Morgan, Jr., 1867–1943.* Charlottesville: University Press of Virginia, 1981.

Freyhan, Robert. *Die Illustrationen zum Casseler Willehalm-Codex, ein Beispiel englischen Einflusses in der rheinischen Malerei des XIV. Jahrhunderts* (The illustrations to the Willehalm Codex from Kassel; An example of English influence on Rhennish painting style in the 14th century). Marburg: Verlag des Kunstgeschichtlichen Seminars, 1927.

Garcia-Guinea, Javier. "Framboidal Pyrites in Antique Books." *Nature* 388, no. 6643 (1997): 631.

Genêt. "The Beautiful Spoils: The Monuments Men." *The New Yorker* 21, no. 40 (1945): 71.

Genieva, Ekaterina. "German Book Collections in Russian Libraries." In: *The Spoils of War: World War II and Its Aftermath: The Loss, Reappearance, and Recovery of Cultural Property.* Editor Elizabeth Simpson, 221–24. New York: H. N. Abrams in association with the Bard Graduate Center for Studies in the Decorative Arts, 1997.

Gilreath, James. "History of a Book: Madison Council Told of First Book Printed in America." *Library of Congress Information Bulletin* 54, no. 9 (1995): 200–202.

Glaser, Hermann, Lutz von Pufendorf, and Michael Schöneich, editors. *So viel Anfang war nie: deutsche Städte 1945–1949* (There never were so many beginnings: German cities 1945–1949). Berlin: Siedler, 1989.

Goebbels, Joseph. *The Goebbels Diaries, 1942–1943.* Editor and translator Louis P. Lochner. Garden City, New York: Doubleday, 1948.

Goßlau, Friedemann. *Verloren, gefunden, heimgeholt: die Wiedervereinigung des Quedlinburger Domschatzes* (Lost, found, returned: The reunification of the Quedlinburg cloister treasure). Quedlinburg: Quedlinburg Druck, 1996.

Habermann, Alexandra, Rainer Klemmt, and Frauke Siefkes. *Lexikon deutscher wissenschaftlicher Bibliothekare, 1925–1980* (Bio-Bibliographic dictionary of German academic librarians, 1925–1980). Zeitschrift für Bibliothekswesen und Bibliographie. Sonderheft 42. Frankfurt am Main: Klostermann, 1985.

Haines, Gerald K. "Who Gives a Damn about Medieval Walls." *Prologue* 8, no. 2 (1976): 97–106.

Hall, Ardelia R. "The Recovery of Cultural Objects Dispersed during World War II." *Department of State Bulletin* 25, no. 635 (1951): 337–44.

–. "U. S. Program for Return of Historic Objects to Countries of Origin, 1944–1954." *Department of State Bulletin* 31, no. 797 (1954): 493–98.

Hammerich, L. L. "Die Trutzreden Hiltibrants und Hadubrants (The defiant speeches of Hiltibrant and Hadubrant)." *Neophilologus* 34, no. 2 (1950): 82–86.

Happel, Hans-Gerd. *Das wissenschaftliche Bibliothekswesen im Nationalsozialismus: unter besonderer Berücksichtigung der Universitätsbibliotheken* (Scholarly librarianship during National Socialism: With special emphasis on university libraries). München: Saur, 1989.

Harris, Arthur. *Bomber Offensive.* London: Collins, 1947.

Hennig, Dieter. "Zur Rückführung zweier Handschriften der Murhardschen Bibliothek der Stadt Kassel und Landesbibliothek" (On the return of two manuscripts belonging to the Murhard Library of the City of Kassel and State Library). *Zeitschrift für Bibliothekswesen und Bibliographie* 20, no. 1 (1973): 24–27.

Henschel, Reinhard. *Gleise und Nebengleise: Von meines Vaters Lokomotiven zu geheime Missionen. Ein Mann besichtigt eine vergangene Zeit* (Tracks and sidetracks: From my father's locomotives to secret missions. A man contemplates a time gone by). Bern: Scherz, 1983.

Hering, Jürgen. "Restitution kriegsbedigt verlagerter Kulturgüter: Ein neues Kapitel zur Rückführung deutscher Bücher aus Rußand." (Restitution of cultural property dispersed during the war: A new chapter in the return of German books from Russia). In: *Bücher für die Wissenschaft: Bibliotheken zwischen Tradition und Fortschritt. Festschrift für Günter Gattermann zum 65. Geburtstag.* Editor Gert Kaiser, 293–303. München: K. G. Sauer, 1994.

Höffkes, Karl. *Hitlers politische Generale: Die Gauleiter des Dritten Reiches. Ein biographisches Nachschlagewerk.* (Hitler's political generals: The Gauleiters of the Third Reich. A biographical reference book). Tübingen: Grabert, 1986.

Holladay, Joan A. *Illuminating the Epic: The Kassel 'Willehalm Codex' and the Landgraves of Hesse in the Early Fourteenth Century.* Seattle: College Art Association and University of Washington Press, 1996.

Homburg, Herfried. *Kassel: Das geistige Profil einer tausendjährigen Stadt* (Kassel: Spiritual profile of a thousand year old city). Kassel: Schneider & Weber, 1969.

Honan, William H. *Treasure Hunt: A New York Times Reporter Tracks the Quedlinburg Hoard.* New York: Fromm, 1997.

Hopf, Wilhelm, Editor. *Die Landesbibliothek Kassel, 1580–1930,* Part II – The manuscript collection by Gustav Struck (The Kassel State Library: 1580–1930). Marburg: N. G. Elwert, 1930.

Hüttenberger, Peter. *Die Gauleiter: Studie zum Wandel des Machtgefüges in der NSDAP* (The Gauleiters: An analysis of the transformation of the Nazi power structure). Schriftenreihe der Vierteljahreshefte für Zeitgeschichte. Vol. 19. Stuttgart: Deutsche Verlagsanstalt, 1969.

Jackson, Stanley. *J. P. Morgan.* New York: Stein and Day, 1983.

Kaiser, Erich. "Das Schicksal des Hildebrandsliedes: Eine moderne Odyssee." (The fate of the Hildebrandslied: A modern odyssey). *Die Lesestunde: Zeitschrift der deutschen Buch-Gemeinschaft* 28, no. 7 (1952): 5.

Kallweit, Adolf. *Die Freimauerei in Hessen-Kassel: Königliche Kunst durch zwei Jahrhunderte, von 1743–1965* (The freemasons in Hesse-Kassel: Royal art spanning two centuries, from 1743–1965). Baden-Baden: Agis, 1966.

Kesting, Fritz. *Stadt und Bad Wildungen im Wandel der Zeit* (The history of the city and spa Wildungen). Bad Wildungen: Wilhelm Bing, 1968.

Kogelfranz, Siegfried, and Willi A. Korte. *Quedlinburg – Texas und Zurück: Schwarzhandel mit geraubter Kunst* (Quedlinburg–Texas and back: Black-marketeering with stolen art). München: Knaur, 1994.

Kolk, Helmich van der. *Das Hildebrandlied: Eine forschungsgeschichtliche Darstellung* (The Song of Hildebrand: A research history). Amsterdam: Scheltema & Holkema, 1967.

Kraus, Hans Peter. *A Rare Book Saga: The Autobiography of H. P. Kraus.* New York: G. P. Putnam's Sons, 1978.

Krause, Friedhilde, and Tatjana Inokent'evna Skripkina. "Margarita Ivanovna Rudomino zum Gedenken (Margarita Ivanovna Rudomino in memoriam)." *Zentralblatt für Bibliothekswesen* 104 (1990): 288–90.

Kroes, H. W. J. "Zum Hildebrandslied" (On the Lay of Hildebrand). *Neophilologus* 33, no. 4 (1949): 212–15.

Kurtz, Michael J. "The End of the War and the Occupation of Germany, 1944–52. Laws and Conventions Enacted to Counter German Appropriations: The Allied Control Council." In: *The Spoils of War: World War II and Its Aftermath: The Loss, Reappearance, and Recovery of Cultural Property.* Editor Elizabeth Simpson, 112–16. New York: H. N. Abrams in association with the Bard Graduate Center for Studies in the Decorative Arts, 1977.

Labach, Michael. "Der Verein deutscher Bibliothekare während des Nationalsozialismus." (The German Library Association during National Socialism). In: *Bibliotheken während des Nationalsozialismus, Teil II.* Edited by Peter Vodosek and Michael Komorowski, 151–68. Wiesbaden: Harrassowitz, 1992.

Leyh, Georg. *Die deutschen wissenschaftlichen Bibliotheken nach dem Krieg* (German scholarly libraries after the war). Tübingen: Mohr, 1947.

Liebers, Gerhard. "Die Bibliotheksverhältnisse in Kassel nach dem Kriege." (Library conditions in Kassel after the war) *Zentralblatt für Bibliothekswesen* 65, 9/10 (1951): 383–87.

Lyndenberg, Harry Miller. "The Ecology of the Pierpont Morgan Library and Its First Director." In: *Studies in Art and Literature for Belle Da Costa Greene.* Editor Dorothy Eugenia Milner, 6–9. Princeton, N. J.: Princeton University Press, 1954.

Madan, Falconer. *Books in Manuscript: A Short Introduction to Their Study and Use; With a Chapter on Records.* London: Kegan Paul, Trench, Trubner and Co., 1893.

Martin, Thomas. "Bemerkungen zur 'Episiola De Litteris Collendis.'" (Commentaries to the 'Epistola De Litteris Colendis'). *Archiv für Diplomatik: Schriftgeschichte, Siegel- und Waffenkunde* 31 (1985): 227–72.

Maurer, Ely. "The Role of the State Department Regarding National and Private Claims for the Restitution of Stolen Cultural Property." In: *The Spoils of War: World War II and Its Aftermath: The Loss, Reappearance, and Recovery of Cultural Property.* Editor Elizabeth Simpson, 142–44. New York: H. N. Abrams in association with the Bard Graduate Center for Studies in Decorative Arts, 1997.

Mayer, Ruth K. "The Roberts Commission." In: Walter I Farmer. *The Safekeepers: A Memoir of the Arts at the End of World War II.* Revised and prefaced by Klaus Goldmann. With an introduction by Margaret Farmer Planton. Berlin: de Gruyter, 2000.

Miller, Lucile V. "Edward and Estelle Doheny." *The Ventura County Historical Society Quarterly* 6, no. 1 (1960): 3–20.

Milner, Art. "Philadelphia's Rosenbach Museum: A Visit to DeLancey Place." *Wilson Library Bulletin* 60, no. 3 (1985): 14–18.

Miner, Dorothy Eugenia. *Studies in Art and Literature for Belle Da Costa Greene.* Princeton, N. J.: Princeton University Press, 1954.

Morris, Leslie A. *Rosenbach Abroad: In Pursuit of Books in Private Collections.* Philadelphia: Rosenbach Museum & Library, 1988.

Musgrove, Gordon. *Operation Gomorrah: The Hamburg Firestorm Raids.* London: Jane's, 1981.

Nicholas, Lynn H. *The Rape of Europa: The Fate of Europe's Treasures in the Third Reich and the Second World War.* New York: Knopf, 1994.

Norman, Frederick. *Three Essays on the Hildebrandslied.* London: University of London, 1973.

Philippson, Ernst A. "Altdeutsche Handschriften" *Journal of English and Germanic Philology* 50 (1951): 248–49.

Renoir, Alain. "The Kassel Manuscript and the Conclusion of the Hildebrandslied." *Manuscripta* 23 (1979): 104–108.

Rosenbach, A. S. W. *A Book Hunter's Holiday: Adventures with Books and Manuscripts*. Boston: Houghton Mifflin, 1936.

–. *Books and Bidders: The Adventures of a Bibliophile*. London: Allen & Unwin, 1928.

Rosenberg, Alfred. *The Myth of the Twentieth Century: An Evaluation of the Spiritual-Intellectual Confrontations of Our Age*. Translation by Vivian Bird. Newport Beach, California: Noontide Press, 1993.

Samuels, Ernest. *Bernard Berenson: The Making of a Legend*. Cambridge, Massachusetts: The Belknap Press, 1987.

Schad, Robert O. "The Estelle Doheny Collection." *The New Colophon: A Book-Collectors' Miscellany* 3, no. 9 (1950): 229–42.

Schoof, Wilhelm. "Die verlorene Handschrift" (The lost manuscript). *Wörter und Sachen: Zeitschrift für indogermanische Sprachwissenschaft, Volksbildung und Kulturgeschichte. Neue Folge* 3 (21) (1940): 53–60.

Schrimpf, Gangolf. *Mittelalterliche Bücherverzeichnisse des Klosters Fulda und andere Beiträge zur Geschichte der Bibliothek des Klosters Fulda im Mittelalter* (Medieval book catalogs of the monastery Fulda and other contributions on the history of the Fulda monastic library in the Middle Ages). Frankfurt am Main: Knecht, 1992.

Secrest, Meryle. *Being Bernard Berenson: A Biography*. New York: Holt, Rinehart and Winston, 1979.

–. "Lessing Rosenwald, Collector of Great Prints, Rare Books." *Smithsonian* 2, no. 12 (1972): 50–57.

Selmer, Carl. "Wie ich das Hildebrandslied in Amerika wiederfand." (How I found the Hildebrandslied in America). *Wirkendes Wort* 6, no. 2 (1955/56): 122–25.

Sowerby, E. Millicent. *Rare People and Rare Books*. London: Constable, 1967.

Starkosch, Avery. "Profiles: Napoleon of Books." *New Yorker* 4 (1928): 25–28.

Sutterlin, James S. "Through Diplomatic Efforts Stolen Historic Manuscripts Recovered." *Department of State Newsletter* 2, no. 142 (1973): 27.

Steinert, Marlis G. *Hitlers Krieg und die Deutschen. Stimmung und Haltung der deutschen Bevölkerung im zweiten Weltkrieg* (Hitler's war and the Germans. Public mood and attitude of the German people during the Second World War). Düsseldorf: Econ, 1970.

Stieg, Margaret F. "The Impact of National Socialism on Libraries." In: *Bibliotheken während des Nationalsozialismus.* Editors Peter Vodosek, and Manfred Komorowski, 11–26. Vol. 2. Wiesbaden: Harrassowitz, 1992.

Strouse, Jean. *Morgan: American Financier*. New York: Random House, 1999.

Süßmann, Gustav. *Das Hildebrandlied – Gefälscht?: Eine Untersuchung* (The Hildebrandlied – a forgery?: An appraisal). Staufenberg: Gustav Süßmann, 1988.

Taper, Bernard. "Investigating Art Looting for the MFA&A." In: *The Spoils of War: World War II and Its Aftermath: The Loss, Reappearance, and Recovery of Cultural Property.* Editor Elizabeth Simpson, 135–38. New York: H. N. Abrams in association with the Bard Center for Studies in the Decorative Arts, 1997.

Terentianus Maurus. *Terentiani Mauri De Litteris Syllabis Et Metris Liber*. Berolini: Reimer, 1836.

Thalmann, Rita, and Emmanuel Feinermann. *Crystal Night: 9–10 November 1938* (Translated from French by Gilles Cremonesi *La Nuit de Cristal: 9–10 November 1938*, Paris: Robert Laffort, 1972). London: Thames and Hudson, 1974.

Thompson, James Westfall. *The Medieval Library*. Chicago: University of Chicago Press, 1939.

Towner, Wesley. *The Elegant Auctioneers*. New York: Hill & Wang, 1970.

Twaddell, William Freeman. "The Hildebrandlied Manuscript in the U.S.A., 1945–1972." *Journal of English and Germanic Philology* 73, no. 2 (1974): 157–68.

Voltaire. *Oeuvres Complètes de Voltaire*. Paris: Garnier Frères, 1877–1985.

Wattenbach, Wilhelm. *Das Schriftwesen im Mittelalter* (Writing in the Middle Ages). Leipzig: Hirzel, 1875.

Weber, Francis J. *Southern California's First Family: the Dohenys of Los Angeles*. Fullerton, California: Lorson's Books and Prints, 1993.

Weber, Francis J., and Josephine Arlyn Bruccoli. "Carrie Estelle Doheny (2. August 1875–30. October 1958)." In: *American Book Collectors and Bibliographers. First Series.* Editor Joseph Rosenblum, 64–69. Dictionary of Literary Biography. Vol. 140. Detroit: Gale, 1994.

Weber, Hans-Oskar. "Landesbibliothek Kassel 1938." (State Library Kassel 1938). In: *Bibliotheken während des Nationalsozialismus, Teil I.* Edited by Peter Vodosek and Manfred Komorowski, 369–73. Wiesbaden: Harrassowitz, 1989.

Wernick, Robert. "The Bookseller Who Couldn't Stand to Sell His Books." *Smithsonian* 23, no. 1 (1992): 106–13.

Wieder, Joachim. "Margarita Ivanovna Rudomino (1900-1990), In Memoriam." *IFLA Journal* 16, no. 3 (1990): 304–6.

Winter, Ursula. "Hildebrandlied und Willehalm-Codex: Zwei Handschriften der Landesbibliothek Kassel und ihre Schicksale." (The Lay of Hildebrand and the Willehalm Codex: Two manuscripts of the Kassel State Library and their fate). *Marginalien: Zeitschrift für Buchkunst und Bibliophilie* 56 (1974): 57–62.

Winterich, John T. "Dr. Rosenbach: the Tycoon of Rare Books." *Harper's Magazine* 212, no. 1270 (1956): 80–88.

Wolf 2nd, Edwin, and John F. Fleming. *Rosenbach: A Biography*. Cleveland: World Publishing Company, 1960.

Ziemke, Earl F. *The U.S. Army in the Occupation of Germany 1944–1946*. Army Historical Series. Washington, D. C.: Center of Military History, United States Army, 1975.

Newspaper Articles

Title entries:

"Ardelia Hall – Obituary." *The Washington Post* (September 10, 1979): Metro, C4.

"Books – Hildebrandlied: manuscript found in the U.S." *Times* (London) (September 28, 1972): 1, col. G.

"Carl Selmer – Obituary." *Staats-Zeitung und Herold – New York* (June 26, 1972).

"Hildebrand wieder daheim." (Hildebrand is back home again). *Hessische Nachrichten* (July 18, 1955).

"Hildebrandslied hinter dicken Panzertüren." (The Hildebrandslied behind heavy steel doors). *Kasseler Post* (July 16, 1955).

"Hildebrandslied wiedergefunden." (The Hildebrandslied has been found). *Kasseler Post* (May 30, 1952).

"Das Hildebrandslied wurde jetzt in den Vereinigten Staaten gefunden." (The Lay of Hildebrand has been found in the United States). *Hessische Nachrichten* (May 31, 1952).

"Karl Kup – Obituary." *The New York Times* (July 7, 1981): Section A, 21, Col. 4.

"Kassel bombed by 100 aircraft." *Times* (London) (September 10, 1941): 4, Col. C.

"Kassel (1,500 Tons) Is Latest R.A.F. Target." *Sunday Express* (London) (October 23, 1943).

"Kassel Gets Pictures Back, for a Price: Veteran's Reluctant Admission of Taking Plunder Clinches Case." *Art Newspaper* 9, no. 82 (1998): 7.

"More Air Blows at Enemy: Another 1,500 Tons on Kassel." *Times (London)* (October 25, 1943): 4.

"Museum Director Fined in Theft Case." *Boston Globe* (December 4, 1991): 40.

"Nach 10jähriger Odyssee: Hildebrandslied zum Teil wieder daheim." (After a ten-year journey, part of the Hildebrandslied is back home). *Hessische Nachrichten* (July 19 1955).

"Nur die zweite Seite des Hildebrandlsliedes kehrt zurück." (Only the second page of the Hildebrandslied returns). *Hessische Nachrichten* (September 13, 1954).

"Petrarch Ms. Sought by Trieste Is Found in Ex-GI's Jersey Shop." *The New York Times* (December 22, 1946): 1, Col. 6.

"Ritter Hildebrand von langer Irrfahrt zurück." (Knight Hildebrand back from long odyssey). *Kasseler Post* (July 16/17, 1955).

[Sun rise] *Times* (London) (October 22, 1943): 5.

Superior Court of the District of Columbia in re: Ardelia R. Hall, Fiduciary No F-22-79 Adult Ward. *The Washington Post* (August 9, 1979): Section Style; Legal Notice: D. 19.

"T as in Treasure, Texas – and Theft." *The New York Times* (July 20, 1990): Section A, 26, Col. 1.

[Weather] *New York Times* (November 10, 1945): 25.

"Why Did Leading US Museum Director Keep Mum Over Paintings Stolen From Kassel." *Art Newspaper* 8, no. 70 (1997): 14.

"Zurück ohne finanzielle Forderungen. *Hildebrandslied* und *Willehalm* daheim" (Back without financial compensation: The *Hildebrandslied* and the *Willehalm* are home). *Hessische Allgemeine* (September 30, 1972)

Author entries:

Gundersheimer, Werner. "Kristallnacht Revisited: A Nightmare, a Legacy." *Washington Post* (November 9, 1988): A10.

Katz, Adolf. "Search for 2 Ancient German Literary Works Ends in Phila." *Philadelphia Sunday Bulletin* (September 24, 1972): Section I, XB5.

Kersten, Kurt. "Das auferstandene Kassel" (Kassel resurrected). *Sonntagsblatt Staats-Zeitung und Herold – New York* (October 17, 1954): 5C, 20C.

Manthey, Marlene. "Das Ende einer literarischen Odyssee" (The end of a literary odyssey). *Wiesbadener Tageblatt* (September 27, 1972).

–. Hildebrandlied heimgekehrt (Hildebrandlied returned). *Die Presse* (Vienna) (September 27, 1972).

Robinson, Walter V. "Theft Admission Ends Tug-of-War Over Artwork." *Boston Globe* (May 13, 1998): A1.

–. "US Tracked WWII Influx of Looted Art. Government Did Little to Prevent Sale of Works Here, Files Suggest." *Boston Globe* (May 9, 1997): A1.

Index

Bei Fragen zur Produktsicherheit wenden Sie sich bitte an:
If you have any questions regarding product safety,
please contact:

Walter de Gruyter GmbH
Genthiner Straße 13
10785 Berlin
productsafety@degruyterbrill.com